Inside the World's Major East Asian Collections

Chandos

Information Professional Series

Series Editor: Ruth Rikowski
(email: Rikowskigr@aol.com)

Chandos' new series of books is aimed at the busy information professional. They have been specially commissioned to provide the reader with an authoritative view of current thinking. They are designed to provide easy-to-read and (most importantly) practical coverage of topics that are of interest to librarians and other information professionals. If you would like a full listing of current and forthcoming titles, please visit www.chandospublishing.com.

New authors: We are always pleased to receive ideas for new titles; if you would like to write a book for Chandos, please contact Dr Glyn Jones on g.jones.2@elsevier.com or telephone +44 (0) 1865 843000.

Inside the World's Major East Asian Collections

One Belt, One Road, and Beyond

Allan Cho
Patrick Lo
Dickson K.W. Chiu

ELSEVIER
CP
CHANDOS PUBLISHING
An imprint of Elsevier

Chandos Publishing is an imprint of Elsevier
50 Hampshire Street, 5th Floor, Cambridge, MA 02139, United States
The Boulevard, Langford Lane, Kidlington, OX5 1GB, United Kingdom

Library of Congress Cataloging-in-Publication Data
A catalog record for this book is available from the Library of Congress

British Library Cataloguing-in-Publication Data
A catalogue record for this book is available from the British Library

ISBN: 978-0-08-102145-3 (print)
ISBN: 978-0-08-102146-0 (online)

Publisher: Glyn Jones
Acquisition Editor: Glyn Jones
Editorial Project Manager: Anna Valutkevich
Production Project Manager: Debasish Ghosh
Designer: Maria Ines Cruz

Typeset by TNQ Books and Journals

Contents

List of Interviewees

Inga-Lill Blomkvist–University of Copenhagen, Copenhagen, Denmark

Carla Bonò–The Giorgio Cini Foundation, Venice, Italy

Hing Chao–International Guoshu Association, Hong Kong, China

Sara Chiesura–The British Library, London, United Kingdom

Cristina Cramerotti–Musée national des arts asiatiques – Guimet, Paris, France

Vladimir Davydov–Peter the Great Museum of Anthropology and Ethnography (Kunstkamera), Russian Academy of Sciences, St. Petersburg, Russia

Mark Elliott–MAA, University of Cambridge, Cambridge, United Kingdom

Katarína Feriančíková–CCK-ISC, Charles University, Prague, Czech Republic

Jie Formoso–National Library of France, Paris, France

Marc Gilbert–Lyon Public Library, Lyon, France

Mary Ginsberg–British Museum, London, United Kingdom

Martin Heijdra–Princeton University, Princeton, NJ, United States

David Helliwell–Bodleian Library, Oxford, United Kingdom

Muneaki Hirano–Japan Center for Asian Historical Records, Tokyo, Japan

Matthias Kaun–Berlin State Library, Berlin, Germany

Sarah Kenderdine–City University of Hong Kong, Hong Kong, China

Harald Kraemer–City University of Hong Kong, Hong Kong, China

Richie Lam–Hong Kong Film Archive, Hong Kong, China

Dat-Wei Lau–Library of the French School of Asian Studies, Paris, France

Soline Lau-Suchet–Bibliothèque universitaire des langues et civilisations (BULAC), Paris, France

Shannon Lee–Bruce Lee Foundation, Los Angeles, CA, United States

Jack Leong–University of Toronto Libraries, Toronto, ON, Canada

Jan Luffer–Oriental Institute, Academy of Sciences of the Czech Republic, Prague, Czech Republic

Toshie Marra–University of California, Berkeley, CA, United States

Bent Lerbæk Pedersen–The Royal Library, Copenhagen, Denmark

Heather Rogers–McGill University, Montreal, QC, Canada

Jeffrey Shaw–City University of Hong Kong, Hong Kong, China

Lisa Song–Hong Kong Baptist University, Hong Kong, China

Raymond So–Hong Kong Sports Institute, Hong Kong (SAR), China

Daniel Sung–National Palace Museum, Taipei, Taiwan, Republic of China

Thomas Tabery–Bavarian State Library, Munich, Germany

Hamish Todd–The British Library, London, United Kingdom

Benedicte Vaerman–KU Leuven University, Leuven, Belgium

Nathalie Vandeperre–The Royal Museums of Art and History of Belgium, Brussels, Belgium

Susan Whitfield–The British Library, London, United Kingdom

Marc Winter–University of Zurich, Zurich, Switzerland

Chantal Wong–Asia Art Archive, Hong Kong, China

Clara D. Yu–Vatican Apostolic Library, Rome, Italy

Authors' Biographies

Allan Cho is the Asian Studies Librarian at Koerner Library's Humanities and Social Sciences division. His work also supports community engagement initiatives and cultural programming at the Irving K. Barber Learning Centre at the University of British Columbia (UBC) Library. Allan also has MLIS and M.Ed. degrees from the UBC, and an MA in History from the UBC history department, where his thesis, 'The Hong Kong Wuxia movie: identity and politics, 1966–1976', focused on the rise of the Hong Kong swordplay films across the Chinese diaspora during the turbulent period of the Cultural Revolution. He is also an instructor in the Department of Library and Information Technology at the University of Fraser Valley in British Columbia, Canada.

Dr. Patrick Lo is currently serving as Associate Professor at the Faculty of Library, Information and Media Science, the University of Tsukuba in Japan. He earned his Doctor of Education from the University of Bristol (UK) and has a Master of Arts in Design Management from the Hong Kong Polytechnic University, a Master of Library and Information Science from McGill University (Canada), and a Bachelor of Fine Arts from Mount Allison University (Canada). He also took part in a 1-year academic exchange at the University of Tübingen in Germany from 1990 to 1991. He is efficient in Chinese (both Cantonese and Putonghua), English and German. Dr. Patrick Lo has presented about 100 research papers and project reports focusing on librarianship, humanities and education at different local and international workgroup meetings, seminars, conferences, etc., including: mainland China, Hong Kong, Austria, France, Germany, Italy, Japan, Korea, Turkey, the US and Sweden, and at institutions including the Library of Congress (US), Austrian National Library (Vienna), University of Vienna, National Library of France (Paris), National Institute of Informatics (Japan), Konrad-Zuse-Center for Information Technology (Berlin), etc. His research interests and areas of specialty include: comparative studies in library and information science (LIS), art and design librarianship and information literacy. His recent publications on LIS include:

Dickson K.W. Chiu received the BSc (Hons.) degree in computer studies from the University of Hong Kong in 1987. He received the MSc (1994) and the PhD (2000) degrees in computer science from the Hong Kong University of Science and Technology. He started his own computer company while studying part time. He is now teaching at the University of Hong Kong and has also taught at several universities in Hong Kong. His research interest is in library and information management with a cross-disciplinary approach involving workflows, software engineering, information technologies, management, security and databases. The results have been widely published in over 200 papers in international journals and conference proceedings (most of them have been indexed by Science Citation Index (SCI), SCI-E, Engineering Village (EI) and Social Sciences Citation Index (SSCI)), including many practical master's and undergraduate project results. He received a best paper award in the 37th Hawaii International Conference on System Sciences in 2004. He is the founding editor-in-chief of the International Journal on Systems and Service-Oriented Engineering. He also serves on the editorial boards of several international journals. He co-founded several international workshops and co-edited several journal special issues. He also served as a programme committee member for over 100 international conferences and workshops. He is a senior member of both the Association for Computing Machinery (ACM) and the Institute of Electrical and Electronics Engineers (IEEE) and a life member of the Hong Kong Computer Society.

Foreword

Cultural institutions welcome everyone regardless of gender, race, ethnicity or means. Although we endure to serve our communities in the broadest sense, simply espousing this attitude in our mission statements is simply not enough. We live in an increasingly globalised society, a 'global village', as some would put it. Libraries, archives, art galleries and museums are in a pivotal position to strengthen their communities through programs, collections and services, and perhaps even more critically by creating environments of inclusion, empowerment and compassion. This timely publication, *Inside the World's Major East Asian Collections: Conversations with the World's Leading East Asian Librarians, Archivists and Curators*, is a collection of interviews embedded with powerful stories of practical and personal practices of managing collections dealing with East Asian materials.

Although the chapters serve as helpful references, the focus of each one is not research-oriented, but effective best practices and in-depth elaborations on historical and heritage institutions that have been developed, tested and proven to be successful in serving the needs and interests of their users and patrons, be it a library, museum, art gallery or archive. Each section is enriched with articles by leading experts from multiple perspectives and all types of cultural institutions from across the world. These selected authors bring a wealth of experience from their work in diverse areas of collection management.

This is an important book because it invites its readership to step out of their own cultural identities and explore the types of East Asian collections around the world that capture and excite our understanding and knowledge of 'Asia'. By reading the stories of successful managers of collections, we can then begin to develop cultural appreciation and awareness of the truly global village we live in. Only then can we design better programs and services that not only encourage use among our clientele, but also provide opportunities for our communities to develop a deeper understanding and empathy for the multiple perspectives of others within their communities.

I have always believed that culture is capable of building bridges when politics and special interests have caused cracks. Therefore, I was really pleased with the participation of our Library, display of the Vatican culture, to this initiative.

Jean-Louis Briguès, O.P.
Archivist and Librarian, Holy Roman Church

Preface

The genesis of this book came from a common theme of the challenges of librarians who face continuous challenges in shrinking budgets, increased workloads and constant change in information technologies. As we gradually worked our way through our discussions, we realised that these themes go beyond just libraries, but also cultural institutions as archives, museums and to a certain extent, art galleries, what is now more commonly known as a whole as LAMs (**L**ibraries, **A**rchives and **M**useums). One might ask, why focus on LAMs? We argue that the present convergence is actually a return to traditional unity. These three institutions (LAMs) share epistemological links dating from the 'Museum' of Alexandria and continuing through the cabinets of curiosities gathered in early modern Europe. But over time, these collections expanded, they became more specialised and their storage was separated according to the form of information and kinds of users. After the 19th century, these institutions professionalised, and intellectual societies and educational programs materialised that crystallised the formal separation.[1] We have come full circle. For us to focus on only one but not the other would be to give an incomplete picture as to the continued merger of LAMs.

Our book, *Inside the World's Major East Asian Collections*, is thus based on a series of direct interviews with different practicing librarians, archivists and museum curators across the world who specialise in East Asian collections. In trying to examine the dynamically shifting role of the cultural institution in the context of managing information, cultural and knowledge exchanges and collaboration on a global scale, we target this book to serve as a reference guide for students, scholars, researchers and professionals who manage East Asian collections, enabling them to gain a glimpse of the vast amount of treasures available for their research and other scholarly activities. As LAMs began their histories mainly as collecting institutions with mandates to preserve and make accessible primary sources valuable for researchers, we want to show in this book how we are coming full circle again with the merger of practices and techniques of managing collections across cultural institutions.

[1] Marcum, Deanna. (2014). Archives, libraries, museums: Coming back together? *Information & Culture: A Journal of History*, 49 (1): 74–89.

Acknowledgements

Growing up in Vancouver as a Chinese Canadian carried with it certain dichotomies: to act Canadian, think Canadian, be more Western; yet learn Chinese, retain Confucian values, speak Chinese at home. But in the public domain, there was only one type of New Year, and that was on 1 January, one type of zodiac, the Western horoscopes of Hellenic origins. Lunar New Year was only as an afterthought somewhat significant because of red pocket money. Our educational system imbued in us the belief that Canada represented the 'two solitudes' of English and French Canadians, its history heavily indebted to the European heritage according to the educational system I had grown up in. At each meeting, we sang 'Oh Canada', our national anthem, which pledged allegiance to the British Queen and the empire.

It was only much later in university that I learned that the history of Canada is in fact multiracial and multiethnic. Pioneers of North America comprised of Hindus, Sikhs, Germans, Chinese, Japanese, Jews and Ukrainians, just to name a few who arrived at the same time as the European colonialists and built the country together, but were left off of the official records. But of course, I had no idea of this complex history, as it was nowhere in the curriculum. I hated those late evenings at Chinese school, where my teacher scolded me for not memorising correctly the number of strokes of each character. So I conveniently (and much to my later regret) dropped it once and for all when I reached high school. I was glad to shed my identity of being Chinese and absolve myself of my heritage.

Having studied history as a graduate student, I eventually came to appreciate the richness of Canadian history from the perspective of the subaltern, the population of the socially, politically and geographically marginalised of the hegemonic power structure of the colonial homeland. But getting access to history beyond just Canadian documents proved to be very difficult. It's only in recent times that the history of Asians in North America is slowly documented, preserved and studied at the university level. It wasn't so long ago that having a course in Asian history was a luxury, let alone a museum or a library dedicated to the Asian language collections. One had to go to Asia to have access to rare materials and learn the language there.

Although Vancouver is considered one of the most 'Asian' cities outside Asia, it is not privileged with vast collections in our museums or libraries. For a local like myself, much of what I learned came from textbooks or television of historical Hong Kong dramas. So when it came time to complete my master's degree in Chinese history, I had to relearn my Chinese using Mandarin, not my native Cantonese, too. As I worked on my thesis about the 'cultural desert' of Hong Kong, it occurred to me that it was ironic that having grown up in a dominantly Chinese population (19.16% of the

2.5 million population of metropolitan Vancouver), my own city had its own cultural amnesia.

So this book project is something of a professional and personal journey. It strikes me as odd that there has been little or no publication about East Asian collections in our globalised society. In interviewing these gatekeepers of many of the finest collections of Asian materials in the world, I'm heartened that Asia's knowledge in the world is in safe hands, and for those scholars like myself in search of Asia, there will always be a home to go to.

I am forever grateful to Patrick Lo for his continuous encouragement of my contribution to this book. Having studied in Canada himself, he is certainly familiar to speak to the trials and tribulations of a Western education, wrought with omissions and gaps in its historical education. It was Patrick who encouraged me to seek my roots and to relate it back to this important book project.

I would like to thank an old university professor, Chu Shao-Kang, as it was his humorous and engaging lectures about modern Chinese history that sparked my interest. As someone who urged me with good intentions not to become a scholar for its lack of opportunities, I owe him a debt of gratitude for sowing seeds of fascination about China. I would also like to extend my sincerest appreciation to my friend and mentor, Dean Giustini, for his unending faith in me as a librarian, who saw my start as a student at his medical library and continued to show trust in me as his colleague and co-author in so many projects.

I would like to dedicate this book to my great grandfather Chow Bing-Fee, who had arrived in Canada in 1912 as a young man penniless, but full of hope and aspiration to earn enough money back home to China by himself, continued his life of hardship so that his family can continue to live. – **Allan Cho**.

Writing this book, *Inside the World's Leading East Asian Collections*, has been an incredible journey for the both of us, incredible in a way that it has allowed us to revisit the fond memories of our field trips to the leading libraries, archives and museums in different foreign countries that sparked intense interest and intellectual curiosity in us during our youth. We would like to extend our sincerest gratitude and appreciation for all the diversely skilled and knowledgeable libraries, archives and museums (LAM) who took part in this interview book project. This book has created such valuable and boundless cultural and professional learning opportunities for these practising LAM professionals to communicate with each other cross-nationally, as well as cross-culturally. These professionals share with our readers their valuable professional practices, experiences and perspectives, enabling us to understand the importance of cross-disciplinarity in the fields of LAM.

Finally, we would like to thank our publisher, Elsevier, and in particular, George Knott (Acquisitions Editor) for having such faith in our book project, as well as his continuous support on the journey of getting this book published by one of the finest academic publishers in the world. – **Dr. Patrick Lo** and **Dr. Dickson Chiu**.

Introduction

When we sought a title for this book, we were careful to live up to the promise of *Inside the World's Major East Asian Collections: Conversations with the World's Leading Librarians, Archivists and Curators*. Of course, it can be a subjective process in labelling who exactly are 'major' or 'leading', but we strove to select those who are considered experts in their field, those who have published extensively in their area of literature, those who have amassed many years of experience in management of their collections and also those who have won awards or acclamation from their peers. We did not make our selections in haste; we also carefully selected interviewees based on a geographical spread that best represented various countries across the world to justify the global focus of our book. That is why we went on a journey to interview experts from the Berlin State Library, the Bavarian State Library, the British Library, the British Museum, the National Library of France, the Vatican Library, the National Library of Denmark, the National Archives of Japan and the National Taiwan Library, just to name a few.

In the context of this book, East Asian collections not only refers to those housed and managed by library, archive and museum (LAM) professionals who are ethnically of East Asian descent, but also their American as well as European colleagues who have devoted their careers to safeguarding cultural heritage collections of immeasurable value. We conducted our research using a mixed-methods approach using semi-structured surveys through face-to-face meetings, Skype and also by email, depending on preferred mode of access by our interviewees. Upon completion of transcribing our interviews, we followed up with our interviewees for clarification and approval for publication of the text.

Aims of this book

This book is intended to serve multiple purposes. In particular, we examine the rise of the 'LAM', and in doing so, we profile leading experts: librarians, archivists and museum curators who specialise in East Asian collections from across the world. In examining the dynamically shifting role of the cultural institution in the context of managing information and collections, this book provides important themes offered by these cultural experts in understanding the necessary professional skills, knowledge and personalities that are required for working in such environments of varying size, scope and composition in LAMs. As galleries, LAMs manage preservation and access of history and culture; their missions and goals as cultural institutions continue to converge.

To achieve this, we examine how the multifarious roles and goals of cultural institutions continue to converge by asking these LAM experts. These are especially apparent as collections are digitised and accessed online; artworks, books, documents, and artefacts all effectively become equal 'information resources', thus creating the need for a broader understanding of these important gatekeepers of heritage and knowledge.

As collecting institutions, LAMs share the common mandate to preserve and make accessible primary resources valuable for researchers and professionals, as well as the public. LAMs are mostly publicly funded, publicly accountable institutions collecting cultural heritage materials. Another aim of this book is to enhance the visibility and recognise the efforts of the LAM professionals as cultural institution leaders, since much of their great contributions in the respective fields to preserving our cultural and documentary heritages have gone unnoticed outside their parent institutions.

Knowledge exchange and research

In North America, there is the Council on East Asian Libraries,[1] while in Europe, there is the European Association of Sinological Librarians (EASL).[2] Such East Asian associations serve as forums for LAM professionals to share information and resources, creating valuable opportunities for them to share ideas and experiences related to career development. Despite the various collaborative and resources initiatives carried out between these two major associations, the opportunities and platforms for professional sharing amongst LAM professional practicing in them and Asia seem rather limited. In addition, many LAM professionals simply do not have the funding support, opportunities or time to share their valuable experiences and expertise. As Sara Chiesura, Lead Curator of the East Asian Collections at the British Library, puts it, 'I would like to thank you for interviewing me and I am eager to read what my colleagues around the world replied to your questions. Sharing knowledge and expertise and being aware of other colleagues' experiences is certainly the best way to improve our skills and to better serve the public as librarians, curators or archivists'.

In addition, a great amount of the research and other works published by the EASL[2] members are not always in English, which is definitely a barrier for international collaboration and knowledge exchange. For scholars and researchers from outside Europe, in particular, this language barrier has further prevented them to collaborate on an international scale, as well as from maximising the use of such invaluable resources available.

In the interviews given by Hing Chao of the Hong Kong Chinese Martial Arts Living Archive and Mark Elliott at Cambridge, they have redefined the roles and job scope of archives, particularly as they are now dealing with intangible cultural heritage: something that is 'living', which cannot be locked up in an archive or museum. To survive

[1] Council on East Asian Libraries (CEAL) – Homepage. Available at: http://www.eastasianlib.org.

[2] European Association of Sinological Librarians (EASL) – Homepage. Available at: http://www.easl.org/index.html.

on their own for future generations, archives must be organised, researched, talked about, promoted and taught to the young generations; otherwise, they risk extinction, physically as an entity and institutionally relevant to their audiences and users.

Career guide

For current students and graduates who are planning to enter a career in LAM, this book could provide them with insights into the careers of different types of LAMs. All the LAM professionals appearing in this book come with many years of training and professional experiences. We asked them to describe in their own words the necessary professional skills, knowledge and personalities that are required for working at the world's different leading LAMs with varying size, nature and composition. For example, for an American university student who majored in Japanese language and Japanese studies, are there other career options in addition to teaching language? For a Chinese master's of library and information science (MLIS) graduate who wishes to seek employment outside his or her homeland, what are the career opportunities and options available? What unique skills should these Chinese MLIS graduates acquire and possess in order to contribute to their future LAM careers? For the second generation of Chinese immigrants who were born, raised and educated in France, like Dat-Wei Lau, who is fluent in Cantonese, Putonghua, French and English, how can one make the best use of such language skills, such as a librarian at the École française d'Extrême-Orient Bibliothèque[3] in Paris? These young and yet aspiring people might be able to find answers and inspiration by reading the interviews of the seasoned LAM professionals appearing in this book.

Digitisation and digital access and exchange

One common theme that repeatedly occurs in this book is the important yet challenging barriers with digital access and digitisation. Experts throughout this book point continuously point out emergence of their work as a sort of 'memory institution' in which they maintain a repository of public knowledge, and digitisation has shifted the critical importance of LAMs as providers of digital libraries and data aggregation services, which serve as recovering the fading or lost memories of common societies.

Of course, to the public, online access to this treasure trove of digital materials make no difference to them whether it comes from libraries, museums or archives; to an uninformed user, they might all look the same. It is this very principle that some scholars have suggested an 'Amazoogle' approach in which an integrated LAMs access system pools resources and provides streamlined service to users via a federated searching model.[4] For example, Canada has merged its National Archives of Canada[5] and the National Library of Canada[6] and combined the functions of both to

[3] École française d'Extrême-Orient Bibliothèque – Homepage. Available at: http://www.efeo.fr/base.php?code=72.

[4] Askin, N. (2015). Collaboration and crowdsourcing: the future of LAM convergence. *See Also*, *1*(1).

[5] National Archives of Canada – Homepage. Available at: http://www.bac-lac.gc.ca/eng/Pages/home.aspx.

[6] National Library of Canada – Homepage. Available at: http://www.bac-lac.gc.ca/eng/Pages/home.aspx.

form the Library and Archives Canada in 2004. With the continued trends towards the digital, it is likely that the development of LAMs will become more prominent in the years to come.

Cultural and knowledge exchanges between the east and west

There are many different modes and formats of learning. Methodologies for practical field research could come in a variety. Adventure travels and tours could also take many different forms. During the course of writing this book, we could not help but imagining and identifying ourselves as the modern-day Marco Polo: traveling from country to country, from culture to culture, getting reacquainted with our own history and culture from a multidimensional perspective by forming meaningful dialogues with these seasoned LAM experts. The experiences and feedback shared by them have also enabled us (the authors) to re-examine how we Chinese people, and our country, should position ourselves from the viewpoints of other cultures in the modern globalised context, how we LAM professionals from East Asia could contribute to the professional community as well as society on an international level.

Research method

The choice of research methods was influenced by the aims of this book project. This study was intended to be exploratory and to reveal a different, richer type of data than that, which a questionnaire survey could not provide. The qualitative (direct interview) approach provided valuable opportunities for the individual practicing LAM experts to describe their unique experiences. The interview answers were created from the participants' own viewpoints. The interviewees took full control over the flow of the entire conversation, and we purposely did not want to control or interfere with the answers to our open-ended questions, giving the participants total freedom to respond in their own words, based on their interpretations of the questions.

The natural and conversational interviews also enabled maximum flexibility for more open, spontaneous and instant exchanges of ideas without any preconceived expectations on our side. More importantly, we could use a series of follow-up questions to clarify their answers and then verify the participants' responses and our understanding. In doing so, we saw 'themes' emerge organically during the course of the conversations and developed a mutual understanding of the concepts being examined.

The goal, of course, was not always the technical explanations behind specific tasks or operations, but rather the immediate and direct experiences of the individuals and the phenomena illustrating the underlying reasons for their actions and decisions. One major advantage of using the semistructured interview questions was that it facilitates probing and ensured that crucial information was not omitted (Neuman, 2009).[7] Furthermore, it enabled interviewees' experiences, attitudes and

[7] Neuman, W. (2009). *Social Research Methods: Qualitative and Quantitative Approaches*. Seventh ed. Boston, Mass.: Pearson Education.

opinions to be fully expressed in their own words, and at the same time, allowing space for a variety of sometimes contradictory points of view to be aired. In addition to allowing the participants to articulate the answers based on their own understandings of our questions, such natural and free conversational interviews also enabled maximum flexibility for more open, spontaneous and instant exchanges of ideas without any preconceived expectations on the interviewers' side. More importantly, we could use a series of follow-up questions (applied to both Skype and email interviews) to clarify their answers, as well as to verify immediately the participants' responses and our own understandings. According to Bryman (2001), one of the strengths of qualitative interviewing is the space it creates to allow 'unexpected' responses to emerge. Therefore, a qualitative approach to data collection and analysis was therefore considered appropriate for the aims and setting of this study.[8] Rossman and Rallis also point out that the interview approach not only provides opportunities for open discussions where both the participants and the researchers can 'construct meaning' together, it is also essential to understand how participants view their world.[9]

Interviews via Skype and email

Email and Skype interviews (each of approximately 60 min in length), conducted over a 12-month period, were the main data gathering techniques used in this book project. Participation in each interview was, of course, entirely voluntary. The interviews were conducted in a semistructured format and were fluid in nature. All participants were asked a similar set of open-ended questions (depending on the backgrounds and the institutions that the individual interviewees were working for), with the aim of maintaining a level of consistency amongst the interview results. The idea was to possibly find common threads amongst the participants' answers. These questions dealt with individual interviewees' own educational backgrounds, current occupational status, professional competencies, specialised areas/skills and most importantly, with the different factors, which motivated these LAM professionals to choose a career in their respective fields. Prior emails were written to the respective participants for seeking permission for conducting the interviews, explaining the purpose of the study, outlining the approximate length of the interviews and so on.

With reference to the interviews that were done in form of email, readers should also take into account that several interviewees who were not English speakers chose to answer their interview questions in their mother tongues, and we, as authors, had to find ways to translate these interviews back into English afterwards, whereas for the other interviews that were carried out over Skype, permissions were also sought for digital voice recording of the interview sessions. The recorded interviews were then transcribed, and then relevant information revealed by individual participants was arranged in common themes. In order to observe the ethical issues associated with research interviews after they have been transcribed, transcripts were sent to the

[8] Bryman, A. (2001). *Social Research Methods*. Oxford: Oxford University Press.

[9] Rossman, G.B. & Rallis, S.F. (1996). *Learning in the Field: An Introduction to Qualitative Research*. Thousand Oaks, Calif.: Sage Publications, p. 124.

interviewees for their review, corrections and approval. For both Skype and email interviews, the central task was to identify the common issues or themes in the experiences related by the participants (Neuman, 2009).[10]

Interviews and afterthoughts

With the convenience brought by modern-day Internet connectivity (Skype and email), figuratively speaking, we covered a vastly more geographical scope than even Marco Polo himself. For example, we began our 'virtual journey' in the globally renowned Vatican, the world centre of the Roman Catholic Faith (we also went via Venice like Marco Polo), went through Germany and France and interviewed LAM professionals stationed in Belgium, Denmark, Czech Republic and up to England. Then we went through the Silk Road, visited the internationally renowned Dunhuang Caves, all the way down to Hong Kong, the Special Administrative Region of China and to Japan via Taiwan. Finally, we make a great leap to North America.

Symbolically, we can say that the Silk Road extended beyond Asia across the Pacific Ocean to North America. As a second-generation Canadian of Chinese descent, one of the researchers of this book, Allan Cho, brought with him a North American viewpoint to this book, one that captures elements of both the Western tradition within the Eastern erudition. In addition, though Dickson Chiu was bought up and has been living in Hong Kong, his father had worked in Canada and his grandfather in the US for a long time, with the majority of his cousins living in North America. To understand the book project's truly global purpose and value, it is important to appreciate the migratory patterns of Asians across the world. As Chinese migrants have been in the regions of North America for more than three centuries, they have shared a unique history with its other 'founding' peoples. In Cho's metro Vancouver, for example, 40% of the Vancouver population is ethnic Chinese, with heterogeneous histories ranging from multigeneration Chinese Canadians to migrants arriving within the last 5 years from around the world. As one walks down the streets of Old Chinatown in Vancouver, Victoria and San Francisco, one sees archaic architecture of the remaining buildings with traces of architectural heritage from early Hong Kong, and by extension, those buildings of Canton, often better kept than their counterparts in the East.

Often left unrecorded or underrepresented in official histories of Canada and America, the Chinese have had a long history and, in fact, were the first traders who arrived in 1788 in what is now Canada. A century later, Chinese gold prospectors settled in San Francisco in the 1849 California Gold Rush in which most of them embarked on their trans-Pacific voyage from the British colony of Hong Kong to Canada and the US. We are finding out now in newly opened archives that these young men joined Chinese brotherhood societies that funded Dr. Sun Yat-Sen's revolution and establishment of the Republican government in 1911. However, this trans-Pacific history also affects Canadian and American history, and their textbooks are now slowly

[10] Neuman, W. (2009). *Social Research Methods: Qualitative and Quantitative Approaches*. Seventh ed. Boston, Mass.: Pearson Education.

rewriting the story of North America, focusing not solely on the Euro-centric viewpoints, and LAMs are clearly leading the way with its cultural collections.[11] This long and continuous history of Asians in North America has been understudied and long ignored within the historical collections of North American institutions.

Our book thus extends the reach to a trans-Pacific lens, one that does not simply focus on North America as a silo; rather, it addresses the role of trans-Pacific migration in multiple directions throughout the Pacific region and eastward across the Atlantic, making a full global journey of people and its material collections. It is therefore truly a marvellous experience to make stops at the University of Toronto[12] to learn about the Hong Kong–Canada collections and to the renowned Ivy League school, Princeton University.[13] Our journey then makes a stop in Europe with an examination of the Asian diaspora. The Lyon Public Library,[14] unlike other municipal libraries in France, holds a vast collection of Chinese collections. Through the work of a local professor, Danielle Li, whose roots in France began when her father, Li Shuhua, arrived there in 1918 and enrolled at the Franco-Chinese Institute in Lyon. When Li Shuhua settled in France to escape the political upheaval in China, not only did Danielle Li become a scholar and citizen, but helped bring the collections from the Franco-Chinese Institute of Lyon to the Lyon Public Library and continue the research of the Chinese in France as secretary general of the same institution that her father went to a century earlier at the Franco-Chinese Institute. The story of the Chinese collections of Lyon is just one illustration of the dynamic interplay between nation building and the accompanying treatment and study of local populations in different countries in LAMs that the interviews in this book has attempted to shed light into the world's major East Asian collections.

[11] Yu, Henry. (2007). "Towards a Pacific History of the Americas." *Amerasia Journal*, *33*(2), xiviii–xix.

[12] University of Toronto – Homepage. Available at: https://www.utoronto.ca/.

[13] Princeton University – Homepage. Available at: https://www.princeton.edu/main/.

[14] Lyon Public Library – Homepage. Available at: https://www.bm-lyon.fr/?lang=fr.

Inside the Vatican Apostolic Library

1

Clara D. Yu
Vatican Apostolic Library, Rome, Italy

Introduction

The Vatican Apostolic Library in Rome is the library of the Holy See, located in Vatican City. Formally established in 1475, although it is much older, it is one of the oldest libraries in the world and contains one of the most significant collections of historical texts. The Vatican Secret Archives were separated from the library at the beginning of the 17th century; they contain another 150,000 items. While the Vatican Library has always included Bibles, canon law texts and theological works, it specialised in secular books from the beginning. Although the East Asian collections are not as well known, this chapter highlights the important work of one librarian (Clara Yu Dong, Fig. 1.1), who manages it so that researchers from around can access it.

Could we begin this interview by getting you to give us a little bit of your background? For example, where did you come from? What have you studied at university? And where/how have you received your professional training to become a librarian?

There is no East Asian department here. I am currently serving as the Researcher, the Librarian and the Curator of the East Asia collections at the Vatican Library. I graduated with a bachelor's degree in Library Science from Wuhan University,[1] a university that is famous for its library and information science (LIS) programmes throughout mainland China. After receiving my bachelor's degree in LIS, I worked for a few years as a librarian at a research institute in China. I then came to Italy to further my studies. I studied pedagogy at the Università di Roma LUMSA[2] and later literature at the Sapienza University of Rome.[3]

Since 1992, I have been working as the East Asian Librarian at the Vatican Library, Curator of Asian collections (excluding West Asian), Researcher, mainly for Chinese manuscripts and other rare books, and also collaborating with the Numismatic Department for Chinese coins (Figs 1.2–1.4).

[1] Wuhan University – Homepage. Available at: http://en.whu.edu.cn.
[2] Università di Roma LUMSA – Homepage. Available at: http://www.lumsa.it/.
[3] Sapienza University of Rome – Homepage. Available at: http://www.uniroma1.it.

Inside the World's Major East Asian Collections. http://dx.doi.org/10.1016/B978-0-08-102145-3.00001-7

Figure 1.1 Clara Yu Dong at her desk in the Printed Books Reading Room (Leonina) of the Vatican Library.
Photographed by Federico Sardella.

Did you study the Italian language in China before coming to Italy? In addition, there are so many European languages that one could choose to learn as a foreign language in mainland China, but why did you choose Italian? As you understand, the speaking population of the Italian language is comparatively small. Unless you are training to become an opera singer, or you are in the food trade business, the opportunity for speaking Italian the outside its native land is very limited; would you not agree?

Figure 1.2 *Vat. estr.-or.* 1, 大方廣佛華嚴經. 卷第五十六. Avatamsaka-sutra, juan 56 (detail). Chinese; 1346; manuscript in gold ink on dark blue paper; 337×122 mm; accordion binding.

Figure 1.3 *Vat. estr.-or. 40*, 清明上河圖 (Along the River During the Qingming Festival) (detail). 16th century; ink and paint on silk; 9854×343 mm (painting 4994×294); scroll.

Well, in my opinion, it is always interesting and useful to be able to speak more foreign languages. Learning a foreign language helps one understand other cultures, as well as meet interesting people. How I became interested in the Italian language? Back in China, I got to know a group of friends, and we used to go to study the language together on weekends. So I continued my studies on weekends, I later won a scholarship to come to further my studies in Italy and the rest is history.

Figure 1.4 *Disegni.Generali.2*, Vincenzo Marchi (1818–1894), View of the Sistine Hall. 1860; watercolor; 464×687 mm; framed.

How many years did you spend on learning the Italian language before going to Italy to study at university?

I estimate about 2 years.

Did you further you education or undertake any professional training related to LIS before taking up your current job as a librarian at the Vatican Library?

I started working for the Vatican Library as a librarian while I was studying at La Sapienza University. My 4-year university study in LIS at Wuhan University, combined with my previous library working experience in China, was already considered sufficient for taking up the librarian job at the Vatican Library. In Italy, a graduate from 4-year university program is called 'doctor', ready to take up professional jobs.

How did you find your job at the Vatican Library? Or was it an open position? Was it via open recruitment? Was there much competition amongst the applicants fighting for the same job?

This librarian position for the Chinese collection at the Vatican Library was open for centuries. For many centuries, the Vatican Library has been receiving large numbers of books and other types of library materials with high historical, cultural, as well as religious values coming not just from China, but also from many different East Asian countries. However, before I came to work for the Vatican Library, there had never been a 'real librarian' with the necessary language skills to process, to interpret, to conduct research on and to catalogue all these materials from China. For this reason, my professor (at the Sapienza University of Rome) recommended me to apply for this

Chinese Librarian position at the Vatican Library. Luckily, they offered me this job, and I happily accepted it without any hesitation.

Could you describe your first day of work as a Chinese Librarian at the Vatican Library? If you cannot remember the technical details, maybe you could describe your very first impression of the Vatican Library. For example, could you share your feelings from the moment you first put your foot into the door of the Vatican Library?

It was absolutely impressive and moving! I will never forget the excitement I felt, knowing that I could actually get behind the closed doors of the Vatican and work for one of the oldest libraries in the world that contains some of the most significant collections of historical texts. The Vatican Library and its Secret Archives have captured people's imaginations for centuries. Many of its contents still remain a mystery to the outside world. Very often, you only hear the mention of such immeasurable Vatican treasures (handwritten correspondences by great masters, such as Michelangelo, Leonardo da Vinci or Henry VIII's love letters to Anne Boleyn) in literature, newspapers, films and television, but being able to work so closely with such important treasures, having such convenient and direct access to this ancient repository of knowledge, being able to learn directly from them and being able to touch them with your own hands, these were undoubtedly enlightening experiences that could not be described in words.

Could you describe your typical day of work at the Vatican Library?

In the beginning, it was very quiet. In the early days, I would just come to the Library and spend most of my time doing research and cataloguing work at my desk in solitude. In comparison to now, there are so many visits from different foreign embassies, ambassadors and government officials representing various countries, not to mention the number of external visitors we have been receiving from different universities, as well as other research institutes worldwide. Because of that, I am now spending much of my working hours away from my desk, doing public relations and other duties for the Library.

Can you tell me why they would want you to be a foreign liaison and do public relations?

My main duty is to perform research and cataloguing the materials (mostly in Chinese) coming into the Vatican Library. However, so much has been changed since the last 10–20 years. I think many of such changes (the Library's daily operations) are caused by the fact that the Vatican Library and its materials have become increasingly open and more accessible to the outside world. In addition to becoming more accessible to people outside the Vatican, we also welcome support and collaborations with different externals partners, researchers and scholars to carry out our large-scale digitalisation projects. In March 2014, the Vatican Library began an initial 4-year project of digitising its collections of manuscripts to be made available online.

Given the enormous size, sheer scope and the unparalleled history of our Library's collections, converting them into the digital format is, without any exaggeration, a 'monumental' as well as a 'marathon' task. Luckily, there are many professionals and experts from outside the Vatican who are interested in forming collaborative partnerships with us. The Vatican Library's ambitious project is to digitise all its 82,000 manuscripts.

Could you elaborate more on the Vatican Digital Library Project (http://digital.vatlib.it/)?

All the manuscripts (including Chinese and Asian rare materials in our manuscript collections) will be digitised. By now, most of our Chinese manuscripts and rare books have been digitised under the Qingshi Project. The Japanese and other Asian materials in our 'Vaticano estremo orientale' collection are also being digitised as part of our manuscript digitisation project in collaboration with NTT DATA. Currently in discussions is a new project of digitising our East Asian, Southeast Asian and South Asian materials in collaboration with four major universities in China, Japan, Singapore and Italy. Besides, in the library we are preparing a project on our digitised documents, making links and inserting texts of comments, etc., interactive, as other people could progressively work on it. Very precious Chinese material, such as **清明上河圖**, Matteo Ricci's **坤輿萬國全圖** and Michael Boym's *Magni Catay*, will be included in the project.

Can you tell us about the highlights of Vatican Library collection?

According to our official homepage, 'The primary task of the Vatican Library, as an institution of both conservation and research, is to keep and conserve as carefully as possible the cultural treasures which have been entrusted to it. Further, the Vatican Library's responsibilities include:

1. increasing its holdings of manuscripts, printed books and coins through acquisitions, exchanges and donations, in accordance with the materials already present in the collections and with the purpose of the institution;
2. studying and promoting knowledge of these materials through the work of the Library's regular and supernumerary staff, and by means of publications; and
3. making available to qualified readers from around the world, with all necessary caution, both the originals and reproductions of the various types of documents and objects preserved in the Library, and providing for these readers all possible and appropriate scientific and technical assistance to their research, continually updating the instruments and aids which are helpful or necessary for their work'.[4]

As a research library for history, literature, law, philosophy, science, music and theology, and also because of our unparalleled long history, we have a countless number

[4] 'Responsibilities of the Vatican Library'. *Rules for Readers in the Vatican Library*. Available at: https://www.vatlib.it/home.php?pag=regolamento.

of precious, important and many world-famous manuscripts. The following are some of highlights from the Vatican Library:

The Vatican Library holds 82,000 manuscripts (as of October 2015). Amongst them, there are famous pieces:

- the papyrus from Egypt of end of 2nd century, the almost complete *Gospels of Luke* and *John*;
- the Codex B of 4th century, one of the most important manuscripts with the complete text of the Bible;
- Codex Borgianus: Pre-Columbian Aztec manuscript, written probably near Puebla (Mexico) at the end of the 15th century;
- Mishneh Torah: Beautifully illuminated Hebrew manuscript of the Mishneh Torah of Maimonides, dated between 1451 and 1475;
- Koran in Kufic: Collection of 73 fragments of the Koran Kufic;
- illustrations of Divine Comedy by Botticelli: Illustrations of The Divine Comedy by Sandro Botticelli for Lorenzo the Magnificent, in the XV century;
- Urbinate Bible: The Urbinate Bible, an undisputed masterpiece of Renaissance book art, made on behalf of Federico da Montefeltro, from the Florentine workshop of the bookseller Vespasiano da Bisticci between 1476 and 1478; and
- Vatican Virgil: Vatican Virgil produced in Rome around AD 400, one of the few surviving examples of ancient illustration of a classic text. The codex, studied by Raphael and purchased by Fulvio Orsini in 1579, arrived in the Vatican Library in 1600.

Presently, the Library preserves over 182,000 manuscripts (including 100,000 archival units); 1,600,000 printed books; around 9000 incunabula; over 300,000 coins and medals; 150,000 prints, drawings and engravings and over 150,000 photographs.

Could you provide a brief introduction to the Chinese language collections of the Vatican Library? Does it have a separate mandate and mission within the Vatican Library, or is it treated the same as a whole library?

Because the Roman Catholic Church had such a long history of missionary work in China as well as in other neighbouring countries, our Chinese collection contains some of the most frequently consulted materials inside the Vatican Library. Many of such frequently consulted materials are, in fact, original manuscripts written in Chinese. In addition to that, we have many old rare books, manuscripts and other precious objects that came from China. For example, the oldest item we have in our Chinese collection is an original 14th-century Buddhist manuscript that survives from the Yuan Dynasty of China.

In fact, the first notice of the existence of Chinese material in the Vatican Library dates back to 1576–77 when Nicolas Audebert, French traveller and humanist from Orléans, copied some documents that were shown to him in the Vatican, including an *Alphabetum idiomatis de Cina*, as recorded in his travel account now in the British Library.[5] In his account, Audebert states that the Vatican Library also preserved *plures* other Chinese books.

[5] The British Library – Homepage. Available at: http://www.bl.uk.

The following is a brief description of the contents of the Chinese collection at the Vatican Library:

- books and archival documents of missionary works;
- other volumes, not missionary works, but often collected and annotated by them: classics of literature, scientific works and Chinese popular encyclopaedias of the 16th and 17th centuries;
- rubbings;
- paintings of the Ming and Qing periods, silk embroidery and other art objects;
- a collection of Chinese coins, consisting of about 3000 specimens from the origin (the oldest are of 5th–4th centuries BC) until the period of Manchukuo; and
- amongst the maps, the most important are those, celestial and geographical, made by the first missionaries, including Matteo Ricci's famous world map of 1602, and many other regional or military maps of late Qing Period.

There is no separate mandate and mission within the Vatican Library for any of the languages. Manuscripts, printed books and other materials in different languages are all treated the same as a whole inside the Library. However, the Library Research Staff is made up of specialists coving different language and subject fields: Greek, Latin, Middle Eastern, Far Eastern, etc.

With reference to the Buddhist manuscript from Yuan Dynasty of China you mentioned earlier, how could it arrive in the Vatican?

According to some sources, this Buddhist manuscript was probably brought back to the Vatican from China around the 16th or 17th century.

Could you tell me about the staffing structure in your department? For example, are you the only librarian overseeing the entire Chinese collection at the Vatican Library? Do you also need to manage the Japanese and Korean collections? In addition, do you also need to process materials in other East Asian languages that are not writing in Chinese characters, for example, Mongolian, Manchu or Tibetan?

Technically speaking, I am not only in charge of the entire East Asian collections, but also overseeing the collections in other Southeast Asian and South Asian languages. Despite having to concurrently manage several collections that span a wide coverage of a variety of subjects and languages, my specialty and research focus still very much remain in the area of premodern Chinese manuscripts and rare books.

As the Librarian who is in charge of the Chinese collection at the Vatican Library, what are your specific roles and duties?

First of all, as a member of Library Research Staff, my core duty is to perform research and cataloguing on the old Chinese manuscripts and other rare books that come to the Vatican Library.

As a reference librarian, I need to answer reference enquiries concerning our Asian collections, but excluding the West Asian collection, which is the responsibility of another library colleague, who is responsible for overseeing the Middle Eastern materials.

As a co-organiser, one of my key roles is to liaise between the Vatican Library and Asian (not West Asian) world, promoting various cross-national and cross-cultural collaborative projects, that is, including: cataloguing, digitisation and publication of manuscripts and other old materials; co-organising conferences, exhibits, receiving external visitors, arranging foreign visits, as well as collaborating with the media.

In addition to original manuscripts, I also need to process the Chinese printed books, taking care of book exchanges, providing assistance for accession of library materials; all these are a big part of my daily work at the Library. I am also responsible for supervising the cataloguing of modern Chinese and Japanese books, a cataloguing project that will soon begin with a new cataloguing system, which will support the input, searching and display of non-Roman scripts.

How many different languages and/or scripts do you need to work with at the Vatican Library on a regular basis?

I do not really know because we have never counted. Moreover, it is not possible for us to find out! As I mentioned earlier, due to the long history of missionary work carried out by the Catholic Church throughout Asia, we have all sorts of manuscripts, books, artefacts and 3-D art objects in almost all possible languages in Asia coming into our Library.

The Vatican Library homepage suggests that photocopies of pages from books published between 1801 and 1990 and photocopies can be requested in person or by email. So how often do you receive such requests for photocopies of books? Do the requesters usually issue their requests for photocopies of books in person or via email?

Well, it is rather complicated question. We do receive requests for photocopies of books on a regular basis. However, we do not deliver the actual photocopies to our requesters by email. Photocopies for private study of pages from books published between 1801 and 1990 may be requested in person or by postal mail. Photocopies are usually made available within the same day or on the following day after a request has been issued. So I think our photocopy request service is relatively speedy. These publishing dates, 1801–1990, only refer to the Western printed books; for Chinese books, only those published after 1911 could be photocopied.

The people who request information from the Vatican Library, who are they? Are the people from different religions groups? Scholars? Academics? Professors or students of theology?

The Vatican Apostolic Library, more commonly called the Vatican Library, is the library of the Holy See, the personal library of the Pope. It was established, in accordance with the intention of the humanist Pope Nicholas V (1447–55), 'pro communi doctorum virorum commodo/for the use and the common interest of learned people' (brief of 30 April 1451).

It is a private library, meaning that the Library and its collections are private properties belonging to the Vatican. Since the modern Vatican Apostolic Library was truly humanist in origin, scope and mission, Nicholas V ordered that it be opened 'for the use and the common interest of learned people' and its collection had to be 'universal' in nature. There was to be a 'universal' representation of a variety of subjects of interest, and thus the collection of books was not to be specialised in theology or church law, as was the case in the great university libraries of Europe at that time, but would have to cover all fields of knowledge as well as various languages of the literature besides in Latin and Greek. In the course of the centuries, the Vatican Apostolic Library has continued to host scholars from all over the world and enriched its assets according to the same criteria.

According to our official website, 'The Vatican Library is the inalienable property of the Supreme Pontiff, and it is by his sovereign will that it is open to consultation. It is not a public institution. It is a library specialized in the philological and historical disciplines; it also has historical holdings in the fields of theology, law and science. It is reserved for scientific research based on the study of manuscripts, printed books, coins and medals, prints, and other graphic and cartographic materials'.[6]

In addition, due to our limited storage space, the Vatican Library only collects books and other materials that are only meant for research purposes. For these reasons, we are not open to the general public, but only to qualified scholars, and we have very strict admission policies for our external readers. For example, university students are not normally granted admission. Exceptions may be made for graduate students preparing a doctoral thesis or studying for the degree of doctor of philosophy (Dr. phil./PhD), as well as for undergraduate students who have a specific need to consult the manuscripts or other materials. Our qualified readers from outside the Vatican are mainly advanced researchers, scholars, doctoral candidates, etc. The Vatican Library can only be accessed by 200 scholars at one time, and it saw approximately 15,000 presences by 4000 scholars last year.

If people wish to do scholarly research at the Vatican Library, they must acquire the proper credentials from their schools or affiliated institutions. For graduate students who wish to use our Library collection, they need to present to us a letter of recommendation issued by their professor or affiliated university, indicating that their institution accepts liability for their students' actions before valid passes are granted for admission. As a long-standing tradition, readers are also requested to indicate the nature of their research project.

For these qualified readers who have been granted valid passes for using the Vatican Library, would there be any fees involved?

It is 100% free! Even since the Vatican Library opened to all qualified readers in 1883 under Leo XIII (who eased the admission process and, at the same time, also

[6] 'Nature of the Vatican Library'. Rules for Readers in the Vatican Library. Available at: https://www.vatlib.it/home.php?pag=regolamento.

opened the Vatican Secret Archives to readers), there are absolutely no costs involved for using the Vatican Library. It is totally free now and will also be free in the future.

What best prepared you for your work at the Vatican Library?

I think my professional education in field of LIS was considered very important. However, there is no substitute for the actual experience gained 'on the job'. Professional education and actual on-the-job experience are both equally important!

Can you tell me what kind of special knowledge and research skills are required for doing your job at the Vatican Library? How is it different, when compared against other special libraries? For example, do you also need to be able to read Latin, in addition to your Italian, English, French and Chinese language skills? The ability to read Latin, it is necessary for your daily work at the Vatican Library?

For the nature and scope of work that I am doing at the Vatican Library, there are no requirements of Latin skills, although a large number of documents entering our Library are still written in Latin until today. Therefore, with a scholarship, I took a 2-year course to study Latin at the Augustinianum Pontifical University and passed the final exam, although the Latin knowledge gained in 2 years could be only in working knowledge level. There are always new skills to learn and new techniques or ability to master, but I am always interested in accomplishing them. To be a good librarian, researcher or curator, I do not think one should ever stop learning new things.

What scholarly and professional LIS associations are you involved with? And how do these professional memberships assist your work at the Vatican Library?

I am a member of EASL (European Association of Sinological Librarians)[7] since 1994. It is really helpful in terms of keeping me up to date with outside world. Even if now, I have not been to any of their annual meetings in the last 10 years, I could still pose a question and ask for advice from other EASL members. I have also been invited to attend conferences held by the Society for Chinese Studies Librarians (SCSL).[8] It is always pleasant to know other LIS colleagues from North America, even though I am not yet a full member of the SCSL. I am also an invited member of the Global Mapping of Macao Project,[9] a project that was initiated and maintained by the Macau University of Science and Technology.[10] Members from both the EASL and the SCSL are very supportive and generous, and they are always ready to help out each other, with issues ranging from resources sharing to providing professional advices for solving particular technical problems, etc.

[7] European Association of Sinological Librarians (EASL) – Homepage. Available at: http://www.easl.org/.

[8] Society for Chinese Studies Librarians – Homepage. Available at: http://www.scslweb.org.

[9] Global Mapping of Macao Project – Homepage. Available at: http://lib.must.edu.mo/gmm/ppt/全球地圖中的澳門項目簡介.pdf.

[10] Macau University of Science and Technology – Homepage. Available at: http://www.must.edu.mo/en/.

Who are the majority users of the Chinese collection at the Vatican Library?

As mentioned earlier, they are mainly professors and researchers, and very often, doctoral students. One must remember that only qualified scholars with proper credentials from their schools or affiliated institutions are admitted to use our Library's collections.

Do you mean that these users from outside the Vatican would come to use your Library to find premodern Chinese materials on other subject disciplines that might not have anything to do with the Christian religion?

Yes, this is absolutely true!

Can you tell us about the typical reference enquires issue by the researchers at the Vatican Library?

Inquiries on our East Asian materials are very different. The nature of their enquiries could range from the in-depth research of single piece of document to request to see all related documents concerning the historical developments of a very specific geographic area in China, to the history of a highly specialised collection.

Are you also a Roman Catholic? Or do you have to be a Catholic in order to work for the Vatican Library? Is your religious faith important for working for the Vatican Library?

Yes, I am a Roman Catholic. One's faith does not affect the work as a librarian.

What is the size of Chinese section of the Vatican Apostolic Library? Could you describe the highlights of your particular Chinese collection?

Today, the Vatican Library's Chinese collection includes about 7000 pieces. Around 2000 of them are original manuscripts, woodblock prints and other printed books that were published before 1911. Six-hundred printed books were published during the Republican Period in China (i.e., 1912–49), and 1000 titles were published after this date (1949). The nonbook collection consists of several hundred maps, rubbings, embroidery, ivory sculptures, photographs and about 3000 coins, etc.

The highlights could be two 'Treasures of the Nation' as defined the UNESCO President and Vice Chinese Minister when he saw our copy of 《清明上河圖》 and the Yuan manuscript copy, '大方廣佛華嚴經'. Other famous and very rare items include: Jesuit maps, such as Matteo Ricci world map, and Adam Schall von Bell's coloured star map.

The librarians at the Vatican Library and the archivists at the Secret Archives, do they need to work together on a regular basis? Or the Library and the Archives are two totally separate units/departments?

The Vatican Secret Archives were separated from the Library since the beginning of the 17th century for various administrative, operational and technical reasons. Staff from both the Vatican Library and the Secret Archives may access each other's collections. However, in terms of administrations and operations, we are two totally separate departments with entirely different collection contents, sets of goals, policies, operational procedures and approaches, etc. Sometimes we (the Library and the Secret Archives) collaborate together, but very often, we work separately as two separate and individual institutions.

Who performs the cataloguing work for the archival materials that are to be kept inside the Vatican Secret Archives?

They are catalogued by the professional archivists working for the Vatican Secret Archives. The concepts of treatment, the set of rules and the record structure for cataloguing library materials are very different from the ones used for describing archival materials; hence, they need to be handled by different people with different training and professional expertise in respective fields.

Inside the Secret Archives, old archival materials, all the way until the end of Pope Pius XI's papacy (1939), are normally inventoried. All documents during a papacy are open for consultation as a block of the mandate. The next to be opened will be that of Pope Pius XII, from 1939 to 1958.

As a librarian of the famous Vatican Library, how do you acquire and evaluate your collection? Is it proactive or do you accept donations/gifts?

This is an issue that is very much restricted by our limited storage space inside the Library; we acquire books that are intended solely to facilitate the study of the much larger collection of manuscripts. The same selection criteria might be applied when it comes to doing book exchanges or accepting a donation from another library or individual.

Could you tell us what challenges and difficulties that you and your library colleagues are currently facing?

The biggest problem we are facing lies in the fact that we are still unable to input original Chinese characters into our online cataloguing system. We have been waiting for a new cataloguing system that could support the input, searching and display of original Chinese characters for many years. Given there is so much Chinese (character) input software available in the market, until this very moment, we still need to transliterate all our East Asian titles/scripts and catalogue them in Roman script in instead, with original scripts. In a few months, we are going to migrate to a new cataloguing system with a completely new OPAC (**O**nline **P**ublic **A**ccess **C**atalogue) interface. When the new system is available, we will be able to catalogue our Chinese and Japanese books in original scripts/characters.

For Chinese manuscripts and rare materials, I have been cataloguing them in printed text, and the catalogue will be published in the form of a printed book. Information in the main fields (title, author, edition, publisher and publication date) will be converted into MAchine-Readable Cataloging (MARC) records, with support provided by the National Central Library[11] in Taiwan, and these MARC records will be uploaded onto the International Union Catalogue of Rare Chinese books[12] (maintained by the National Central Library, Taiwan). Other regular Chinese printed books will be catalogued in our local OPAC with the new system that supports non-Roman scripts.

However, they are not the pressing challenges that we are facing. The most pressing challenge is conservation work. Many of our Chinese previous rare books are in critical condition, owing to the acidic components found in the pages, and we are looking for either financial or additional manpower support for performing conservation work for saving these valuable book items.

Which part of your job do you find most rewarding?

I am proud to say I enjoy all aspects of my work and have a particular interest in doing research on such culturally rich materials that come into the Vatican Library. In addition, being able to exchange ideas with other esteemed scholars, co-organising or participating in conferences and exhibits, etc., all these are, no doubt, valuable experiences.

How many librarians are there in total working at the Vatican Library?

We have less than 100 staff in total working at the Vatican Library. But many carry the job title as Collaborator. With various projects, now we need to collaborate with many different people outside of the Library, both internally and externally, onsite as well as offsite.

At the Vatican Apostolic Library, is there a balancing act in terms of managing priorities between the various areas of language expertise/collections in regards to the other Asian language collections (i.e., Japanese, Korean, etc.). What are your experiences at the Vatican Apostolic Library in this regard?

There are absolutely no balancing acts and priorities in terms of the way we manage our collections. The size of holdings at the Vatican Library is absolutely huge. During the past centuries, only a small-portion part of the manuscripts and rare materials have been properly studied and catalogued. They are undoubtedly treasures of knowledge and the ultimate key to understanding various aspects of humanity. For the purpose of supporting the 'use and the common interest of the learned people' from all over the world, the Vatican Library welcomes scholars to study our East Asian collections, without any distinction of race, religion, origin or culture. We welcome support and help from anyone who could contribute their knowledge and inputs.

[11] National Central Library (Taiwan) – Homepage. Available at: http://www.ncl.edu.tw/mp.asp?mp=2.
[12] Union Catalogue of Rare Chinese Books – Homepage. Available at: http://rbook2.ncl.edu.tw.

In 2010, you were in Beijing for discussions about a project to edit works concerning Chinese history from the 17th to the beginning of the 19th centuries, which are kept in the Vatican Library. What is your progress and are you still working with the Chinese government on this project?

This project began in 2008. It will be published in the form of digitised texts and also in facsimile form on paper. Four series will be published, that is, including about 700 titles of the 1300 photographed. The first series of 44 volumes, including about 170 titles, were published and first presented in Rome in January and then in Beijing in April. His Excellency Archbishop Bruguès the Librarian, Dr. Piazzoni the Vice Prefect and I went to Beijing for the event. The second series will be published in the near future.

The current Librarian of the Vatican Library is Jean-Louis Bruguès, who is a Catholic Priest, not a librarian. How does that work for a library such as yours? Do you need to communicate directly with the Archbishop on a regular basis on different technical issues related to the daily operations of the Library?

Jean-Louis Bruguès is the current Librarian (President) of Vatican Library; he is an Archbishop. He is not only the Librarian of the Library, but also Archivist of the Vatican Secret Archives. However, the Prefect and the Vice Prefect oversee the Vatican Library's daily operations. And the Librarian (Jean-Louis Bruguès) reports directly to the Pope.

Was the Archbishop also trained in the field of LIS or archival science?

No. He is Dominican and came from a strong academic background.

A Library of the Venice and the Giorgio Cini Foundation's Far East Centre for Comparative Studies of Cultures and Spiritualities

2

Carla Bonò
The Giorgio Cini Foundation, Venice, Italy

Introduction

The Fondazione Giorgio Cini (The Giorgio Cini Foundation) is a nonprofit, cultural institution based in Venice, Italy. It was established to promote the redevelopment of the monumental complex on the Island of San Giorgio Maggiore, and encourage the creation and development of educational, social, cultural and artistic institutions in its surrounding territory. The Centre for Comparative Studies of Cultures and Spiritualities (CCSCS) at The Giorgio Cini Foundation was set up in 1958, as the natural evolution of the existing Institute 'Venice and the East', with a goal to promote the study of the civilizations of India and the Far East.

Venetian-born Carla Bonò is currently serving as a librarian at the CCSCS, and obtained professional librarian training at the Biblioteca Nazionale Marciana. In the following interview, Ms. Bonò talks about the language skills and professional knowledge that are required to serve as a librarian at a European research centre that is devoted to the comparative studies of cultures and spiritualities.

Could you begin this interview by first introducing yourself, for example, your training and background, and your major roles and duties at the CCSCS, The Giorgio Cini Foundation? For example, which part of Italy do you come from?

I am a Venetian, and I have served as a librarian at the Giorgio Cini Foundation[1] since 1 February 1965, after working for some years as a secretary to a well-known criminal lawyer, Professor Francesco Carnelutti, who was also the President of the Centre of Culture and Civilization at the Giorgio Cini Foundation.

[1] The Giorgio Cini Foundation – Homepage. Available at: http://www.cini.it/en/.

Inside the World's Major East Asian Collections. http://dx.doi.org/10.1016/B978-0-08-102145-3.00002-9

Figure 2.1 Scholars consulting texts in the Buddhist section.

Please provide a brief introduction to the CCSCS and its association with the Giorgio Cini Foundation? What are the goals and missions of the CCSCS? Has there always been a Library since the very first day the CCSCS was established?

The CCSCS was set up in 1958 as the natural evolution of the existing Institute 'Venice and the East', with a goal to promote the study of the civilizations of India and the Far East. Over the years, the CCSCS has placed a strong emphasis on establishing an ongoing dialogue between East and West, between people, civilizations and religions. It also serves as a point of reference for scholars from all over the world, providing them with our rich library resources and other seminars, conferences and publications related to the field of comparative studies of cultures and spiritualities (Figs 2.1 and 2. 2).

The Centre places strong emphasis on the following:

1. The comparative approach, seen as the main antidote to all forms of 'fundamentalism', and the promotion of dialogue between civilizations, intended not only as an exchange and comparison of different concepts, but also of different political experiences, theoretical and aesthetic, etc.
2. The religious and spiritual dimension and the wisdom traditions of civilization, which are the subject of study and comparison. The term 'wisdom traditions' refers to the answers that humans have given, in different cultural contexts, to question the meaning of their existence in the world, the ideals of perfection of the self and the existential paths suitable to achieve them.
3. The recognition of the transformative potential of religious traditions. Faced with the crises (ecological, economic and moral) afflicting our society, only the religious and spiritual traditions seem capable of arousing emotions and generating energy needed to produce radical changes of paradigm.
4. The enlargement of perspective to major wisdoms and traditions of the world, not only in the Eastern, but also highlighting in particular those who have contributed over time to define the European identity.

Figure 2.2 Chinese woodblock prints.

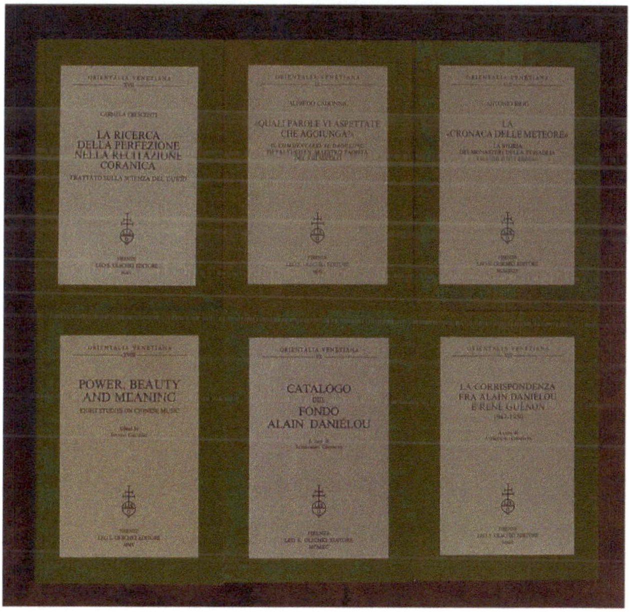

Figure 2.3 Selection of books from the 'Orientalia Venetiana' Series, published by Istituto 'Venezia e l'Oriente'.

It is associated with the Institutes of the Foundation (which include the Institute of Art History, Institute for the History of the Venetian State and Society, Institute for Music Theatre and Opera and Italian Antonio Vivaldi Institute).

In 1984, The Venice and the East Institute (now CCSCS), began publishing its own Collection of Oriental Studies called the *Orientalia Venetiana* (Fig. 2.3), which ended in 2005 with the 18th volume. Titles published in the Collection include: *Turfan and Tun-huang: the texts: Encounter of Civilizations on the Silk Route*; *China and Iran from Alexander the Great to Tang Dynasty;* Alfredo Cadonna: 'What words do you expect me to add?' The Commentary to Daodejing Bai Yuchan, Taoist master of the 13th century; Ester Bianchi: The Iron Statues Monastery. 'Tiexiangsi'. A Buddhist Nunnery of Tibetan Tradition in Contemporary China; Antonio Attisani: A ce lha mo.

Study on the forms of theatricality Tibetan; Luciana Galliano: Power, beauty and meaning: eight studies on Chinese music; Alessandro Grossato: The correspondence between Alain Daniélou and René Guénon (1947–1950); Alessandro Grossato: Catalogue Fund Alain Daniélou; Antonio Rigo: The 'Chronicle of Meteora'. The history of the Monasteries of Thessaly between the 13th and 16th centuries; etc.

Over the years the Institute has had different leadership, or 'managers', including Professor Paolo Beonio-Brocchieri (yamatologo), Professor Amalia Pezzali (indologa), Professors Agostino Pertusi and Antonio Rigo (bizantinologhi), Professors Lionello Lanciotti and Alfredo Cadonna (sinologists).

What is the current size of the East Asian Collections at the CCSCS Library? Could you describe the highlights of the CCSCS Library collection?

We currently have about 36,000 volumes. Among the highlights, I would like to mention the Tibetan Buddhist Canon (Tibetan Tripitaka, vols 151), the Chinese Buddhist Canon (Taisho Daizokyo, vols. 100), the *Encyclopedia of Japanese Buddhism* (*Dai Nippon Bukkyo Zensho*, vols 135), *Urga Kanjur* (in Tibetan, vols 103), *Mongolian Kanjur* (vols 108), *Taoist Canon* (Daozang, vols 60), collections in Chinese Si Bu Cong Kan and Cong Shu Ji Cheng, the Fund 'Alain Daniélou' (collection of manuscripts in Sanskrit musicology) and microfilms from the Imperial Library of Beijing (Microfilm Collection of the National Library of Peiping Rare Books).

The library founded by the Institute also has some of the most important magazines, namely: 344 titles on the Far and Near East and 86 titles of the Bizantinistica and Studies of South-East Europe. Many of them begin with the very first volume of the collection. These include:

Journal of the American Oriental Society, (1843–present)
Le Muséon, (1940–present)
Journal of Oriental Studies, (1954–present)
Bulletin de l'Ecole Française d'Extrême-Orient, (1901–present)
Bulletin of the Museum of Far Eastern Antiquities, (1929–present)
Japanese Journal of Religious Studies, (1974–present)
Monumenta Nipponica, (1938–present)
Bibliotheca Philologica et Philosophica Buddhica, (2010–2012)
Judaica, (1945–present)
Vetus Testamentum, (1951– present)
Bibliotheca Orientalis, (1943–present)
Biblical, (1920–1991)
T'oung Pao, (1908–present)
Monumenta Serica, (1935–present)
Oriens Extremus, (1954–present)
Journal Asiatique, (1873–present)

Journal of the Economic and Social History of the Orient, (1958–present)
The Journal of the Music Academy, Madras, (1930–1968)
The Muslim World, (1928–1997)
The Taiwan Folkways, (1994–present)
Hanxue Yanjiu Tongji, (2001–present)
Aegyptus, (1920–present)
Lĕšonenu, (1928–2002)

What best prepared you for the position of librarian at the CCSCS?

I attended a (professional librarian training) course at the Biblioteca (Nazionale) Marciana located in Venice.

Could you please describe a list of technical skills (including language skills) and professional knowledge that you require for your job as a librarian at the CCSCS?

Knowledge of classical languages (such as ancient Greek and Latin), knowledge of Library Science and computer literacy skills etc.

Are you also a fan of Marco Polo, and always had a fascination for his journey to the Far East which took place over 800 years ago.

Yes, I have always been interested in Asian cultures. Obviously, in the Library of the Institute we have a number of volumes of sinology concerning the famous Venetian traveller, Marco Polo, etc. (Fig. 2. 4).

Do you have any statistical figures indicating the number of university students who are currently learning East Asian languages, or undertaking courses in Asian Studies in Italy in general?

Figure 2.4 Different editions of Marco Polo's 'Il Milione' (17th century onwards).

No, but there are thousands of students at Ca' Foscari University,[2] Venice, studying Oriental languages (Chinese, Japanese, Hindi, Persian, Arabic, Armenian and Greek etc.). Many of them have come here to study at our institute, for generations, actually.

What scholarly and professional associations are you a part of, and how do they assist you in your work?

I am not part of any professional association.

Who are the majority of the Asian collection users? That is, who comes to see you at the CCSCS Library? Are they mostly professors or students from higher education institutions? Or are they people from outside the postsecondary sector, i.e., the general public?

Most users are students and university professors. Many of them who were students in the past (and have become specialists in their fields), are now teaching in various universities in Italy and abroad.

Could you give examples of typical reference/research enquiries issued by the researchers or scholars at the CCSCS Library?

Typical search requests concern the philological reading of the texts, the consultation of articles enclosed in the several journal collections to Oriental and research in ethnomusicology.

As the librarian overseeing the collection, how do you acquire and evaluate your collection? Do you proactively collect or do you accept gifts?

The acquisition and evaluation of collections was made by academic experts who have partnered with The Fondazione Cini. Nowadays, it is almost the same, even if the purchase volume is virtually frozen for lack of money (though we keep almost all magazine subscriptions). Of course we also accept gifts (e.g., from 'Toyo Bunko' in Tokyo and The International Research Institute for Advance Buddhology Soka University[3] located in Tokyo).

In institutions with Asian Collections, it is inevitable that there is a balancing act in terms of managing priorities between the various areas of language expertise/collections in regards to the other Asian language collections (that is, Japanese, Korean, etc.). What are your experiences as a librarian in terms of balancing and prioritising? Do you need to?

Areas that are prevalent are Sinology, Buddhist Studies and Indology. I personally have not taken an active role in decision-making.

[2] Ca' Foscari University of Venice – Homepage. Available at: http://www.unive.it/nqcontent.cfm?a_id=10497.

[3] Tokyo and The International Research Institute for Advance Buddhology Soka University – Homepage. Available at: http://iriab.soka.ac.jp/orc/english.html.

Figure 2.5 General view of the different areas of the library (Islamic, Chinese, Japanese, Indology and Buddhist studies).

Figure 2.6 Aisle view of the archive of the periodicals.

How is the collection catalogued and accessible for users? With a non-roman script, what challenges does this present to cataloguing? Are there any?

Everything is translated and/or transliterated into Roman characters. Access to users is provided through catalogues by author and subject (paper ballots). At the moment The Giorgio Cini Foundation is promoting a huge work of cataloguing and digitalization on several branches of the CCSCS Library, such as Alain Daniélou's Archive and Tiziano Terzani's Archive. These Archives are now partially available online.

What are the difficulties and challenges that you and your CCSCS colleagues are currently facing?

The difficulty, now common to many, is to obtain all the resources that are necessary to implement organic projects and ambitions.

Figure 2.7 Professor F. B. Fukui with librarian C. Bonò in the Cloister of the Giorgio Cini Foundation (June 2001).

Are there any collaborative projects currently being carried out between the CCSCS Library and other libraries (both inside and outside of Italy)?

There are partnerships with various universities in Italy and some research centres such as IsIAO CESMEO in Rome and Turin, The Institute of Oriental Philosophy[4] in Tokyo, Italian Cultural Institute in Kyoto etc.

Which part(s) of your job as the Librarian at CCSCS do you find most rewarding?

I truly enjoy helping young students and scholars in conducting their research (Figs 2.5–2.7).

[4] Institute of Oriental Philosophy – Homepage. Available at: http://www.iop.or.jp.

From the Shang to the Qing at the British Library

3

Sara Chiesura
The British Library, London, United Kingdom

Introduction

The British Library holds a vast collection of materials in Chinese, Japanese, Korean, Manchu and Mongolian including manuscripts, printed books, periodicals, sound recordings, maps, newspapers and archives. It also actively collects contemporary publications on a wide range of subjects in the languages of East Asia and about the countries and cultures of the region. As Lead Curator of the East Asian Collections at the British Library, Sara Chiesura (Fig. 3.1) highlights the Chinese Collection which includes a unique series of more than 400 oracle bones (jia gu/甲骨). These bones date from 1600 to 1050 BC (Shang Dynasty) making them the oldest items in the British Library. As the oldest objects in a museum can say a lot about that institution, just how far back its historical identity reaches reveals the importance of the British Library in our understanding of China.

Could we begin this interview with you introducing yourself? For example, your training and background, and your major roles and duties as the Lead Curator of the East Asian Collections at the British Library?

I graduated from the Department of Asian and North African Studies at Ca' Foscari University of Venice[1] in 2005, majoring in Chinese language. Before my degree I spent one year in Kunming, in Yunnan Province, and after graduating I lived and travelled in Asia for almost 5 years, mostly in the People's Republic of China. During this time I worked with both Chinese and international institutions. In my spare time I travelled in South East Asia and Japan.

From 2010 to 2013 I worked for a Confucius Institute[2] as the Events and Language Programs Manager. I also worked as a teacher of Chinese language to adults and high school students as well as the project manager of the Confucius Classroom Project in high schools. At the end of 2013 I was selected as the Curator of the Chinese Collections at the British Library,[3] and later I continued my career at the Library as Lead Curator.

[1] Ca' Foscari University of Venice – Homepage. Available at: http://www.unive.it/nqcontent.cfm?a_id=10497.
[2] Confucius Institute – Homepage. Available at: http://confuciusinstitute.unl.edu/institutes.shtml.
[3] The British Library – Homepage. Available at: http://www.bl.uk/.

Inside the World's Major East Asian Collections. http://dx.doi.org/10.1016/B978-0-08-102145-3.00003-0

Figure 3.1 Sara Chiesura.

The major duties of my current role are to develop and manage the Library's Chinese Collections and therefore to select current acquisitions, to project manage international collaborations and partnerships and to make the collection available both to researchers and the general public through cataloguing, digitisation projects, exhibitions and events.

For the kind of work that you are doing at the British Library, why are international collaborations so important? Who are the major partners that you collaborate with on a regular basis?

International collaborations are important for many reasons, especially in the case of collections which are originally not from the UK. First of all, it is important that researchers around the world are aware of the content of our collections, so working with other institutions improves our outreach. In some cases collections from the same region, from a single previous collector or from one archive, have, during the centuries, been split between different institutions around the globe. It is important to keep a strong relationship with institutions with similar collections, or parts of collections, that in some way 'complete' each other, for example the *Yongle Dadian*. Furthermore, we can always learn and share skills and practices with other libraries or museums. For example, we will soon welcome in our team a PhD student from Shandong University[4] who, thanks to his specific knowledge, will help us to catalogue a particular type of material in the collection. Another example is the project on the

[4] Shandong University – Homepage. Available at: http://en.sdu.edu.cn/.

Figure 3.2 Sara looking at a Ming dynasty printed concertina.

oracle bones. Next week we will host colleagues from the National Library of China[5] to discuss new methods for conservation and storage of the bones.

How, and at what age, did you develop an interest for the Chinese language and culture?

It was the attraction of the unknown that inspired me to study the Chinese language and culture when I was 18. I have always been fascinated by Asia, which in my teenage mind was a place of mystery, great landscapes and mountain temples but also a modern megalopolis, so a place of captivation for varied and different reasons. I was attracted by the fact that I did not know much about it and it was on the other side of the world, the perfect excuse to escape from the mountain village I come from in Northern Italy with a backpack and a dictionary in my pocket.

I wanted to explore and experience different worlds, languages, foods and cultures and China was just the perfect place. Chinese characters have also been a source of fascination. They looked beautiful, balanced and complicated at the same time and the thought of being able to read through those apparently unintelligible little lines was a great incentive to start.

Are you a second career curator/librarian i.e., have you had other careers before you started working as a curator for the British Library?

This is my first experience as a curator (Fig. 3.2), since I had not worked in a library or a museum before being selected for the position at the British Library. I had previous experience in the cultural promotion and cultural engagement fields and in working in international partnerships with Chinese institutions.

[5] National Library of China – Homepage. Available at: http://www.nlc.cn/newen/.

Figure 3.3 The British Library building in London.

Based on your online biography, you are Italian, from Venice. How did a young Italian woman like you end up working as the Curator of the East Asian Collections at the British Library?

After a few years working in China, and 3 years back in Italy, I felt that I needed a change. Being European I have the right to work in other countries of the European Union, and London is an international and vibrant city with lots of exciting cultural activities, world known museums, libraries, theatres and events going on all-year-round.

The British Library is a prominent institution with exceptional and rich collections of great historical value, so when I was selected for the position I did not think twice and flew to London 1 week later (Figs 3.3 and 3.4). I always wanted to work in a cultural institution and have always been a keen visitor of libraries, galleries and museums. After 2 years, I have to say that it was a good decision, both for my career development and personal life.

What I love the most about working at the British Library is probably the dynamic and international environment of this institution, and the fact that every day I can learn from readers and colleagues' experiences and knowledge. I feel honoured to work for a public institution which is freely open to everyone who is interested in doing research with our collections, or only in being inspired from them.

How would you describe the British Library? Do you sometimes feel like you are working for the United Nations? Or serving as an important crew member onboard the Starship Enterprise? How do you deal with so many different cultures, languages, scripts, people from all ethnic backgrounds and most importantly different ways of thinking?

Figure 3.4 The King's Library tower in the public area of the British Library in London.

Working here is certainly something I am proud of. The Library considers the different backgrounds of its staff and readers an opportunity for learning and innovation, and having a diverse environment is an occasion for cultural enrichment. It reflects the diversity and the richness of our collections (for example, more than 300 languages are represented across our Asian and African Collections!) and makes the working environment very stimulating. It also echoes the dynamism and the international vibe of London as a global city.

What is the current size of the Chinese Collections? Could you also describe the highlights of the Chinese Collections at the British Library?

The East Asian Collections include material in Japanese, Korean, Chinese, Mongolian, Manchu and other 'minor' languages from East Asia. The materials include manuscripts, printed books, periodicals, maps and newspapers, and also sound recordings and archives.

The Chinese Collection is composed of more than 100,000 printed books, 2500 periodical titles and approximately 20,000 manuscripts. The earliest acquisition of Chinese materials were from the collection of Sir Hans Sloane, founder of the British Museum. The collection is composed of a wide variety of items including manuscripts, printed books, rubbings, maps, scrolls, bank notes, letters, posters and paintings.

Among the highlights of the Chinese Collection we find a unique series of more than 450 Shang Dynasty (商朝 c.1558–1046 BC) oracle bones, which are the oldest items in the Library. They were collected by two missionaries, Samuel Couling and Frank Chalfant between 1903 and 1908, and entered the British Library Collections (at that time part of the British Museum[6]) in 1911. This year we have digitised them and the entire oracle bones collection is available online for readers and researchers.

[6] The British Museum – Homepage. Available at: http://www.britishmuseum.org/.

Another collection highlight, if talking about East Asian printing, is the *Diamond Sutra* (金剛經), the world's oldest dated 'book' (it is in fact a scroll). Dating from AD 868 this book forms part of the Stein Collection. The beautiful frontispiece is now exhibited in the Library Treasures Gallery and it has been restored and digitised completely as part of the International Dunhuang Project (IDP).[7] High resolution images of the scroll are available on the IDP website.

The third highlight I would like to mention is the *Yongle Dadian* (永樂大典): the 'Great Canon of the Yongle Reign', commissioned by the Yongle Emperor (明成祖) in 1402 and completed in 1407. The Library holds 24 volumes of the second edition (1562–72) of this unique manuscript, corresponding to 49 chapters. The *Yongle Dadian* volumes at the British Library have also been entirely digitised and they are freely available to be consulted on the Library website.

What best prepared you for your work as the Lead Curator of the East Asian Collections at the British Library?

Apart from strong language and subject knowledge, I think that this job requires a high level of flexibility, an open-minded attitude, the ability to work under short deadlines and the ability to deal with colleagues, partners and readers from different countries and experiences. In this light, I think that my international background and the fact that I had experience of working in different countries helped me to have the right approach. You certainly also have to love what you do, and in my case this is quite easy as I really enjoy working for the public and working with culture.

People working for the British Library are sometimes called curators and sometimes librarians. What are the major functional differences between the two?

The British Library now uses the term 'Curator' to refer to the team members who are responsible for the management of a collection. Their duties include liaising with the Conservation team for care of the collection, undertaking the selection of titles for acquisition, speaking with the media about the collections and curating exhibitions. It is a broad term, but probably also the most accurate given the nature of our collections (the library was part of the British Museum until 1973), and given that we work not only as a library (and so the job involves cataloguing, replying to readers' enquiries and so on) but also as a museum (with both permanent and temporary displays, national and international loans, show&tell for visitors and students and so on). Furthermore, the Library Collections do not only include books but also physical objects (line bones, artifacts, paintings, banknotes and so on) so in this case the term curator is more appropriate, and it gives the idea of the broad range of activities involved.

Do professional librarians working at The British Library also need to be holders of an American Library Association-accredited Master of Library and Information Science (MLIS) degree?

[7] International Dunhuang Project (IDP) – Homepage. Available at: http://idp.bl.uk/.

It depends on what the main duties are for the particular role. Some jobs, like the position of Cataloguer, are usually directed at people who have an MLIS degree, strong skills in cataloguing and/or extensive experience in a library. Other roles are open to people with different backgrounds who have specific languages skills or other strengths depending on the specific requirements. In the case of the Curators, the MLIS degree is non-compulsory but there are other mandatory requirements such as good knowledge of the languages involved and their literature, a first degree level qualification in the relevant discipline, the ability to work both independently and in a team and good information technology skills.

The Library makes sure that we have the training that we need, not only when we first enter the role, but also as ongoing training and development. In my case, I received training in MARC21 cataloguing when I first arrived and I work in close contact with our Metadata team to be able to work at the required standards.

Recently, we successfully completed some cataloguing projects with a cycle of paid internships. We were able to temporarily employ interns with strong language skills in some 'minor' languages included in our collections (i.e., Ethiopic and Mongolian), which our permanent team had struggled to catalogue because of the range of languages and scripts involved. The interns did not necessarily have previous experience in cataloguing, but, thanks to a series of documents created and developed by our metadata team and after basic training, they could complete the information required simply by typing in a spreadsheet which was eventually converted to a MARC record.

How many different languages have you mastered? Are you also trained to read premodern Chinese literature? How vital are such foreign language skills in terms of performing your job as a curator at The British Library?

I speak and read Italian, English, Chinese and Spanish. At University I attended two courses on Classical Chinese, which turned out to be very useful for my current role. Chinese language is vital for my daily work, especially when cataloguing and selecting materials for the new acquisitions, but also when communicating with partners in China. Chinese modern and premodern literature is also a subject I studied at university. In order to deepen my knowledge and keep updated on the current research trends, I also try to read a lot and attend seminars and lectures focusing on historical periods or literary works which are included in our collections.

(1) Language Skills, (2) Knowledge in History, (3) Research Skills or (4) Knowledge in Archaeology. According to your experience, which has proven to be the most important in order to do your job well?

All the skills you mentioned are very important for our work since we are dealing with collections which can, and need to, be interpreted from many different aspects. We can look at an item from a language, historical or archaeological perspective, so I would say that knowing language, history and archaeology and having research skills are all important abilities for being a good curator. The flexibility to shift from one perspective to another and the ability to adapt these skills to different parts of the collections are also important.

Please describe the staffing structure of the East Asian Department at the British Library?

The team is part of the Asian and African Collections, which includes material from South Asia, South-East Asia, East Asia, Central Asia, the Middle East and Africa. There are about 40 people working in the Department, including both permanent and temporary staff. It's a very lively and exciting team to work in, with many colleagues of different nationalities and from different backgrounds.

Currently, our East Asian team is composed by five people. The Head of the East Asian Collections supervises our team and, together with the Curator of the Japanese Collections, manages the material in Japanese and Korean. As Lead Curator, I am responsible for the Chinese, Mongolian and Manchu Collections, and I work together with the Curator of the Chinese Collections and the Curator of the Manchu and Mongolian Collections. The team is divided in two main areas, one focusing on Japanese and Korean, the other one concentrating on Chinese, Mongolian and Manchu, but we obviously have many intersection points in our collections so we often work together on several projects.

Two temporary members are also currently part of the East Asia team: one intern for Korean, who is helping us to catalogue the material in Hangul, and one post-doctoral researcher, who is cataloguing and researching our Maoist propaganda posters collection.

East Asian material from the Stein Collection is also included in the IDP, which is also part of the Asian and African Collections Department. Here, a team of approximately eight people is taking care of digitisation of items of the Stein Collection, in partnership with international institutions with similar collections.

Could you describe your typical day at work? Is there ever a typical day at work?

One of the most exciting aspects of my work is 1 day is rarely exactly like another one. Some duties are carried out on a daily basis (cataloguing, answering readers' enquiries and planning new acquisitions), but for the rest of the time it really depends on the projects we are working on in that particular week or month.

If we are planning a digitisation project, then we liaise with the digitisation studio and the licensing team; if there is an exhibition, we spend more time preparing labels and working with the exhibition team and the conservators in charge of handling and transporting the items; if there is an international agreement on the table, then we spend more time drafting the agreement and working with our international partners and legal offices.

It depends what's in the diary and what the deadlines for delivering a particular project are. We usually engage with our audience through our departmental blog, where we write about the collections or new projects, and through social media like Twitter.

Investing the time and manpower to engage with our audience through our departmental blog, where we write about the collections or new projects, and through social media like Twitter. What benefits would it bring to your work, and the role of the British Library in society, in the long run?

At the Library every department has a so-called 'Departmental blog'. Contributing to the blog is an important part of our work as curators, because it gives us the possibility to connect with our readers, to show the results of our research and to further stimulate external research. Blogs are usually short and contain a lot of visual material and they are not only aimed at researchers, but also at the general public. Social media are also important communication channels for us. They are easy to use, flexible and immediate and give us the opportunity to engage with audiences from all around the world and especially the younger students and researchers.

What scholarly and professional associations are you a part of, and how do they assist you in your work?

I am a member of the China Library Group (CLG) and the European Association of Sinological Librarians (EASL). The first group meets twice a year and include the librarians and curators specialising in Chinese in the UK. The second association includes all the sinological librarians and curators in Europe; an EASL conference takes place once a year in September, in one European library or university which invites the other associates. I am also a member of the Universities' China Committee in London and the National Committee for Information Resources on Asia (NACIRA).[8]

Being part of these associations is very important for my work as they allow me to be in touch with several colleagues, discuss issues or problems that we might share and receive assistance or suggestions from the other members. It is also a good way to keep updated on the latest trends in the research and information management fields not only at a national, but also at an international level.

Who are the majority users of the East Asian Collections at The British Library? That is, who comes to see you about your collections? Are they mostly professors or students from higher education institutions? Or are they people from outside the postsecondary sector, i.e., the general public?

According to our last survey, the majority of the Library's readers are doing academic research at a postgraduate level, and I believe this is true also for the East Asian Collections. Given the nature and the history of our collections, which have a strong focus on rare or unique materials, most of the readers are professors, researchers or PhD students who are doing research on primary sources.

Nevertheless, sometimes I receive enquiries from undergraduates who would like to see material from the Ming and Qing dynasties or earlier, not necessarily for research but for their enjoyment and inspiration. Access to the Library Reading Rooms is free and anyone with an interest in our collections can register for a Reading Pass.

[8] National Committee for Information Resources on Asia – Homepage. Available at: http://nacira.org.uk/.

Could you give examples of typical reference/research enquiries issued by the researchers or scholars at the East Asian Collections at the British Library?

Research enquiries are mostly about our rare books collection, given the variety of the catalogues involved. Sometimes researchers based outside the UK need to preorder an item for which the shelf mark is needed. Being located outside of London they don't have access to the cards and microfiches catalogues, so we help them to locate the material they need. Other times readers are looking for a suggestion about a certain topic, or they are looking for visual material to accompany their forthcoming publication. For enquiries in general, we cooperate with our colleagues in the Reference Services Team who are also working in the Reading Rooms, so they have a daily contact with the readers.

There is also an Oriental Section of the British Library, managed by Hiroko Brittain in Boston Spa. What are the differences in terms of the collections and services between the Oriental Section (Boston Spa) and the East Asian Collections of the British Library (London)?

The Library's two main sites, St Pancras in London and Boston Spa in Yorkshire, are part of the same institution and they do not differ in terms of structure or services.

Speaking about the collections, we can say that most of the historical collections are held in the basements in London, while most of the contemporary acquisitions and the newspapers are held in Boston Spa, where we recently opened a new high-tech storage building for the Newspapers Collection. The main reason is logistical. Most of our readers in London need to consult rare items, so having them located in the basement of the same building is more convenient. An item can be ordered from one of our Reading Rooms in St Pancras and received within 1 h. However, there is not space for everything in St Pancras so the contemporary acquisitions are stored in Boston Spa. Items can be ordered from St Pancras and are delivered within 48 h. We also have a Reading Room in Boston Spa, and both the sites can receive items from the other when ordered by a Reader or a staff member.

Some of the staff are located in London, while others are located in Boston Spa. Staff in operational departments like IT, Human Resources, Metadata management and so on are usually located in Boston Spa, while most of the curatorial staff, exhibition teams and events teams are based in London. However, it is not uncommon for colleagues from the same team to be located on different sites and communicate daily with emails and online video conferences.

Hiroko recently retired from the Library, so all team members of the East Asian Collections are currently based in St Pancras.

How does the collection catalogue and provide access for users? With a non-roman script, what challenges does this present to cataloguing? Are there any?

The Library's main catalogue is called *Explore the British Library* and it contains more than 56 million items. It can be freely accessed from the home page of the

Library website. Another catalogue, also available on the website, is dedicated to the archives and manuscripts.

The Chinese Collections catalogues are both in electronic and card format. The material acquired before 1966 was catalogued on cards using the Wade–Giles transliteration system. This catalogue contains about 20,000 titles, of which many are rare and important items from the Ming and Qing dynasties. In 1966, the Library adopted *pinyin* as the transliteration system for Chinese characters. The pinyin cards catalogue produced from that year until 1993 contains about 50,000 items. These two catalogues are available to consult in the Library's Asian and African Studies Reading Room in St Pancras.

In 1993, the Library started using an electronic system for cataloguing the Chinese Collection items. Initially, the system used was *Allegro*. The items catalogued in *Allegro* are available to consult in a web-based catalogue: the UK Union Catalogue of Chinese books, which includes not only the British Library items, but also the items in the Chinese Collections of other UK institutions such as Oxford, Cambridge, SOAS and so on. Current acquisitions of printed books are now catalogued in a system called *Aleph*, which operates in MARC21 and is the system under the *Explore the British Library* catalogue.

The manuscripts in the Chinese Collections are divided in two main areas. The Stein Collection manuscripts are catalogued and digitised as part of the *IDP* (based at the Library). There are approximately 600 manuscripts in Chinese which are not part of the Stein Collection, and they are listed in a series of printed catalogues. Contemporary acquired manuscripts are instead catalogued in the Integrated Archives and Manuscripts System (IAMS), which makes the records available on the Library website.

The main challenges regarding the Chinese Collections catalogues are the formats of the records rather than the non-roman script used. Most systems now integrate and display non-roman scripts without problems, so in my case the biggest challenge lies in converting the large amount of records on cards (about 70,000 titles) to electronic ones, and in making the conversion from the Wade–Giles transliteration to the current standards. Converting the card catalogues to electronic records means that readers will not need to physically be in the Library, or spend time going through thousands of cards, to know what is in the collection. They will also be able to preorder the material they want to look at online.

We are currently cooperating with a series of institutions in mainland China and Taiwan for the retroconversion of our Chinese Collections catalogues. Furthermore, we recently launched a crowdsourcing platform called *LibCrowds*, where we ask users to help us by matching a record they are shown on a scanned card with existing electronic records in the Online Computer Library Center database. We are already seeing good results. For example, through the crowdsourcing platform we were able to receive approximately 2000 completed records in about four months, and we are now ingesting them in our system. They will be available online in a couple of weeks for everyone to see and share.

The themes and information needs of libraries, archives, and museums (LAM's, as some have referred to them) have increasingly converged. What are your experiences and thoughts about these cultural institutions, whose work and best practices now often overlap?

The British Library is an institution that shares a lot in common with public museums and archives. Given the nature of its collections, the Library engages with the public in many different ways. The Library was part of the British Museum until 1973, so we naturally find 'museum' characteristics in our collections.

Not only do people come here to access the collections in the Reading Rooms, but also to enjoy a talk, an evening event or to visit our exhibition spaces: the Treasures Gallery, which can be freely accessed and exhibits a permanent display of the Library's most precious and renowned items (from the Diamond Sutra to the Gutenberg Bible), and the Folio and PACCAR Galleries, where we organise themed exhibitions. The Reading Rooms can be accessed only with a Reading Pass, but the other spaces can be enjoyed by everyone. There are cafeterias and shops, a conference centre and a learning centre, so the site really works as a public space in a broader sense.

In our daily job, we probably have lots in common with museum curators, as we not only catalogue the materials and answer to reader's requests and questions, but we also organise exhibitions, events, conferences, tours and 'show and tell' sessions. We also work in cooperation with our Loan Registrar for lending items to other institutions, with the Library's Conservation Centre and with the Imaging Studio. We also cooperate with other libraries, museums and universities or other institutions devoted to culture and learning.

Recently, I have been managing a project funded by the UK Department of Culture, Media and Sport (DCMS[9]) on the conservation, digitisation and exhibition of the Library oracle bones collections. This activity is part of a bigger project of skill sharing with Chinese institutions, and it involves the British Library, the British Museum, the V&A (Museum)[10] and the Tate. I attend regular meetings with my colleagues from these institutions where we share knowledge and practices and we are now organising a workshop together. This experience has been enlightening, as I learned how much my work has in common with the work of my colleagues at the other institutions in London. I could see that we generally share the same challenges and strengths in working with East Asian Collections and with international partners.

Which part(s) of your job as the Lead Curator of the East Asian Collections at The British Library do you find most rewarding?

I am very happy and proud when I feel that I do something useful and enjoyable for readers and the public. This usually happens when we succeed in digitising an item and making it available online for everybody to study and see, or when, after months of hard work, we open an exhibition and I see people enjoying it, looking at the labels I wrote and learning something from it. It is also very rewarding when we get positive feedback from someone. Now and then readers write to us to express gratitude and appreciation for our work which for example, enabled them to write a PhD thesis or

[9] UK Department of Culture, Media and Sport – Homepage. Available at: https://www.gov.uk/government/organisations/department-for-culture-media-sport.
[10] Victoria and Albert Museum – Homepage. Available at: http://www.vam.ac.uk/.

an article. Those are the moments when you know you did something worth doing, no matter how much work and effort it required.

It is not uncommon to see librarians with no interest in music or visual arts, taking up positions as heads/directors of music and visual arts libraries. They are hired because they are effective administrators or managers or good at IT, and not because of their knowledge or research skills in related fields. Being an effective administrator versus being a respectable scholar with well-grounded knowledge in the field, which do you think is more important to serve as a good curator?

I think that a curator needs both management and research skills, as well as being rather flexible in their everyday work. My daily duties really cover both of the aspects. For example, in order to reply to readers' enquiries, to select the materials for new acquisitions, to interpret the materials in the collection, to present a conference paper or to prepare an exhibition, you would certainly need a strong basis of knowledge in the field. However, at the same time you would also need time management and project management skills, and you should be able to administrate funds, manage the work of others and organise your work within short deadlines. The challenge is therefore to maintain a balance between scholarly research and administrative/management work.

Do you have any questions for me? Is there anything you would like to share with the readers before we conclude this interview?

I would like to thank you for interviewing me and I am eager to read how my colleagues around the world replied to your questions. Sharing knowledge and expertise and being aware of other colleagues' experiences is certainly the best way to improve our skills and to better serve the public as librarians, curators or archivists.

Further Reading

Blogposts written by Sara Chiesura on for the Asia, Pacific and Africa Collections, the British Library. Available at: https://bl.academia.edu/SaraChiesura.

A Combined Library, Archive, and Museum – Exploring the British Library

4

Hamish Todd
The British Library, London, United Kingdom

Introduction

Hamish Todd (Fig. 4.1) leads the curatorial team responsible for the British Library's collections from East Asia. The British Library–through the combination of the collecting traditions of the old British Museum Library and the India Office Library and Records–possesses one of the finest single resources for Asian studies in the world. Since British Museum Library's inception, the British Museum Library and the India Office Library have both enjoyed the privilege of legal deposits of printed books, periodicals and newspapers from colonial India, which expanded the collections enormously during the second half of the 19th and first half of the 20th century. The British Museum Library also benefited from similar legislation relating to Sri Lanka, Mauritius, Fiji, Hong Kong, Malaysia etc. The effectiveness of the colonial legacy's legal deposit eventually dwindled by the 1930s and it was not until the 1960s that systematic collecting–largely through straightforward commercial channels backed up by some exchange agreements–was revived. The India Office Library and the British Museum Library (from 1973 onwards part of the British Library) continued to independently collect both English-language and Asian-language material right down to 1982, when the India Office Library was transferred to the British Library.

Could you begin this interview by first introducing yourself, for example, your training and background, and your major roles and duties as the Head of the East Asian Collections at the British Library?

I read Japanese at Cambridge University[1] and graduated in 1983. I then spent two years in Japan as a participant in the British English Teachers Scheme (a precursor of the Japan Exchange and Teaching (JET) Programme[2]), which offered UK graduates

[1] University of Cambridge – Homepage. Available at: http://www.cam.ac.uk.
[2] Japan Exchange and Teaching (JET) Programme – Homepage. Available at: http://jetprogramme.org/en/.

Inside the World's Major East Asian Collections. http://dx.doi.org/10.1016/B978-0-08-102145-3.00004-2

Figure 4.1 Hamish Todd.

the opportunity to work in schools, colleges and other organisations in Japan, primarily to teach English. I worked at Suntory,[3] a brewing and distilling company, teaching English to staff members and translating correspondence and advertising material.

On my return to the UK in 1985 I worked as a translator, and then in December 1986 I joined the British Library[4] as one of two Japanese language curators in the Department of Oriental Manuscripts and Printed Books. I have been with the British Library ever since although my job title and the name of the department have undergone several changes over the years. In 2000 I became Head of the Japanese Section, then in 2010 Lead Curator for Japanese and Korean.

Since April 2015 I have been Head of East Asian Collections. As such, my primary role is to lead, develop and manage the Library's collections of material relating to East Asia (China, Japan and Korea). I also act as the lead curator for Japanese Collections and am responsible for the Korean Collections. I lead a team of four other curators, two for Chinese, one for Japanese and one for Manchu/Mongolian, as well as project staff and interns. Together we work to develop, preserve and exploit the Library's holdings in the East Asian languages to build international collaborations and partnerships, and to make the collections available to users through record creation, digitisation, exhibitions and events.

How, and at what age, did you develop an interest for the East Asian languages and cultures?

From a young age I have been fascinated by languages and scripts, I remember family holidays to Greece and North Africa where I was intrigued by the strange symbols that I could not read. At one point I was determined to study hieroglyphics and be an Egyptologist but decided the weather might be too hot! At high school our history curriculum included Asian history and it was there that I first really became interested in East Asia, especially Japan. Its history, culture, language and writing

[3] Suntory – Homepage. Available at: http://www.suntory.com.

[4] The British Library – Homepage. Available at: http://www.bl.uk.

seemed so different and challenging. In the late 1970s, when I was considering what to study at university, I bought a number of 'Teach Yourself' language books and in the end Japanese won out over Arabic, Hebrew and what was then called 'Serbo-Croat'.

How many different languages have you mastered? You began your career as the Japanese Curator at the British Library. From 2000 to 2014 you then became the Lead Curator of the Japanese and Korean Collections. Given your experience and the positions you took at the British Library, I take that you are also fluent in both Japanese and Korean?

At school I learned French, German, Latin and Ancient Greek, all of which have proved very useful over the years, either when travelling or for helping with the vagaries of English spelling! I have also learned Dutch and Danish, since the Netherlands and Denmark are two countries that I love to visit and where I have good friends. Of course, the foreign language that I am most fluent in is Japanese. I especially enjoy the challenge of reading the non-standard forms of Chinese characters and kana scripts that I encounter in the course of my work.

Since being given responsibility for our Korean Collections I have made efforts to learn Korean, but my knowledge of the spoken language is not as good as I might wish. Fortunately, the widespread use of Chinese characters in premodern Korean texts allows me to understand our important collection of antiquarian material and is also a great help now that I deal more with Chinese matters.

Are you a second career curator/librarian – meaning have you had other careers before you started working as a curator for the British Library?

As I mentioned earlier, I worked in Japan as an English teacher for two years and then as a translator after I came back to the UK.

Could you please provide a brief introduction to the East Asian Collections at The British Library?

The British Library's East Asian Collections include material in Chinese, Japanese, Korean, Mongolian, Manchu and other 'minor' languages. They cover a wide range of subjects and formats including manuscripts, printed books, periodicals, maps and newspapers. They range in date from Chinese oracle bones, which are 3500 years old, to the most up-to-date electronic resources. Apart from what is technically the 'East Asian Collections', material in these languages and relating to the countries of East Asia can also be found in other departments of the Library. So for example, there are rich resources in the Sound Archive, the Map Collection and Archives and Manuscripts.

What is the current size of the East Asian Collections? Could you also describe the highlights of the East Asian Collections at The British Library?

Calculating the total size of our East Asian Collections is problematic. Firstly, not all material has yet been included in online catalogues. Secondly, the collections are not all kept in one location. However, a rough estimate would be as follows:

Languages	Printed Books	Manuscripts	Serials/Official Publications
Chinese	100,000	22,000	2500
Japanese	80,000	500	6000
Korean	15,000	50	700

My colleague Sara Chiesura has commented on the Chinese highlights in her interview, so here I will mention some key items from the Japanese and Korean Collections.

The pre-1868 antiquarian holdings of 4000 printed works and 400 manuscripts are the most important part of the Japanese Collection. One undoubted highlight is *Feiqe monogatari*, a series of extracts from the Tale of the Heike, printed by the Jesuit Mission in Amakusa in 1592–93 using movable type. Works produced by the Jesuit Mission Press are known as *Kirishitanban* or 'Christian publications' and are very rare. Only 73 copies are known worldwide and the British Library is fortunate to have seven of them. Our *Feiqe monogatari* is the only extant copy in the world. What makes it particularly significant is that it is printed in the Roman alphabet not Japanese script, so it offers a valuable insight to the pronunciation of the Japanese language at that time.

Among our Japanese manuscripts, the most important are the 19 lavishly illustrated *Nara ehon*, versions of popular tales which were produced from the mid 16th to late 17th centuries. Among them is an early manuscript of the *Ise monogatari*, probably written around 1520–60, and *Tengu no dairi* which tells of Minamoto Yoshitsune's visit to the palace of the Long Nosed Goblins. All these *Nara ehon* have been digitised and can be viewed on the British Library's Digitised Manuscript pages http://www.bl.uk/manuscripts/.

As the highlight of the Korean Collection I would select *Kisa chinp'yori chinch'an ŭigwe* (records of the ritual presentation and banquet in the *kisa* year) written in 1809. This manuscript was created for the Korean Royal Court as a record of the ceremonies conducted in the first and second months of 1809 to mark the 60th anniversary of the consummation of the marriage of Lady Hyegyŏng (1735–1815), widow of Crown Prince Sado (1735–62), and grandmother of the reigning King Sunjo. The ceremonies organised in 1809 were part of the latter's desire to make amends for the past ignominies his grandmother had suffered and no expense was spared. The manuscript provides a faithful record in words and images of the arrangements, participants and objects involved in the formal presentation of cloth (*chinp'yori*) and in the banquet (*chinch'an*). It has now been digitised and is available on our Digitised Manuscripts website.

What best prepared you for your work as the Head of the East Asian Collection at the British Library?

The best preparation for my role as Head of the East Asian Collections has been the years of experience working in the British Library and in the field of Japanese studies librarianship. One of the key elements of the work of a curator is knowledge of the collections for which he/she is responsible, and this can only be acquired with time and by learning from colleagues. I certainly learned a huge amount from my predecessor and I see it as an important part of my role as Head of the East Asian team to help my colleagues develop too.

The British Library is a large and complex organisation so it is crucial to have a good understanding of its history and how the various parts work together. At the same time the skills required by a librarian or curator are constantly changing. When I first started at the British Library in 1986 the most sophisticated technology I had to master was an ancient typewriter, a catalogue card and a pen! Now so much of what we do involves digital media and web-based projects and I am constantly learning. I am very grateful that other members of my team and the department are so 'tech-savvy'.

I think it is vital to be flexible and open to new ideas and opportunities. For those of us who have been in the profession or an organisation for many years there is sometimes a tendency to think 'we tried that before but it did not work'! New technology, collaborations and an innovative approach to funding can often make the formerly impossible possible!

Do you also work closely with the East Asian curators/librarians at the British Museum, the National Library of France, the National Library of China or National Diet Library of Japan for different cross-national collaborative projects?

The East Asian team maintains close contacts with libraries, museums, universities and other institutions within the UK and around the world.

We regularly work with colleagues from the British Museum[5] and frequently lend collection items to each other's exhibitions. Given our shared history, the British Museum and British Library could be called 'sister organisations' and many of what are now British Library collections were originally acquired by the British Museum. We have loaned Chinese, Japanese and Korean items to the British Museum's exhibition *Ming: 50 years that changed China* which ran from September 2014 to January 2015. As my colleague Sara Chiesura mentioned, we are currently participating in a UK government-funded project to share skills with China along with the British Museum, the Victoria and Albert Museum[6] and the Tate Galleries.

Naturally, the national libraries of East Asia are key organisations for us to work with. The British Library has a Memorandum of Understanding with the National Library of China (NLC),[7] which is a partner in a number of our projects. The International Dunhuang Project (IDP)[8] has a long and fruitful relationship with the

[5] British Museum – Homepage. Available at: http://www.britishmuseum.org.
[6] Victoria and Albert Museum – Homepage. Available at: http://www.vam.ac.uk.
[7] National Library of China – Homepage. Available at: http://www.nlc.cn/newen/.
[8] International Dunhuang Project (IDP) – Homepage. Available at: http://idp.bl.uk.

NLC and the East Asian team is now working with NLC on a number of cataloguing and digitisation initiatives, among them one centred on the British Library's collection of Chinese oracle bones. Colleagues from NLC are sharing their expertise on the best practice for cataloguing and housing these precious items with our curatorial and conservation staff.

Similarly the British Library has worked closely with the National Diet Library of Japan (NDL)[9] over many years. I and several other British Library staff have benefited from training opportunities provided by NDL. I spent 3 months at NDL early in my career as part of an official staff exchange between the two institutions and it provided a valuable grounding in many aspects of Japanese studies librarianship, as well as creating a network with many leading figures in our community. Other British Library and UK librarians have also been able to take advantage of such arrangements. In June 2015 we hosted a workshop conducted by a reference specialist for UK Japanese studies librarians.

Our relations with the National Library of Korea (NLK)[10] also go back many decades and there is a formal Memorandum of Understanding between the two institutions. We are currently planning a project with NLK to digitise some of our rare books and manuscripts and I attended the Overseas Koreanology Librarians Workshop,[11] which NLK organised and hosted in October 2015.

With all three national libraries we have long-standing exchanges of official and government publications, which have proved an excellent way to obtain these important but often hard to acquire materials. In addition, we frequently welcome staff from the national libraries to the East Asian Collections, and are often involved when they visit colleagues in other areas of the British Library, since the working relationships are not limited to the Library's Asian and African Collections.

Curators versus Librarians – people working for the British Library are sometimes called curators and sometimes librarians – what are the major functional differences between the two?

The British Library uses the term 'curator' for some of its staff, partly for historical reasons and partly to reflect the nature of our roles. The core collections and departments of today's British Library were originally part of the British Museum until 1973, when the British Library was founded as an independent body. The Museum terminology of 'curator' rather than 'librarian' has continued to be used for those staff who are responsible for management and care of a specific collection. It reflects the fact that our collections contain not just books and manuscripts but a wide range of material including artefacts, archives, sound recordings, photographs, paintings, oracle bones and so on. 'Curator' also seems an appropriate term to convey the range of our duties which, alongside obviously librarian-type activities such as acquisitions and cataloguing, also includes tasks more normally associated with a

[9] National Diet Library of Japan – Homepage. Available at: http://www.ndl.go.jp/en/.

[10] National Library of Korea – Homepage. Available at: http://www.nl.go.kr/english/.

[11] Overseas Koreanology Librarians Workshop – Homepage. Available at: http://nias.ku.dk/news/overseas-koreanology-librarian-workshop.

museum, for example arranging exhibitions and displays, organising 'show and tell' sessions for visitors and liaising with conservators over preservation and treatment of the collections.

In the British Library, we use 'librarian' in a more general sense to distinguish those staff who work with the collections from those who fulfil other roles within conservation, imaging studios, and operational, technical and support services.

Following restructuring of the Library's senior management, the term 'Chief Librarian' has been introduced for the post in charge of all collections-related departments, while the Chief Operating Officer heads the other sections such as Reading Room Services, Finance, Human Resources, Collection Storage, Document Supply and Customer Services. Both of these report to the Chief Executive who is the overall head of the British Library.

For the professional librarians working at the British Library, do they also need to be holders of an American Library Association-accredited Master of Library and Information Science (MLIS) degree?

As far as I am aware there is no requirement for British Library staff to hold an American Library Association-accredited MLIS. It may be included as a 'desirable' qualification in recruitment but not as 'essential'. For curatorial (librarian) posts at the British Library more emphasis is laid on knowledge of the appropriate language or discipline, relevant research or practical experience and other 'competencies' identified by Library management. For example flexibility, the ability to work independently or as part of a team, problem-solving skills etc.

The Library also sets great store by ensuring that staff receive appropriate training, either 'on the job' or through organised courses and workshops.

(1) Language Skills, (2) Knowledge in History, (3) Research Skills or (4) Knowledge in Archaeology. Based on your experience, which has proven to be most important in order to do your job well?

In fact all of these skills are necessary for my work as a curator. A knowledge of the linguistic, historical and, in some cases, archaeological context in which an item was created is very important in understanding, managing and exploiting the collections in my charge. At the same time research skills are needed for much of the bibliographic and interpretative work I do as well as to help me understand the needs of readers and users.

Please describe the staffing structure of the East Asian Department at The British Library? For example, what are the working relationships between the Head of the East Asian Collections, the Lead Curator of the Japanese and Korean Collections and the Japanese Curator? Also what is your working relationship with Sara Chiesura?

The East Asian team is part of the Asian and African Collections, alongside curatorial teams responsible for Middle Eastern and Central Asian Collections, South Asian Collections, SouthEast Asian Collections, African Collections, the IDP and the Prints,

Drawings and Photographs section. Our team consists of five people: the Head of East Asian Collections, who manages the team and is also in charge of the Japanese and Korean Collections, supported by the Curator of Japanese Collections; the Lead Curator of East Asian Collections is responsible for the Chinese Collections and works closely with the Curator of Chinese Collections and the Curator of Manchu and Mongolian Collections.

This nomenclature is perhaps a little confusing as the British Library recently changed the names of some of the posts. There was formerly (1) a Lead Curator for Japanese and Korean, (2) a Lead Curator for Chinese, (3) a Japanese Curator and (4) a Chinese Curator. I was appointed to the new role of Head of East Asian Collections that absorbed the functions of the Lead Curator for Japanese and Korean. The post of Lead Curator of Chinese Collections was renamed Lead Curator of East Asian Collections.

In addition, we often have a number of staff working with us on a temporary basis as interns or on special projects.

Outside the East Asian Collections proper a number of staff work on East Asian material. For example the IDP has a team of seven who work on cataloguing, digitisation and conservation of the Central Asian/East Asian Collections, acquired by Sir Marc Aurel Stein in the early 20th century.

Could you describe your typical day at work? Is there ever a typical day at work?

It is one of the joys — and challenges — of my job that no two days are ever the same. It all depends on what projects we are working on in the team, what deadlines we have and how busy we are with visitors and delegations.

There are some regular or recurring activities which form the core of my curatorial work: selecting material for acquisition, cataloguing antiquarian material, answering a wide variety of reference enquiries from readers and the general public, assisting colleagues in the Acquisitions team and elsewhere in the Library with tasks that require a knowledge of Japanese or Korean, identifying collections items in need of conservation and so on. Or I might be asked to provide valuations for collection items going on loan or to give an expert opinion on export licenses.

I am regularly contacted by members of the public who have Japanese or Korean items that they want me to identify. Sometimes they send a photo; sometimes they bring the item in person. It is always an interesting challenge and requires a good deal of detective work. It can also need some tact when a precious heirloom turns out not to be the hidden treasure they are hoping for! Fortunately British Library staff are not permitted to give financial valuations so I just gently hint that an item may be of primarily sentimental or curiosity value. Generally people are simply keen to find out more about their mystery objects.

Representation and promotion of the collections are important elements of a curator's work so I may be giving a presentation or a lecture, or writing a post for our Asian and African Studies blog about an interesting collection item or project we are involved in. I often have to receive visits from VIP delegations, academic researchers, university students or other groups with an interest in our East Asian Collections.

Frequently this involves organising 'show and tell' sessions which is one of the really rewarding and enjoyable aspects of my job.

As Head of East Asian Collections, I also have to attend a lot of meetings — some more interesting than others — to do with the strategy and planning part of my job. For example there may be discussions with our legal and licensing teams or our Imaging Services colleagues when we are involved in a digitisation project, or with other Collection Heads over issues that affect the whole department.

What scholarly and professional associations are you a part of, and how do they assist you in your work?

I find it hugely valuable to know so many knowledgeable and dedicated people both in the UK and overseas to whom I can turn for information and guidance. I have been fortunate to be involved with a number of organisations including the Japan Library Group (JLG),[12] of which I am chair, the Korea Library Group (KLG), the National Committee for Information resources on Asia (NACIRA)[13] in the UK and the European Association of Japanese Resource Specialists (EAJRS),[14] all of which allow colleagues to share information, expertise and experiences. In recent years I have also benefited enormously from participating in conferences and organisations in the US. I regularly attend the Council of East Asian Libraries meetings and am currently a member of the Committee on Japanese Materials, as well as serving on the Executive Committee of the North American Coordinating Council on Japanese Library Resources (NCC). I have learned a great deal from North American colleagues with their wide range of skills and experience.

As East Asian Studies librarians around the world face many of the same technological issues and challenges of 'how to do more with less?', I believe it is increasingly important that our community works together to offer support and expertise. Whatever the advances of technology, much of what we achieve continues to rely on personal networks and our willingness to share our knowledge.

Who are the majority users of the East Asian Collections at the British Library? That is, who comes to see you about your collections? Are they mostly professors or students from higher education institutions? Or are they people from outside the post-secondary sector, i.e. the public?

As a national library we have a wide range of users. Given the nature of our East Asian Collections the majority are academic researchers or postgraduate students. However, independent researchers, undergraduates and members of the general public often make use of our collections and seek our advice. A large number of our users are from

[12] The Japan Library Group (JLG) – Homepage. Available at: http://www.jlgweb.org.uk.

[13] National Committee for Information resources on Asia (NACIRA) – Homepage. Available at: http://nacira.org.uk.

[14] European Association of Japanese Resource Specialists (EAJRS) – Homepage. Available at: http://eajrs.net.

East Asia since much of our material is unique, very rare or impossible to access in the country of origin.

Access to British Library collections is free of charge so anyone with an interest in our East Asian holdings can register for a Reading Pass.

Could you give examples of typical reference/research inquiries issued by the researchers or scholars at the East Asian Collections at the British Library?

The majority of our reference enquiries relate to our antiquarian Chinese, Japanese and Korean Collections. Given the history, size and complexity of our collections, and the fact that everything is not yet catalogued online, we are often asked for help identifying particular items or to find material on a research topic.

However, the types of reference enquiries I deal with are very varied: recently, for example they have ranged from how Japanese folding books (*orihon*) were read in the Edo Period to religion in North Korea and from trying to decode ownership seals to looking for evidence of the Chinese Trading Factory in Nagasaki on some of our early Japanese maps.

There is also an Oriental Section (British Library), managed by Hiroko Brittain in Boston Spa. What are the differences in terms of collections and services between the Oriental Section (Boston Spa) and the East Asian Collections of the British Library (London)?

There was formerly an Oriental Section at the British Library's site in Boston Spa, Yorkshire, which handled acquisitions and processing of journals in East Asian languages for the British Library's Document Supply Service, mainly in the fields of science, technology and medicine. However, following the retirement of its former head, Hiroko Brittain, a restructuring took place and the work of the Oriental Section was combined with others so it no longer exists as a separate entity nor is there any specialist East Asian language expertise. Members of the East Asian team in St Pancras are now called on to help with Romanisation and other queries.

How does the collection catalogue and provide access for users? With a non-roman script, what challenges does this present to cataloguing? Are there any?

This is one of our greatest challenges! The British Library main catalogue, *Explore the British Library*, contains more than 56 million items and is freely available online. A second online catalogue *Explore Archives and Manuscripts* provides access to non-print material such as manuscripts, archival documents and photographs. However, not all East Asian material is included in these. A large part of the collection can still only be searched on cards or in printed catalogues. As my colleague Sara Chiesura explains in her interview there are a number of innovative projects going on to help with the conversion of the 70,000 catalogue cards to records that can be added to our two main online catalogues.

For Japanese Collections the situation is less daunting. Since the early 1990s the British Library, along with other Japanese studies libraries in the UK, has participated in the UK Japanese Union Catalogue Project through which we registered our holdings with the National Center for Science Information Systems (NACSIS),[15] now the National Institute of Informatics (NII)[16] in Tokyo. Since then UK libraries have added over 250,000 records and the union catalogue project has been expanded to include holdings of 30 institutions in eight countries. This is a cooperative cataloguing system so we also contribute records, principally for our newly acquired antiquarian material, which can be of use to libraries in Japan and elsewhere. All of these records can be viewed on the CiNiii Books website http://ci.nii.ac.jp/books/. Through collaboration with the NII in 2011 we were able to import over 26,000 records into our Aleph system and these are now available via *Explore the British Library*. All current acquisitions of printed material, both modern and antiquarian, are catalogued in Aleph, often using records downloaded from Online Computer Library Center (OCLC)[17] or NACSIS. So the situation for Japanese is that all books and periodicals published since 1900 are available online. Work is proceeding on cataloguing our earlier material. Access to this is via the following printed catalogues: *Catalogue of early Japanese books in the British Library* compiled by Kawase Kazuma and Okazaki Hisaji (Tokyo, 1996) which includes pre-1868 printed books and manuscripts, and *Descriptive Catalogue of Japanese Books in the British Library Printed before 1700*, by Kenneth Burslam Gardner (London and Tenri, 1993) which contains detailed descriptions of 637 items printed in Japan up to and including the end of the Genroku Period (1704). Our 500 Japanese manuscripts are in the process of being added to our online catalogue *Explore Archives and Manuscripts*.

For Korean language material a handlist of the antiquarian material is available and it is hoped that these 250 or so items can soon be added to *Explore the British Library*. Records for manuscripts are available online in *Explore Archives and Manuscripts*. Most modern printed books are available in our main online catalogue and we currently have an intern working to convert the remaining 500 cards.

The challenges presented by East Asian scripts are two-fold. Firstly there are the problems which we face as cataloguers, particularly with premodern material, in reading or deciphering the huge number of Chinese characters and their many variants and, especially for Japanese, the cursive forms of *kanji* and *kana*. Secondly there are the technical difficulties of inputting them into our library systems and catalogues, which are primarily designed for roman script languages. However, as technology advances these problems are being solved. Recently, we have been working to create online records for our holdings of Mongolian books and manuscripts, many of which are written in traditional Mongolian script. Since this should be written vertically and

[15] National Center for Science Information Systems (NACSIS) – Homepage. Available at: http://itt.nissat.tripod.com/itt99012/nacsis.htm.

[16] National Institute of Informatics (NII) – Homepage. Available at: http://www.nii.ac.jp/en/.

[17] OCLC – Homepage. Available at: https://www.oclc.org/home.en.html.

is a dynamic script in which letters change their form according to their position in the word this has presented challenges for our IT and Metadata teams.

The themes and information needs of libraries, archives, and museums (LAMs, as some have referred to them) have increasingly converged. What are your experiences and thoughts about these cultural institutions whose work and best practices now often overlap?

As I have explained, the British Library was created from the British Museum Library in 1973 and our collections are similar to those of a museum in their breadth of formats and range of material. The Library also includes extensive archives so it could be said that we are a combined 'LAM'! In many ways therefore, our work is a mix of traditional librarian and curatorial activities including collection development, cataloguing, research, conservation and exhibition and event organisation.

I believe that the fundamental priorities of museums, libraries and archives are the same, to develop, record, preserve and exploit their collections and there is much that we can learn from each other. We also face many of the same challenges: how best to engage with new audiences, especially the 'Internet Generation', how to utilise new technology and, in Europe at least, how to make the most of our shrinking financial and human resources.

Which part(s) of your job as the Head of the East Asian Collection at the British Library do you find most rewarding?

The most rewarding part of my job has to be the privilege of working with our amazing collections on a daily basis. I really enjoy showing them to users and visitors, explaining what they are and why they are significant and then seeing the audience's interest and enthusiasm.

I also get a great deal of satisfaction from solving puzzles, for example helping a researcher to find exactly what they have been looking for, finding out more about a collection item, deciphering the preface of a Japanese book, working out what the characters on a seal mean and so on. For me there is something deeply satisfying, almost therapeutic, in the process of cataloguing, of examining a book or manuscript, trying to understand its history, significance and content and then expressing that information in a way that will be meaningful to others.

So often our library managers are obsessed with statistics and finding ways to quantify activities. Sadly, so far no one has come up with a system to measure the delight of researchers when a librarian helps them find the elusive item or information they have been searching for!

Another exciting aspect of my new role as Head of East Asian Collections is learning more about the Chinese Collections and working with the curators on the various collaborative projects in which they are involved. I find working with my team a rewarding and stimulating experience. We come from different backgrounds and generations and have different expertise, experience and outlooks but together we make a productive and creative team, a complementary mix of linguistic and collection knowledge, innovative ideas, experience and practical skills.

It is not uncommon to see librarians with no interests in music or visual arts, taking up positions as heads/directors of music and visual arts libraries. They are hired because they are effective administrators or managers or good at IT, and not because of their knowledge or research skills in related fields. Being as effective administrator or being a respectable scholar with well-grounded knowledge in the field, which do you think is more important to serve as a good curator?

Ideally a good curator should combine both administrative skills and expertise in a relevant field of study, although it is not always easy. I am sure most of us can think of examples of excellent scholars who have no idea about managing their time or budgets and of administrators with no understanding of, or interest in, the staff or the organisation they are managing!

At the British Library we are expected to have a thorough knowledge of our collections which underpins our activities but, increasingly, we are also expected to be efficient managers of staff, budgets, time and other resources. Many of us are called upon to develop, raise funds for and manage complex projects which requires a range of new skills. To be able to do this effectively it is vital to have adequate training and support, and to learn from the experience of colleagues who may be further down the road in this regard. We are lucky at the British Library to be able to call on colleagues with a wide range of skills to help us with areas such as fundraising, financial management, human resources, legal matters and copyright/licensing issues.

How Popular Books From Ancient China Were Rescued by Sir Thomas Bodley: A Tale of the Bodleian Library, Oxford University

5

David Helliwell[1], *Heather Rogers*[2]
[1]Bodleian Library, Oxford, United Kingdom; [2]McGill University, Montreal, QC, Canada

Introduction

The University of Oxford is known for being the oldest existing university in continuous operation in the English-speaking world. Supporting the studies, teaching and research of the entire university community are the Bodleian Libraries, notable for being the largest and oldest university library system in the United Kingdom having been a legal deposit library for 400 years. Named after Sir Thomas Bodley (1545–1613), an English diplomat and scholar, the entire Bodleian Library system encompasses 30 libraries across Oxford, i.e., including major research libraries and faculty, departmental and institutional libraries. Chinese scholar and librarian David Helliwell (Fig. 5.1) has been managing the Chinese Collections at the Bodleian Library for over four decades. In the following interview, Helliwell tells us how a piece of newspaper from Hong Kong instilled in him an interest in the Chinese language over 60 years ago, as well as how a large collection of Chinese popular books — originally looked down on by the aristocratic class and scholarly communities in the Ming Dynasty — ended up in the Bodleian Library collection.

Could we begin this interview by you providing a brief self-introduction? For example, your training and background, and how you became the Curator of the Chinese Collections at the Bodleian Library, University of Oxford?

I went to university to read Chinese studies. In the early days, courses on Chinese Studies offered by British universities were almost entirely classical. Nothing had changed in the older British universities at that time, and we were only taught about ancient Chinese history and classical civilization. There was very little, almost nothing, about modern and contemporary China. But everything began to change after I graduated. The university courses now are all completely different, but I was trained as a classical Chinese sinologist.

Inside the World's Major East Asian Collections. http://dx.doi.org/10.1016/B978-0-08-102145-3.00005-4

Figure 5.1 David Helliwell.

What made you become interested in Chinese studies? For example, being European would you not rather study French, Spanish or German, i.e., modern languages spoken by neighbouring countries of the UK?

Well, I did learn many of these European languages at school. I learned French, Latin, and also German, but I soon became very fed up with them. I would lose interest in a language as soon as I figured out how it worked. But the Chinese language absolutely fascinated me, it was the Chinese characters (writing and the scripts) that I was first attracted to. I thought the Chinese writing scripts were absolutely incredible, and I wanted to know how the Chinese writing system worked. As you can see, I like to study a language like a piece of clockwork or a jigsaw puzzle. Maybe I should have studied linguistics or mathematics at university instead.

In other words, your interest in languages lies not in communicating with other people but for the joy that is similar to decoding a riddle? Or the satisfaction derived from solving a mathematical puzzle?

Well, that was exactly what my sinological training gained at university during the 1960s was all about. We were trained not to communicate in Chinese with other 'living' people, but to extract information about ancient China from these premodern Chinese texts.

With your Chinese language skills and knowledge about China, have you ever thought about working for the British foreign services or even for the MI6[1]? Was it by chance that you became interested in the Chinese writing system?

[1] MI6 (Military Intelligence, Section 6) – a British intelligence agency which supplies the British Government with foreign intelligence.

Well, no! I remember when I was at primary school, almost 60 years ago, one of the children had a bit of a newspaper from Hong Kong. It was really very rare because nobody had seen a Chinese newspaper at that time, and she kept tearing little bits out and gave them to her classmates saying, 'Look you've got some Chinese here'!

Was learning a foreign language, especially like Chinese, considered a 'cool' thing to do amongst children and teenagers in the 1960s? Or would one get ridiculed by peers for having such an unusual interest in languages from the Far East?

China was not cool then, and it isn't cool now! Japan is cool, but China is not cool! I am sorry to say that. I went to a state grammar school. You took an examination at the age of 11. If you passed it, you then went to a so-called grammar school and had quite an academic education. That was the education I had.

Could you describe the experience of your very first Chinese lesson, for example, the first day of your Chinese class?

It was at Durham University.[2] I was 18 years old then, and I remember that it took me nearly a week to learn just six Chinese characters. Three years later, I graduated with a bachelor's degree in Chinese studies from Durham University.

What was your career plan right after you graduated from university? Did your parents talk to you about your academic interests, and your decision to major in Chinese Studies at university?

No, they did not say anything at all. As long as I was doing what I wanted, they did not care. Because it was quite different from today. Remember, it was the 1960s, and anything and everything was possible during the 1960s! In the 1960s, nobody thought about money. If you went to university, you would automatically get a job afterwards without any problems. On the contrary, it is quite different nowadays. Young people only think about money, or at least at Oxford University they do. They do not just want a job. They want a job that gives them a lot of money.

Could you tell us about your education in Chinese Studies at Durham University during the 1960s?

We had about seven or eight lectures or classes a week, and we were expected to teach ourselves. In addition, we had weekly tutorials. We went to see our tutors to talk about things — to talk about China — to discuss what we had studied as well as what we were studying. We also had individual tuition, which would go on for at least an hour. Sometimes it went on for half or a whole day.

After finishing my bachelor's degree at Durham University I spent 2 years in Japan, because I wanted to live in the Far East for a while. Unfortunately I could

[2] Durham University – Homepage. Available at: https://www.dur.ac.uk/.

not go to China, because it was at the peak of the Cultural Revolution. I suppose I could have gone to Taiwan but to me, Taiwan wasn't really China. I also had to make money to support myself. I wanted to spend 2 years in the Far East, so I went to Japan and taught English to make a living. I then returned to the UK to do my PhD.

Living in Japan was an incredible experience. I absolutely loved it and I love it even more now. It is very clean and everything works in Japan. It is a fair society compared with England. People are civilized and Japanese people know how to behave.

It was before the Internet, before Youtube, before any online audio dictionaries or digital interactive language learning apps. So how would one go about finding materials to learn about China or to learn a foreign language?

We simply went to the university library and looked for a book to learn from. But we were only learning about classical or premodern China. We were only learning the facts of Chinese history and classical civilization, and the views of these facts may change with fashion. However, the basic historical facts will never change, and we were learning that for the first time. We were not doing any research, but we were teaching ourselves the basic details about Chinese history and classical civilization, and the professors in Chinese Studies at Durham University were all Europeans.

Our curriculum in Chinese Studies at Durham University was divided into two parts. The basics of Chinese language, and remember we were only learning classical Chinese. Then we had to learn the classical Chinese texts, for example texts from the classical Chinese philosopher Mengzi/Mencius (孟子) (372–289 BC), and parts from the *Shiji* (史記). We had lectures on general Chinese history and Chinese art. In summary, we learned about classical Chinese philosophy and the ways of thinking.

Which aspects of the Chinese culture/civilization or which schools/periods of Chinese philosophy really captured your interest?

I became interested in a Han Dynasty Confucian philosopher named Dong Zhongshu (董仲舒, 179–104 BC). Two years after I finished my bachelor's degree, after spending some time in Japan, I went back to Durham University to begin my PhD programme studying this philosopher. After 2 years at Durham University I realised that I had lost interest in Dong Zhongshu, so I finished the research work I had done and earned a Master of Letters (MLitt) degree, before taking up my current job at the Bodleian Library, University of Oxford. For my MLitt graduation thesis I translated Dong Zhongshu's biography in the *Hanshu* and I wrote a lengthy introduction to his way of thinking.

How did you end of working as the Curator of the Chinese Collections at the Bodleian Library?

The PhD programme at Durham University was a three-year course. Actually, most people would take longer, but my funding was only for a maximum of three years. At the end of my second year, this job (Curator of the Chinese Collections) at the Bodleian Library was advertised. I did not want the job at that time however, my PhD supervisor forced me to apply for it because he said, 'If you do not get this job, you will not get a job in Chinese studies because there will not be any for a long time', and this was perfectly true.

In the early days, one did not need a library qualification [Master of Library and Information Science] to work in a library. In fact, in good libraries such a degree was regarded as a disqualification, and not a qualification. You were expected to know your subject well. But a big change has taken place between then and now. When I first entered the library field, people said to me, 'Oh, what is your subject?' Whenever a new person came to the library, people said, 'What is your subject?' If you asked that question now, it would be considered grotesque, because people do not have 'subjects' any more. They call themselves library managers now and that is a big change.

How many different languages have you mastered?

Only one, that is English!

When you first took up your job as a librarian at the Bodleian Library, was there a mentor you worked closely with, to acquire all the skills and knowledge needed for managing an academic library?

Yes, when I first went to the Bodleian Library there was already a person in charge of the Chinese and Japanese language collections. He did both subjects (i.e., Chinese and Japanese) and I went to help him. After six months he was promoted to an administrative position in the Library, so I became the person in charge. In the beginning I was supposed to be in charge of both Chinese and Japanese Collections.

Working as the Curator of the Chinese Collections at the Bodleian Library, in addition to serving as a 'subject specialist', are you also regarded as a scholar? A gatekeeper of Chinese culture? Or a guardian of Chinese materials of high cultural and historical values?

We (library curators) are regarded as scholars, and we eventually became full faculty members of Oxford University. In other words, I am a librarian but also a full member of the Faculty of Oriental Studies.[3]

As a full faculty member of the Faculty of Oriental Studies at the University of Oxford, do you also need to teach students or conduct lectures or seminars on a regular basis?

[3] Faculty of Oriental Studies, University of Oxford – Homepage. Available at: http://www.orinst.ox.ac.uk/.

I do not do any teaching, but some of my colleagues do. Not in Chinese, but in other Western subjects.

How do students who went to the University of Oxford to do Chinese Studies during the 1960s compare with students nowadays? How are their interests, goals and mentalities different from each other?

In the 1960s and 1970s China was a third world country with no hope for the future. There were no jobs, nobody was interested in the country and there was very little trading and business going on. China was simply not known.

Students in the old days were like me. Some of them were able to go into jobs doing Chinese; but most were not. Many of them went into the civil service. They went to work for companies in completely different fields. You see their degrees in Chinese Studies were simply regarded as a qualification. It was a sign that they were bright and they would make useful employees, but their knowledge wasn't valued. It was of no interest at the time.

On the contrary, it is quite different now. These days, most of the students who graduate in Chinese Studies are not interested in Chinese culture and civilization at all. They are only interested in China in order to make money, so they go to London and work in the city. They work for commercial companies. They are only interested in China as a means of doing good business.

What about the students who chose Egyptian Studies or Arabic Studies at Oxford University during the 1960s and 1970s? What kind of career paths did most of them end up following?

More or less the same as the Chinese Studies graduates. For example, I had a good friend at college reading Arabic who eventually became a civil servant. I had two other friends who were studying Geography: one went into the Royal Navy and eventually became a naval officer, the other went into hospital administration. It was nothing to do with their subjects, and that was the same with Chinese.

At first I just regarded what I did at the Bodleian Library as a job. In fact, I was not very happy with the work at the Bodleian Library in the beginning. It is only recently that I have become happier.

I often considered quitting the job. Even after six weeks I thought of quitting, but my parents persuaded me to stick with it. I wanted to quit because I found the work to be very boring. In addition, I wasn't in charge of the work. Basically, it was very repetitive! I wanted to change things, but I could not because I wasn't in charge. Everything changed when the person in charge got promoted. And eventually, I became in charge and gradually, I could get things done as I wanted.

Could you describe the working environment at the Bodleian Library at Oxford?

In the early days working at the Bodleian Library was like being in jail, despite the Library's beautiful and historical setting. The building I was working in was very dirty, old and run-down. It was a terrible building. The library building has now been completely transformed, it is very beautiful (Figs 5.2 and 5.3).

Can you give a brief introduction of the Chinese Collections housed at the Bodleian Library?

The Bodleian Library has one of oldest Chinese Collections in the world, as we have been collecting Chinese books continuously since 1604. The first books were brought back to Europe by the Dutch East India Company. During the 17th century, the Dutch East India Company would send trading missions to South East Asia, and they would bring back these old books from different Chinese communities scattered throughout South East Asia.

Why would they European merchants donate these Chinese books to the Bodleian Library?

Figure 5.2 The old Bodleian Library (interior).

Figure 5.3 The old Bodleian Library (exterior).

They did not donate them. They sold them to the Bodleian Library. Remember, they were merchants. They were only interested in money!

Why would the University of Oxford pay money to buy these old Chinese books from the merchants?

We did not. We persuaded rich people to buy them for us. That is what we always do. We have no money! The reason why we have more of those books than anybody else is because of Sir Thomas Bodley (1545–1613), the person who founded the Bodleian Library. At the time, those valuable premodern Chinese books were collected not as books but as valuable, rare curiosities. In other words, merchants had the same view of those books as I had as a little girl with that little bit of a Chinese newspaper.

These books were very common in premodern China, but they were of no practical value to us at the time. Now they are extremely rare. When these books first came to Europe, Bodley saw them and acquired them from the European merchants. These books were considered very common and popular down-market books in premodern China, and were read by Chinese merchants. The Chinese scholarly communities in the old days did not take these books seriously, and were simply not interested in such books. The Chinese scholars and the upper classes were very selective and aristocratic in their reading interests and tastes. Hence, they did not fill their bookshelves with common, down-market stuff. They were only interested in respectable scholarly materials, which is why many of those books found in the Bodleian Library now are unique surviving copies. Traditionally, the Chinese were very aristocratic in the way they built their libraries. Real scholars did not collect books that were read by the common people.

At the Bodleian Library we collected everything that came our way, because we did not know what it was.

When these old Chinese down-market books were first brought to the University of Oxford, did anyone at the Bodleian Library have the knowledge and language skills to process them?

No! Simply no one! After these books were brought to the University of Oxford, for at least 200 years, no one at the Bodleian Library had the knowledge or language skills to process them. As a result, they were simply shelved together for easy retrieval, we are talking about only 2 m of shelves for foreign materials.

The Bodleian Library has one of the largest premodern Chinese Collections in Europe, and we probably have the largest collection of Chinese Protestant missionary publications in the world. The 19th century missionaries who went to China wrote a lot of books in Chinese, and those books are turning out to be extremely interesting. Currently, many Chinese people are interested in those books and we have at least 1400 different editions.

These include many unique surviving copies. Almost every week, a scholar somewhere asks me for a digitisation of those books. The people interested in these books fall into two categories: One lot of scholars is interested in East–West cultural exchanges of the 19th century as evidenced in the work of the missionaries. Missionaries were usually very educated people, and they were not only trying to introduce Christianity to the local people, but were also taking Chinese ideas and knowledge about China back to Europe. So they were very interesting people. The other group of people who are interested in them are religious people added "in which there are many"America. There are also people in the Far East who are interested in the Christian religion, and in converting the Chinese people to Christianity. So there are two kinds of people who are interested in those books. I have catalogued all the books and we are currently digitising as many as we can.

What kind of subject headings do you use for describing these premodern Chinese materials?

Basically, Chinese books are classified according to the classification system used by the Chinese scholars of the premodern era. But we do not assign subject headings for describing these premodern Chinese materials.

Are you the solo librarian overseeing the Chinese Collection at the Bodleian Library?

Well I was until three years ago, and then the Bodleian Library received a large donation from a Chinese benefactor, so now there are two of us. In addition to this work on premodern books, I also had to maintain a large collection of modern Chinese books at the Bodleian Library.

When I was first appointed almost all our books came from Taiwan, as very few books were published in Mainland China during, as well as after, the Cultural Revolution. However, everything began to change during the 1980s, and now there are too many (Chinese) books to handle as an overwhelming number of books are published in Mainland China every year. I started buying modern Chinese books on a large-scale between the 1980s and 1990s. Then, of course, another issue arose: electronic resources. We had to find a lot of money to provide electronic resources, and these now would take up most of our book budget. The buying of physical books has gone right down. I think the same thing is happening in many other places. In 2012–13, the Bodleian Library found money from a private foundation in Singapore, Tan Chin Tuan.

They provided a four-year budget to enable me to catalogue our premodern books. These unique premodern Chinese materials are very important for our Library. Every single library is buying modern books, they are everywhere and are not so important. What makes a library collection unique is its historic collections! In these historic collections you can often find things which you can't find anywhere else. So it was considered very important to describe these collections and present them to everybody in digital format. So that has been my job for the last four years. They also found money to appoint a new person to take over my job, i.e., to take over the running of the modern Chinese Collections.

Are you saying that compared to 20 years ago, your role and responsibilities as the Curator of Chinese Collections at the Bodleian Library have changed drastically?

Yes, completely changed! It is very useful, because I am now just looking after the premodern Chinese books. In other words, I am doing exactly what I was educated to do and exactly what I want to do.

Could you describe your job nature and your typical day at work at the Bodleian Library?

Yesterday I sat in front of my computer for about 6h without a break, without speaking to anybody. Sometimes I go to the faculty and speak to people, or I have a coffee with a colleague or something, but I could spend most of my days at the Bodleian Library without having to speak to other people. Occasionally I am asked to deal with a reader who might have a particular inquiry. And of course, I am answering emails all the time.

What kind of feelings do you actually get when you are working with these old premodern Chinese materials? Do you feel like as if you are playing with some very complicated jigsaw puzzle?

Yes, exactly. It is for me just playing with a puzzle. Classical Chinese is not a universal language like music. I am afraid, it is almost incomprehensible. So I do not get into the texts very much because of my limited abilities. I can't open a classical Chinese book and just read it. It's quite impossible. In fact, there are very few Chinese who can do that now. As a Curator of the Chinese Collection, what I am trying to do is to fit that book into a jigsaw puzzle. It is to present the book to the rest of world through the Internet in such a way that it can be found.

How would you describe your role in this scholarly community? Do you see yourself as a facilitator? A mediator of some kind, making the materials available on the Internet and allowing individual users to interpret the contents themselves?

I never think about those things. I neither need nor wish to justify my job. Sometimes I am surprised that people actually pay me to do what I do. It is incredible, really! Who would pay for such a thing?

Could you tell me about the challenges and difficulties that you and your colleagues are facing at the Bodleian Library?

A shortage of money to buy materials and bureaucracy! For example, I need to attend a lot of meetings, and I'm always trying to avoid them.

How do you usually say 'NO' to these meetings? Can you actually say 'NO'?

I have two techniques: One is to just not go. The second is to go, and to be very provocative at the meetings and to cause trouble! Then if you do not go, nobody would mind. In fact, they are glad if you do not go to these meetings at all. In fact, these meetings never do anything. They just sit around talking, that's all. Nothing actually happens. The talk is seldom translated into actions. The secret for success in the past was to appoint somebody who was reasonably competent and just tell them to get on with it.

In library and university settings, there is very little need for the sort of management that you get in commercial industries. If you were organising a big company with lots of processes going on, with workers whose jobs are not really to think, but just to man a production line, then you might need that kind of management approach.

But you simply can't introduce that sort of approach into a library or university environment. These days, there is too much bureaucracy. People going into the (library) profession do not enjoy the same autonomy as I did when I first entered. Nowadays, people are not promoted for the quality of their work in a subject area, and I think this is a very big problem for the younger colleagues. You cannot be promoted in the way that I was promoted, by being good at your subject and good at what you do. In order to be promoted you have to go into some sort of managerial role.

They also try to use numbers to justify their decisions, the rigorous use of quantitative techniques to assess project progress, efficiency, effectiveness and productivity etc. However, in my opinion, that is a really silly approach because numbers are very easy to invent. The numbers being presented do not have to be true. You can say a number, and how can they prove it or disprove it? Numbers are very silly indeed. People invent numbers all the time.

Given the cultural and historic values of your Chinese Collections at the Bodleian Library, do also need to put up exhibitions to showcase your valuable collections to people both within and outside the University?

Yes, certainly!

How often does the Bodleian Library organise such exhibitions, and who would decide the theme of the next exhibition?

The Bodleian Library has become a sort of showcase for the University of Oxford, where tourists can simply go in and off the street and see the most beautiful things like the *Magna Carta*, the *Gutenberg Bible*, and all kinds of precious items.

Does the Bodleian Library also charge people money for admission to look at these rare book exhibitions?

No, our exhibitions are totally free of charge.

Does the Bodleian Library continue to purchase valuable rare books on a regular basis to enrich the collection?

Yes, we certainly do. Unfortunately, we have no real budget for that. But sometimes a book dealer or an individual might offer us a book for a certain price. If I think that the book should be added to our collection, I will try to find the money to do that. I am usually quite successful in that regard. People also donate many things to us. For example, in April this year we were given a box of missionary materials by a retired law professor living near Oxford, whose grandfather had served as a missionary to Hankou during the late 19th century. I have just finished cataloguing those materials. I would say at least two-thirds of those materials seem to be quite rare and unique. Because they are neither found in WorldCat nor CALIS. They also cannot be found in other library catalogues. I only finished cataloguing them in late October, and by early November a reader from Taiwan asked for scans of two of them. If you search using Google, it will automatically lead you to the Bodleian Library catalogue to find the book.

Are you saying that a major part of your job is to provide photocopies or digitised copies of these rare Chinese materials to both internal and external users?

I have quite a big budget for digitising our Chinese Collections. In fact, I have more money for digitisation than the library can support, because the Library has not really got a very good infrastructure for digitisation. The fee for scanning is quite expensive. In fact, it is ridiculously expensive! But I have a budget for scanning which is done in the Library by our studio. As the cost of scanning is so high, if a reader asks me for a scan of a rare book, I pay for it out of my library budget. The reader then pays nothing because I am simply adding it to our digital library. My justification is that if a scholar considers this book important, by definition that is something we ought to scan.

Could you tell us more about the majority of the users of the Chinese Collection at the Bodleian Library?

Our users are mostly undergraduates. Our Chinese premodern collection is used mostly by visiting scholars, who are here to study particular manuscripts, printed books or other rare items, or people who wish to access our digital collections online. At Oxford University, although we have nearly 1000 overseas Chinese students from the People's Republic of China, for the most part, they are not actually doing Chinese studies. They are mostly studying Economics, Engineering, Medicine and other subjects. We also have to think about providing different resources for different student groups to meet their needs. This is why electronic resources are so important, because they want access to our databases in their own languages as well as to the materials in Western languages.

How do faculty members in the Chinese Department at Oxford University see you and your role as the Curator of the Chinese Collections? Do they see you as their intellectual equal? Their teaching partner? Someone who has grounded knowledge in the subject and is responsible for developing a collection of Chinese materials for supporting their teaching and research? Could you elaborate on this?

The senior Chinese curators (there are currently three of us) are full Faculty members, and are accepted as such. We do not currently do any teaching, but could do so if asked. Some library colleagues in other disciplines (Western manuscripts for example) do teach in their faculties, and even supervise doctoral students from time to time.

During your years at Oxford as the Curator of the Chinese Collections, did you ever get to meet or serve any famous Chinese scholars or novelists from Hong Kong, China or Taiwan? If you have, could you describe your encounters with them in detail?

Famous people are always coming to Oxford, including Chinese scholars. I often get to meet them, but seldom have significant dealings with them. The most famous Chinese scholar I ever entertained was Chang Bide (or Ch'ang Pi-te as we then spelled it). Here goes, but you may not want to print it all! It was Chang Bide, then a Director of the National Palace Museum in Taipei, who gave us a copy of the complete reprint of Siqu Quanshu (四庫全書). Shortly after, he visited Oxford, and we showed him around for a few days.

He looked at our rare book collection and was quite impressed by it. He said that from it, we could learn all that we needed to know about traditional Chinese printing and book production. Indeed, this was the collection that I studied in order to teach myself. It's well known that he liked to drink. We took him to lunch one day and ordered white wine however, I noticed that the contents of his glass were darker than ours. He had laced it with whisky from a hipflask that he always carried around for this purpose! To get him to the airport we hired a chauffeur driven car, which we had paid for in advance. However, when he got there I heard that he gave the driver all the British currency that he had left, over £50, which was quite a lot of money. It was surely the driver's lucky day!

Do you have any other interesting stories to share? For example, did you ever get to meet members of the Royal Family at the Bodleian Library? In addition, because of the Bodleian Library's architecture and history, it has been made a favourite location for a large number of filmmakers. Did you see or help out when they were shooting any of the following motion pictures: Another Country, Harry Potter, Madness of King George III or Brideshead Revisited?

Yes, I invigilated part of the filming of the first *Harry Potter* film in the Old Library. We had to make sure that the film crew were not chewing gum. Apparently people who chew gum often stick it under tables and chairs — quite disgusting.

Last year I also showed the Selden Map to Prince William when he came to open the China Centre Library. I attach a (rather bad) picture taken by a colleague.

With all your training and education in classical Chinese, your job was to function like a schoolmaster, making sure the film crew were not chewing gum? Are you serious?

The rule is that a senior member of staff had to be present, they were filming in a historic building with rare books on the shelves close by.

Preserving the Ewenki and Orochen People at the University of Cambridge

6

Mark Elliott
MAA, University of Cambridge, Cambridge, United Kingdom

Introduction

The Museum of Archaeology and Anthropology (MAA) at the University of Cambridge houses the University's collections of local antiquities, together with archaeological and ethnographic artefacts from around the world. Dr Mark Elliott (Fig. 6.1) is a curator with responsibility for the Asian, European and African ethnography collections (see Elliott working with Asian collections in Fig. 6.2). Having carried out ethnographic research in India, Elliott's research interests cover South and Southeast Asia, focussing on historical anthropology and collections history as well as the development of museum collections and museum practice. In this chapter, Elliott talks about the MAA's East Asian collections, with particular emphasis on the Ewenki and Orochen materials.

Could we begin this interview by first introducing yourself, for example, your training and background and your major roles and duties at MAA at the University of Cambridgc[1]?

Dr Mark Elliott (ME): My name is Mark Elliott and I am Senior Curator for Anthropology at the MAA (at the University of Cambridge), with responsibility for ethnography collections from Asia, Africa and Europe. My role involves research, interpretation and exhibition of the collections, working with colleagues to ensure that they are appropriately cared for and developing collections so that they remain live and relevant to visitors, scholars and source communities. I also teach graduate students in the University (of Cambridge). I'm originally from Ireland and studied social anthropology at the University of St Andrews[2] before a PhD in social anthropology here in Cambridge. My doctoral research was in South Asia, specifically the city of Kolkata in West Bengal, India, looking at interactions between people and things in museums and ritual contexts, such as Hindu puja. I joined MAA in 2003 and

[1] Museum of Archaeology and Anthropology (MAA) at the University of Cambridge – Homepage. Available at: http://maa.cam.ac.uk/.

[2] University of St Andrews – Homepage. Available at: https://www.st-andrews.ac.uk/.

Inside the World's Major East Asian Collections. http://dx.doi.org/10.1016/B978-0-08-102145-3.00006-6

Figure 6.1 Dr Mark Elliott.

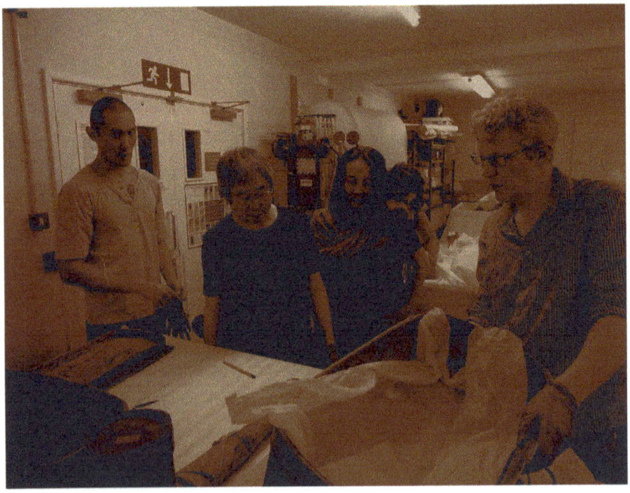

Figure 6.2 Dr Mark Elliott engaging with Orochen collections, working with Hing Chao He Mu and Bai Ying.

have worked across all collections of the Museum (Fig. 6.3), most recently acting as Exhibition Coordinator for the Museum's redisplay in 2010–12. I've held the post of Curator since 2012.

As a European, how did you become interested in Asian anthropology?

ME: I ended up working in Asia by accident, or perhaps it's better to say 'organically'. I was interested in museums as field sites, or cultural artefacts, and wanted to pursue a PhD, exploring interactivity in such environments, and also how museums

Figure 6.3 Main Anthropology Gallery, Museum of Archaeology and Anthropology, University of Cambridge.

might be 'different' outside the Euro–American context with which I was familiar. A friend from Kolkata told me about the Indian Museum in the city, the oldest and largest in India, known as the Jadu Ghar, or 'House of Magic', and regularly visited by people from rural villages and pilgrims as well as people from the city, especially on festival days. I chose it as a field site, learnt Bengali and as much as I could about Indian history and Indian museology, and came back with an intense interest in the people and material cultures of India. Travel and work in the years since my PhD have consolidated by interest and also my experience and knowledge, although this is an ongoing process. The most significant factor, though, is my continued confrontation to the collections that MAA looks after. Every time I encounter an artefact, it is a new discovery and asks new questions. These experiences continually renew my fascination, and my role at MAA is to try to enable others to experience the collections in the same way. But crucially, I am a curator for anthropology, not a curator for Asia. My work involves engaging with collections from across the world, and in fact, it is the connections and relationships between people, places and things that fascinate me and which I try to communicate in exhibitions, for example.

As a European, what were the major barriers or challenges you had to overcome in order to be good at what you are doing or to excel in your field?

ME: Unsurprisingly, perhaps, the most significant barriers are scale, language and distance. I cannot hope to be a specialist on all regions from which collections in my care originate. To be an expert on 'India' would be extraordinary, and frankly unrealistic, let alone claiming expertise on 'Asia' (or indeed Africa or Europe. I was born in Europe, but that does not make me an expert on it). I regularly engage with collections from places that I have never visited and whose languages I do not speak. One of the biggest challenges is how we deal with this. I feel we have a responsibility to the makers, collectors, donors and former owners of artefacts to ensure that they are preserved and also understood and made accessible. The only way to do this is through collaboration with scholars and source communities. This brings its own challenges. Language and physical distance (between Cambridge and Nagaland, for example, or Cambridge and Hulunbuir) can often present insurmountable barriers, but where there is the shared will, enthusiasm and, of course, funding for this kind of work, the mutual benefits are extraordinary.

What are the most common methodologies and research practices currently being used in the field of Asian anthropology?

ME: This is such a large and diverse field; I do not think I can give a solid answer. In terms of museum anthropology, or museum ethnography, in Cambridge and the UK, I think there has been a trend in recent years towards greater engagement with the stakeholders of collections, perhaps local diaspora communities or, as in the case of Cambridge, collaborative research with source communities in the countries and regions from which the collections originated. MAA has a strong track record in this kind of work in Oceania and North America, where the emphasis is on relationships. The 'relational museum' approach highlights historic collections as assemblages of people, relationships and things, prompting attention to the complex and often contested histories as well as the shared heritage of overseas collections in European institutions. The nature of anthropological collections in countries like the UK, overwhelmingly consisting of artefacts from people and places outside of Europe, can and should result in a global, or at least international, focus. My experience of many collections of anthropology in Asia is that their attention is focused within national borders, or sometimes transnational regions. I think there is great potential for increased communication across borders and a focus on processes and relationships internationally and cross-culturally; I am seeing more and more interest in this kind of work from museums in Asia, and this is a fantastic step, both for those museums, our museums and the communities whose heritage they care for.

Researchers in Asia versus researchers in Europe/North America: are there any major differences in terms of the approaches (themes/research practices/concepts/perceptive) used by the researchers for carrying out their research works in these two regions?

ME: Certainly. I've already alluded to the inevitable differences in perspective engendered by particular histories of colonialism, nation building and the accompanying treatment and study of indigenous populations in different countries. The context of our ongoing work with Ewenki (鄂温克族) and Orochen (鄂倫春族) communities in China and Russia is, in fact, an international research and networking project funded by the Leverhulme Trust[3] that addresses concepts of identity and indigeneity in these two nations, and thus, the associated theories and methodologies adopted and adapted in each context. It has brought together scholars and curators in England, Scotland, Russia and China to consider 'etnos' and 'minzu' as deployed by states and anthropologists. While the Museum's work with the photographic collections from Ewenki and Orochen communities has focused on visual and oral histories, framed by an interest in the 'return' of

[3] The Leverhulme Trust – Homepage. Available at: https://www.leverhulme.ac.uk/.

Figure 6.4 Exhibition: Buddha's Word: The Life of Books in Tibet and Beyond.

images to communities, no one can ignore the often complex and difficult legacies that anthropology, anthropologists and ethnographic collections have in each context.

American anthropologist and novelist, Dr Liza Dalby, who specialises in Japanese culture and her research publications on geishas: are there any similarities and differences between Dr Dalby's research approaches/methods and the ones being used for researching on the Ewenki and Orochen people?

ME: One way of answering this question might be in terms of imagination. Dalby's work highlights the productive interplay between ethnography and fiction, something that social and cultural anthropology has been aware of (though not always comfortable with) for some time now.

Please provide a brief introduction to the MAA's East Asian collections at the Cambridge University.

ME: The Museum holds collections of artefacts, photographs and documents from every inhabited continent and almost every period in human history and prehistory. While the historical research and exhibition focus of the museum has, particularly in recent decades, been on local archaeology and ethnographic collections from Oceania and North America, we also care for large and important collections from Asia.

What is the size of the Asian collections? Could you describe the highlights of the collection, including the Ewenki and Orochen materials?

ME: There are approximately 40,000 catalogue records for Asian artefacts in the Museum's database. Well-known collections are those from Nagaland in Northeast India and the Tibetan and Himalayan collections, which were the subject of an exhibition in 2014 called Buddha's Word: The Life of Books in Tibet and Beyond (Fig. 6.4). We also look after important research collections from anthropologists, many of them

Cambridge-based, who worked across Asia: A.R. Radcliffe-Brown's collection from the Andaman Islands are an significant part of the important Andaman and Nicobar collections, for example, and, of course, Ethel John Lindgren's collections of artefacts and photographs from Inner Mongolia are unique.

What best prepared you for the position as Curator at the MAA?

ME: My studies in social anthropology and my doctoral research in India, of course, gave me the qualifications and some of the knowledge and experience I needed to work as a curator. But for me, it was subsequently working in a museum in other roles that was most transformative. One can approach artefacts, photographs and collections as aesthetically interesting, historically fascinating or provocative, for example, and we can bring all sorts of theories to bear on them regarding their materiality or agency. However, encountering collections is often a lesson in the fragility, vulnerability, complexity and sometimes awkwardness of things. There are challenges from a straightforward collections management point of view, or from the perspective of research and interpretation. Sometimes an object is too heavy or too fragile to carry. Often it is hard to understand or interpret clearly, for any number of reasons. Sometimes the documentation is incomplete, wrong or missing, and you might spend a day or days trying to solve a problem and perhaps never succeed. This taught me to be flexible, I hope, and patient, though not always. It also taught me that museums, and indeed archives or libraries, are places with history where processes and techniques are employed that can be transformative of the artefacts and people that inhabit them.

What scholarly and professional associations are you a part of, and how do they assist you in your work?

MAA is an institutional member of a number of national and international networks, such as **As**ia–**E**urope **Mus**eum Network (ASEMUS)fn44[4] and the UK National Museum Directors' Council,[5] which create opportunities for skill sharing and collaboration. In addition, staff are individual members of subject-specialist networks that cut across regions and disciplines, such as the UK Museum Ethnographers Group[6] and the South Asian Art Group.[7] The networks created through such associations can help us in identifying objects, sourcing expertise for research enquiries, advice on practical problems like suggesting a particular brand of equipment for a particular job or building short- and long-term collaborations.

Who are the majority of the East Asia collection users? That is, who comes to see you about your Asian collections? Are they mostly professors or students from higher education institutions, or are they people from outside the postsecondary sector, i.e., the public?

[4] ASEMUS – Homepage. Available at: http://asemus.museum.

[5] National Museum Directors' Council – Homepage. Available at: http://www.nationalmuseums.org.uk/.

[6] Museum Ethnographers Group – Homepage. Available at: http://www.museumethnographersgroup.org.uk/en/.

[7] South Asian Art Group – Homepage. Available at: https://uksaag.wordpress.com/.

Our galleries are open to all, free of charge, and well over 90% of our visitors are from outside the University. We host thousands of schoolchildren in group visits and workshops, which is a key priority for MAA and many other museums. We also welcome hundreds of visiting researchers to work with the collections at MAA each year. An increasing number of these visitors are interested in material from Asia, particularly as research and exhibition projects highlight the richness and importance of the material we care for. Many of these visitors are research students and scholars from Cambridge and other universities in the UK and beyond. We also use collections in teaching university undergraduate and graduate courses. The most important visitors are those from source communities or communities of origin. There are many barriers preventing indigenous people from accessing their heritage in UK museums, whether in terms of distance and cost of travel or on restrictions of movement, and we are committed to finding alternative ways to make collections accessible. Three decades ago, MAA was closely involved in what may be the first example of 'digital repatriation' of museum collections to source communities: the Cambridge Experimental Videodisc, which gathered together images of artefacts and photographs, along with historic archives relating to Naga peoples of Northeast India, and sent them to the state of Nagaland.

As the Curator overseeing the collection, how do you acquire and evaluate your collection? Do you proactively collect or do you accept gifts?

The Museum has always been dependent on donations of collections, often from anthropologists and other scholars who have devoted years of their lives to research within a particular community. Like many museums, we have little or no budget to purchase new acquisitions, and, in any case, we would be cautious of purchasing historic artefacts on the art and antiquities market when provenance cannot always be firmly established. Today, the majority of new acquisitions still come via donations. We tend to prioritise artefacts and collections that somehow relate to our existing holdings; space and resources are always limited. However, in recent years, we have secured external grants to collect and commission new works by indigenous artists and makers from the communities from which historic collections came. This is an exciting and important opportunity to keep the Museum's collections live and relevant for current and future generations.

How does the collection catalogue provide access for users? With a non-Roman script, what challenges does this present to cataloguing? Are there any?

MAA was one of the first museums in the UK to put its catalogue online, and we are in the process of a long overdue upgrade of a system, which now feels rather antiquated. The biggest challenge that I have is that much of the Asian collection at MAA is largely unresearched, and metadata can be inconsistent. My key objective in the coming years is to generate support for improving collections' documentation through survey and collaborative research. MAA holds relatively little textual or documentary material in Asian languages, and working with scripts has thus rarely been a significant issue. Where inscriptions on objects are recorded and translated, this information is provided on our catalogue. However, as engagement with the Asian collections grows and a greater number of voices are accommodated around the artefacts, this may need to change in coming years.

The themes and information needs of libraries, archives, and museums (LAMs, as some have referred to them) have increasingly converged. What are your experiences and thoughts about these cultural institutions whose work and best practices now often overlap?

The first thing that comes to mind is that museums, libraries and archives each have to deal with 'Big Data'. Managing large collections, many of which will only be rarely, if ever, 'used' and handling the increasingly complex assemblage of documentation and metadata that surrounds each object is a challenge. There is a lot of work going on to 'digitise' collections and put them online, often in bespoke databases and platforms. One of the issues here is consistency and longevity. The Internet is littered with sites that have been created to bring together collections and make them accessible to new audiences in new ways, but with limited budgets, the ends of projects are left to wither. It would be wonderful if there was a more sustainable way to do this. But I also think that there can be an enormous gulf between what might be called 'research' and what might be called 'curatorial' or 'collections management'. Depending in part on the discipline or agency to which museums, libraries or archives are attached, there is often little understanding that the process of curatorship or managing a collection is research in a fundamental way. If I encounter an object in the collection and either discover something new about it or make a new connection, that's research. If I manage to sort out a documentation problem that reveals part of the history of the object, the collection or the museum, that's research. Museums, libraries and archives are critical sites of knowledge production and control, which have shaped and continue to shape academic disciplines. That has not really answered your question, I suppose.

Which part(s) of your job as curators do you find most rewarding?

Encountering an object, making a discovery and sharing it with people.

Ewenki and Orochen, their traditional ways of life, the wisdom behind their daily practices (survival skills) and the concept of being content and happiness, all so remote from the ways we urban people live, what could we possibly learn from Ewenki and Orochen people? Why should we continue to invest so much manpower and resources to learn about them?

I do not necessarily think Ewenki and Orochen people are 'so remote from the ways we urban people live'. They are people, after all, and their creative responses to life's challenges should be of interest to those of us who are neither Ewenki nor Orochen. Of course, it might be that contemporary reindeer herders, for example, might be able to challenge and inform urban people's wasteful way of life that is damaging the world in which we live it. But it's all too easy to view indigenous peoples in whatever part of the world as distant, other, exotic. Indeed, you might say that it is this distancing, this othering, which has allowed governments throughout the world to treat indigenous peoples in ways that we now regret. More fundamentally, however, from a museum's point of view, we have their stuff! It might have been obtained through various formal and informal processes that were more or less connected with state intervention in their traditions and human rights. We have a duty of care to these collections, and that means that manpower and resources should be devoted to making them understandable and accessible.

Worldwide and Cost-Free Access to the Geographically Scattered Materials From Dunhuang and Other Sites in Chinese Central Asia

7

Susan Whitfield
The British Library, London, United Kingdom

Introduction

The Mogao Caves are one of the most culturally significant Buddhist cave temple sites located in Dunhuang, Gansu Province, northwestern China; a city that is situated in a rich oasis containing the Crescent Lake and the Mingsha Shan (literally meaning 'Singing-Sand Mountain'). In addition to the numerous murals and sculptures of immense cultural value, the Mogao Caves are also notable for their large collections of religious and other secular manuscripts, recovered by foreign archaeologists and explorers travelling along the Silk Road during the early 1900s. Currently, large collections of such Dunhuang documents and artifacts are spread across major libraries, museums and research institutes throughout the UK, France, Germany, China, Japan and Russia. Established in 1994, the International Dunhuang Project (IDP) is a international collaborative effort to conserve, catalogue and digitise manuscripts, printed texts, paintings, textiles and other artifacts collected from Dunhuang and other various archaeological sites located at the eastern end of the Silk Road. As of 1 March 2016, the online IDP database comprised 137,812 catalogue entries and 483,721 images. While many of them are in Chinese, a large number of these IDP documents are in various other languages and scripts including Tibetan, Tangut, Uigur, Sanskrit, Tocharian, Sogdian and the then little-known Kharosthi and Khotanese. In the following interview Dr Susan Whitfield (Fig. 7.1), Director of IDP at the British Library, discusses the joys and various challenges faced in Dunhuang Caves to give researchers and scholars worldwide free access to these geographically scattered materials.

Inside the World's Major East Asian Collections. http://dx.doi.org/10.1016/B978-0-08-102145-3.00007-8

Figure 7.1 Dr Susan Whitfield.

Could you begin this interview by first introducing yourself? For example, your training and background, and your major roles and duties at the British Library[1]? Did you have other careers before you started working for the British Library?

My first undergraduate degree was in Philosophy and Psychology, and I intended to continue graduate work in philosophy. However, I travelled to East and South-East Asia over one summer and after this decided to take a year out to learn Chinese. I soon realised I also needed to learn classical Chinese to understand the culture. One thing led to another and I completed another degree in Chinese, then went on to do a PhD in Chinese Historiography.

During this period I had several jobs including translation, indexing, editing, computer support and newsletter design. But my main work over this period was working on the statistical analysis of clinical trials.

I started work part-time at the British Library when still completing my PhD. Shortly after, I was employed on an external grant to coordinate the activities of the newly formed International Dunhuang Project (IDP)[2]. The IDP became a separate curatorial section of the British Library and I have been Curator and Director of the IDP for over a decade.

I have a curatorial role looking after the collection and ensuring its accessibility to readers. I also have to manage the project, its partners, staff and funds, build and maintain relations with partners in the UK and worldwide, carry out research, give lectures and fundraise. I also work on database design, implementation and updating and on the website.

How, and at what age, did you discover a strong interest in Dunhuang and the Silk Road?

I visited Dunhuang when travelling in China as an undergraduate in 1984, but my interest was not piqued until I was completing my second degree and started to realise the importance of the Silk Road for understanding Chinese history and culture. This has only been reinforced since.

[1] The British Library – Homepage. Available at: http://www.bl.uk/.

[2] International Dunhuang Project (IDP) – Homepage. Available at: http://idp.bl.uk/.

As a European, what were the major barriers or challenges you had to overcome in order to be good at what you are doing, or to excel in your field?

I'm not sure that being European put up any barriers in itself.

How does your list of publications (particular the books) on Dunhuang and the Silk Road relate to your work at the British Library?

My research is essential both to curating the collections, and to maintaining the profile of the IDP. The former enables me to understand the collections, to make decisions about their preservation and also understand the needs of scholars. The latter is vital for building relationships and trust with other institutions and scholars worldwide, for promoting the project and, of course, for fundraising. My books include exhibition catalogues, conference proceedings (for example, on forgeries and conservation) and histories using the British Library Collections as one of the primary source materials. All these are directly related to my work.

Please provide a brief introduction to the Dunhuang Collections at the British Library? For example, the size, scope and highlights of the Dunhuang Collections at the British Library.

The collections under the IDP curatorial section are the manuscripts acquired by Stein and others from sites in Chinese Central Asia, not just Dunhuang. The Central Asian Manuscript Collections consist of over 50,000 items in over 20 languages and scripts, on several different media (paper, wood, leather, birchbark, palm leaf etc.). They date from the first century BC to the 19th century, and range in size from fragments less than an inch square to scrolls over 70 feet long (Figs 7.2–7.5).

Could you tell us more about the International Dunhuang Project (IDP), and in your capacity, the research and cataloguing of the Central Asian Manuscripts at the British Library? What are some of the highlights of this collection?

Please see the recent articles in the *Encyclopaedia Iranica*[3] and in the *Journal of Dunhuang and Turfan Studies* on IDP. There is also a good introduction in *The Journal of Web Librarianship* 1.1 (2007):113–122.[4]

What best prepared you for the position of Director of the IDP?

It was a job that developed over time, but the combination of computer/programming skills, organisational skills and research skills have been vital. More than anything however, has been a belief that the aims of this project were feasible, despite considerable scepticism from many!

[3] *Encyclopaedia Iranica* – Homepage. Available at: http://www.iranicaonline.org/articles/international-dunhuang-project.

[4] http://www.tandfonline.com/doi/abs/10.1300/J502v01n01_09.

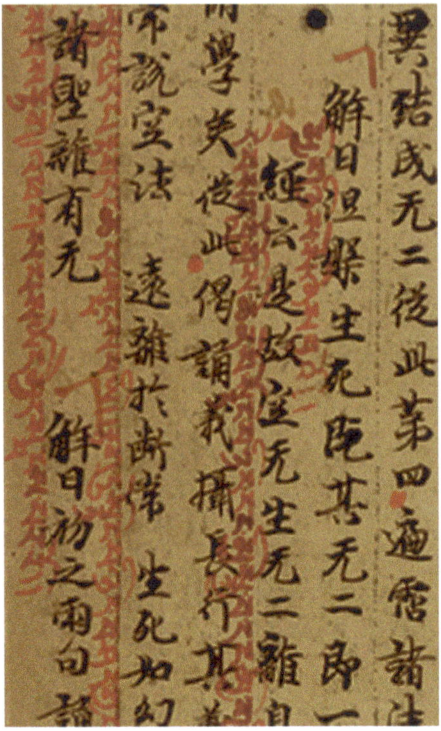

Figure 7.2 A Chinese–Tibetan manuscript.

Figure 7.3 Diamond sutra.

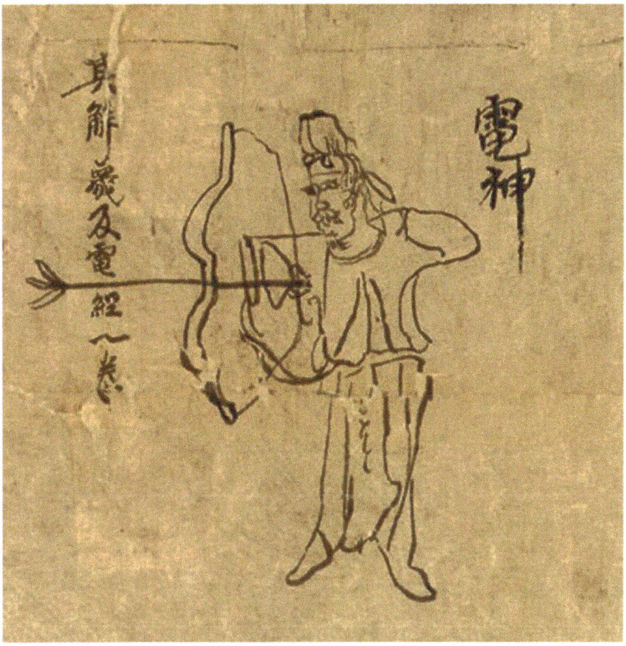

Figure 7.4 Dianshen, thunder god.

Figure 7.5 Tangut manuscript.

What scholarly and professional associations are you a part of, and how do they assist you in your work?

I am a member of several associations and their main role, especially in the early years of my career, was to keep me in touch with developments and to provide contacts.

Who are the majority of the your collection's users? That is, who comes to see you about your collections? Are they mostly professors or students from higher education institutions? Or are the people from outside the postsecondary sector, i.e., the public?

Users of our database comprise both members of the scholarly community and members of the public (you can look at the results of our user survey on the website, http://idp.bl.uk/survey/report.html). Readers coming to the British Library to view manuscripts are generally scholars, students and academic faculty. We also hold educational workshops for schoolchildren.

Could you give examples of typical reference/research enquiries issued by researchers or scholars interested in this area of research? Or is there never a typical reference enquiry for Dunhuang/Silk Road studies?

There is no typical enquiry, they come in all shapes and forms: history of the saluki; on variant forms of Chinese characters; the burial practices of Zoroastrians; the pigments used in the wall paintings or the load of a camel etc.

In the past few years, the British Library has been engaged in the digitisation of some of its collections. What are some of the projects, and what future plans are there for the digital collections? Could you tell us about the Library's recataloguing and full text digitisation of the Chinese ancient books and manuscripts project?

Hopefully my colleagues in the Chinese section have answered this one!

In your research, you've argued that China is more fragmented and diverse than unitary narratives might have us believe. How did you become interested in China and Central Asia in particular, and in what ways has your interest in Central Asia made you rethink Chinese history?

As I mentioned above, as soon as I started looking at the history, religion and material culture of China, I realised I could not understand it without understanding the history, religion and material culture of China's neighbours. This is not particular to China, I believe that there was a connected world across Afro-Eurasia and that while some developments happened in isolation, many did not. I would therefore now always keep an open mind about the influences that have led to the creation of any narrative or object.

How is the Dunhuang Collection catalogued and accessible for users? With a non-roman script, what challenges does this present to cataloguing? Are there any?

The IDP offers free online access to images and catalogue entries of archaeological artefacts (including manuscripts) from Chinese Central Asia. The website and metadata are given in eight languages, including several with non-Roman scripts. Sometimes this has raised issues with software compatibility and display across different systems and browsers etc. but these have always been surmountable and are getting easier now that Unicode is better developed.

It is worth noting that we do not see our role as curators in providing definitive catalogues for this material. We cannot possibly have the skills nor is scholarship at a stage where there is always consensus. We therefore include the key metadata with the objects and then associate the items with whatever catalogues are available, historical and modern. So one item might have several catalogue entries associated with it. These might contradict each other. It is up to the scholars and users to assess these. We cannot have the knowledge to make these decisions, nor would we want to: our role is to look after the objects and to provide access.

What are some of the technical challenges that you face in this position, particularly in terms of preservation and digitisation?

Preservation and digitisation have not really thrown up technical challenges. In terms of digitisation, we waited until technology was developed sufficiently to provide good quality images before using digital cameras. The photography is generally straightforward. The challenge of the long-term preservation of the digital archive and of the IDP resource is another matter: again, this is not as much an issue of public sector resourcing and planning as it is of technology.

Please give a brief account of the history, and the latest developments in the IDP? Was the IDP initiated and launched by the British Library?

Please see recent articles in the *Encyclopaedia Iranica*[5] and in *Journal of Dunhuang and Turfan Studies* on IDP. You can also see articles on the IDP's beginnings and its subsequent history in http://idp.bl.uk/archives/news43/idpnews_43.a4d.

What are the major challenges and difficulties of being the Director of the IDP? For example, do you have to serve as a diplomat, i.e., convincing people from different nationalities and cultural backgrounds to work together? Do the political agendas between different governments sometime interfere with the developments or budget allocations of the IDP?

The IDP arose out of a conference between curators and conservators of all the major collections of Central Asian Manuscripts, who all agreed that more collaboration was required. It thus had the support of all the major holders from the start. The main issues were for everyone to make time for the collaboration and, once we went online, to input material into the database. The IDP has continued to operate largely on a 'bottom-up' system, first getting the support of curators, conservators and scholars for its work.

[5] *Encyclopaedia Iranica* – Homepage. Available at: http://www.iranicaonline.org/articles/international-dunhuang-project.

I have relied more on my enthusiasm and belief in this project to build trust between all the partners rather than diplomatic skills.

To date, politics has not interfered with the work. Most of the funding continues to be external.

Has it become increasingly difficult to find young scholars to take up research in this field, because of the limited career path/options?

No, I would say it is becoming easier as the Silk Road becomes more popular. However, it is difficult to find scholars to take up some areas of research, e.g., Tangut studies, palaeography etc.

Do you see yourself as a historian, researcher or librarian?

Historian and curator (both include researcher).

Which part(s) of your job as the Director of the IDP do you find most interesting and rewarding?

Working with the collections; working with the IDP team in the UK and with colleagues, students, scholars and others worldwide; seeing material come online and receiving feedback from people using it.

What are the most important skills, knowledge or character traits that are required to be a good leader of the IDP?

Patience, persistence, enthusiasm, energy, diplomacy, writing skills, management skills, technical skills, the ability to carry out numerous tasks at once, more patience, persistence, energy and enthusiasm.

Propaganda Art as a Powerful Weapon for Promoting Nationalism, Patriotism and Hatred Towards the Enemy

8

Mary Ginsberg
British Museum, London, United Kingdom

Introduction

Successful propaganda art can be informative, persuasive or even deceitful and manipulative. As negative as it might sound, propaganda can also be used for spreading positive messages like fighting for women's rights, racial equality, community health advocacy, as well as encouraging people to vote, etc. According to American political scientist and communications theorist Bruce Smith (2016), although biased in nature, effective propaganda can be used as a powerful psychological mechanism for influencing and altering the attitude of a population towards a specific cause, position or political agenda in an effort to form a consensus to a standard set of belief patterns. In the following interview, Mary Ginsberg (Fig. 8.1), author of *The Art of Influence: Asian Propaganda*, discusses her unique curatorial experiences in organising exhibitions of propaganda art at the British Museum, as well as exploring the political reasons behind the appeal of extremist ideologies embedded in propaganda art.

Could you begin this interview by first introducing yourself, for example, your training and background, and your major roles and duties at the British Museum?[1]

I am the interim curator for Chinese paintings and prints and the Central Asian collections while the permanent curator is away for a year's study leave. My major duties are care of the collections, research, maintaining and improving the database (which is accessible online) and working with visiting scholars and students.

I have worked in a number of roles in here at the British Museum over a 15-year period, generally fixed-term projects, or as a volunteer.

[1] The British Museum – Homepage. Available at: http://www.britishmuseum.org/.

Inside the World's Major East Asian Collections. http://dx.doi.org/10.1016/B978-0-08-102145-3.00008-X

Figure 8.1 Mary Ginsberg.

Could you tell me how the British Museum first recognised your talents and recruited you to work as part-time curatorial staff for them, and subsequently organised several major exhibitions on propaganda art for the Museum?

I'd been working as a volunteer while doing my MA at SOAS (School of Oriental and African Studies).[2] Just as I finished my MA, they needed an exhibition assistant for a year. I worked on several others over the years. I did the propaganda show as guest curator during one of my volunteer stints. It would be very generous to say they recognised my talents. I would not put it that way; I considered myself hugely lucky that they'd have me.

I understand that you also attended the Sotheby's Institute of Art.[3] The education you received in art history, compared with the curricula provided by a traditional academic institution, for example, Yale University,[4] Columbia University[5] or SOAS, University of London, how are they different from each other?

As an undergraduate, I double majored in Russian Studies and Chinese Studies at Yale (University). My focus was political socialisation in communist countries, which is what led to my later interest in propaganda art. At Columbia (University)'s School of International Affairs (now School of International and Public Affairs),[6] I specialised in East Asia and International Business. I then spent 15 years as a banker, mostly in Asia,

[2] SOAS, University of London – Homepage. Available at: https://www.soas.ac.uk/.

[3] Sotheby's Institute of Art – Homepage. Available at: http://www.sothebysinstitute.com/.

[4] Yale University – Homepage. Available at: http://www.yale.edu/.

[5] Columbia University – Homepage. Available at: http://www.columbia.edu/.

[6] School of International and Public Affairs, Columbia University – Homepage. Available at: https://sipa.columbia.edu/.

before formally taking up the study of Art History in the SOAS–Sotheby's diploma course (as it was then structured, mixing academics and markets), followed by a master's degree at SOAS.

Could you describe your job scope and areas of responsibilities at the British Museum? In addition, could you describe your typical day at work at the British Museum?

I am not a curator of propaganda art. The British Museum does not have such a position. When I guest curated *The Art of Influence: Asian Propaganda*, it was as a volunteer. As temporary curator for paintings, prints and Central Asia, my typical day involves meeting students or visiting scholars; answering public enquiries; and meeting with colleagues on issues of collection care, conservation, public programmes or data management. Sometimes, I get to do a bit of research, but not often.

At what age and how did you develop an interest for propaganda art?

I'd always studied propaganda, but it wasn't till I was in my 40s, working on the British Museum's collection of Chinese ephemera, that I realised the connection between my undergraduate studies and propaganda art. The first significant book on Chinese art and politics was Ellen Johnston's Laing's *Winking Owl* in 1988. In my undergraduate years, political scientists did not 'do' art.

Could you compare the Chinese propaganda art (created in Communist China and North Korea) against the Soviet Union or American propaganda art, with the aim of highlighting their individual stylistic uniqueness/differences?

What a huge question. I think the early Soviet graphics are among the best propaganda designs ever made, a huge diversity of passionate expressions. Socialist realism as prevailed in the USSR from the 1930s was formulaic and much less interesting. Of course, most communist countries adopted a form of socialist realism, which showed the world as it should be, not necessarily as it was. China's propaganda in the 1950s was engaging and imaginative (e.g., Fig. 8.2), unlike the endlessly repetitive art of the Cultural Revolution (1966–76). North Korea followed much of China's style. It's action-packed and colourful, but too much of the same thing over and over. Vietnam and Cuba followed their own styles for propaganda, reflecting their own artistic traditions. Comparing communist propaganda with American and Western Europe, not to mention Nazi Germany, is a whole book's worth; I'd bore you to death.

How would you define 'Propaganda Art'? Is it something that is easily definable?

I am not one who thinks all propaganda is bad; it's not always lies. The goal of propaganda, and propaganda art, is to create involvement. In times of war and revolution, propaganda is essential, and in the countries I've studied, where literacy levels were low in turbulent times, visual propaganda, rather than text, is particularly important.

What best prepared you for your work at the British Museum?

Figure 8.2 Zhang Ding, 'Children New China', 1950, woodblock print.

Museum work is largely learned on the job. As a volunteer and part-time curator over the years, I got help from any number of other curators and scholars. As guest curator of a whole show, I was very grateful to have the support of curators, museum assistants and exhibition design specialists.

What is the size and scope of the propaganda art collection at the British Museum? Could you also describe the highlights of propaganda art collection at the British Museum?

I can only speak for Asia. The Japanese collections are pretty comprehensive, covering most of the 20th century. The Chinese collections are very strong in some areas, but there are gaps. Particularly important is material, on both sides, from the Asia–Pacific War (1931–45). There is a very strong collection of Vietnamese war drawings from the 1960s and 1970s. There are excellent North Korean posters, paintings and prints, but not from before 1990. Most of the Indian propaganda material relates to independence. An example of Indonesian propaganda art can be seen in Fig. 8.3.

You curated an interesting exhibition, **The Art of Influence: Asian Propaganda, in 2013**. Could you comment on this exhibit on rarely seen political art from Asia?

It was unusual in that it crossed all boundaries and borders in Asia. Many of the themes were politically sensitive, and some of the works were offensive to certain viewers. It is a credit to the British Museum that they face sensitive issues head-on. Much of the material was anticolonial, so also anti-Western. We tried to offend everyone equally.

How do you know if your exhibitions or propaganda art are well received by the audience or not?

Figure 8.3 Indonesian anti-bomb poster, 1959.

You know by the number of visitors, the formal reviews and the social media commentary. I think about 150,000 people saw *The Art of Influence*. That is pretty good, considering it was only on for 3 months, in a kind of tucked away gallery in the British Museum. The visitor blogs and tweets were fun, but I was happily surprised by some of the more conventional reviews. An unexpected mention was in *Forbes Magazine*, not their usual sort of thing, to say the least.

What scholarly and professional associations are you a part of, and how do they assist you in your work?

I am on the Council of the Oriental Ceramic Society,[7] which engages in many aspects of Asian art. I am a member of the Association of Asian Studies.[8]

What type of contact does the British Museum have with mainland Chinese authorities or researchers?

[7] Oriental Ceramic Society – Homepage. Available at: http://wp.ocs-london.com/index.php/about-us/.
[8] Association of Asian Studies – Homepage. Available at: https://www.asian-studies.org/.

The British Museum works with many museums and other cultural organizations in China. Several MOUs[9] are in place with national museums. Scholars and other museum staff collaborate under the British Museum's International Training Programme[10] and other museum-to-museum exchanges.

Because of the nature of the topic, do you or the British Museum have much feedback or pressure from mainland Chinese authorities?

No pressure. The cultural staffs of several Asian embassies in London visited the exhibition, *The Art of Influence: Asian Propaganda*.

How did the British Museum go about to collect the propaganda art pieces from different countries during the past decades?

Different types of propaganda have become available at different times. A good example is the art of the Second Sino–Japanese War (1937–45). China was effectively divided into three parts (nationalist, communist and Japanese-occupied areas). The British Museum acquired collections from all three, but it took 30 years. The British Museum has relatively little material from the 1950s; it comes to auction occasionally, but it is otherwise hard to acquire. People did not collect it the way they did Cultural Revolution posters (e.g., Figs 8.4 and 8.5), nor do they fake the 1950s art the way they do the Cultural Revolution stuff.

A different case is the art of the Democratic People's Republic of Korea (North Korea). Until 2000, almost no foreigners were allowed to visit the country, nor was the art exported in any meaningful way. The British Museum now has one of the best museum collections of North Korean art (e.g., Fig. 8.6), but nothing produced before around 1990.

Another great collection in the British Museum comprises drawings and posters from the American War in Vietnam (Fig. 8.7). This is a discrete group of works, almost entirely produced from 1965–75. Vietnamese artists produced wonderful revolutionary art well before the 1960s and since the country's unification, but the British Museum has little of this material yet.

Are there any positive responses from mainland China about the collection? Are there even any ongoing donations? Any plans for collaboration with governmental archives/museums on this collection?

We have many staff exchanges working on museum collections and object loans for exhibitions in both directions. However, these relate to the art of earlier periods, and so far, there has been no collaboration on political works.

The themes and information needs of libraries, archives and museums (LAMs, as some have referred to them) have increasingly converged. What are your experiences

[9] MOU – Memorandum of Understanding.

[10] British Museum: International Training Programme – Homepage. Available at: http://www.britishmuseum.org/about_us/skills-sharing/international_training.aspx.

Figure 8.4 Chinese Cultural Revolution poster, 'Anti Lin, Anti-Confucius'.

and thoughts about these cultural institutions whose work and best practices now often overlap?

The object is accessibility across collections and all media. It's amazing what is available without leaving your desk. Except where copyright restrictions prevent it, the British Museum makes its collections available to all, online. Other museums do the same. Universities put the full contents of many essential books online, and services like JSTOR and Questia make everyone's research so much easier. I can access full historical archives and poster collections online for many countries. Other countries are far more restrictive, whether for policy reasons or lack of technological resources.

Which periods or styles of propaganda art in Asia interest you most?

Wartime art and the art of new regimes (first years after a revolution). Also propaganda of daily life, and political art which relies on tradition. My special research area is propaganda with and for children.

Figure 8.5 Chinese Cultural Revolution poster, 'Learn from Daqing'.

Figure 8.6 Posters enlarged from postage stamps, Democratic People's Republic of Korea (North Korea).

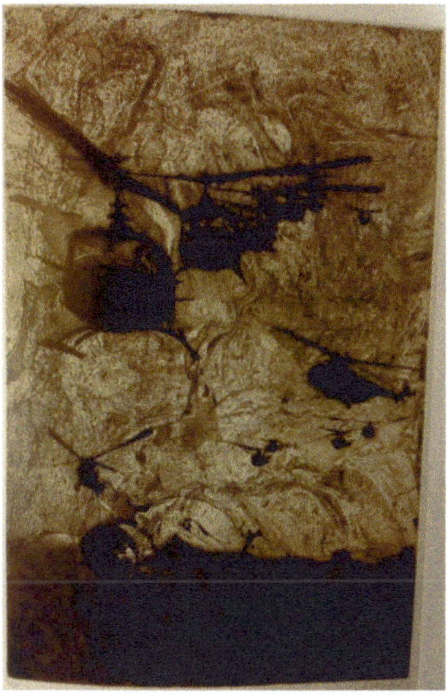

Figure 8.7 Sigmund Abeles, 'Kids with Helicopters', 1967, anti-Vietnam War etching.

Which part(s) of your job at the British Museum do you find most rewarding?

I very much enjoy trawling through the propaganda collections of all the Asian countries and finding new connections among various media, messages and artists. Working with objects and research projects are more interesting than correcting the database, but all the day-to-day tasks are essential.

What are the major challenges and difficulties currently faced by you and your colleagues?

Resource allocations. Too much to do and not enough time or money for all the potential projects. But isn't this true everywhere, in a world with exponentially increasing information and opportunity?

Do you think propaganda art is also moving increasingly towards digital? If that is the case, what are the future roles of an art curator of propaganda art like you?

In some countries, much propaganda art is digital. Digitally manipulated photography has produced some excellent works of dissent. These can be collected and displayed in hard copies, as other art can.

Digital art is increasingly curated in galleries and other public spaces, on laptops, tablets and all varieties of monitors. I am a director of the Lumen Prize, the preeminent international digital art competition, and the best works from the competition are exhibited in several cities around the world each year. The digital phenomenon is just beginning.

The artwork and masterpieces held at the British Museum and the collections housed at the National Gallery, London[11] and the Tate Gallery,[12] how are they different from each other?

The British Museum is a museum of the world, its history and cultures, from earliest times to the present day. It has fine art, but also artefacts of daily life. The others are more specialised: the National Gallery houses one of the world's greatest painting collections, the Tate Britain is for British art from 1500 and Tate Modern holds international modern and contemporary art.

It is said that a great piece of art would feed a person's soul. So when one looks at a piece of powerful propaganda art, what kind of psychological effects would it have on a person's mind?

Propaganda has pejorative connotations in the West, taking on meanings of deception, manipulation and coercion. Of course, propaganda can be used for sinister exploitation of behaviour and attitudes. However, it also inspires action and belief in a common cause. Propaganda wins wars, igniting patriotism. Dissident propaganda sparks revolutions, engaging with repression and inequity, exposing the flaws in official propaganda. Propaganda, and propaganda art, create involvement; that's a fairly neutral interpretation.

What are the feelings engendered by effective propaganda?

Depending on the side you are on, propaganda inspires loyalty/love of cause, country/identity and belonging/hope for future, or it provokes fear/hatred of enemy/anger at injustice.

Can you name a piece of propaganda art where its images and messages are so powerful that they are etched in your consciousness as a viewer, and these images or messages are so powerful that they have in some way changed the course of your life? Or you can never forget the messages behind it?

Several works have had extraordinarily powerful effects on the audiences of their time. Two works immediately spring to mind: both were antiwar protests. Picasso's 1937 *Guernica* is probably the quintessential work in that respect and has influenced antiwar artists to this day.

From the Vietnam War years, the best-known example is the 1972 photograph of a young girl running naked after a napalm attack. Everyone knows the photo, but almost no one could tell you the girl's name (Kim Phuc) or the AP photographer's (Nick Ut). It is often said that the Vietnam War was fought on American television; were those powerful images news reportage or propaganda?

[11] The National Gallery, London – Homepage. Available at: http://www.nationalgallery.org.uk/.

[12] Tate Gallery – Homepage. Available at: http://www.tate.org.uk/.

Aesthetic elements versus political elements/messages: with your 'trained eyes' as a curator, when you are looking at a piece of propaganda art; which elements do you look into first? Or which elements speak/appeal to you more?

I look at the message. One of the reasons propaganda appeals to me is that I am usually pretty sure I understand what it is about, unlike with much of contemporary art. The early Bolshevik posters were surely among the greatest graphics ever produced, not only because of their obvious passion, but the enormous variety, imagination, humour, boldness and style in the revolution's cultural production, etc. Once propaganda becomes repetitive, flabby and formulaic, it loses persuasive power.

Propaganda that relies on folk art—traditional motifs or stories—appeals to me greatly. Firstly, it's sympathetic: the images are familiar to most people, so they make them more comfortable with radical change. This is especially important for older people. On the other hand, as a critic of propaganda, it amuses/bemuses me to see how governments appropriate and distort tradition to suit their purposes.

This exhibition, **The Art of Influence: Asian Propaganda**[13] and its subsequent book, were they initiated by you or by the British Museum? Did you get a lot of support from the British Museum for doing the exhibition and this book?

I suggested it several years before we did it. Our Department was looking for exhibition themes that went across Asia, rather than say, Chinese paintings or Indian textiles. Other examples were Buddhism and ritual vessels. Propaganda is a sensitive subject with potential to offend just about everyone, but once it was agreed, of course the British Museum and all related departments supported it. The British Museum Press was terrific!

Would you also say that the Renaissance masterpieces created by Leonardo di Vinci and Michelangelo (for example, The Last Supper fresco, and the Sistine Chapel ceiling, etc.) are propaganda art for the Roman Catholic Church?

I would not dare to comment on Renaissance art or the uses to which art was put by the royal and religious patrons for whom those artists worked. I would say that the average person today does not consider them to be propagandists, but great artists, less interested in the political motives. Having said that, no art can be completely divorced from the political circumstances of the time of its production.

[13] The Art of Influence: Asian Propaganda: http://www.britishmuseum.org/whats_on/past_exhibitions/2013/asian_propaganda.aspx.

There's No Other Way but to Use the Berlin State Library

9

Matthias Kaun
Berlin State Library, Berlin, Germany

Introduction

The East Asia Department is an independent division of the Berlin State Library. Established in 1922, the department is responsible for the acquisition and development of literature in the languages of East Asia (Chinese, Japanese, Korean, Mongolian, Tibetan, minority languages of China etc.). In addition, the East Asia Department acquires literature on East Asia in Western languages. The East Asia Department manages the collection focusing on East and South-East Asia. As an academic scholar and Head Librarian, Matthias Kaun (Fig. 9.1) is uniquely qualified to assess in Germany to assess and lead a stellar collection.

Can you begin this interview by first introducing yourself: your training, your background and your major roles and duties at the Berlin State Library?[1]

I studied sinology, Chinese language, Asian history and public law, and earned my master's degree a number of years ago. Just before I finished my PhD, I applied for library training. I'd had long-standing ties with the East Asia Department (Berlin State Library)[2] since I was a student, which helped me be successful. And so I succeeded. They only invite four people every year for this kind of library training: a civil service library training that is organised by the library. I began training at the library in 2000, and continued at the Cologne University of Applied Sciences.[3] There, I trained for a second university degree in library science. I completed this in 2002 and became a civil servant in the East Asia Department (Berlin State Library) for the China section (Figs 9.2 and 9.3).

In 2006 I became Head of the Department, which is now organised into different sections including China, Japan, Korea etc. We have between 20 and 25 people working in the department. We are responsible for all different services including cataloguing, organising metadata in all Asian languages etc. We are a kind of 'library within a

[1] Berlin State Library – Homepage. Available at: http://staatsbibliothek-berlin.de/en/.
[2] East Asian Department, Berlin State Library – Homepage. Available at: http://staatsbibliothek-berlin.de/en/about-the-library/abteilungen/ostasien/.
[3] Cologne University of Applied Sciences – Homepage. Available at: https://www.th-koeln.de/en/homepage_26.php.

Inside the World's Major East Asian Collections. http://dx.doi.org/10.1016/B978-0-08-102145-3.00009-1

Figure 9.1 Matthias Kaun.

Figure 9.2 Berlin State Library (exterior).

Figure 9.3 Berlin State Library (interior).

library'. My department is also responsible for a national East, Central and South-East Asia Collection which is partly funded by the German Research Foundation. The idea is that our library serves as a kind of national hub for German researchers. Our collection, which concentrates on the humanities and social sciences, is easily accessible for all who need access to this special material. And here I do not make any difference between print and E-content.

Before we go any further, could you tell me why you decided to study Chinese? I think it wasn't a very popular subject 20 years ago. Is my speculation correct?

It wasn't very popular at that time. I would say that I studied Chinese by chance; it just happened more or less. I did not start with Chinese; the idea was to become a teacher at a big university. It was an autumn day when I went there and I met a professor. He invited me to his office and we were talking about this and that, and he said, 'I'm a new professor here at the university, teaching Asian Studies and Asian History'.

After he asked me to join his lectures, I became interested in Asian history and decided to stay there and began studying Chinese and Asian history.

But for a European, it wasn't that common. Usually, when you were a child, you'd be exposed to French, English or Latin. Asian Studies—Chinese or Japanese—would be very unusual. At that time your parents were not mission people, so you never had the chance to visit this part of Asia at a very young age. What was the appeal to you?

My father did often go to China when he was younger, but that did not influence my decision to study China Studies. However, even today I have noticed that most of the students who study Chinese do not necessarily have a personal relationship with China. They, like myself, just want to do something different and explore their intellectual interests.

You talked a little bit about your background and how you got started in your career, but what best prepared you for your job as Director of the East Asian Collections at the Berlin State Library?

I would say that being, and staying, open-minded is important. But ultimately, we need a professional background in our subject. To be an expert in your field is necessary: field means both Asian studies and library science, although I try to avoid the term library science.

How do you define 'professional background', because the scope of Chinese Studies is so vast?

Let me explain more deeply what I mean by professional. We have a team of specialists here, for the China section we have three colleagues who are in charge of the Chinese Collections. They have a professional background in, say, premodern Chinese literature i.e., premodern Chinese philosophy, premodern Chinese texts or other types of premodern materials. Others are educated in the field of modern Chinese studies, which does not necessarily mean to say they speak only modern Chinese since we all do that more or less. Professional in the sense of a strong understanding of the broader economic and social sciences in our field of study. We have a mixture of expertise among the staff, a kind of diversity management within the area we cover as librarians, because we can't fulfil all these as one person. It is impossible. We all have our own different areas of expertise and personal interests, which should not be neglected.

There are different requests coming from the research community. For example, we're not experts in Chinese law but we have knowledge in areas that we can draw from. I can help because I studied public law in Germany, but I am not an expert in Chinese law. We have to deal with these requests as best as we can as professionals. As professionals in our own intellectual areas, we show people a way to find the materials they need or identify materials they might need.

Can you give me a typical example of a research enquiry issued by a scholar in Chinese studies?

There are no typical questions as such, but I can give you lots of questions that I have collected over the years. For instance, there are enquiries regarding our Manchu materials as we have a strong focus on Manchu materials in our collection. We do receive enquiries like 'I am looking for material on the Chinese–Russian relationship or Chinese–Indian relationship in the 1950s and 1960s'. As you can see, questions are diverse.

Why do they need to send you an email to ask you instead of just checking against the catalogue?

When you're talking about articles and journals, it is easy to find them across different databases; you can just simply run a search. Yet there are lots of materials from East Asia that can't be searched easily or freely on the Internet. You need to have information competence. We have to train our users here. The catalogue is just one access point to the collection; it alone will not answer all your questions. Our CrossAsia search offers a broader search. Normally, the search results are sufficient. But even here: You need to know what to search.

Are you saying that you need to help users find materials not just within the Berlin State Library, but also outside the State Library and on the Internet?

Users come to us, and we go into institutes all over Germany to train people how to use the library. We introduce databases and how to search and use them. This is a very important part of our daily work but is very tiring and cost intensive. Discussion and direct feedback with the community is immensely important. We have a list of databases and we put database descriptions on our website, and I would say it is useful. You can be sure that some of our users—most of our users—really acknowledge that.

I am certain that we have users working in a field who are already experts in different topics. Let's say stone inscriptions, for instance. Who is the expert on stone inscriptions? I would say none of us. We offer content on stone inscriptions, from publications to databases, especially from the Chinese University of Hong Kong Library[4] which has a brilliant database on stone inscriptions. We know you might find something there, but we're not experts on it.

If there is a student who needs some sort of knowledge we can help him with 'Look here, click here, try it out and then if you need some further help, maybe we can help'. If we can't help, we have an online forum where people can connect with other people, researchers can get in touch with other researchers and try to help them resolve the problem. At some point, we are not the experts. We're experts in licensing, metadata and searching, but if it comes to really deep knowledge, we are not the experts. Here again, we try to connect people who use our CrossAsia service. We offer a forum for asking questions and integrating our community.

During your time as an administrator at the Berlin State Library, what are some of the challenges that you've faced? I.e., technical, collections-wise or people-wise?

The major thing that is really impressive is the change of electronic access. We have a long history of electronic access and in fact, some of it is 'old-fashioned' now. But this was not the case 15 years ago. Compared to more conservative libraries, when it comes to acquisition and acquisition policy, I would say that we are often at the forefront of the development of the East Asian libraries in Germany and Europe. Electronic access is a challenge but ultimately a very positive one as it brings content to our users. However, with all the different E-resources, we also face lots of technical problems, particularly with encoding or standards, and especially with metadata standards. The sheer amount of materials that we have should not be viewed as a problem, but rather as a new type of challenge. While we can offer more than 120 million different materials online, we still have to maintain and administer it; it is not an easy task.

I understand that the Berlin State Library also has many rare books from China. Can you tell me about the origin of these rare items? Germany did not have many colonies like France or Great Britain so did you acquire them through auctions, through colonisation or purchasing from the publishers?

In our library, the first books were acquired by missionaries and even bought at auctions in the Netherlands. But the question is: why would a royal library start to collect material in Chinese? In our case, our (Prussian) king said that he wanted to have the books because he wanted to learn, and he wanted to benefit from them for economic reasons. He wanted to build economic relations with Asia, especially China. That was the reason why he acquired Chinese books. The first ever catalogue published by our library was the catalogue of its Chinese books.

[4] The Chinese University of Hong Kong Library – Homepage. Available at: http://www.lib.cuhk.edu.hk/.

Was it during the 18th century that it started?

No. It started in 1661 and our first catalogue was published in 1683. In the mid-19th century, a German bookseller went to China, Hong Kong and South China and acquired materials for us and the Bavarian State Library.[5] He divided it into two parts: one part came to Berlin and one part went to Munich. Interestingly, the reason why it was divided was that he could not agree on a price for the collection. Unfortunately, the biggest disaster occurred in Berlin during the Second World War (WWII), because huge parts of the collections were lost or divided into different parts.

During WWII, our collection was brought out of Berlin to different places. At the end of WWII, parts of the collection were found in Poland, near Krakow, and some were taken to the former Soviet Union, today Russia. So parts of our collection are still in Berlin and other parts are in Krakow. We have just finished a project together with the Jagiellonian Library in Krakow. We digitised the former parts of our collection which are now in Krakow so we can recatalogue it, and we are waiting for funding so we could start a similar project with Russia. But with Russia, we have no real idea where to find the parts of our collection. Material could be in St. Petersburg, but we do not know for sure. So it is more difficult.

When you said that the Germans and the Russians could not identify the collection, do you mean they could not identify the content?

We have many Chinese experts in Russia and they know exactly what's in the collection. Rather, there is a political issue emerging regarding who is the owner of this material. When we started our project in Krakow, we left all political discussions behind because we just wanted to digitise the material, describe it, mark records for the titles and then offer it to the public. In Russia, it is a problem because the Russian Parliament says that all materials taken into Russia after WWII signifies that Russia is now the owner of those materials. So there's no easy way of cooperation. I went to Moscow in 2006 and I could identify our own titles there. We really hope that we will be able to find a way to cooperate with Russia. We would love to reidentify the material and maybe digitise it for both sides, Russia and ourselves.

Is it a balancing act in terms of managing priorities between the various East Asian languages and collections?

Yes and no. But we can say that we have a hierarchy when it comes to the budget. We have strong Chinese Collections, and the publishing market is a big part of it. We now have a good demand from the Japanese side, but the market situation is totally different. The Chinese market is the biggest market in the world in terms of publications. The Japanese market might be the most expensive market in the world, but it is not as big as the Chinese market. The Taiwan market is also not as big as the China market. The Korean markets are not that big, but there are very good E-resources. The Central

[5] Bavarian State Library – Homepage. Available at: https://www.bsb-muenchen.de/en/.

Asia market is a steady special market, especially when it comes to Mongolian or Uygur materials.

So we have a system and we develop our own policy according to the demands and the different market situations. It is complicated because we try to be flexible but of course we also have budget restrictions.

Which part of your job at the Berlin State Library do you find the most rewarding?

It is a really special job that I have here, and I would say that when it comes to the East Asian library world, it is the best job in the world (as long as we have central and national responsibilities). It is rewarding because our services are used by all researchers in the field of East Asian Studies in Germany. CrossAsia is really successful. I would say that we fulfil a kind of national library service for East Asian Studies and far beyond, because we're not only talking about Chinese or Japanese Studies, but also economic subjects and people who are working in the field of Chinese economics, society, law and so on. Transdisciplinary and transcultural questions are much more significant in numbers than ever before.

This job is really fascinating because I have to fulfil all these different activities and support all the institute libraries in Germany. But also be a kind of umbrella infrastructure or backbone infrastructure which those libraries and researchers can rely on. Library has all these different E-resources and acquire all those big sets of book volumes, but it is still important to offer this to all of the research community. That is our main duty. It is not competitive like the US model; it is more complementary. That is very rewarding.

What are the roles and missions of the East Asian Department at the Berlin State Library?

I represent the Berlin State Library, but I am not representing an important department if you compare it with our manuscript or music department. I am only the director of a small department, but we have the largest budget. From my point of view, there is a very good reason to have our own library for East Asian culture in Germany. Our main mission is still planning, running and offering excellent service and infrastructure to the research community that need access to this special material.

Can you tell me what a typical day at work is for you?

This morning I checked my emails. After this I went to a meeting at 9:00 a.m. on a conversion project: a card conversion and a catalogue conversion project. Then I came here and had a talk with my colleague who just returned from a meeting at the University of Oxford. She gave me a very brief report on the meeting, then I met another colleague who I asked to download some materials from our databases. I then went to lunch with three colleagues from our administration team, which was fun. Afterwards I had a short meeting with my colleague and some colleagues from the

IT department on our cataloguing service. It is all mundane and tomorrow is more or less the same.

Different meetings, different talks and different work. A normal day for the library starts at 9:00–9:30 a.m. and I stay here until 6:00–7:00 p.m. I normally continue to work at night because I need to write applications for grants, but I do that at home. I can't do that in the office because there are too many people around and phone calls coming in. I try to check my emails in the evenings as well because I want to reply to China as soon as possible because of the time difference. That is a typical day.

What kind of emails would you get from China and who would sends you these emails?

This morning I received emails from the China International Book Trading Corporation (CIBTC)[6] and Unihub, a database company in Beijing. We purchased databases from them many, many years ago, and they want to continue it. I also received one email from Laos because we have a cooperation with the National Library of Laos.[7] That is it from East Asia for today.

Ten years ago, the European Union (EU) allocated a lot of funding for the state libraries and different national libraries to build new projects, especially projects that related to the national heritage of different national museums and libraries. What about your department? Did you receive similar funding?

No, but this year we applied for an EU project. It is a very interesting project with different partners from all of Europe. The main partners were ourselves, the Leiden University Library[8] in the Netherlands, the Max Planck Institute for the History of Sciences[9] and some other institutes from Spain and Finland. The idea is to offer a backbone infrastructure to support all kinds of activities in the humanities and social sciences using East Asian materials.

We received a decision from the EU, and they said, 'No we will not fund the project because we have some problems with the technical set-up'. That was the main reason, but we are still working on it. I am not convinced by big projects because they are too cost intensive. I strongly believe that we will continue with this project but on a smaller scale. I am interested in it for many reasons. One is that we could offer great services to the German research community because we could offer even more than others like Harvard University.[10] We have licensed these kinds of materials, and what we noticed was that we have a European imbalance. European countries, such as Switzerland and the Netherlands, do not have programmes that are as well supported as ours. When it comes to the UK, they tend to compete with other

[6] China International Book Trading Corporation (CIBTC) – Homepage. Available at: http://www.cibtc.com.cn/gtweb/enaction.do.

[7] National Library of Laos – Homepage. Available at: http://www.nationallibraryoflaos.org/.

[8] Leiden University Library – Homepage. Available at: http://bibliotheek.leidenuniv.nl/.

[9] Max Planck Institute for the History of Sciences – Homepage. Available at: https://www.mpiwg-berlin.mpg.de/.

[10] Harvard University – Homepage. Available at: http://www.harvard.edu/.

institutions; I do think we should really cooperate and find good quality resources instead of competing.

The idea is to bring these resources to European libraries. For example, we introduced CrossAsia to the European markets by negotiating and establishing European consortiums, which few institutions could have financed by themselves. As a result, I am now thinking about different models which would level the field, or close this gap, between the German situation and the rest of Europe. The other problem in Germany is that we really need a digital infrastructure, because when we license this material we have hosting and archival rights. We have tons of data here and we now need a system that allows us to 'control', administer and maintain it. On the other hand, we need a system that gives us access to this material by a special and controlled interface, to meet the demands of researchers in the field of Digital Humanities.

Could you tell us the difference between archival rights and hosting rights? What are the implications for supporting research, especially for Digital Humanities scholars?

We have this already with CrossAsia, we harvest material from all over the world now. Let me give you an example to clarify what I mean. There was a problem with the *Renmin Ribao* (人民日报), a Chinese newspaper database, a few years ago. If you searched for words that are not allowed to be searched (for censorship purposes in China), it was annoying. But when it comes to finding materials for research from these types of databases, it becomes a big problem. While the Berlin State Library normally has hosting and archiving rights, it still needs a system that allows users (without violating the copyright) to have access to the materials or integrate those texts' copyright licenses into their own environments, and do so without violating the original contract.

That is a tricky situation for us. So there's much more than creating a repository or harvesting system. It is really about a system that offers a technical interface and that can offer access to materials that researchers can work with without violating copyright. That is what we are now thinking about. We have a concept for that and we are trying to bring it into action. Hosting and archiving mean more or less the same to us now in the CrossAsia context. We are less interested in hosting a special application and databases system, but we are interested in hosting and archiving the pure content which normally means metadata and machine readable full-text in a standard format.

What professional associations are you a part of? What about the other East Asian librarians in Europe? What do you talk about?

I am a member of the Association of Asian Studies (AAS) ,[11] the European Association of Sinological Librarians (EASL) [12] and the Europe Association for China Studies (EACS).[13] I'll give you an example, my colleague just came back from

[11] Association of Asian Studies (AAS) – Homepage. Available at: https://www.asian-studies.org/.

[12] European Association of Sinological Librarians (EASL) – Homepage. Available at: http://www.easl.org/.

[13] Europe Association for China Studies (EACS) – Homepage. Available at: http://www.chinesestudies.eu/.

the University of Oxford last week. EASL meetings are socialising meetings, much more so than the Council of East Asian Libraries (CEAL)[14] meeting. We talk about different situations in Europe and in America. We are talking about smaller institution libraries.

What do you mean by 'socialising meeting'?

Every situation is different in Europe. We are not talking about professional librarianship; there are very few professional librarians in the EASL. My Berlin colleagues are professional as are those in Munich, Paris and Oxford, but that is all. All my colleagues are good at fulfilling their duties in their libraries, but talking about bigger and common projects is not really a problem. The EASL is really for socialising, just to meet people, say hello and that is it. The EASL is no professional organisation.

To meet once a year, it is almost like a family. We're talking about a small organisation here. I try to join the CEAL meetings regularly because I am very much interested in what's going on in different places. The CEAL meetings are more or less influenced by private institutions, mainly libraries of Harvard University,[5] the University of British Columbia,[15] Stanford University[16] and similar big institutions like the University of California, Los Angeles (UCLA)[17] and the University of Californai, Berkeley[18] etc.

Germany has 16 different states. Berlin State has its own library and Bavaria has its own state library, they're both large and have very important collections. I am wondering about the Bavaria State Library, which also has a large East Asian Collection. Is that comparable to the Berlin State Library's?

The answer is: yes and no. We had comparable collections of premodern materials, but our collection is now more or less divided into different parts whereas the Bavarian State Library has a complete collection of their premodern materials in Munich. However, if it comes to modern services, modern books and modern journals, they have more or less ceased in their engagement in these areas. They reduced their interest in supporting Chinese or East Asian Studies in Germany, maybe as a result of our strength in these areas. This is logical since our collection is already strong and we invest a lot of money in this area, so they would rather concentrate on different areas of expertise. However we should keep in mind that the collection in Munich is part of the Bavarian State Library (BSB) collection; our collection is also partly financed by central means from the German research Foundation. And therefore we have different situations. The BSB is doing a lot in the field of their Asia Collection like their engagement in digitising the collection.

[14] Council of East Asian Libraries (CEAL) – Homepage. Available at: http://www.eastasianlib.org/.
[15] The University of British Columbia – Homepage. Available at: https://www.ubc.ca/.
[16] Stanford University – Homepage. Available at: http://www.stanford.edu/.
[17] The University of California, Los Angeles (UCLA) – Homepage. Available at: http://www.ucla.edu/.
[18] University of California, Berkeley – Homepage. Available at: http://www.berkeley.edu/.

Is there any collaboration between the Berlin State Library and Bavarian State Library?

Not really, even though we know each other. They have a big digitisation project in Bavaria together with Google. They have digitised most of their Chinese Collections. For example, I tried to receive all the records for indexing like I tried to for Harvard's digitised collection. For Munich, I have to use their big open data set. So I would say that we like each other and we can talk, but when it comes to real cooperation and exchanging data, we all know that cooperation on the working level is hard and complicated.

What about the German National Library?[19] Do they have an important East Asian Collection?

No, it is a different set-up because they were founded by publishers 100 years ago. They are only concentrating on material published in Germany, and material that is related to Germany. So they might have some collections in Chinese on German or about Germany, but they do not have a Chinese Collection or Indian Collection. They're really concentrating on German language materials.

I have to ask you about your collection development policy. How do you decide what new books to buy and what new electronic databases to buy? How do you determine the needs of your users?

That is an easy and complicated question at the same time. We are not so much of a department or collection within the Berlin State Library, but we are a collection for all of Germany. We have our own collection development policy. We really try to select all titles in the field of humanities and social sciences, and support all researchers in East Asian Studies and beyond. That means that we allow everybody to contact us and give us ideas on what we should buy, or if they have a set that they can't buy because it is too expensive, we would buy it for them and send it to the library through our interlibrary loan service. So that is very easy because it is a direct contact.

Beyond that, we have our own policy which means that we want to have a good collection of East Asian material which not only supports Chinese Studies or Japanese Studies, but all subjects. In Europe, when it comes to modern collections, institute libraries really fulfil local research and teaching needs etc. We, as the Berlin State Library, want to provide an East Asian Collection from archaeology to *manga* studies for as long as we can. And even material not normally purchased, like popular magazines. We have this kind of material, but we have to reduce it for budget reasons. However, there is the idea to have an example of this kind of material and offer it to the German research community. We try to be in touch with our research community, try to be flexible enough to go to conferences, to meetings with researchers, get into contact with them and try to advertise our services and get feedback on what is needed and what kind of expectations we are faced with. So far, the feedback is good and we hope we will be able to continue.

[19] German National Library – Homepage. Available at: http://www.dnb.de/EN/Home/home_node.html.

As a German citizen managing an East Asian Collection, what are the major challenges you are facing or the key advantages?

The major challenge is our system, which was running for more than 50 years and was supported by the German Research Foundation, has now stopped. Funding of the old programme ends by the end of 2016, and we applied for a new programme. We have to redevelop our services more or less. We will know by the end of December 2015 whether we will be able to continue with the new programme in 2016. I am convinced that we offer a very good infrastructure, but it needs a stable financial backbone and requires more than a three-year project (which will be funded by the new programme). There are some investments that we want to do and we are really willing to invest in it; I hope we can continue.

Who are the majority of your users?

It has changed a little bit because we had a change in our education system here. Now we have the BA (bachelor's) and MA (master's) education system. We noticed that the BA students are not really able to work with our very special resources, because they have a lack of language and reading skills in Chinese, Japanese and Korean. We lost part of our users because students in the sixth or seventh semester at the university now normally read Western-language materials. Nevertheless, we are here to support them.

I guess nearly every professor in East Asian Studies uses our services. Not every day, but they have to use our system; I would say there's no way out. The same is true for PhD students or post-doctoral researchers. Researchers use it maybe more often than the professors. When it comes to figures, our user group has been stable for the last 5 years.

Opening up the Bavarian State Library's East Asian Collections to the World

10

Thomas Tabery
Bavarian State Library, Munich, Germany

Introduction

The Bavarian State Library (Bayerische Staatsbibliothek) holds a rich collection of Chinese, Japanese and Korean books and manuscripts, overseen by Dr Thomas Tabery (Fig. 10.1), curator of the East Asia Collection. It is the Chinese collection that stands out, in terms of both quality and quantity. Currently, it comprises around 230,000 printed volumes and over 3000 manuscripts including a large number of Chinese rare books and manuscripts. In the last years the library has made great efforts to make its East Asian materials more clearly visible and more easily accessible for the public and the scholarly community around the world. Bibliographic descriptions of Chinese and Japanese titles have been improved and extensive digitisation projects launched. As a result, today, the majority of out-of-copyright Chinese titles (titles published before 1875) as well as a large number of Japanese titles of the Bavarian State Library are fully digitised and freely accessible online.

Could you begin this interview by first introducing yourself? For example, your training and background, and your main functions and duties at the Bavarian State Library?

After finished my studies in linguistics, philosophy and sinology in Wurzburg, Nanjing, Beijing, Paris and Leipzig, I held the positions of research assistant at the Institute of East Asian Studies, Leipzig University,[1] and of visiting lecturer at the HHL Leipzig Graduate School of Management.[2] I received my PhD from Leipzig University for my thesis in the field of Chinese history of thought, and I completed my training in library and information science (LIS) at the Konstanz University Library[3] and the Bavarian Library Academy.[4]

[1] Leipzig University – Homepage. Available at: http://www.zv.uni-leipzig.de/en/.

[2] HHL Leipzig Graduate School of Management – Homepage. Available at: http://www.hhl.de/en/home/.

[3] Konstanz University Library – Homepage. Available at: https://www.kim.uni-konstanz.de/en/.

[4] Bavarian Library Academy – Homepage. Available at: https://www.bsb-muenchen.de/en/about-us/head-office-departments/library-academy/.

Inside the World's Major East Asian Collections. http://dx.doi.org/10.1016/B978-0-08-102145-3.00010-8

Figure 10.1 Dr Thomas Tabery.

Since 2008, I have been working at the Bavarian State Library[5] in Munich. As Deputy Head of the Oriental and Asia Department and as Curator of the East Asia Collection I have, amongst others, the following responsibilities:

- Firstly, collection building and the establishment of a new supplier structure for books and journals from the People's Republic of China and the Republic of China, Taiwan.
- Secondly, project management. Two examples would be the retroconversion of our Chinese and Japanese card catalogues, which has been completed by an external service provider, and the recataloguing and digitisation of large parts of our collection of Chinese ancient books and manuscripts.
- Thirdly, to expand and ramp up cooperation with libraries from East Asia.

Please provide a brief introduction to the Oriental and Asian Collections at the Bavarian State Library with a focus on your East Asian Collections

Founded in 1558 as the Court Library of the house of Wittelsbach, the Bavarian State Library today ranks among the most significant European universal and research libraries (Figs 10.4 and 10.5). It houses several special collections, among them an exceptional Oriental and Asian Collection with 600,000 volumes of printed works and 18,400 manuscripts with an enormous variety of vernacular languages from a large geographic area including Northern Africa, the Near and Middle East, and from Central, Southern, South-East and East Asia etc. These holdings are supplemented by literature in Western languages which relate to these regions.

Munich has a long history of collecting Oriental and Asian materials. Since its foundation, the Court Library—later the Bavarian State Library—held one of the most important collections of Oriental literature in Europe, due to the Widmanstetter and Fugger Collections acquired before. During the 17th and 18th centuries, the acquisitions of Oriental literature was sporadic and anything but systematic. Things changed in the 19th century: the secularisation of Bavarian monasteries and clerical dukedoms, the transfer of the Mannheim Court Library to Munich and several specific and purposeful large-scale purchases allowed the library to establish an extensive Oriental and Asian Collection.

[5] Bavarian State Library – Homepage. Available at: https://www.bsb-muenchen.de/en/.

Let's have a closer look at our Chinese, Japanese and Korean holdings. The oldest documentation of Chinese titles in the library goes back to the year 1618. To this day, the Chinese Collection is continually being expanded., It currently comprises 230,000 printed volumes and 3000 manuscripts. What is special about it? It contains one of the largest collections of Chinese ancient books and manuscripts in the Western world, among them many rare and valuable specimens (Figs 10.2 and 10.8).

The Japanese Collection consists of roughly 90,000 printed volumes, containing several hundred printings from the pre-Meiji period. The small Korean Collection, of around 3000 titles, includes 600 volumes that were printed before 1900. The majority of those titles date back as far as the 17th century. Both the Japanese and as the Korean Collection were only started after 1945.

Could you describe the highlights of the Oriental Collections?

Well, it is difficult to keep this brief. Many highlights can be found, for example, our 4400 Islamic manuscripts from the eighth to the beginning of the 20th century, whose provenance reflects the Islamic world from Spain to Java. Here, the ornamental Korans and the Persian miniature manuscripts deserve special attention.

As one of only a few libraries outside Yemen, our library owns 800 ancient Sabean wood inscriptions, which were partly deciphered only in recent years.

The collection of early Oriental printed works is outstanding. It comprises numerous incunabula from the beginning of Oriental book printing in Europe and the Orient.

Especially noteworthy is our Yiddish Collection, which was acquired primarily after the Second World War (WWII), and our Hebrew Collection, which ranks among the most important Hebrew Collections in the world and was one of the few Hebrew libraries in Germany to survive WWII.

The Tibetan texts encompass an original block print of the so-called Lhasa Kanjur, and a complete set of copies of all printed slabs held by the East Tibetan monastery of Derge. The large collection of Tibetan book covers is of particular significance.

To mention some important unique objects: the Bavarian State Library holds the only complete manuscript of the Babylonian Talmud, which survived the destruction of Hebrew books during the Middle Ages; the illustrated cosmography by al-Qazwini (1280); an Armenian book of gospels with miniatures (1278); an 83 m long roll containing the Indian epos Mahabharata; gold and silver leaves from Burma and a Tibetan manuscript with the thumb print of the fifth Dalai Lama.

Other unique items are our manuscripts of peoples from South-East Asia, like the Yao or the Shan. With approximately 2800 Yao manuscripts, the Bavarian State Library holds one of the largest collections of this kind in the world.

What are the highlights of the East Asia Collection?

Amongst the most valuable Chinese items, you can find about 20 printings from the Song (960–1279) and Yuan Dynasties (1279–1368). Most of them are Buddhist texts, many of which were part of early canonical editions that are no longer available as a

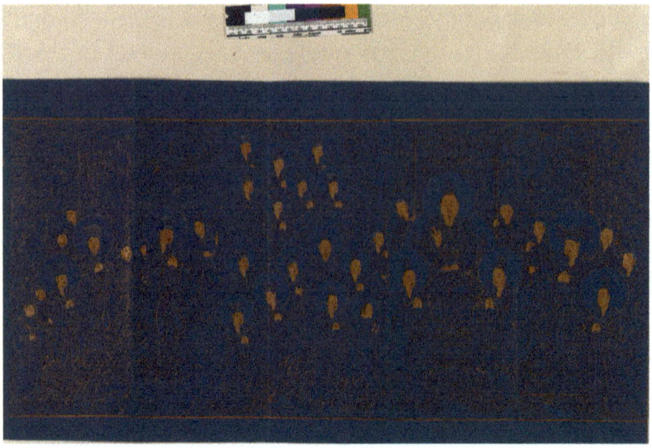

Figure 10.2 Daoist text in blue-gold, Ming dynasty (Cod.sin. 136).

whole today, while some fragments are scattered across the world. In addition, there are more than 100 Ming dynasty (1368–1644) printings which cover the wide spectrum of the rich Ming Dynasty's printing history, and several hundred Qing dynasty printings including a number of printings of Western missionaries in China. The oldest Chinese print owned by the Bavarian State Library dates from 975. The most valuable of the Chinese manuscripts are doubtlessly three Dunhuang manuscripts dating from the Tang Dynasty (618–907).

The strength of the old Japanese Collection lies in its balance, as is evidenced by a wide range of genres. A specimen of the oldest Japanese print from before 770, a Buddhist scroll with an incantation (a so-called dharani) is kept in a carved wooden pagoda. Another early and remarkable item is a blue-gold sutra from the Heian period in the 12th century. Among the richly and elaborately illustrated book productions from the Edo era, 44 painters' books are particularly outstanding. They contain drawings by famous artists in virtuoso coloured xylographs.

The oldest Korean specimens are chapters of the Buddhist canon printed on Ganghwa Island in 1237, whose printing blocks are still preserved in the Haeinsa monastery, and a catalogue of medicinal products printed with clay printing types in 1433.

You are a scholar in your own right, a Chinese specialist. How does your research and scholarship inform your work as a curator?

Due to my own experiences, I am familiar with the requirements of a research library and with the specialised needs of scholars. I have felt these moments of happiness myself when I discover special materials in library collections. This is why we try to make our East Asian materials as easily accessible as possible, and continue to further expand our special collections not least by acquiring very specialised materials. The latter is not an easy task in times of rising book prices and declining budgets.

What scholarly and professional associations are you a member of, and how do they assist you in your work?

I am a member of the German Association of Chinese Studies (DVCS),[6] the Association of German Librarians (VDB)[7] and the European Association of Sinological Librarians (EASL).[8] In my daily work, I benefit from the exchange of ideas and experiences with specialists and colleagues.

Who are the majority of the Asian Collection users? That is, who comes to see you about your collections? Could you give some examples?

The Bavarian State Library regards researchers, scholars, lecturers and students worldwide as its primary target groups. The use of our Asian materials proves this right. Our users come from universities and other research institutions not only within Germany, but from all over the world. Here are some examples: a researcher from the United States who compared our different editions of a famous Chinese painting manual; a group of Japanese and Chinese specialists of Daoist studies who had a close look at our collection of religious manuscripts of the Yao people and a historian from Guangzhou who discovered publications from the Guangzhou area in our collection which date from the 18th and the 19th century and that no longer exist in China.

In institutions with Asian Collections, it is inevitable that there is a balancing act in terms of managing priorities between the various areas of language expertise/ collections with regard to the other Asian language collections (i.e., Japanese, Korean etc.). What are your experiences as a librarian in terms of balancing and prioritising? How do you acquire and evaluate your collection?

Due to budget cuts a few years ago, we were forced to focus our acquisitions on selected areas. Taking the East Asian Collections as an example, it was decided to further expand the Chinese Collection and to sharply reduce Japanese and Korean monograph acquisitions. The reasons for this were the quantity and the quality of the Chinese Collection and its relatively high usage figures.

However, further enhancement of the Chinese Collection is challenging: On the one hand, our financial resources are limited; on the other hand, there are growing numbers of scholarly titles, accompanied by increasing book prices in China.

In accordance with the historical development of the collection, the current acquisitions focus on the arts disciplines of imperial China up until the year 1912: history, philosophy, religion, literature, the fine arts and archaeology. There are standing orders for our Chinese and Japanese journals. Monographs and electronic resources are proactively selected according to our collection profile and purchased from a number of suppliers from the People's Republic of China, the Republic of China (Taiwan) and Japan.

[6] German Association of Chinese Studies – Homepage. Available at: http://www.ruhr-uni-bochum.de/oaw/dvcs/index_en.html.

[7] Association of German Librarians – Homepage. Available at: http://www.vdb-online.org/verein/info-en.php.

[8] European Association of Sinological Librarians – Homepage. Available at: http://www.easl.org/.

How is the collection catalogued and accessible for users? With a non-Roman script, what challenges does this present to cataloguing? Are there any?

Dealing with non-Roman script was difficult, or even impossible, in German catalogue systems until a few years ago. This is what the Bavarian State Library did to cope with this situation. In 1990 the library started to catalogue its East Asian acquisitions in the RLG Union Catalogue Research Libraries Information Network (RLIN),[9] the shared electronic catalogue of a group of American research libraries. Why was that? This database was chosen because at the time RLIN was the only international library catalogue in which Chinese and Japanese characters could be added to the record, and in which a significant amount of metadata for East Asian titles was already available. After RLIN was integrated into OCLC WorldCat[10] in October 2007, the newly acquired East Asian titles of the Bavarian State Library were catalogued in WorldCat until the end of 2008. We have subsequently migrated all of our WorldCat records to our own library catalogue.

1 January 2009 marked a turning point: from that point on Chinese titles have been directly catalogued in the Aleph database of the Bavarian Union Catalogue[11] in original Chinese script as well as in Pinyin transcription, as Aleph was Unicode capable at that time.

The retroconversion of our old Chinese and Japanese card catalogues into electronic form was carried out by an external service provider who created around 100,000 electronic records in both vernacular language and transcription. The project was completed in 2012. Since then, all of our Chinese and Japanese titles have been electronically catalogued in original script and transcription.

With regard to non-Roman scripts in library catalogues, many problems have been solved, but there are still some left. For example, the correct indexing by search engines and the problem of tokenization of strings of Chinese characters.

In the past few years, the Bavarian State Library has strongly committed itself to the digitisation of its copyright-free collections. Could you outline this approach?

Digitisation has become a standard method for providing worldwide access to printed and handwritten information. The Bavarian State Library pursues the strategy of comprehensively digitising its copyright-free holdings, following two complementary approaches: Firstly, there is the in-house digitisation at the library's Munich Digitisation Center.[12] Here, the digitisation of manuscripts, incunabula, printings of the 16th century and of all other valuable holdings is carried out. Secondly, copyright-free printings of the 17th, 18th and 19th century are scanned as part of a public–private partnership between the Bavarian State Library and Google. To date, around 150,000 volumes have been digitised by the Munich Digitisation Centre, and nearly 1 million volumes by Google (status as of November 2015).

[9] RLG Union Catalog (RLIN) – Homepage. Available at: http://www.oclc.org/research/activities/holdings-gateway.html.

[10] OCLC WorldCat – Homepage. Available at: https://www.worldcat.org/.

[11] Bavarian Union Catalogue – Homepage. Available at: https://opacplus.bib-bvb.de/TouchPoint_touchpoint/start.do.

[12] Munich Digitisation Center – Homepage. Available at: http://www.digitale-sammlungen.de/index.html?&l=en.

This strategy also applies for Chinese works: Digitisation of Chinese ancient books and manuscripts, dating from the 18th century and earlier, was realised by the library's Munich Digitisation Centre with financial support from the German Research Foundation.[13] A total of 12,000 printed volumes and many manuscripts have been digitised. The digitisation of another 13,000 Chinese volumes dating from the 18th and 19th centuries was carried out by Google.

As a result, since the end of 2015, a total of 25,000 volumes of out-of-copyright Chinese printings (i.e., works published before 1875) of the Bavarian State Library have been fully digitised. Thus one of Europe's major collections of Chinese ancient books and manuscripts is accessible online worldwide.

Could you tell us more about the library's recataloguing and full text digitisation of the Chinese ancient books and manuscripts project?

Our oldest Chinese books and manuscripts, originating from the 7th to the 18th century, were comprehensively catalogued and fully digitised between 2011 and 2015 as part of a project funded by the German Research Foundation. A total of 12,000 printed volumes and a large number of manuscripts have been digitised, with more than 1 million digital images produced.

All titles to be digitised were recatalogued, which means that extensive bibliographic descriptions, according to the "Cataloguing guidelines for creating Chinese rare book records in machine readable form,[14]" were created. According to these guidelines a broad scope of characteristics was included in the bibliographic description.

The digitisation was carried out by the library's Munich Digitisation Centre, one of the largest digitisation centres in Europe. The digitisation workflow not only comprised the scanning process (Fig. 10.3), but also quality control of every single image and the capture of structural data (table of contents). In each digitised volume, important structural features (for example, chapter headings, prefaces and epilogues, illustrations or

Figure 10.3 Scanning.

[13] German Research Foundation – Homepage. Available at: http://www.dfg.de/en/.

[14] http://www.eastasianlib.org/ctp/webinars/ChineseRareBook/CRBP_guidelines.pdf.

Figure 10.4 The Bavarian State Library (exterior).

Figure 10.5 The Bavarian State Library (interior).

ownership seals etc.) were captured as structural metadata, which subsequently allows users to directly access specific structural and content-related parts of the digitised items.

In the area of digital long-term preservation, the Bavarian State Library works together with the Leibniz Supercomputing Center[15] in Munich where all electronic documents of the library are saved.

All digitised titles are accessible free of charge via the Digital Library and the online catalogue of the Bavarian State Library, the Bavarian Library Network (Gateway Bayern), WorldCat, the Union Catalogue of Chinese Rare Books of the National Central Library[16] in Taipei, virtual libraries including CrossAsia[17] and Europeana[18] as well as via commercial search engines.

[15] Leibniz Supercomputing Centre – Homepage. Available at: https://www.lrz.de/english/.

[16] National Central Library – Homepage. Available at: http://enwww.ncl.edu.tw/.

[17] CrossAsia – Homepage. Available at: http://crossasia.org/.

[18] Europeana – Homepage. Available at: http://www.europeana.eu/portal/en.

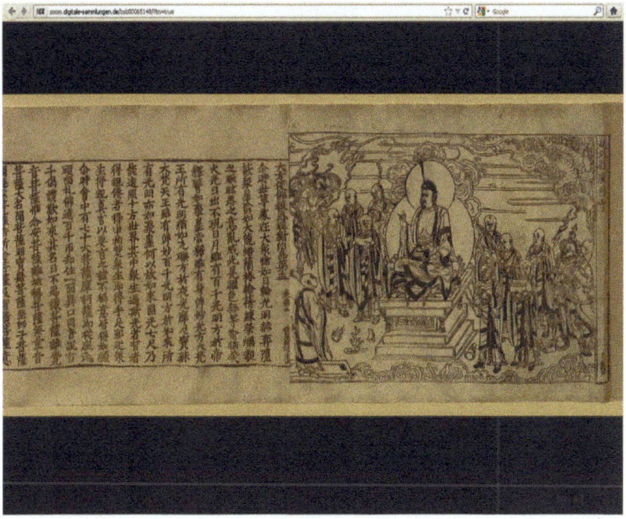

Figure 10.6 Frontispiece of Jin-Tripitaka (Res/4 L.sin. C 266.

Figure 10.7 Zooming in the frontispiece.

In addition, we have set up a separate website, the Digital East Asia Collections (http://eastasia.digital-collections.de). Here, zoom technology is used to present oversize materials. You can zoom in and out of the digitised scrolls and foldouts (Figs 10.6 and 10.7).

All images are available as JPGs with 72 dpi. Free PDF downloads are possible. TIF files (300 dpi) can be provided by the Bavarian State Library, e.g., for reproductions.

Figure 10.8 Painting Manual of the Mustard Seed Garden (Jie zi yuan hua zhuan), 1679 (4 L.sin.K 290).

The Digital East Asia Collections website also contains digitised versions of Chinese and Japanese printings from the 17th, 18th and 19th century which have been created in the context of the public–private partnership with Google.

Tell us more about the public–private partnership with Google.

With its service Google Books (previously known as Google Book Search), Google is the major player in the field of retrodigitisation. Google Books is a digitisation project of industrial scale, a true mass digitisation project. Book selection takes place only according to their fitness for scanning from a conservatory perspective, and according to certain requirements of size and volume posed by Google's proprietary scanning technology.

The public–private partnership between the Bavarian State Library and Google started in 2007. Other library partners are the libraries of Columbia University,[19]

[19] Columbia University – Homepage. Available at: http://www.columbia.edu/.

Harvard University,[20] University of California,[21] Stanford University,[22] Keio University,[23] the National Library of Catalonia etc.[24]

At the end of 2015, around 1 million copyright-free volumes (dating from the 17th to the 19th century) of the Bavarian State Library's holdings have been digitised by Google, including approximately 13,000 Chinese volumes and a significant number of Western titles on East Asia. Google keeps a digital copy of each work scanned which is integrated into Google's services, while the library gets a copy that is made freely available via the library's online catalogue.

What are some of the technical challenges that you are facing, particularly in terms of preservation and digitisation?

Various digitisation techniques had to be used depending on the texture of the paper, depending on whether there were thin, separate fascicles or thick, Western-style bound volumes that contain several fascicles or depending on the size. Foldouts up to 7 m or scrolls up to 11 m in length had to be scanned.

In view of the growing number of digitisation projects, the major challenges of digitising Chinese Collections are not technical. Rather, amongst other things, the challenges ahead are to do with improving the visibility of the digitised collections, integrating them into established and widely used search environments and ensuring the long-term preservation of digitised objects. The digital long-term preservation is a major challenge.

You mentioned cooperations with East Asian Libraries. Could you tell us something about that?

Our contact with East Asian libraries led to a number of official cooperations. In March 2012 the Bavarian State Library and the National Central Library in Taipei concluded a cooperation agreement, which is oriented amongst others towards the exchange of experts, experience and technologies in various areas of library and information activities. The metadata of our Chinese rare books have been integrated into the international 'Union Catalogue of Chinese Rare Books' maintained by the National Central Library. Moreover, in November 2014, the 'Taiwan Resource Centre for Chinese Studies' at the Bavarian State Library was opened.

In January 2013, a cooperation agreement with the Hong Kong Public Libraries was signed with the purpose of implementing joint projects in the field of innovative technologies.

[20] Harvard University – Homepage. Available at: http://www.harvard.edu/.

[21] University of California – Homepage. Available at: http://universityofcalifornia.edu/.

[22] Stanford University – Homepage. Available at: http://www.stanford.edu/.

[23] Keio University – Homepage. Available at: https://www.keio.ac.jp/en/.

[24] National Library of Catalonia – Homepage. Available at: http://www.bnc.cat/.

Initiated by the partnership between the Free State of Bavaria and the Chinese province of Guangdong in October 2014, the Bavarian State Library signed a cooperation agreement with the Sun Yat-sen Library of Guangdong Province. The cooperation focuses on joint projects and on the mutual exchange of know-how, for example, in the field of digital services or restoration technologies.

Aside from this, we are in close contact with other libraries, for example, the Shanghai Library[25] and the China Academic Digital Associative Library (CADAL)[26] at Zhejiang University.[27]

Which part(s) of your job at the Bavarian State Library do you find most interesting and rewarding?

What I really like about my job is being responsible for our exceptional East Asia Collection with its long history and with its many fascinating objects.

[25] Shanghai Library – Homepage. Available at: http://www.library.sh.cn/web/index.html.
[26] China Academic Digital Associative Library (CADAL) – Homepage. Available at: http://www.cadal.cn/bqggg/copyright.htm.
[27] Zhejiang University – Homepage. Available at: http://www.zju.edu.cn/english/.

A History That Dates Back to the 13th Century in Switzerland's Zurich Central Library

11

Marc Winter
University of Zurich, Zurich, Switzerland

Introduction

Founded in 1917, Zurich Central Library is one of the largest libraries in the field of humanities and social science in Switzerland. In addition to being the main library of the city of Zurich, it is also the library of the University of Zurich. In short, it is Zurich's cantonal, municipal and university library. Dr Marc Winter (Fig. 11.1), a sinologist who specialises in premodern Chinese and who trained in librarianship, is currently serving as the Chinese librarian at the Institute of Asian and Oriental Studies (Figs 11.2 and 11.3), University of Zurich. In the following interview, Winter explains how China and Asia services and holdings at the Zurich Central Library provide researchers in the city with a pathway for understanding East Asia.

Could you begin this interview by first introducing yourself? For example, your training and background, and your major roles and duties as the Chinese librarian at the Zurich Central Library and the University of Zurich Library?

My name is Marc Winter, I studied sinology (Chinese studies concentrating on language and philology)[1] with a focus on premodern Chinese, did my MA on the *Sunzi Bingfa* (孫子兵法), PhD on the *Dictionary Shuowen Jiezi* (說文解字) and a habilitation (thesis to be eligible for tenure professorship) on Qing Dynasty Confucianism. All of these degrees were obtained at the University of Zurich. During my studies, I spent four years in Nanjing in the People's Republic of China (1988–90 and 1993–95). After finishing the habilitation, I did a Master of Advanced Studies (MAS) training programme on library management and information science.

My duties include the acquisition, curation, cataloguing and loaning of the Chinese language holdings of the institute. In addition I also cooperate with other parts of the institute's library such as the Japanese and Western language library, which generally houses books on China, Japan and Asia in non-original languages (Figs 11.4 and 11.5).

[1] University of Zurich – Homepage. Available at: http://www.uzh.ch/en.html.

Inside the World's Major East Asian Collections. http://dx.doi.org/10.1016/B978-0-08-102145-3.00011-X

Figure 11.1 Dr Marc Winter.

Figure 11.2 Library circulation counter, Institute of Asian and Oriental Studies China/East Asia.

Apart from the core library work I also train students in information literacy, research techniques and reference works on China and Asia.

Could you give me a brief account of the history of the Zurich Central Library? Why is this also the main library of the University of Zurich? Can you describe the affiliation between the Zurich Central Library and the University of Zurich Library?

The Central Library (in Zurich)[2] was founded as the deposit library for local publications, and as the copyright library for items published in the city and the canton (like a

[2] The Central Library in Zurich – Homepage. Available at: https://www.looren.net/en/library/zurich-central-library/.

Figure 11.3 Inside of the library, Institute of Asian and Oriental Studies China/East Asia (photos 1 and 2).

Figure 11.4 Rämistrasse 59, Zurich, where Indian, Islamic and gender studies have their offices and where the Western language library is located.

Figure 11.5 Zurichbergstrasse 4, where Chinese and Japanese studies are located.

province) of Zurich in the 19th century. It has also been the main university library to the University of Zurich since the founding of the University in 1833, because both were, and are, funded by the canton. The University of Zurich Library only opened in 1980 on the outside campus and specialises in science, thus for humanities the Central Library still functions as the main university library. It also acquires expensive databases, which any single institute could not fund. However, for many university institutes it is normal to have a small specialised collection of books on the field of research of the institute.

The (Zurich) Central Library has a history that dates back to the 13th century, when the books from the monastery (on the grounds of which the main buildings of the library still stand) were the core of the collection. In 1831, the monastery was abolished and the library with 14,000 titles and 3500 volumes was the foundation when the Central Library was incorporated in 1835. Today it has over six million documents. For more information, see: http://www.zb.uzh.ch/profil/historischer-bestand/index.html.de.

Acting as the main library of both the city and the University of Zurich is unique. Does it mean that you are serving dual roles, i.e., being an academic and public librarian at the same time?

No, the Central Library is an academic library, the public libraries in Zurich are the Pestalozzi Libraries, which are completely separate. The only public aspect is that we have a few native Chinese readers who use the literature in the institute for recreational reading. I am in no sense a public librarian, I am an academic librarian serving the needs of academic readers, i.e., the students, faculty and researchers of Chinese humanities.

How, and at what age, did you develop an interest in the Chinese language, history and culture?

During my teenage years or even earlier. I have a childhood memory of Mao Zedong's burial on the news, I became fascinated with Kung Fu and was interested in a language that was so very different from the Indo-Germanic languages I had learnt at school.

After I took up sinology in 1986 (age 19), I started to become interested in contemporary Chinese politics and the military. However in 1989, when I was in China for my first year, all the interest I had in contemporary China as an academic subject was quelled and I turned to Classical studies, my interests being Chinese leishu (類書) (often referred to as Encyclopaedias) and the development of Confucian textual studies.

I have also practiced Chinese martial arts myself. Could you tell me whether learning Chinese martial arts has in any way helped you appreciate and understand Chinese culture or philosophy?

Not really. I must say, practicing Iaido (居合道) has helped me in many ways with my daily life, in particular how to address confrontations and how to gather the strength to pull through. I would also say that understanding Zen philosophy and the strong sense of hierarchy in Asian society has helped me be more patient when practicing, however, I cannot think of a way it helped me in the direction you ask.

How many different languages have you mastered?

German, English, Chinese, French, Italian, both varieties of Swiss-German and classical Chinese.

Do you have any statistics indicating the number of people who are learning Chinese, or other East Asian languages, at university level in Zurich, and in Switzerland as a whole?

In 2015 the institute had a total of 117 students, and the number of students has been stable (100–150) since 1992, when a second chair for Chinese studies was created. However, there are students in Geneva and in Bern who also study Chinese, so no, I cannot give you a representative figure of any accuracy.

Could you describe your typical day at work as the librarian at the Zurich Central Library and the University of Zurich Library?

I arrive at the office around 8:30 a.m., send out automated recalls for books, answer my e-mail and then—provided there are no meetings—I start working with books. This involves either ordering or cataloguing books. The flow of work is interrupted by users who bring back or take out books, these sometimes need to be recatalogued since about one-third of the holdings are not in the electronic ALEPH catalogue. If no meetings are scheduled for the day, I work through until 5:00 p.m. when the library closes. For lunch I usually take about half an hour and eat in-house.

What is the current size and scope (subject coverage) of the Zurich Central Library and the University of Zurich Library?

The Central Library, with over six million documents, has gigantic holdings on any given academic subject. I do not know their budget for East Asia, but I am sure it is more substantial than the Institute's. The Institute has holdings on China and Asia in original language and Western languages. For original language holdings there are approximately 40,000 titles in 95,000 volumes, whilst for Western languages there are less, around 50,000 volumes of which maybe 30,000 are on China and the rest are on Japan, Korea and Asia. We collect books on Chinese literature and language, minority languages, history, philosophy, religion, geography, ethnography, reference works, etc. There is a very general humanities scope with a focus on language and literature.

What best prepared you for the position as the librarian at the Zurich Central Library and the University of Zurich Library?

Studying sinology, working with libraries in China and buying lots of books myself. Also the MAS training programme helped me develop my own understanding of library processes, independent from my colleagues.

Could you tell me about the staffing situation in your department?

The Chinese language library has a staffing of 150% (currently three people), that is the equivalent of one and a half person's. The same is true for the Western language library (currently four people), which also collects books on Japan. There are two professorships on China with research assistants, teaching staff and administrative posts.

What scholarly and professional associations are you a part of, and how do they assist you in your work?

The European Association of Sinological Librarians (EASL),[3] the yearly conferences of which I always attend. Other than that I'm a member of the DVCS (Deutsche Vereinigung für Chinastudien/德國漢學協會),[4] and I used to be a member of the European Association for Chinese Studies (EACS).[5] The EASL helps in getting library work done, discussing and organising acquisitions and exchanging everyday tricks and helpful minutia.

Who are the majority users at the Zurich Central Library?

The general academic public: students, faculty, researchers and the general public looking for academic works.

Who are the majority users of the Chinese Collection and the University of Zurich Library?

Students and faculty staff of the institute, interested members of the general public (in particular enthusiasts for Chinese medicine etc.) and native Chinese readers.

[3] European Association of Sinological Librarians (EASL) – Homepage. Available at: http://www.easl.org/.
[4] Deutsche Vereinigung für Chinastudien (德國漢學協會) – Homepage. Available at: http://www.ruhr-uni-bochum.de/oaw/dvcs/.
[5] European Association for Chinese Studies (EACS) – Homepage. Available at: http://www.chinesestudies.eu/.

How large is the Chinese immigrant population in Zurich or in Switzerland in general? What are the social backgrounds of these Chinese immigrants in Zurich? What kind professions have they taken up after settling down in Zurich?

In the canton of Zurich, there were (in 2014) 152 inhabitants from Taiwan and 3308 citizens of the People's Republic of China; out of these, 326 were born here, the others abroad. I cannot tell you about their social background. From what I see in the library, there are many Chinese students who study engineering or science, but this is judging from the small segment of Chinese people who choose to use the library, so my observations are in no way representative.

What are the social backgrounds of the Chinese immigrants in German-speaking parts versus French-speaking parts? Are there any major differences?

I cannot tell you. I work in the library, therefore I have no access to statistical data of the nature you enquire.

Could you give examples of typical reference/research inquiries issued by users of the Zurich Central Library and the University of Zurich Library?

At the library, patrons either come with a very specific title they want, or they have no idea what they want and need assistance in research.

Were there situations in the past where users from the Zurich Central Library and the University of Zurich Library were fighting for the same resources?

The Central Library buys books on China in Western languages in large numbers, the institute decides which resources we want at the institute as a second copy. There is no fight: it is true cooperation. The institute tends to buy more material from smaller publishing houses, since large packages from Routledge or Brill are bought by the Central Library anyway. The University of Zurich Library has no holdings on East Asia that I'm aware of.

The library offers information literacy (IL) skills classes to students at the University of Zurich. Are users outside the University also entitled to take these IL classes?

No, since they are too specialised on the needs of students of premodern Chinese. The IL courses at the Central Library are open to the general public.

How do users of the Zurich Central Library and users of the University of Zurich Library differ from each other, in terms of their information needs and library user behaviours?

Again: this is comparing a huge general academic library with millions of books with an institute library focussed on servicing the needs for Chinese studies/sinology, so it is hard to compare. The University of Zurich Library is not the institute I work at.

As a librarian at the Zurich Central Library and the University of Zurich Library, how do you acquire and evaluate your collection?

Catalogues, Zotero recommendations from researchers, subscriptions to series and specific wishes of users. When recommendations come in we check whether they fit in with the rest of the collection.

Are users of the Zurich Central Library also interested in using the Chinese or East Asian Collections of the Library?

Some of them definitely are. They could come to the institute library if they ask. However, having a common catalogue with the Central Library has put the institute library up on the map more prominently.

How is the collection catalogued and accessible for users? With a non-Roman script, what challenges does this present to cataloguing? Are there any?

The ALEPH catalogue allows the cataloguing of duplicated fields, so we have all the records in Chinese script and Pinyin. Older holdings, not represented in the online catalogue, are on card. They are catalogued using Wade-Giles, which can be testy.

The themes and information needs of libraries, archives, and museums (LAM's, as some have referred to them) have increasingly converged. What are your experiences and thoughts about these cultural institutions whose work and best practices now often overlap?

I am completely unaware of this situation, I have to say.

Has the current refugee situation in Europe had any major impact on the range and nature of services provide by cultural institutions in Switzerland, let's say libraries in particular?

No.

Which part(s) of your job as a librarian at the Zurich Central Library and the University of Zurich Library do you find most rewarding?

Tailoring the catalogue to the need of users and helping students find what they did not know existed.

Do you have any questions for me? Is there anything you would like to add before we finish this interview?

I wanted to make it clear which situation I work in. Claudia, whom you contacted first, works at the Central Library (the big one), as the East Asia 'reference', which is a curator of the collection. Since she only works with Western language materials, she thought it would make more sense for me to be represented as the librarian for Chinese studies. I work at the institute, which is yet another separate library from the University of Zurich Library (the one at the science campus). At the institute we have these mentioned stacks and work in two separate teams, in which I fill 50% (in the Chinese language library) and 30% (in the Western counterpart). In the first there is also my colleague Katharina 'Cathy'Thoelen who has curated the collection for the last 30 years.

The Pestalozzi Library[6] is a chain of libraries, basically started as charity work which has since become the public city library network. It is entirely different from both the University Libraries (i.e., the University of Zurich Library and all institute libraries) and the Central Library. To confuse things even more, there is also the polytechnic university and it's institutes, but I will not mention them any further.

[6] The Pestalozzi Library – Homepage. Available at: http://www.pbz.ch/info-en-weiteren-sprachen/englisch-english/.

Collecting Asia at the Oriental Institute of the Academy of Sciences of the Czech Republic

12

Jan Luffer
Oriental Institute, Academy of Sciences of the Czech Republic, Prague, Czech Republic

Introduction

The Oriental Institute of the Academy of Sciences of the Czech Republic (ASCR) is a public and nonuniversity research institute, founded by the Czechoslovak Parliament in 1922, with the aim to cultivate and build up scientific and economic relations with the Orient. In 1929, a library was opened to support the research activities carried out by the Oriental Institute. Overseeing the daily operations of the Oriental Institute Library is Dr. Jan Luffer, who, as a 13-year-old boy, discovered his unexplainable interest for the Asian languages and cultures via popular media from Japan. In the following interview, Dr. Luffer shares with the readers how he combines his personal interests and language skills into a career as a librarian for one of the leading institutes in Central Europe that is dedicated to the research of the Orient.

Could we begin this interview by first introducing yourself, for example, your training and background, and your major roles and duties at the Head of the Library at the Oriental Institute of the ASCR[1]?

My university studies and my professional experience as a librarian can be seen as two parallel lives. I hold a PhD in folklore studies and publish articles and books on folk legends and other folk narratives (including a book on Japanese folktales). At the same time, I am working as a Head of the Library (at the Oriental Institute of the ASCR), and occasionally publish some texts also from this field. I started in 2003 at the National Library of the Czech Republic,[2] where I worked in the Authority Department and helped to establish the general Czech rules for personal names authority files. In 2008, I came to the Library of the Oriental Institute of the ASCR and my tasks widened;

[1] Oriental Institute of the Academy of Sciences of the Czech Republic (ASCR) – Homepage. Available at: http://www.orient.cas.cz/.
[2] National Library of the Czech Republic – Homepage. Available at: http://www.en.nkp.cz/.

Inside the World's Major East Asian Collections. http://dx.doi.org/10.1016/B978-0-08-102145-3.00012-1

I had to take care of several employees and a big, impressive library. I also liked the unique Asian and African characteristics of the documents; although I am not specialist in Oriental studies, I feel an affinity to their subjects.

Could you give us an introduction and brief account of the Oriental Institute of the ASCR? Has there always been a Library since the first day the Head of the Library at the Oriental Institute ASCR was established?

The Institute was founded officially in 1922, but actually came into existence in 1928, and the Library immediately followed in 1929. Initially, its aim was to promote cultural and economic relations between our country and the Orient, but after 1945, the Institute became purely scientific and focused on the history and culture of Asia and Africa. The Institute publishes two journals, namely the *Archiv orientální* (since 1929) in world languages and *Nový Orient* (since 1945) in Czech. In December 2015, a foreign branch of the Institute was established in Taiwan.

The students who are studying Asian or African languages or studies at your Academy, what kind of careers would they take up in Czech after they have graduated from the ASCR?

I am not the proper person to answer that, but from my limited point of view, I see that some of them work as translators or teachers of the language.

How many different languages and scripts do the library collections of the Oriental Institute currently cover?

It is difficult to tell; there are too many of them, including European (e.g., English, German, Czech, etc.), Asian (Chinese, Arabian, Hindi, etc.) and African (Shona, Ndebele, etc.) languages.

Please tell me about the staffing structure of the Library at the Oriental Institute of the ASCR.

Currently, there are three full-time employees and one part-time in the Library: the Head of the Library, a person in charge of cataloguing books and providing services to readers, a person in charge of periodicals and a colleague taking care of the Chinese Lu Xun Library (at the Oriental Institute, ASCR) (Fig. 12.1).

How many different languages have you mastered?

It would be too daring to say I mastered any language. I have quite good command of English and passable knowledge of German and Russian. For several years I learned Japanese, which would have become useful here, but all I can do is read hiragana and katakana.

Figure 12.1 Lu Xun Library of the Oriental Institute of the Academy of Sciences of the Czech Republic.
Photo by Stanislava Kyselová, Academy of Sciences of the Czech Republic photo.

How and at what age did you develop an interest in foreign languages and cultures, and learning the Japanese language in particular?

The Japanese language is a part of my interest in Japanese culture. It started when I discovered origami as a 13-year-old boy (which I like even today) and then continued through books, movies, training kendo, learning language at the university and doing some research on folktales and folk legends later. The newest contribution is an anthology of translations of Japanese short stories made by various translators that I edited, and we are going to publish it early in this year (2017) as a special volume of our journal, *Nový Orient*.

Concerning other languages (including also Latin and Old Church Slavonic), it was part of my college studies of Czech language and literature, although in some cases (Japanese, Russian), the study was only voluntary.

Compared with other European countries that are of similar population size to the Czech Republic, the Czech Republic seems to have far more academic and research institutes that are devoted to Chinese or East Asian studies. Could you describe the reasons behind that? Does it have many things to do with the fact that the Czechoslovakia was a loyal ally and a satellite state of the former Soviet Union and the Soviet Union had a close relationship with Communist China, North Korea, as well as Vietnam?

I am afraid I cannot agree with this idea. During the communist regime, we had two such institutes, the Oriental Institute and a department at Charles University,[3] and at present, we have four; two new departments at universities were founded after 1989, the last of them just some 3 years ago. I think this is an appropriate number compared to our conditions. Being a satellite state of the Soviet Union did not affect the research at our Institute, at least not in a good way. Czech Asian studies followed the impetus given by the tradition before the year 1945, and the positive relationships with China and Northern Korea in the 1950s, leading to founding of a Chinese and a Korean library at our institute, were realised without a Soviet intermediary. Anyway, after the Sino–Soviet split in 1960, it was highly improbable that the Soviet Union would have supported contacts with China.

Do you have any statistics indicating the number of people who are learning Chinese or other East Asian languages at university level?

I have no such statistics available. I am only aware that the dominant East Asian language and culture taught at universities is Chinese.

How many different libraries or information centres does the ASCR have? Are there other individual branch libraries set up for supporting the learning and research of other academic disciplines at the ASCR?

[3] Charles University in Prague – Homepage. Available at: http://www.cuni.cz/UKENG-1.html.

There are more than 50 institutes of the ASCR, and I believe that the majority of them have a library, although some of them are not public, and there are big differences. By far, the largest include the Library of the Oriental Institute (Figs 12.2 and 12.3), and the Institute of History, whereas all the other libraries have, at most, half the amount of documents. There is, of course, the main library of the ASCR, which is the largest and offers a general collection of primary scientific literature.

Figure 12.2 Study room of the General Library of the Oriental Institute of the Academy of Sciences of the Czech Republic.
Photo by Stanislava Kyselová, Academy of Sciences of the Czech Republic.

Figure 12.3 Storage of the General Library of the Oriental Institute of the Academy of Sciences of the Czech Republic.
Photo by Stanislava Kyselová, Academy of Sciences of the Czech Republic.

Figure 12.4 Dr. Jan Luffer, Head of the Library of the Oriental Institute of the Academy of Sciences of the Czech Republic.

Could you describe your typical day at work as the Head of the Library at the Oriental Institute of the ASCR?

I am not sure which day I could call typical, so I can describe to you what happened yesterday. We obtained 19 boxes of books of Jaroslav Průšek (1906–1980), a famous sinologist. We sorted them and brought the Chinese books to Lu Xun Library, where my colleague, together with the help of a foreign student on an internship, checked them. Then I registered new books purchased via the Internet, prepared the documents of our foreign journal subscriptions for our economic department and answered requests by mail (Fig. 12.4).

What is the current size of the Library at the Oriental Institute of the ASCR?

Concerning metres of books and journals, it is very close to 4000; as to their numbers, it is about 230,000 of volumes in total, and about 60,000 of them are Chinese publications at the Lu Xun Library (see Fig. 12.5 for a display of Far Eastern prints and manuscripts).

What best prepared you for the position as the Head of the Library at the Oriental Institute of the ASCR?

What prepared me for this position is the experience and contacts from working previously at the National Library, together with the will to learn new knowledge.

What scholarly and professional associations are you a part of, and how do they assist you in your work?

I am not a member of any association. If I need any assistance, I know I can rely on the main library of the ASCR and the National Library of the Czech Republic.

Figure 12.5 A small display of prints and manuscripts from the Far East.

As the Head of the Library at the Oriental Institute of the ASCR, how do you acquire and evaluate your collection?

This usually means a combination of gifts, exchanges and purchases. If there is a foundation or an institution willing to donate books, we try to accept them. Starting from the year 2014, we have been obtaining hundreds of books in Chinese from Taiwan Resource Centrum for Chinese Studies (臺灣漢學資源中心).[4]

How does the collection catalogue provide access for users? With a non-Roman script, what challenges does this present to cataloguing? Are there any?

[4] Taiwan Resource Center for Chinese Studies (臺灣漢學資源中心) – Homepage. Available at: http://trccs.ncl.edu.tw/e-index.aspx.

The acquisitions are catalogued using RDA (Resource Description and Access) and Aleph (automated library system), and they are accessible via most important Internet catalogues, like the Union Catalogue of the Czech Republic. However, only 10% of the collection has been available in digital format; the number of books is high, whereas the number of librarians managing the collection is low. Nonetheless, the rest of documents are also available via the Internet, but only as scanned cards from our card files. There are rules for transcription of non-Roman script, which every library in this country should follow. In some cases, the rules are clear: Chinese in Pinyin and Japanese in modified Hepburn, and in other cases, there are no common rules, for example, Hindi and Mongolian, and we have to help ourselves with the assistance of our orientalists. We try to preserve specific traits of the script and the language and prefer more exact ways of transcription.

The themes and information needs of libraries, archives and museums (LAMs, as some have referred to them) have increasingly converged. What are your experiences and thoughts about these cultural institutions whose work and best practices now often overlap?

It is certainly difficult for libraries to compete with tablets and cell phones connected to the Internet. The solution seems to be to create something that YouTube and Facebook cannot, a social place for meeting people (tea/coffee room, cultural programme, gallery, etc.) and a place where you can rely on information you get, preferably from more areas. Some big municipal libraries, like the one in Prague, already work this way and they do not suffer from the lack of visitors. Unfortunately, this is not the way for specialised scientific libraries. They have to offer a deep immersion into their field of study: the newest and important books, essential journals and electronic databases of articles, reference indexes, etc.

The current refugee situation in Europe, has it caused any major impacts on the range and nature of services provided the cultural institutions in the Czech Republic, let's say, libraries in particular?

This topic has been, of course, very productive in our media during the year and reflects widely in our society. However, I am not aware about any influence on libraries. The only reflection was a call for books in Arabic for refugees issued by the Municipal Library of Prague.[5] Our library took part in this event (I guess how many other libraries could do it?) and donated some nonscientific books of this kind.

Which part(s) of your job as the Head of the Library at the Oriental Institute of the ASCR do you find most rewarding?

Working in a pleasant social environment and building a very interesting library is altogether the most rewarding.

[5] Municipal Library of Prague – Homepage. Available at: https://www.mlp.cz/en/.

Documenting the Cultural Exchange of Czechoslovak–Chinese Relations

13

Katarína Feriančíková
CCK-ISC, Charles University, Prague, Czech Republic

Introduction

The Chiang Ching-kuo Foundation (CCKF) for International Scholarly Exchange is a nonprofit organisation established in 1989 in honour of the late President Chiang Ching-kuo, with its headquarters set up in Taipei, Taiwan. The Chiang Ching-kuo International Sinological Center (CCK-ISC)was established at Charles University in Prague, Czech Republic, in cooperation with Charles University in 1997 as the first major CCKF overseas branch. The main objective of the Centre is to promote sinology in Europe with the aim of enriching and further developing research and study of Chinese culture. The Institute of East Asian Studies (IEAS) was first founded in 1945 as the Department of Philology and History of East Asia, Charles University in Prague. At the IEAS, students may choose to study sinology, Japanology, Koreanistics and ethnology with specialisation in Vietnamese Studies. Managing the operations and services of the CCKF and IEAS libraries is the multilingual Librarian, Katarína Feriančíková (Fig. 13.1), who spent her university years studying sinology and Chinese drama. In the following interview, Katarína discusses how her work as an academic librarian facilitates the cultural exchanges of Czechoslovak–Chinese relations.

Could we begin this interview by first introducing yourself, for example, your training and background, and your major roles and duties as the Librarian at the CCK-ISC[1] at Charles University in Prague?

I obtained a master's degree in sinology. Then I passed examinations in PhD studies concerning traditional Chinese drama. However, I have not yet completed my PhD dissertation. I also passed various courses, concerning librarianship [three modules of librarian system Tinlib, two modules of Aleph (automated/integrated library system), English for Librarians, Needs of Handicapped Users of Library]. My major roles and

[1] Chiang Ching-kuo International Sinological Center (CCK-ISC), Charles University – Homepage. Available at: http://cck-isc.ff.cuni.cz/en/about-us.html.

Inside the World's Major East Asian Collections. http://dx.doi.org/10.1016/B978-0-08-102145-3.00013-3

Figure 13.1 Librarian Katarína Feriančíková.

duties at the CCK-ISC are as follows: acquisition, loans, bibliographical search and cataloguing.

At what age and how did you develop an interest in the Chinese language, history and culture?

About the age of 17.

Could you give us an introduction and brief account of the history of the CCK-ISC and its affiliation with Charles University? Has there always been a library since the first day the CCK-ISC was established?

The CCKF for International Scholarly Exchange[2] is a nonprofit organisation headquartered in Taipei, Taiwan. It also maintains a regional office in McLean, Virginia near Washington D.C. in the US. The Foundation was established in 1989 in honour of the late President Chiang Ching-kuo.

[2] Chiang Ching-kuo Foundation (CCKF) for International Scholarly Exchange – Homepage. Available at: http://www.cckf.org.tw/en?set_language=en.

Figure 13.2 Library of CCK-ISC. It is an office of CCK-ISC, reading room of the Library and classroom for students of sinology.

CCK-ISC was established at Charles University in Prague,[3] Czech Republic, in cooperation with Charles University in November 1997 as the first major branch of CCKF overseas. The Centre organises programmes held at Charles University, coordinates the [Global Environment Facility (GEF)] Small Grants Programme[4] and cooperates in CCKF Fellowship. Support given to the IEAS[5] (at Charles University in Prague) helps to expand the Library, which is open to scholars and students from the region. Other grants and projects are administered directly from the Taipei Headquarters.

The Library was not a part of the CCK-ISC from the very beginning. The building of the library collection started in 1999, 2 years after foundation of CCK-ISC. The CCK-ISC collection (Fig. 13.2) is one of the two collections of the Library of the IEAS at the same University in the same building (according to http://cck-isc.ff.cuni.cz/en/about-us.html, cited 6 December 2015).

Could you give us an introduction and brief account of the history of the IEAS and its affiliation with Charles University? Has there always been a library since the first day the IEAS was established?

The predecessor of IEAS was founded in 1945 as the Department of Philology and History of East Asia. Then the department changed names and studies. The contemporary name IEAS started to be used in 1990s. It is possible to study four majors in IEAS, namely sinology, Japanology, Koreanistics and ethnology with specialisation in Vietnamese Studies. The building of IEAS Library collection started in 1947. Since 1999, IEAS has two collections. The first one is IEAS itself (Figs 13.3 and 13.5); the second one is CCK-ISC Library.

3 Charles University in Prague – Homepage. Available at: http://www.cuni.cz/UKENG-1.html.

4 The GEF Small Grant Programme – Homepage. Available at: https://sgp.undp.org/.

5 Institute of East Asian Studies, Charles University in Prague – Homepage. Available at: http://oldweb.ff.cuni.cz/FF-7888.html.

Figure 13.3 Library of Institute of East Asian Studies.

Figure 13.4 Shelves containing books published in the Peoples' Republic of China in 1950s, in the Library of Institute of East Asian Studies.

Figure 13.5 Library exterior.

Are you currently serving as the Head Librarian at CCK-ISC? If yes, could you tell us about the staffing structure at the CCK-ISC Library?

The librarian of IEAS Library—that is me—also works for the CCK-ISC collection. Also, there is one assistant, and other students of the IEAS helps to register and catalogue newly arrived publications, when necessary.

Are you also currently serving as the Head Librarian at IEAS? If yes, could you tell us about the staffing structure at the IEAS Library?

Yes, I am also the Head Librarian at IEAS. I am the only full-time regular employee. Part-time irregular employees change in turns. In school year 2015–16, the part-time employees are as follows: five cataloguers and three assistants. The cataloguers and assistants, with one exception, take turns after 1 or 2 years, since they are students. One cataloguer has been working in the Library for more than 10 years. The cataloguers work about 20 h per month; the assistants work 32 h per month. The job of assistants is usually as follows: registration of newly arrived publications, help with administration, stock revision, customs clearance, etc.

How many different languages and scripts do the library collections of the IEAS Library currently cover?

Especially Chinese and English; also Czech, Korean, Japanese, Russian, German, French, Vietnamese, Slovak, Polish, Italian, Latin, Laotian, Swedish, etc.

What is the current size and scope (subject coverage) of the IEAS Library?

Humanities concerning Chinese, Japanese, Korean, Vietnamese and Southeast Asian studies, namely studies in literature, history, philosophy, art, social sciences; translations into European languages; textbooks; etc.

Who are the majority of patrons and users at the IEAS Library?

The majority of users at the IEAS collections are students and teaching staff of IEAS. Fewer readers are affiliated in the other departments than IEAS, in the Faculty of Arts, Charles University or in the other faculties of the University in Prague, Czech Republic or in Korea and Japan, and the library is used very rarely by public readers.

How many different languages and scripts do the library collections of the CCK-ISC Library currently cover?

Especially Chinese and English; also Czech, German, French, Russian, Korean, Slovak, Polish, Italian, Latin, Japanese, etc.

How many different languages have you mastered?

Four (Czech, Chinese, English, Russian). Slovak is my native language. However, Czech is very similar to Slovak.

Compared with other European countries that are of similar population size to Czech, Czech seems to have far more academic and research institutes that are devoted to Chinese or East Asian studies. Could you describe the reasons behind that? Does it have many things to do with the fact that the Czechoslovakia was a loyal ally and a satellite state of the former Soviet Union, and the Soviet Union had a close relationship with Communist China, North Korea, as well as Vietnam?

Since I studied sinology, let me speak about sinological institutions. In my opinion, the following factors have influenced the amount of academic and research institutions in the Czech area:

1. Jesuits;
2. good relationship with China and Taiwan; and
3. enthusiasm and professionalism of sinologists.

To explain: the interest in China in the Czech lands of the former Austro–Hungarian Monarchy (AHM) may be traced back into the 18th century when Czech Jesuit Karel Slavíček (1678–1735) visited China as a missionary. He was a universal scholar, also interested in Chinese astronomy and music.

The predecessor of sinology in the Czech lands in AHM and from 1918 in the former Czechoslovak Republic, Oriental Studies, may have started by the end of 19th century. At the time, Prof. Rudolf Dvořák (1860–1920), the founder of Czech Oriental studies, published his first works in Oriental studies, including Chinese studies. Two years after the academic passed away, in 1922, the Oriental Institute (of the Academy of Sciences of the Czech Republic) was founded.

A founder of modern Czech Sinology, Prof. Jaroslav Průšek (1906–80) started his academic career in the Oriental Institute in 1930s. After World War II, the relations between Czechoslovakia and China were good. The good relations influenced cultural exchanges between former Czechoslovakia and China, that is, including Chinese studies.

In 1945, Prof. Průšek founded the Institute of Philology and History of Far East, that is, the present IEAS. His students belonged to the first generation of Czech sinologists. The generation was very enthusiastic and wrote a number of studies about Chinese history and culture and translations from Chinese.

However, after the entry of Soviet troops into the former Czechoslovakia in 1968, the level of Chinese studies dropped. The studies were limited almost only to the translations of Chinese newspapers. Also, in compliance with the state policy, sinologists were supposed to criticise Mao Zedong's policy. However, sinologists published some studies in Chinese literature, history, theatre and philosophy. Some of the sinologists could not publish publicly. That is why the publications, written by them, were signed by another sinologists. Also, it was difficult to gain publications published in the West, and sinologists often could not attend conferences in the West. However, despite to the difficult conditions, the first generation of sinologists raised their followers.

The year 1989 meant a start of social and economic changes towards liberalisation in the former Czechoslovakia. At the same time, Czechoslovak–Chinese relations have improved, also in terms of cultural exchange, including Chinese studies. Real sinology was renewed in the Czech lands of the former Czechoslovakia and later, from 1993, in the independent Czech Republic. It means that sinologists, specialised in Chinese history, literature, art and philosophy, started to present lectures and continued to write studies and translations. Despite financial difficulties, it was easier to gain Western and Chinese literature.

Furthermore, except Prague (Charles University), it is possible to study Sinology in Olomouc (Palacký University[6]) and Brno (Masaryk University[7]). Also, the Oriental Institute, now a part of the Czech Academy of Sciences,[8] continues to exist. All of the four centres of Chinese studies also invite visiting professors from China, Taiwan, Europe and the US. Speaking about sinology in Prague, the foundation of CCK-ISC contributed to the improvement largely.

Do you have any statistics indicating the number of people who are learning Chinese or other East Asian languages at the university level?

The statistics for the year 2015 is as follows:

	Number of Students Currently Studying	Number of Students Who Interrupted Study	Number of Students	Number of Students
Institution / Language	Charles University, Prague		Masaryk University, Brno	Palacký University, Olomouc
Chinese	63	17	125	245
Korean	69	4	0	29
Japanese	81	10	100	219
Vietnamese	18	0	0	39
SUBTOTAL	231	31	225	532
TOTAL (all mentioned languages)	**1,019**			

Please note that the numbers of students in Chinese, Korean and Japanese languages means the numbers of students in sinology, Koreanistics and Japanology. The number of students in Vietnamese in Prague indicates the number of students studying *with Specialisation in Vietnamese Studies*. In Olomouc, the number in Vietnamese indicates the number of students of Vietnamese language, not Vietnamese studies.

It is possible to compare actual numbers with the situation in previous years. For example, Charles University in Prague accepted 15 students in 1991, and then the number decreased; however, up to now, students has increased slightly. The number of first-year students in Olomouc increased from 10 in 1993 to 92 in 2007.

Could you describe your typical day at work as the Librarian at the CCK-ISC?

I do not think there is a typical day in the library. However, every day consists of the following activities:

- preparing booked publications for readers;
- selecting Czech publications for order and forwarding list of new foreign publications to teaching staff;

6 Palacký University – Homepage. Available at: http://www.upol.cz/en/.
7 Masaryk University – Homepage. Available at: https://www.muni.cz/.
8 The Czech Academy of Sciences – Homepage. Available at: http://www.cas.cz/index.html.

- writing e-mails; and
- loans (circulation services), etc.

Irregular necessary activities are as follows:

- delivery of mail in the main building of the faculty;
- orders of publications;
- registration of newly arrived publications;
- bibliographical search;
- sale of publications with discount;
- data for interlibrary loan of books in Chinese (check of catalogue records in Czech transcription and Pinyin);
- checking the work of students;
- preparing small displays of publications; and
- help with conferences, etc.

What is the current size and scope (subject coverage) of the CCK-ISC Library?

Humanities concerning Chinese studies, namely, studies in literature, history, philosophy, art, social sciences; translations into European languages; textbooks; etc.

What best prepared you for the position as the Librarian at the CCK-ISC?

Study of sinology, qualification courses and annual meetings of the European Association of Sinological Librarians (EASL).[9]

What scholarly and professional associations are you a part of, and how do they assist you in your work?

I am a member of the EASL. The membership is useful, especially in terms of acquisition and cataloguing.

Who are the majority of patrons and users at the CCK-ISC Library and the CCK-ISC itself?

The majority of users at the CCK-ISC collections are students and teaching staff of sinology in IEAS. Few readers are affiliated in other departments than IEAS in the Faculty of Arts, Charles University,[10] or in the other faculties of the University in Prague, Czech Republic, or in Eastern Europe, and the Library is used very rarely by public readers.

Could you give examples of typical reference/research inquiries issued by the researchers or scholars at the CCK-ISC Library?

There is no typical reference/research inquiry at the CCK-ISC Library. Readers want to know what is in both the CCK-ISC Library and IEAS Library. Some examples

[9] European Association of Sinological Librarians (EASL) – Homepage. Available at: http://www.easl.org/.
[10] Faculty of Arts, Charles University in Prague – Homepage. Available at: http://oldweb.ff.cuni.cz/FF-7614.html.

of reference inquiries: publications concerning Chinese sacral architecture, 大字报, pedagogy in China, comics in China and Taiwan, Chinese journals in archaeology, etc.

Could you give examples of typical reference/research inquiries issued by the researchers or scholars at the CCK-ISC Library?

There is no typical reference/research inquiry at the IEAS Library. Readers want to know what is in both the CCK-ISC Library and IEAS library. Some examples of reference inquiries: publications concerning Japanese clothing, bibliography of sinologist and theatrologist Dana Kalvodová, periodicals concerning Korea, etc.

As the Librarian at the CCK-ISC, how do you acquire and evaluate your collection?

The prevalent way of acquisition is purchase; the other way is donation.

The Library is a very small collection of about 4000 titles of books, 37 titles of serials and 1 database. As for the media, we own printed form, CDs, DVDs, slides and audiocassettes, etc. However, for students and employees of CCK-ISC, the collection is quite useful, since it owns the majority of books relevant for study and newest books published abroad. Some of the books are the only exemplars in the Czech Republic.

As the Librarian at the IEAS, how do you acquire and evaluate your collection?

The prevalent way of acquisition is purchase; the other way is donation and exchange. The IEAS Library has a small collection of about 21,000 titles of books and 70 titles of serials. As for the media, we own printed form, CDs, DVDs, audiocassettes and films. More than 2000 books, published in the People's Republic of China in 1950s (Fig. 13.4), may be the most valuable part of the collection. Also, we value more than 800 books published in the People's Republic of Korea.

How does the collection catalogue and provide access for users? With a non-Roman script, what challenges does this present to cataloguing? Are there any?

The collection is included in the catalogue of the Charles University in the link http://ckis.cuni.cz/. The Chinese publications are catalogued in aggregated Pinyin, and the syllables are connected according to 现代汉语词典. Since the best way of catalogue search is via Chinese characters, it is a challenge to catalogue in Chinese script.

The themes and information needs of libraries, archives and museums (LAMs, as some have referred to them) have increasingly converged. What are your experiences and thoughts about these cultural institutions whose work and best practices now often overlap?

Whenever I receive an announcement concerning exhibition, lecture or other similar activity dealing with Chinese culture, I forward it to readers of our Library.

Also, twice or thrice a year, I prepare small display of publications of the Library on a different topic. Sometimes the topic is connected with a significant anniversary (e.g., foundation of Republic of China in 1911) or a significant person (writers Gao Xingjian and Mo Yan); sometimes the topic deals with a lecture of a visiting professor (e.g., German Sinology).

The current refugee situation in Europe, has it caused any major impacts on the range and nature of services provided the cultural institutions in Czech, let's say, libraries in particular?

No, the refugee situation in Europe has not caused almost any impact on the cultural institutions in Czech. There are only some small private activities. For example, my friend takes children of refugees outside the refugee camp near Prague as a volunteer for trips from time to time. The friend said that there are almost no publications to read in the camp in languages spoken in Western and Central Asia. That is why I collect the books, de-accessioned by the Institute of Near Asian Studies in our University, to bring them to the refugee camp.

From Collection Building to Web Development and Network Building in the Nordic Asian Studies Community

14

Inga-Lill Blomkvist
University of Copenhagen, Copenhagen, Denmark

Introduction

The Nordic Institute of Asian Studies (NIAS) is an academically independent Nordic resource centre focusing on the research on modern and contemporary Asia from an area studies perspective. In addition to serving as a research institute, another core function of NIAS is to connect people and other local and overseas institutions with expertise on Asia. In short, NIAS seeks to broaden knowledge of modern Asia in the Nordic region through conferences and workshops, accessible information resources, commentary on current affairs and contact with media, government and businesses, etc. Managing NIAS Library and Information Centre (NIAS LINC) is Inga-Lill Blomkvist (Fig. 14.1), who devoted several years studying the Chinese language at universities in both Sweden and mainland China. In the following interview, Ms. Blomkvist discusses her participation in building a Nordic information portal for Asian studies and a professional network in the Nordic and international community.

Could we begin this interview by first introducing yourself, for example, your training and background, and your major roles and duties at Library and Information Centre at the NIAS[1]?

I began studying Chinese at Stockholm University[2] in Sweden from 1979 to 1981 and then went to Beijing as an exchange student and stayed there for over 3 years. I have a Bachelor of Arts degree with Chinese as my major, and I graduated as a librarian in 1995. I have also done 1 year of Japanese studies at university level and several short courses in the field of library and information science and web design while working.

[1] Nordic Institute of Asian Studies (NIAS) – Homepage. Available at: http://nias.ku.dk.
[2] Stockholm University – Homepage. Available at: http://www.su.se/english/.

Inside the World's Major East Asian Collections. http://dx.doi.org/10.1016/B978-0-08-102145-3.00014-5

Figure 14.1 Inga-Lill M. Blomkvist.

Since 1996, I have been working at the NIAS Library with many different aspects of the library and websites of the institute, but mainly with e-resources for research on East Asia and web development.

Please provide a brief introduction to the Library and Information Centre at the NIAS.

NIAS is a Nordic institute, funded mainly by the Nordic Council of Ministers,[3] which is the official body for Nordic (Denmark, Finland, Iceland, Norway and Sweden) intergovernmental cooperation. NIAS was founded in 1968 and has, since the start, been situated at and hosted by the University of Copenhagen.[4] The research and the collections of the Library are focused on modern and contemporary Asia from an area studies perspective. Via our library services, interurban loans and a continuous 2-week scholarship programme for MA and PhD students, we provided information support, literature and journals for the Nordic Asian studies community. Since 2005, we have established a Nordic NIAS Council (NNC)[5] with, as of now, 26 Nordic universities and research institutes as members, including the major Nordic universities with Asian studies programmes. Through our information platform, the AsiaPortal (www.asiaportal.info), we provide online services and we also subscribe to specialised e-resources for Asian studies for our NNC member institutions. In 2014, NIAS LINC was converted into a 100% online library, working with providing e-resources for, first of all, our NNC member institutions, but also for the whole Nordic Asian studies community. NIAS Library's printed collections of books and periodicals were at the same time transferred to the Royal Library. We are continuously working to expand our online collections.

[3] Nordic Council of Ministers – Homepage. Available at: http://www.norden.org/en/nordic-council-of-ministers.

[4] University of Copenhagen – Homepage. Available at: http://www.ku.dk/english/.

[5] Nordic NIAS Council (NNC) – Homepage. Available at: http://nias.ku.dk/nnc.

What is the size of the Asian collections? Could you describe the highlights of the collection?

Our online collections are available to our patrons via our online information platform, www.asiaportal.info. We have a collection of some 100 e-resources on the AsiaPortal, partly licensed, partly freely available, a collection of approximately 100 titles of e-books from NIAS Press available to our NNC member institutions and a journal collection, which we are working to update. The AsiaPortal is also a window to Nordic research on Asia and presents news and events from the Nordic Asian Studies community, the *In Focus* blog[6] with shorter and longer contributions from Nordic researchers, a link collection of Nordic open access (OA) papers and articles[7] and an OA journal, *Asia in Focus – a Nordic journal on Asia by early career researchers*,[8] which was established by the Library in 2015.

Our highlights are the NNC licences to databases for Asian-language material in Chinese, Japanese and Korean, where we are able to provide access to e-resources for researchers and students at the NNC institutions which they do not have access to otherwise and which are very important for them to have access to.[9]

What best prepared you for the position as librarian at NIAS?

The combination of studies in Chinese and Japanese with a librarian's degree and the practice while working as a student at the Stockholm University Library[10] and the Library of the Museum of Far Eastern Antiquities in Stockholm.

The Library at NIAS is an academically independent Nordic research and resource centre, and it is still integrated as part of the University of Copenhagen. What is the relationship with the Copenhagen University Library?

NIAS is an independent library with its own websites, resource collection, server systems and staff. We are physically housed at the University of Copenhagen, and make use of their services. NIAS has previously had a contract for Library management software with University of Copenhagen Library, which it provides for external Libraries such as NIAS. This in turn made our collection visible on the University of Copenhagen online catalog.

We have, through the years, cooperated with Copenhagen University Library regarding acquisition of material by a division of labour where we acquired printed and online resources for studies within social sciences and on modern and contemporary

[6] http://www.asiaportal.info/blog/.
[7] http://www.asiaportal.info/nordic-publications/.
[8] http://www.asiainfocus.dk/.
[9] Japan Foundation – Homepage. Available at: http://www.jpf.go.jp/e/.
[10] Stockholm University Library – Homepage. Available at: http://su.se/english/library/.

Asia, while they acquired material in Asian languages and for the humanities and sciences. Since 2014 we continue to acquire specialised Asia-focused e-resources within humanities and social sciences for the University of Copenhagen as well as the other NNC institutions, while our physical collection has been transferred to the Faculty Library of Social Sciences at the Copenhagen University Library.[11] We are considered as part of the university network, even as an independent institute, and our staff at NIAS have access to all the university library resource services.

What scholarly and professional associations are you a part of, and how do they assist you in your work?

I am a member of[12] the Swedish Association of Information Specialists (SFIS) (member of the board of SFIS South),[13] European Association of Sinological Librarians (EASL), Danish Union of Librarians (BF), DIK Association (Sweden; professional association/trade union for university graduates in the fields of documentation, information and culture), Southeast Asia Library Group (SEALG)[14] and the European Association of Japanese Research Specialists.[15] From SFIS, I get a network of colleagues in Sweden, and, together with DIK information of developments in the libraries in Sweden, BF provides the same information for Denmark and also professional short courses. EASL, EAJRS and SEALG provide networks and colleagues who can help with finding information and advice when needed. All networks provide 'competitive intelligence' from the international field.

Could you describe your working relationship with Bent Lerbæk Pedersen, East Asian Librarian at the National Library of Denmark[16]?

Bent is a very important colleague for me, as he has a long and profound experience as research librarian for Asia, and China and Korea foremost. I turn to Bent to get his evaluation of e-resources and opinion on the researchers' interest in various e-resources, as he has had many contacts in his professional role at the Royal Library.

You had given a presentation at the Internet Librarian Conference in the UK about AsiaPortal, which is known as a Nordic cross-disciplinary Library 2.0 project focused on information sharing and user interaction portal. Could you tell us more about it? How has it evolved since it first began?

[11] Faculty Library of Social Sciences at the Copenhagen University Library – Homepage. Available at: http://kub.kb.dk/socialsciences.

[12] http://www.sfis.nu/english.

[13] http://www.easl.org/.

[14] Southeast Asia Library Group (SEALG) – Homepage. Available at: http://www.sealg.org.

[15] European Association of Japanese Research Specialists (EARJS) – Homepage. Available at: http://www.eajs.org.

[16] The Royal Library – the National Library of Denmark and Copenhagen University Library – Homepage. Available at: http://www.kb.dk/en/nb/.

The presentation was at the Internet Librarian Conference in London in 2007, which was soon after start-up of the AsiaPortal. The aim of the AsiaPortal is that it should function as a one-stop platform where our Nordic patrons would find the information sources they need for their studies/research, and also as a platform for information sharing within the Nordic Asian studies community, as well as a window to research on Asia in the Nordic countries for an international audience.

The development of the portal has, right from the start-up, been central to our library services, and we have gradually moved all but the basic information about NIAS Library over to it. As the library collections now are 100% digital, the AsiaPortal is the main platform for our services. On the AsiaPortal we particularly emphasise the e-resources as access to these specialised resources is very much appreciated by our patrons. Other than the e-resources, the AsiaPortal is the home to the *In Focus* Blog, which provided the inspiration for the establishment of the OA journal, *Asia in Focus*. In our work with the blog we experienced that there was a need for a forum for early career researchers, MA or PhD students, to get published and to get guidance in the publication process. The establishment was also in line with NIAS mission as embodied in, for example, the SUPRA Programme (**SU**pport **P**rogramme for **A**sian **S**tudies),[17] which includes a scholarship program for two MA or PhD students to visit NIAS for a fortnight in order to receive advice and assistance from NIAS Library in finding relevant information for their theses and access to NIAS′ networks, and advice and feedback from NIAS' researchers. The scholarship programme is very popular and more than 40 students and researchers visit NIAS every year through the programme. It has been running in its present form since 1993 and has been one factor which has enabled and strengthened NIAS' network of researchers in the Nordic countries, as many of the former stipends now hold senior positions.

Who are the majority of the Asian collection users? That is, who comes to see you about your Library and Information Centre's users? Are they mostly professors or students from higher education institutions, or are they people from outside the post-secondary sector, i.e., the public?

The printed collection of NIAS Library could be used by anyone as a public library, but was mainly used by students and researchers, either from NIAS and University of Copenhagen or other academic institutions in Copenhagen and the region, including the South of Sweden, or stipends on the NIAS SUPRA scholarship program or other visiting scholars. Our online collections are partly freely available for anyone to use and we can see that we have visitors from the Nordic countries, the US, Asia, Europe and from all over the world; partly, we provide licensed e-resources which are used by our NNC member institutions, and their staff, students and affiliated persons.

Could you give examples of typical reference/research inquiries issued by the researchers or scholars at the Library and Information Centre at the NIAS?

[17] SUPRA – Homepage. Available at: http://nias.ku.dk/what-supra.

It is often researchers or students who need help with finding material on a specific issue, mostly in Chinese or Japanese, or in English but about China or Japan, as we are the strongest in our e-resources there. Also, supervisors and NNC[5] contact librarians know that this is my specific area of expertise, for example, 'Where can I find the last Chinese 5-year plans in English?' or 'How can I find translations to English of speeches by Chinese leaders?'. Often, I am also asked to help find a specific article or book.

As the librarian overseeing the collection, how do you acquire and evaluate your collection? Do you proactively collect or do you accept gifts?

As we do not have a printed collection anymore, we do not get such gifts. But when we did, we always evaluated the gifts first, as space is limited and cataloguing requires staff resources. We evaluated if the gift fitted our collection's prioritised areas, if it was already available in other Danish libraries and if it was of special interest in some other way. For our e-resources, we look at the broader interest of the whole Nordic community and, in particular, the NNC institutions. When developing the collection and the AsiaPortal in general, but especially in the selection and evaluation of the resources, we cooperate closely with the network of contact librarians at the NNC institutions we have established, the NNC Library Group. We also get suggestions for new e-resources to be included in the collection from colleagues and researchers, which we then normally ask for a trial to.
For evaluation of the resources we look at usage statistics and feedback from the NNC librarians, and from users of the AsiaPortal—we provide ample opportunities online to give feedback. Final decisions are taken in cooperation with the NNC libriarians.

In the past few years, the NIAS has been engaged in the digitisation of some of its East Asian collections. What are some of the projects and what future plans are there for the digital collections and/or publishing?

At NIAS Library, we are planning to extend our collections in general, and particularly want to do so on South Asia and Southeast Asia. We want to update our journals collection with OA journals and licenses to journal titles not otherwise available in the NNC libraries' collections and update our collection of free online resources in general and the Nordic publications collection in particular. We will also continue to work with our OA journal, *Asia in Focus*. *Asia in Focus* is also available via the common publication platform of the Nordic Council of Ministers http://norden.diva-portal.org/.

The archives of NIAS journal *NIAS-nytt/Asia Insights* (1993–2009) are partly available via the NIAS website, http://nias.ku.dk/asia-insights-nias-nytt, but former issues are also indexed by Proquest; see http://search.proquest.com/publication/28017.

Foremost, NIAS Press has been working on digitisation projects and is supplying:

1. e-content to a range of library suppliers;
2. e-content to the NNC community available, only for them via the Asiaportal;
3. free e-content via the common publication platform of the Nordic Council of Ministers, http://norden.diva-portal.org/; and
4. NIAS Press is also actively working on making consumer e-books available on the major online platforms, e.g., Kindle, Apple iBooks store, etc.

In institutions with Asian collections, it is inevitable that there is a balancing act in terms of managing priorities between the various areas of language expertise/collections in regards to the other Asian language collections (that is, Japanese, Korean, etc.). What are your experiences as librarian in terms of balancing and prioritising? Do you need to?

Creating a geographical balance is an issue and a very acute issue for the Library right now. With a printed book collection and a journals collection, we could cover the geographical areas of Asia more evenly. Without these components in our collection, the balance is more challenging.

There is a wide area of e-resources: printed, licensed or freely available e-resources. For freely available resources, there exist resources for all of Asia from Central Asia to East Asia and from North Asia to Southeast Asia, but naturally, there is no consistency in content or format. The available resources are hard to keep track of to set the guidelines for the collection for such a wide focus area as ours, covering all of Asia, humanities and social sciences, and mainly from the modern period onwards, and it is hard to keep such a collection updated. When it comes to licensed e-resources, there are a number of local providers in native languages in China, Japan, Korea and Taiwan, but for South Asia, Central Asia and Southeast Asia, very little. For native language resources, we can negotiate licenses, as our number of potential users is very small, even though there are 26 NNC member institutions. We are also fortunate to be generously supported by mainly the Japan Foundation and Fudan-European Centre for China Studies, located at NIAS, but also by the Korea Foundation[18] and Chiang Ching-kuo Foundation. International providers have e-resources in English, but these often become too expensive for our budget. This leaves us with a need to cover the other geographical areas apart from East Asia via other resources, mainly OA resources. We will invest in our freely available e-resources collection and rebuild a journal collection from titles that are OA or particularly desirable for our patrons. We are also looking at other options to balance the collection.

How does the collection catalogue and provide access for users? With a non-roman script, what challenges does this present to cataloguing? Are there any?

We do not have a catalogue for NIAS e-resources collections, but provide access to them via our AsiaPortal. Our e-resources are used by the NNC institutions, and if they want to enter titles in their catalogues, that is possible, but so far, getting metadata for cataloguing for material from the databases we provide access to has not been requested.

The themes and information needs of libraries, archives and museums (LAMs, as some have referred to them) have increasingly converged. What are your experiences and thoughts about these cultural institutions whose work and best practices now often overlap?

The NIAS Library has not cooperated with museums and archives. It seems to me that LAMs still have clearly defined roles with archives and museums providing

[18] Korea Foundation – Homepage. Available at: http://en.kf.or.kr/?menuno=3722.

primary sources for researchers while libraries provide secondary sources and research tools. But with digitisation projects in libraries, of course, there is some overlap and we have common interests in the development of OA, copyright legislation and IT technology for information science, such as digitisation and data management. It is also clear that there is an increasing convergence between libraries and publishers.

Which part(s) of your job as curators do you find most rewarding?

I thoroughly enjoy that my job consists of so many diversified aspects, from license negotiations to network building in the Nordic and international community to collection building to web development. An important bonus for me is the freedom to develop new projects within the limits of available resources. Working so close to the researcher community and helping to provide visibility for research results, for example, with the journal *Asia in Focus*, and developing content and functionality on the web, in general, I find particularly rewarding.

A Royal Library That Is Open to Everyone in Denmark and Worldwide

15

Bent Lerbæk Pedersen[1], *Heather Rogers*[2]
[1]The Royal Library, Copenhagen, Denmark; [2]McGill University, Montreal, QC, Canada

Introduction

The Royal Library (Det Kongelige Bibliotek) was founded in 1653 by Frederik III, King of Denmark (1609–70), as a personal library and opened to the public in 1793. Bent Lerbaek Pedersen (Fig. 15.1) is a long-time research librarian in the Far Eastern section of the Royal Library, Copenhagen, and has mainly worked with (and published about) its Chinese holdings. The Chinese collections at King's Library began as a need by the Danish court at the time for an understanding of their trading partners in Qing Dynasty, China. Over the years, the Library has grown, and Bent Lerbæk Pedersen outlines in detail how the Library's Chinese collection has contributed to the Danish understanding and research of China.

Could you begin this interview by first introducing yourself, Bent, your training and background and your major roles and duties at the Far East collections at the Royal Library of Denmark[1]?

I was educated at Copenhagen university in Chinese culture, which does not actually exist anymore, and was one of the few students who completed this educational programme. During my employment at the Royal Library of Denmark, I received librarian training for half a year, and from that, I continued to work in the business of libraries. What I did at that time was to purchase books from China especially, catalogue the books and then also take care of different kind of questions to the collections. At that time, we only had the (printed) card catalogues, and it was somewhat confusing to our patrons, so we have to guide them on how to find things. But nowadays, it's a little bit different because we have online catalogues, so we do not get so much of those types of questions anymore. My work has shifted to more specific inquiries from users, particularly to help and guide them in examining certain types of works or certain types of books about research areas.

[1] The Royal Library of Denmark – Homepage. Available at: http://www.kb.dk/en/.

Inside the World's Major East Asian Collections. http://dx.doi.org/10.1016/B978-0-08-102145-3.00015-7

Figure 15.1 Bent Lerbæk Pedersen.

Your library is called the Royal Library (of Denmark). Is it because it was founded by King Frederik III of Denmark, or does it have any relations to the library located inside the royal palace with materials previously used or donated by members of the Danish Royal Family?

It was founded as a King's private library in 1660s. Because Denmark had just gone through a war, it received a lot of books as part of the war booty, so the King decided to make a library in the castle in Copenhagen. His thinking at the time was to inaugurate a special building for the library, planned in the 1670s. Although it was initially for the use of King and his supervisors, it became open to the public in 1793. Of course, 'public' in that sense meant people who had the right connections and could read, write and read. Since that time, it has been separated from the royal castle since the Library is actually physically located outside the castle. Fortunately, because the castle was burned down twice, the collection survived because it was not physically part of the castle. Today, the Library is seen as a special place in Denmark.

According to you, the Royal Library of Denmark used to belong to the Royal Palace and was meant to be used by the Danish King and the members of the Royal Court only. You also mentioned that this Royal Library was set up during the mid-17th century, and they already had valuable books and other precious materials that came from Qing Dynasty, China. My questions are: What were the original aims of setting up this Chinese collection inside the Royal Library at that time? What kind of benefits would they gain from building this Chinese collection inside the Royal Library? In addition, was the Danish Court trying to develop an understanding of the Qing Dynasty of China culturally, politically, religiously and socially, with the hope of doing trading business or forming diplomatic relations with China? Or they were trying to spread the word of the Christian God?

There was no separate Chinese section in the Royal Library; the Chinese books and documents were just a part that could be shown to visiting guests by the King.

The Danish court was mostly interested in trade. The spread of Christianity to China from Denmark was not first really organised until the latter part of the 19th century.

The Danish Royal Court was only interested in trading with China. So what were the Danish Court trading with China at that time? Tea and silk or other goods? Was trading done via sea?

Tea, porcelain, silk and a few furniture pieces. Trading was carried out by sea. Denmark was, at that time, a strong seagoing nation.

During the 17th century, what kind of people at the Danish Royal Court would have the language skills and knowledge to understand and manage these collections from the Far East?

There was no knowledge of Chinese at the Danish Royal Court both in the 17th and the 18th centuries. Only a few civil servants might have known a little Chinese.

A few civil servants from the Royal Court might be able to speak and read Chinese. How did they acquire the Chinese language skills? How would they find someone to teach them Chinese in Denmark during the 17th century in Europe?

I do not know if there was anyone in the civil service who know a little Chinese, but if they did, it was by trade both within Europe and Far East. We had a lively trade with the Netherlands.

The official name of the organization as of 1 January 2006 is the Royal Library, the National Library of Denmark and Copenhagen University Library. So, is the Royal Library of Denmark a national library, an academic library or a public library?

The Royal Library of Denmark is also the National Library of Denmark,[2] and part of the Library is the Copenhagen University Library,[3] both institutions in one. The National Library (of Denmark) part receives all books printed in Denmark as the Legal Depository. Selected parts of books printed in Denmark are purchased for the University Library for lending, as Danish books in the National Library only can be seen in our research reading room. We tie our collection to the University of Copenhagen, where we then share our purchases with our pooled funding of money.

So the National Library of Denmark itself is considered a research library. It's not, in a sense, a public library, but that does not mean that that you can't use it as a public patron. Everyone is allowed to use our Library. A big part of our collection is actually open for lending. But if a book is 100 years old, it's not allowed to be out of the Library. You have to use it in our reading room or Rare Books and Manuscripts department.[4]

[2] The National Library of Denmark – Homepage. Available at: http://www.kb.dk/en/nb/.

[3] Copenhagen University Library – Homepage. Available at: http://www.kb.dk/en/kub.

[4] Centre for Manuscripts & Rare Books, The National Library of Denmark – Homepage. Available at: http://www.kb.dk/en/nb/laesesale/CMB/index.html.

Why do not we delve into a little bit about your background as a librarian? At what age and how did you develop interest for East Asian languages and cultures?

When I was about 17 years old, I was interested in poetry; I was actually interested in the translated poetry of the Chinese poet, Li Bai (701–762), so fellow students and I developed a discussion group to study Chinese poetry. When it was time to apply for the university, I thought, why not try Chinese and, by extension, Chinese culture. It became an excellent fit, so that, I suppose, it was this interest in poetry that actually attracted me to Chinese studies.

Chinese poet Li Bai (701–62): as a university student, why did you find his poetry so appealing? In your opinion, are there sentimental values behind his works that would speak to all people, regardless of their ethnic and cultural backgrounds? In addition, over the years, you have gained a better mastery of the Chinese language and culture? Has this, in any ways, helped you deepen your understanding and appreciation towards Li Bai's work? In addition, your interest in Chinese art: what styles (Confucius, Taoist and Buddhist) and periods of Chinese art interest you most? In addition to being aesthetically pleasing, do they speak to you on a spiritual level? If yes, please describe in detail.

Li Bai's poems are simple and straight to the point. After entering the University of Copenhagen, I concentrated on Chinese culture in general, but developed an interest in forming decoration on Chinese architecture and early Chinese lacquer wares. I find it fascinating to follow the development of patterns, for example, from a naturalistic drawn bird to an abstract form, which you can see among others on lacquer wares from late Zhou and Han. It is an aesthetic enjoyment to trace these types of changing forms.

How many different languages have you and did you master in school and right now? Are such foreign language skills vital for performing your daily work at the Library in your position?

Well, in the school we could choose between different types of European languages. English, of course, was one of the more popular ones, and then either French or German, so I knew a little bit French, a little bit German and, of course, a lot of English. But it was in university that I learned Chinese.

Could you describe a typical day at work for you?

Over time, I realised that regardless of how you plan for your day, it rarely goes according to plan because I get all sorts of inquiries from users. In the past, it could be by telephone or (postal) mail, but inquiries are mainly by email today. It can be about almost anything.

It could be how to locate a book, or more specific questions include, do we have this type of item in the Library? Then I have to help guide the patron to actually find books inside the Library.

Another example is when the directors of the Library need some kind of information for making a policy or whatever it could be, I have to be ready to give them this at any time and all the time, of course. When I am on duty at the reading room, I help my users and guide them in using the resources, which do not necessarily have anything to do with my Chinese and Japanese studies knowledge.

Could you provide us a brief introduction to the collections at the Far East collections at the Royal Library of Denmark?

The Chinese, Japanese and Korean collections form a holistic collection based on old traditional types of subject areas (see Figs 15.2–15.7 for works from the collections). We also have a base collection for the study of ancient China in philosophy, history, linguistics, etc. Because of my education in Chinese culture, I have also developed an interest in archaeology and art, and so I have been trying to develop a collection on some basic works on art and archaeology, but it's not one, which we could call a large collection. In that sense, we fulfil basic works on China so one can start research at Library, and then move onto libraries from Europe or from China if you need more materials in a more in-depth area of study.

What is the size of the collections? What are some highlights?

If one calculates how many volumes we have, then I say maybe 80,000 in the Chinese collection, maybe 50,000 in Japanese and maybe 20,000 or 30,000 in Korean

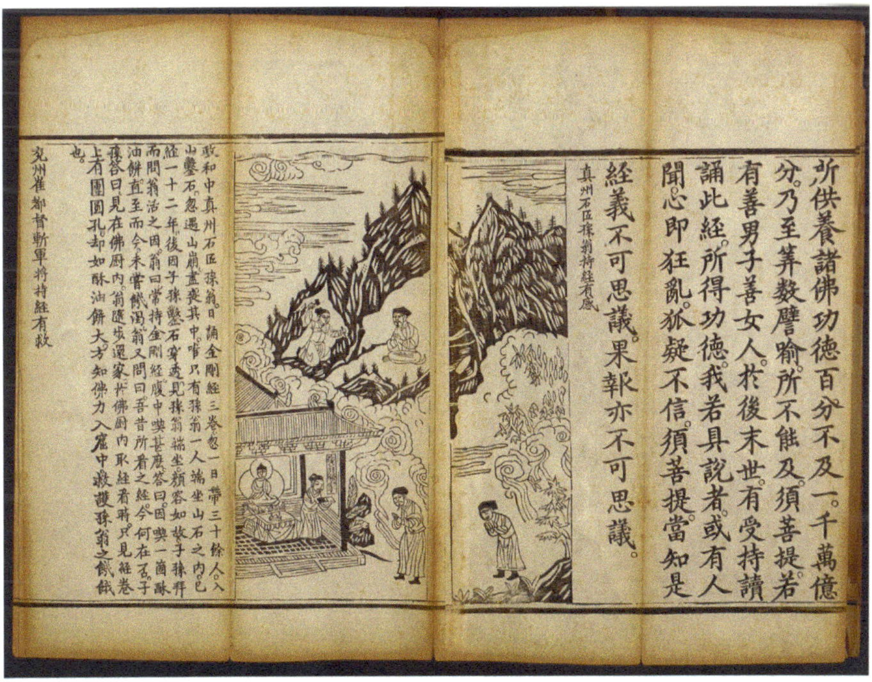

Figure 15.2 Jin'gang banruo boluomi jing, printed 1591.

Figure 15.3 Yao zhongshen tu, painted in 1793 (a set of 25 hand-painted scrolls) from the Yao minority in Guilin province.

Figure 15.4 Sanchuan (cloth banknote issued in Communist Sichuan–Shaanxi area in 1933).

collections. But it is very difficult to say because this number does not account for the digital materials in the online databases, and they include Korean, Japanese or Chinese materials, etc.

Where we're a little bit weak in is the East Asian modern studies area collections, especially in politics. Although we have tried to develop this area of the collection, it is a difficult subject to capture, and in my experience, these new or so-called modern areas of interest are difficult to collect because there's a lot of

Figure 15.5 Mi Laosu (Mickey Mouse) cartoon, printed in Shanghai, 1946. Probably a redrawn version of 'Editor in Greif'.

Figure 15.6 Hyaku Kannon, painted by Kano Tansen (1686–1728), dated 1721.

what I call rubbish. For example, a title could not be giving much important information other than a few nominal ideas. Thus, we can never know until we actually purchase the item.

What would you say is a highlight of the collection?

We have 16 manuscripts from Dunhuang, which were donated to our Library by a Danish telegrapher in 1916, which are quite interesting. Nice calligraphy is also something that I like very much, because I'm very much interested in (traditional Chinese) art. Calligraphy is undoubtedly an important form of art in China.

Figure 15.7 Tokaido gojusan-tsugi, drawn by Utagawa Kunisada (1786–1864), printed in Edo, 1852.

Chinese calligraphy, why do you find it so interesting? In terms of its key concepts, do you think in some ways are similar or comparable to the modern abstract expressionism that appeared in Europe and North America in the late 19th and early 20th century?

Well, you can see Chinese, Japanese and Korean calligraphy as forms, abstract forms if you like, but the meaning and the sound of the characters also add to the pleasure to view a piece of calligraphy. Of course, some types of calligraphy are difficult to read, so there the forms alone are important. My knowledge of modern abstract expressionism is not very big, but some of the Western artists were clearly inspirited by Far Eastern art and calligraphy.

Could you tell me about the staffing structure of the Far East department of the Royal Library of Denmark?

Well it's a bit of a sad history. When I was employed in the Library in 1970s, we were in what was then called the Oriental collection. We had nine full-time staff members employed, but today I'm the only one left in the Oriental collection. That means I represent 100% of the entire East Asian language studies areas, including Asia, North

Africa, Arabic, Italian and so on. We've been cut down so much so that I am the only one left in the Library.

What are the major difficulties and challenges that you and your library colleagues are currently facing?

I think it's the same for most libraries around the world. It's about digitisation and e-books. In terms of e-books, how do we cope with all of these different types of electronic materials that are coming to us? Most of these databases we can buy access to are extremely expensive, and how do you select the one database, which is benefiting for our readers? That is a major problem.

Fortunately, it is not a large problem for us as we have a Nordic Collaboration[5] and it has an institute which takes care of these type of things, so we sit in the background and advise them on what we think readers would like so I do not have to choose them myself. We have chosen certain things, and we have gotten very, very positive feedback from our users, so they are, of course, quite happy. But unfortunately, the prices of such materials are going up and the budget for the Library is going down.

So we have a problem there, and that, by the way, is not limited to just East Asian resources. It also covers European and Western sources. It's a general trend in libraries. The price goes up and the library receives less money each year, so that is a challenge for the library world and for me too, of course.

What scholarly and professional associations are you a part of and how do they assist in your work?

As a professional librarian, I belong as a member to the European Association of Sinological Librarians.

How does that assist you with your work in terms of connecting with other librarians?

It is nice because you get the personal contact, and if you get some kind of question, where, you know, my collection can't cover it, or you do not really know it, then I just know which colleague I can contact. It can be in France; it can be in Great Britain. It can be in Austria and so on. Because I know a particular individual, I get an immediate response when I go to him or her for assistance, especially since it will be professionally good advice. So that's good.

Who are the majority of Far East collections users, and that is, perhaps to clarify, who comes to see you about your collections? Are they mostly professors or students from higher educations? Or are they people from outside the postsecondary sector, namely, the public?

[5] NIAS, the Nordic Institute of Asian Studies, is an academically independent Nordic research and resource centre, focusing on modern Asia from a predominantly social sciences perspective. NIAS is an integrated part of the University of Copenhagen with the status of a centre under the Department of Political Science. http://nias.ku.dk/nordic-collaboration/university-copenhagen.

Well, it's a mix. I would say the biggest group we have is actually students and then maybe researchers or professors is next. Because we're a part of the Danish network, we get a lot of questions and requests from public libraries. Because it's a free service that everyone can go to, we do not know necessarily know who are our users. Is it a researcher who lives someplace outside Copenhagen? Or is it just a person who is just interested in a particular subject area? So we do not know. However, we do know that geographically, a lot of our readers are actually from China, Japan and Korea who come for short periods of time to do research in Denmark. They sometimes come to request certain books or ask for certain things, such as for their research, for leisure or entertainment. It's a bit mixed, so our user group consists of very different types of people. It can be 'lay' people or it can be highly educated people.

Do you have any statistics of the number of people studying Chinese the number of people studying Chinese or Japanese languages at university in Denmark? Are they available? Do you know?

There is probably some kind of official figure. I would think at the moment, there are about 100 individuals who are active in Chinese studies, about 80 in Japanese and maybe 20 in Korean. But we also have Southeast Asian languages, so we also have these types of users of the Library, too.

But although there are actual 'official' statistics, they might not be accurate in that they do not indicate who is actually an 'active' and an 'inactive' learner. In principal, everyone can attend a class at the university. Of course, these who go there are enlisted in the university as a student. For example, when I began university in 1970, my university had a lot of people from outside the university who attended classes, but who were not actually registered in the classes.

You talked a little bit about the users, your typical day at work and some of the things you do. Can you give examples of research inquiry issued by scholars or researchers at the Far East Division at the Royal Library of Denmark?

Some of them are quite specific. We do have those types of questions, which a patron asks for a type of work or a specific title, which they could just as easily find in an online catalogue. Yet, there are also those, which are immensely interesting, ones that we must do some further research in the subject area and help guide the user to find those books and materials, which we have in our collection or outside the Library.

Since we have other types of libraries in Copenhagen that also have Chinese and Japanese materials, we might refer them there if we do not happen to have it in our Library. Those are very interesting research questions, and I find it very rewarding if I can help people conduct their research because it's not always so easy to know that one library outside the Royal Library has actually collections of Chinese materials as well, especially if the user does not know that it's available out there, and I happen to know it exists.

As the Librarian of the Far East collections, how do you acquire and evaluate your collection? This is particularly interesting as you are the solo librarian there. How do you acquire and evaluate your collection?

As I mentioned earlier, we're not so strong in the area of Far East modern politics and economics. If you want to study China, Chinese culture, Chinese history or Chinese philosophy or religion, we might have the basic works that would give you a good start. Otherwise, we would look to other libraries in Europe and tap into the interlibrary loan system, which can help us easily get books from other libraries free of charge, especially if you're a student or researcher. For the local community users, they would pay a certain fee to get those books, but it's still a very good service for those who need it. My colleagues and I can also point to other libraries if they need to have the materials.

In the past few years, the Far East division of the Royal Library of Denmark has been engaged in the digitisation of some of its collections. What are the projects and what future plans are there for future digital collections?

Because our division is only a small part of the Royal Library, we do not have much money for that type of digitalisation, so we have to fight every time to get something lined up for digitisation. We prioritise what our users need access to for digitisation and especially those materials, which only are available in the Library's reading room. If there is enough money, we can get it digitised, but I must fight for it. I have to fight for it to get this done.

For example, our digitised Dunhuang manuscripts are actually not located in the Royal Library collections. It's actually part of this International Dunhuang Project (IDP)[6] because we cooperated with them in order to have it digitised. We partnered in the funding of this digitisation project; we digitised the manuscripts and IDP made the online access because it would be open to a global audience and not just limited to the Royal Library in Copenhagen. Nobody actually knows that we owned the scrolls, but what's important now is that everyone in the world can see this international project.

Could you describe the fascinations towards the Dunhuang caves and their treasures amongst the scholarly community in Europe?

The Dunhuang materials are important for both the study of Daoist and Buddhist religions and also for the Chinese administrative system in early times. I am personally attracted to the magic materials and the calligraphy. Some of the Dunhuang materials are unique, for example, we have a unique part of Juan 15 of the *Huayanjing lun* (*Avataṃsaka Sūtra*/華嚴經 Fig. 15.8) in our small collection of 14 Dunhuang scrolls, including 16 manuscripts, etc.

[6] Dunhuang International Project – Homepage. Available at: http://idp.bl.uk.

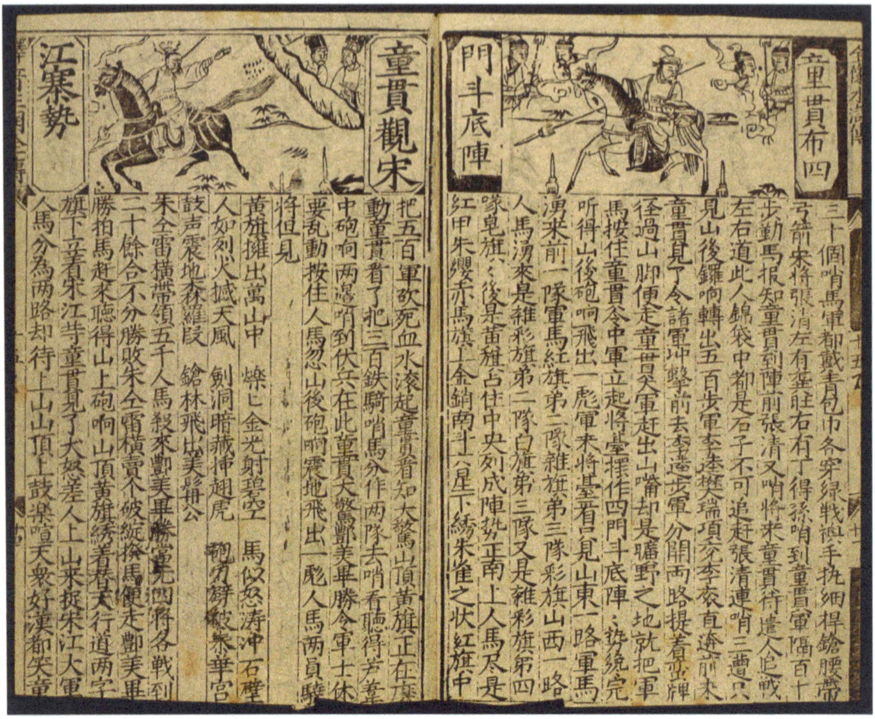

Figure 15.8 Juan 15–19 of Quanxiang Shuihu chuanzhuan, printed c.1600.

How does the collection catalogue and provide access for users? Now, particularly with a non-roman script, what challenges does this present to cataloguing, or are there any at all that you faced in your years as a librarian?

We have an online catalogue, and it started with Pinyin, only with Pinyin transcription for Chinese, Hepburn for Japanese and the Reischauer for the Korean ones. The majority are still only in these transcriptions, but 8 years ago, we added Chinese characters or Hangul for the Korean one. These transcriptions are increasing, too. At the moment, I'm using what you call my 'free hours' to add Chinese characters to the Chinese catalogue. Close to one-third of the Chinese collection has Chinese characters where they are searchable in the catalogue, and the Japanese has about one-third transcribed, where the Korean collection has only 20% or so, but I add as many characters as possible on a continuing basis. This is important since we are a member of the WorldCat (www.worldcat.org), where our books are available by search, so we get quite a lot of requests, even though we do not have scripts for a lot of the titles.

Because our collection is searchable online, I think we can search for most titles, but one of the problems is the searching of individual characters, for instance, how do you, in Chinese, put the translation into a Romanisation? I do it separately, every word or not. I put them together because I still find it odd that *renmin* (人民), for example, is split into *ren* (人) and *min* (民). I mean I see it as a concept, *renmin*, one word, not two.

The themes and needs of libraries, archives and museums, or LAMs, as it's somehow referred to them, have increasingly converged. I mentioned this earlier on as well; I guess we should put galleries in as part of that. What are your experiences and thoughts of cultural institutions whose work and best practices now all often overlap?

In Denmark, we have a strategy to cooperate as much as possible, no matter if you are an archive, library, art museum or historical museum. For instance, we have the Danish National Museum, which actually has quite a lot of books as well. In fact, we have a project of printed catalogues on East Asian materials housed in the National Museum (of Denmark),[7] the Royal Library and the Danish National Archives,[8] so in that sense, we have been in collaboration since the 1960s. So, in this case, a printed catalogue is cross-listed in all of these cultural institutions. As you can see, cooperation among us is very important.

Lots of the connections have already been there for a very long time, but I think it is because our library system's philosophy is that every citizen in Denmark can use the library system, and that belief also extends to archives and to museums. As a result, this cooperation between these different institutions is our tradition and is extremely important.

According to information found on the web, between 1968 and 1978, the Library saw one of the largest books thefts in history. Someone had managed to steal some 1600 historical books worth more than 50 million, including prints by Martin Luther and first editions by Kant, Moore and John Milton. Can you describe the security system of the Royal Library during its early days and why such precious items could be stolen by a regular user?

First, I have to say, the thief was my former boss. He was employed by the Library, and so we think, at that time at least, that the employed were loyal to the institution, but he wasn't. He was taking books out.

So the security was, of course, quite lax in the 1960s when he was employed. I think he was employed in 1968, and according to what we can find out, he started at the time to take books home. At that time, the security was not the same level that we have today because society was different back then. People did not steal from public libraries or museums. You had to really be a hard-core criminal to do that type of thing, so the security was not so strict, but after the late 1970s, after the discovery of lost books in the Library, our security was totally changed. There was much stricter control of people when they left the Library. They checked what patrons took out of the Library. Today, we have chips embedded in the library books, which set off an alarm if you take them out of the Library without permission. So in that sense, the security is much stricter now today.

We have in the Library, in the reading rooms, security cameras filming people all the time, and people working in the reading rooms are supervising what people are

[7] The National Museum of Denmark – Homepage. Available at: http://en.natmus.dk.

[8] The Danish National Archives – Homepage. Available at: https://www.sa.dk/en/about-us/danish-national-archives.

doing, and if you want to have some access to some special materials, you have to have a special pass, which you must register as a special user, and we take a photo of these particular patrons in order for us to process those passes. Moreover, if the patron is coming from outside Denmark, we take a copy of his identity, passport or ID cards or whatever he might have on hand. So regulations are much tighter today than before, when only staffed employees could steal from the Library.

Now, it is not uncommon to see librarians with no interest in music or visual arts taking up positions as heads and directors of music and visual arts libraries. They're hired because they're effective administrators, good managers and good at IT, and not because of their knowledge or research skills in related fields. Now, there are also librarians who are hired to manage East Asian Library collections, only because they can speak and read these languages, and not because they have an active scholarly or cultural interest in the materials themselves. Now here's the question: being an effective administrator versus being a respected scholar, with well-grounded knowledge in the field, which do you think is more important to serve as a good librarian, being a respectable scholar or being a good administrator?

I think you have to be a scholar because an administrator does not know the content of the collection. I remember when I started, I did not have knowledge of the more ancient Chinese history. I had just a general knowledge of the area. But after working for many years, I have acquired quite a lot of knowledge of what the different eras would contain which works, what can they be used for and how they might benefit a student or researcher. An administrator is not interested in that type of thing. They just want to make sure that books are signed out, where I can give an academic or researcher much more direct and a personal kind of advice and help him do his research. Luckily, our current director of the Library is very much oriented into research. He thinks that we must be able to help researchers and students; they are ultimately our core users.

You also talked about your training and your background. What best prepared you for your current position as a librarian?

I think it was when I was a student, I obtained a student job in the Institute's library. I realised and saw how a library functions. It was very interesting work, and I think from that point on, I was quite interested in the job in a library. When I became a regular employee and received library training, it all really helped me understand how an entire library functioned and how the life in that type of world existed, how things worked and how you understood it. That was all very interesting to me. From my training as a student assistant to librarian training, both were very important experiences for me.

Which part of your job as librarian do you find the most rewarding? We've talked about challenges, but what are the most rewarding aspects of your job as a librarian?

A happy patron! Someone who can express that they have gotten good help. Another thing I also find today is even more interesting is the sense is that I can provide, via our Library's website, something that can help people to understand what type of resources we have and what we actually can provide, so I make available smaller items available on our website, which I think are interesting to our users. It can be a digitised item, for example, or it can be a library research guide on how to locate things in the Library or on the web.

Exploring the Hidden Treasures

16

Benedicte Vaerman
KU Leuven University, Leuven, Belgium

Introduction

Founded in 1425, the KU Leuven University is considered the largest, oldest and most prominent university in Belgium. In 1968, the KU Leuven University split into the following two institutions, namely:

1. KU Leuven University, Dutch-speaking, situated in Leuven; and
2. Catholic University of Louvain, French-speaking, situated primarily in nearby Louvain-la-Neuve.

Managing the collections and daily operations of the East-Asian Library, is the multilingual Benedicte Vaerman (Fig. 16.1), who, as a teenager, discovered her initial interest in Asian culture through Japanese art and literature. In the following interview, Ms. Vaerman candidly discusses the essential skills and knowledge, as well as the personality traits that are required for working as a successful East-Asian librarian for onc of the oldest academic institutes in Europe.

Could we begin this interview by first introducing yourself, for example, your training and background, and your major roles and duties at the East-Asian Library, KU Leuven University?[1]

I obtained an MA in sinology here at the KU Leuven University and continued studying the Chinese language for more than a year in Taiwan. When I returned to Belgium, I worked in a research project, which later stopped due to the freezing of the project funding as a reaction to the Tiananmen Massacre, which took place in Beijing in June 1989. At that time, there was only a very small Chinese library here at the University, and our research institute had established its own Documentation Centre on Contemporary China somewhere else. When I had to go looking for a new job, I could start working partly in the existing Chinese library and partly in the Documentation Centre. I continued to develop both collections and harmonised their cataloguing system. In 1996, after renovating and expanding the former Chinese library, the collection of the Documentation Centre was also moved there,

[1] KU Leuven University – Homepage. Available at: http://www.kuleuven.be/english.

Inside the World's Major East Asian Collections. http://dx.doi.org/10.1016/B978-0-08-102145-3.00016-9

Figure 16.1 Benedicte Vaerman.

and we established an East-Asian Library inside the main building of the Central Library of the KU Leuven University.[2] The first years of the new library were hectic because we received extensive donations. We received lots of journals, newspapers and books from institutions and private people that had been collecting material about China before. This was very welcome because the collection was lacking all the basic material that was edited before the 1970s, when KU Leuven University had split in two. The French-speaking part of the University was established in another town, called Louvain-la-Neuve, and all the former collections on the Far East had gone there.

I have been running the East-Asian Library since the very beginning, mostly in cooperation with a part-time colleague working on the Japanese and Korean collections. Volunteers and job students are helping with cataloguing, re-shelving and other duties. I am responsible for the library management as well as for the collection development on China.

At what age and how did you develop an interest in the Chinese language and culture?

I developed an interest, initially in Japanese art, as a teenager. In Belgium, it was not possible to study only Japanese studies in university at that time; you had to register for Chinese studies and choose Japanese as your second language. That is exactly what I did. Afterwards, I became fascinated and interested in Chinese culture. I still am very much interested in Japan too, but I have never succeeded to develop my Japanese language knowledge more.

[2] Central Library of the KU Leuven University – Homepage. Available at: http://bib.kuleuven.be/english/bibc.

Can you describe the experience of your very first Chinese language lesson in Belgium? What was it like?

We had a very good teacher of the Chinese language; it was great fun.

Do you have the statistical figures indicating the number of people studying Chinese language at your university and in Belgium in general?

Impossible to say; there are too many different institutions where you can learn Chinese in Belgium, even if the country is small. KU Leuven University has, however, the best Chinese language training of them all. Every year, we have around 40 to 60 new students in the first year.

The students who study East Asian languages at your university, after their graduation, what kind of career will they enter into?

There are very broad possibilities, just as other students in the human sciences disciplines.

Please provide a brief introduction to the collections at the East-Asian Library, KU Leuven University? What is the size of the collections? Could you describe the highlights of the East Asian collection?

The collection of the East-Asian Library has developed a lot since its establishment, growing from a small reference library to a more mature collection of more than 100,000 items (see Figs 16.2 and 16.3), of which about 70,000 are on China, 30,000 on Japan and less than 10,000 on Korea.

Acquisition on China focuses on books and reference works for the study of sinology, including the Chinese language. In Western languages, we buy mostly material concerning modern and contemporary China, which serves a very broad public, including people from outside the university. For acquisitions in the Chinese language, we focus on Chinese philosophy (ancient and contemporary), and on contacts between China and the West since the Ming because our professors, Nicolas Standaert and Carine Defoort, are running long-term research projects on these topics. Researchers from all over the world are coming specially to our Library to consult our collections on East–West contacts.

The collections on Japan and Korea have changed dramatically since the appointment of a good reference librarian, which resulted in a much better balanced collection and a booming use of the collections on Japan and Korea. Sadly, after only 2 years working as a full-time librarian, it was just recently decided that he will be reduced to working half-time at the East-Asian Library (Fig. 16.4).

For the development of the collection in general, donations have been all along very important. Apart from the many Belgian institutions and private persons who donated their collections, we receive yearly donations from Chinese, Japanese and Korean institutions, as well as from international private companies and persons.

Figure 16.2 Reading room of the East-Asian Library.
Photo by Dirk Motmans.

Figure 16.3 Buddha statue near the entrance of the East-Asian Library.
Photo by Dirk Motmans.

Figure 16.4 View of the Central Library building in winter. The East-Asian library is at the second floor.
Photo by Dirk Motmans.

What best prepared you for your work at the East-Asian Library, KU Leuven University?

In my view, doing research myself prepared me very well to be a good librarian because it helped me understand what researchers need. Contact with our patrons is very important too because topics of interest, working methods and tools change very quickly and one needs to keep our finger on the pulse. Finally, reading and hearing what is going on in the world, visiting and using other libraries, talking with other librarians, discussing about modern information needs and practices, it's all part of a never-ending process of trying to do a good job.

How many different languages have you mastered?

My mother tongue is Dutch, and this is also the language of our university. At home, I speak French; for my work, I use a lot of English and Chinese.

How much Chinese/Japanese language or history on East Asia do you need to know in order to serve as the Librarian for the East-Asian Library?

The more the better because cataloguing Chinese collections, knowing where to find Chinese classical Chinese texts and how to catalogue older material can be very complicated. The necessity of solid topic knowledge and a broad cultural background, and the fact that you need to build it up through years, is often not taken in account by general library management. There is a general tendency of downgrading reference librarians and replacing them with cheaper staff.

Please describe the staffing structure at the East-Asian Library. Are you the solo Librarian working at the East-Asian Library?

I am the only full-time staff; my colleague who is specialised on Japan and Korea works now again part-time. Luckily, Chinese, Japanese, Korean and Belgian volunteers regularly come to help with cataloguing and other cores. Sometimes we also hire student helpers.

Could you describe your typical day at work? Is there ever a typical day at work?

In general, I sit behind my computer, trying to catch up with all the emails waiting for an answer, orders to be issued, reports to be written and lists to be checked. And then, there are many meetings to go to, very often foreign visitors to welcome and many readers to help. The ever-rising cost of databases is a big challenge to us, and it takes a lot of energy to find the necessary funding for it. This is the kind of acquisitions work that is sometimes done in cooperation between different faculties or in consortia with various European institutions.

What scholarly and professional associations are you a part of, and how do they assist you in your work?

Of course I am part of the university library community, and therefore I am assisted by local specialists in IT, in rare and precious books, in e-resources and, hopefully, later, also for acquisition and cataloguing. For specific advice on the 'Chinese' part of my job, I have no colleagues here, and I generally refer to my colleagues of the European Association of Sinological Librarians (EASL).[3] I have been part of this yearly meeting for many years, and therefore I know which library in Europe has what kind of materials and what my European colleagues are good at. If necessary, I call or write them, or I contact some friends in China to help me out.

Who are the majority of the East-Asian Library, KU Leuven University users? That is, who comes to see you about your collections? Are they mostly professors or students from higher education institutions? Or are they people from outside the postsecondary sector, i.e., the public? I was checking your University's homepage (http://www.kuleuven.be/english/faculties_schools); it seems that KU Leuven University does not offer any programmes on East Asian studies. Am I to understand that the services and collections of the East-Asian Library are meant to support the foreign language programmes at KU Leuven University (see http://ilt.kuleuven.be/english/)?

You can actually study for a BA, MA and PhD in sinology and Japanese studies in Leuven, and quite a few people are doing so. These students, their faculty and researchers, are, of course, the main users of the Library. Because the Library also buys a lot of Western-language books on contemporary China, many students from other faculties will also come to borrow books about China. For example, a sociology student will come here for a book on migration issues inside China because the library with sociology books might not purchase as many titles on this topic.

Furthermore, the university also has a large community of Chinese students and researchers who use the Chinese books and databases very actively. Finally, the East-Asian Library is the only active library on China in Belgium, and it therefore attracts a lot of people from outside the academic community with a wide variety of points of interest. We also play a role of information centre to these people, to the press or to local Chinese associations. We will tell them who the Belgian specialists are in Chinese art or in contemporary politics, forward the address of a Chinese language school or help with the identification of a Chinese object. Artists, including architects, also might come for inspiration and explanation on oriental arts.

The Library is also a place of identification for the students and faculty of sinology and Japanese and Korean studies. Foreign guests and visiting professors will often visit or hold a talk in the Library. In 2009, then Chinese Vice President Xi Jinping visited the Library (see Fig. 16.5).

Considering the growing importance of electronic data, in the near future, the Library may be evolving more towards a multifunctional platform, where talks are held, films are projected, book or literature clubs are gathering and students are having workshops and practical seminars. The librarian will more and more keep in touch with students and researchers through online contacts, regardless whether they will be staying in China or in Leuven.

[3] European Association of Sinological Librarians (EASL) – Homepage. Available at: http://www.easl.org/.

Figure 16.5 Visit of (then) Vice President Xi Jinping to the East-Asian library in 2009, shaking hands with the (then) rector of KU Leuven University.
Photo by KU Leuven University/Rob Stevens.

Could you give examples of typical reference/research inquiries issued by the researchers or scholars at the East-Asian Library, KU Leuven University?

Typical questions will be: What are the translations existing of a certain Chinese text, what are the best books on a specific topic and how can readers obtain a certain book/article, which is not included in our collection? We also help people to locate a text in a *Congshu*, teach and help people to search specific databases, advise students on working methods, help them with finding difficult characters and check and correct *Pinyin* or other transcriptions and general data on China when used by nonsinologist researchers in their publications. Questions are sometimes very diverse, and therefore, it is important to know many people and institutions around to refer to.

As Librarian at the East-Asian Library, KU Leuven University, how do you acquire and evaluate your collection?

I try to take time to speak to the users of the Library; I read a lot and I keep in touch with other librarians in Europe doing the same work. This helps me to know what to buy and what are our needs. I will often forward information from editors to our faculty, on databases, for example, and ask them if they would be interested. For the acquisition of databases, I will first ask for a trial version, try it out and forward it to specialists of the topic. Evaluation of the collection is done in roughly the same way: by asking, reading, comparing and checking other collections, proposing and testing, etc.

In the past few years, the East-Asian Library, KU Leuven University has been engaged in the digitisation of some of its collections. What are some of the projects and what future plans are there for the digital collections?

Because the East-Asian Library does not have a lot of precious books on China, we are not active in digitisation. Precious books are not kept in the East-Asian Library, but they are kept in a special department for precious books. In the coming years, we plan to digitise the precious books on China at the university library. I will work together with this department on these projects.

How does the collection catalogue and provide access for users? With a non-Roman script, what challenges does this present to cataloguing? Is there any?

We catalogue with ALMA, and our OPAC (**O**nline **P**ublic **A**ccess **C**atalogue) is called LIMO, based on PRIMO.[4] Access to the databases is generalised throughout the KU Leuven University intranet. As a university library, we have to follow the procedures, rules, working methods and standards from the rest of the university. Needless to say, this is generally not adapted to using Chinese and Japanese, which generates regularly a lot of extra work for us.

We have had a lot of problems in the past with the cataloguing of Chinese books because our former systems did not support characters and non-Roman scripts. Therefore, we started cataloguing much later than other departments, and we still have not succeeded in completing all necessary retro-cataloguing. Since 2014, when Leuven University has adopted ALMA, we again have a lot of problems with the display and the indexing of our Chinese and Japanese data. We try to adjust this in cooperation with the library IT department. Sadly, by now, we still cannot retrieve Chinese and Japanese bibliographic data from other catalogues, which results in a very heavy workload.

The themes and information needs of libraries, archives and museums (LAMs, as some have referred to them) have increasingly converged. What are your experiences and thoughts about these cultural institutions whose work and best practices now often overlap?

In general, I think there is no problem of overlapping when each institution has its own focus. Especially in a small place like Belgium, where interest in China is still quite rare, we need insight from different institutions in order to have a more holistic knowledge base about China. Therefore, it is an advantage if different universities, museums and cultural institutions can offer a variety of approaches to Chinese culture for the public. What should be done, and I tried to introduce it already among the China libraries in Belgium, is making clear who does what and abiding to these arrangements. Ghent University,[5] for example, buys a lot of material about Buddhism in China, and the Belgian Institute of Higher Chinese Studies in the Cinquantenaire Museum[6] has been buying books on Chinese art. That's where we will send people

[4] PRIMO is a centralised index or resources portal that provides convenient one-stop, relevance-ranked results from many of the Library's online and print collections in a single search.

[5] Ghent University – Homepage. Available at: http://www.ugent.be/en.

[6] Belgian Institute of Higher Chinese Studies – Homepage. Available at: http://www.china-institute.be/index.html.

when they are researching Chinese Buddhism and art. And students of Ghent and Brussels can come to Leuven when they need classical Chinese texts or books on contemporary society in China.

Which part(s) of your job as a librarian at the East-Asian Library, KU Leuven University do you find most rewarding?

The nicest moments are those when I see people are borrowing the books and using the databases I have bought because it makes me feel useful. Discussions with researchers and students are important too because we learn so much from each other, and sometimes I have the feeling that I can make a difference. Last but not least, the contact with the books is, of course, ever interesting: the pleasure to get to know my collection, the curiosity that arises when I discover new points of view and recently acquired books or when I take the time to explore the hidden treasures in my own collection.

The Most Royal of Museums in Belgium

17

Nathalie Vandeperre
The Royal Museums of Art and History of Belgium, Brussels, Belgium

Introduction

The Royal Museums of Art and History (RMAH) of Belgium is a group of museums in Brussels, Belgium, that includes the Museums of the Far East, dedicated to Oriental art and culture, specifically that of China and Japan. One of the principal focuses of the museums' collection, Chinese export porcelain, is housed in the Chinese Pavilion. While this Chinese Pavilion, a chinoiserie building, focuses on Chinese art originally designed for export to the West, the Japanese Tower similarly displays Japanese art, mostly porcelain created for export to the West. The RMAH also have Chinese and Korean collections in yet another museum site, the Cinquantenaire Museum. This chapter details the work of one curator, Nathalie Vandeperre, who manages the East Asian collections, and with it, helps enable researchers' and the public's understanding of Asian in Belgium.

Could we begin this interview by first introducing yourself, for example, your training and background, and your major roles and duties at the Royal Museums of the Far East (Belgium)[1] and the RMAH of Belgium[2]?

My name is Nathalie Vandeperre (Fig. 17.1). I graduated with an master's degree in sinology from the University of Leuven[3] in 1992, and completed this with a special diploma in cultural studies. My first employment was as librarian of the Belgian Institute for Advanced Chinese Studies (located inside the RMAH of Belgium). Later, I worked at the Educational Department of the RMAH, and started to get acquainted with the Asian collections through conferences, etc. In 1999, I joined the East Asian Department. My first assignment was the installation and opening of the Museum of Japanese Art, which is located on a site with three historical buildings on the outskirts of Brussels: the Chinese Pavilion, the Japanese Tower and a third building, where we opened the Museum of Japanese Art (Figs 17.2–17.4). Since then, I became interested in exotic architecture, chinoiserie and the Chinese and Japanese export art collections that are on display in the Pavilion and the Tower.

[1] Royal Museums of the Far Fast (Belgium) – Homepage. Available at: http://www.kmkg-mrah.be/museums-far-east.
[2] Royal Museums of Fine Arts of Belgium – Homepage. Available at: http://www.fine-arts-museum.be/en/.
[3] University of Leuven – Homepage. Available at: http://www.kuleuven.be/english.

Inside the World's Major East Asian Collections. http://dx.doi.org/10.1016/B978-0-08-102145-3.00017-0

Figure 17.1 Nathalie Vandeperre.

Figure 17.2 Chinese Pavilion.

Due to budget restraints, the staff of the East Asian department (China, Japan, Korea) has been seriously reduced: I have one part-time colleague focussing on educational work for the East Asian collections, and one technical assistant.

Figure 17.3 Japanese Tower.

Figure 17.4 Museum of Japanese Art.

At what age and how did you develop an interest for East Asian art and cultures of the Far East in general?

I started to study sinology out of curiosity for the 'unknown'; after my bachelor's degree (age 20), I knew I wanted to study more cultural or artistic topics instead of the more modern and economical side. Working in a museum is like a dream come true!

These two groups of museums are each referred as museums (plural) and not museum (singular), which is referred as museum(s)—which is because of the different collections devoted to the same/similar theme? Or because of the museums' different location sites or physical buildings, despite their collections all belong to the same theme or administrative unit?

The RMAH are indeed located on four different sites in Brussels:

1. the Cinquantenaire Museum[4] (main building, with departments of Antiquities, European Fine Arts, National Archaeology and non-European Arts);
2. the Musical Instruments Museum[5];
3. the Halle Gate[6]; and
4. the Museums of the Far East.[7]

The last one consists of three buildings built in 1900–10 in one park: the Japanese Tower (Japanese export art collections), the Chinese Pavilion (Chinese export ceramics collections) and the Museum of Japanese Art (Japanese collections). The site is part of the East Asian Department at the RMAH.

All of the collections and staff in all four sites are part of the RMAH, one of the federal (national) Belgian museums.

'Royal': Does it mean that these museums were founded by the Belgium Royal Family? Or collections of the museums used to belong to the royal palace of Belgium, and they are currently on loan to the museums?

They are royal because they were founded as national museums soon after the Belgian independence in 1830. In Belgium, being a kingdom, the national museums are called 'Royal', but the provenance of the collections is not royal.

Could you describe Belgium's relationship with China and Japan during the past few centuries? Trading and other types of diplomatic relations between the China and the Belgium, when were they first established?

In terms of China, Belgian entrepreneurs were present in China at the beginning of the 20th century, building railroads and trams and founding banks. These industrials often were collectors and brought their collections back to Belgium. Our late King Leopold II saw many opportunities in the Far East and encouraged them. Belgium had

[4] Cinquantenaire Museum – Homepage. Available at: http://www.kmkg-mrah.be/cinquantenaire-museum.
[5] Musical Instrument Museum (Brussels) – Homepage. Available at: http://www.mim.be/museum.
[6] Halle Gate – Homepage. Available at: http://www.kmkg-mrah.be/halle-gate.
[7] Museums of the Far East – Homepage. Available at: http://www.kmkg-mrah.be/museums-far-east.

diplomatic representatives in China's major cities at the turn of the 20th century. After the damage of the Boxer Rebellion in 1900, Belgium also received indemnities, and that is how the Belgian Institute for Advanced Chinese Studies was created in 1929.

For Japan, Belgium celebrates 150 years of diplomatic relations with Japan in 2016. Before, there were hardly any contacts with Japan (same for most countries except the Netherlands).

What is the current size of the collections amongst these two museum groups? Could you describe the highlights of the collection of the Curator of the Museums of the Far East? How does this collection differ from the China–Japan–Korea collections at the RMAH?

For our Japanese collections, we have 12,000 of inventoried items; however, some of them might contain multiple objects but still count as one item (for example, a whole ceramic set would be inventoried as one item). The exact number of items has not been counted yet. The most precious part, the ukiyo-e collection, has over 7500 prints, many of them in pristine condition. The Museum of Japanese Art shows a rotating presentation of prints, textiles, painting, armours, sword fittings, lacquer, ceramics and Buddhist art, etc. The Japanese Tower displays Japanese export art: Imari ceramics and Meiji art that was on show in the first international exhibitions in the west.

For our Chinese collections, there are currently some 6000 inventory items. Almost half of them are Chinese export ceramics, displayed in the Chinese Pavilion. The other half of the collections date from Neolithic to the 20th century, including ceramics, jades, bronzes, textiles, paintings, Buddhist sculpture, wall paintings and furniture. They are currently on display in the Chinese galleries at the Cinquantenaire Museum (Fig. 17.5).

Our Korean collection has some 100 items, most of them ceramics, offering a panorama of tradition from Three Kingdoms to Choson. These are currently on display at the Cinquantenaire Museum.

Figure 17.5 Cinquantenaire Museum.

What best prepared you for the position of Curator of the Royal Museums of the Far East, and also for the China–Japan–Korea collections at the Royal Museum of Art and History?

My work at the educational department was excellent preparation. In addition, although I took one course on Chinese art at university that was only very small and merely an introduction, it proved to be good preparation for this position.

The Museums of the Far East are currently under renovation. What type of work do you conduct while this renovation is in progress?

At this point, the work has not started; there are no plans and no financing so far. My role now is more like lobbying and trying to attract attention of the authorities and make sure they do not forget about it while it is closed.

What scholarly and professional associations are you a part of, and how do they assist you in your work?

I am a member of the board of directors of the Belgian Institute for Advanced Chinese Studies. They have an excellent library, which I use almost every day, and a network of scholars. I also remain in close contact with professors at the University of Leuven.

Who are the majority of the Museum's patrons and users? That is, who comes to see you about your collections? Are they mostly professors or students from higher education institutions? Or are they people from outside the postsecondary sector, that is, the general public?

There are all sorts of patrons. Tourists particularly comprise a large audience, but there are also students from Belgian universities. Since there are no other large Chinese and Japanese collections in other Belgian libraries, our library is popular in this area since it is quite rich on the subject. Other users include colleagues from abroad, who visit mainly for our Japanese prints collections. Another segment of users include collectors who are asking for information about their own collection.

Could you give examples of typical reference/research inquiries issued by the researchers or scholars at the Far Eastern department at the Museum?

A type of reference inquiry that is new in the last few years is the topic of the provenance of collections. Recently, I am fielding more inquiries about collectors and sales of particular art works and collections. I find this an interesting topic as well, but it takes much archival work.

As Curator of the Chinese, Japanese, and Korean collections, how do you acquire and evaluate your collection?

In terms of acquisitions, due to budget restrictions, mainly by gifts; we hardly buy anything. As for evaluation, the value of objects, I find that very hard. To do so, I try to browse through sale catalogues. Unfortunately, we do not have a budget to hire experts to do this for us. However, I do know some foreign colleagues who do hire experts.

Do you also have libraries or information centres set up inside these royal museums, with the aim of supporting the ongoing research activities carried out amongst the museum staff, as well as to promote self-learning amongst the general public (museum users in particular)?

Yes, we have a very good Chinese library, a good library on Japanese art, both accessible for students and amateur researchers.

In the past few years, the Royal Museum of Art and History has been engaged in the digitisation of some of its collections. What are some of the projects of the Far Eastern department and what future plans are there for its digital collections?

We are in a digitisation process, and part of it is available for the public through our website at www.carmentis.be. I try to work also with international databases, for example, Ritsumeikan University for the ukiyo-e prints and Hosei University for Japanese Buddhist art. Digitisation is a work in progress and will take many more years to complete these projects.

How does the collection catalogue and provide access for users? With a non-roman script, what challenges does this present to cataloguing? Is there any?

The cataloguing system for the museum collections does not adopt non-roman script, so that kind of information is a transcription item for library catalogue (also, we would not have the specialised staff to do the digitising).

The themes and information needs of libraries, archives and museums (LAMs, as some have referred to them) have increasingly converged. What are your experiences and thoughts about these cultural institutions whose work and best practices now often overlap?

I find myself very lucky to have my office located inside the Japanese library and just next to the Chinese library, and I could not do my job without them. I wish I had more time to get acquainted with new publications, like I did when I was a librarian myself. But my successor at the Chinese library is doing an excellent job, and having her pointing out interesting new material to me is most precious.

Which part(s) of your job as curator do you find most rewarding?

Showing the collection to the public through (small) exhibitions is very rewarding, especially when you meet with the visitors. Helping out students can be too.

A Unique Chinese Collection for the General Public at the Lyon Public Library in France

18

Marc Gilbert
Lyon Public Library, Lyon, France

Introduction

The collections now housed in the Lyon Public Library appeared over the centuries in various parts of the city. Whether private libraries or collections of religious institutions, their history is inextricably bound to that of the old city of Lyon. Although it is unusual to find a wide collection of Chinese in France's municipal libraries, Lyon Public Library is an exception due to its links with the Far East, and more particularly with China, maintained over several centuries. Its Chinese language librarian, Marc Gilbert (Fig. 18.1), offers insights into how the Library developed such a strong collection of materials published during the peaks of different social and political turmoil that took place in mainland China in the 20th century, including the Revolution of 1911, the Republican era, May Fourth Movement, Civil War, Communist Party, Great Leap Forward, Cultural Revolution, Chinese economic reforms, etc.

Could we begin this interview by first introducing yourself, for example, your training and background, and your major roles and duties at the Chinese Librarian at the Lyon Public Library?

I specialised in Chinese studies. In 1998, I graduated with a bachelor's degree from Beijing (Peking) University[1] after spending 4 years at the Department of Chinese Language and Literature.[2] I also have a master's degree in Chinese Language and Literature from Institut National des Langues et Civilisations,[3] Paris.

I worked for 2 years (2000–02) at Taipei Ricci (Institute)[4] Library. This was my first professional experience in a library. I was in charge of setting a new LMS (library management system or integrated library system) and cataloguing the collection of this private research library specialising in Chinese studies.

[1] Peking University – Homepage. Available at: http://english.pku.edu.cn.
[2] Department of Chinese Language and Literature, Peking University – Homepage. Available at: http://chinese.pku.edu.cn/.
[3] Institut National des Langues et Civilisations (INALCO) – Homepage. Available at: http://www.inalco.fr.
[4] Taipei Ricci Institute – Homepage. Available at: http://www.riccibase.com/.

Inside the World's Major East Asian Collections. http://dx.doi.org/10.1016/B978-0-08-102145-3.00018-2

Figure 18.1 Mark Gilbert.

Figure 18.2 Lyon Public Library (exterior).

I have been working at the Lyon Public Library (Fig. 18.2) since 2010. As the Head of Chinese Collections, I am in charge of acquisitions, cataloguing, counselling researchers and readers, hosting official delegation from China or Taiwan, organising exhibitions and following up our partnerships with three major Chinese libraries (Shanghai, Beijing and Guangzhou).

Learning about China from books is often very different from actually visiting the country because people tend to romanticise and idealise about a place they wish to visit. Could you describe your very first impression of China? For example, your very first week/month in the city of Beijing and your initial reactions with the students at Peking University, how are their learning modes different from the French students'?

I arrived in China in August 1992; I was not at Peking University then, but at Beijing International Studies University.[5] I remember it was very hot and very humid. I was surprised to see horse-drawn carts in the close suburb of Beijing. At this time, we could not stay with Chinese students, but at the foreign students' dormitory. Still, it was easy to meet Chinese students, especially around sport facilities, considering that most of them came to that university in order to learn foreign languages. I was amazed by their capacity to reach a very good level, in French for example, without being able to leave the country.

Do you have any statistical figures indicating the number of people at university who are interested in learning the Chinese language in France, or in Lyon in particular?

I do not have access to these figures. Chinese is still taught at junior high schools, high schools and universities in Lyon.

There are so many European languages. In addition, France used to have many colonies; why would the junior high and high schools in Lyon choose to teach Chinese to the French students? Are the teenagers interested in learning Chinese in France? What are the practical reasons behind this school policy?

I believe interest in Chinese language and culture is growing, as Chinese political and economic influences have become increasingly important. It is a matter of opportunity, I suppose.

At what age and how did you develop an interest in the Chinese language and the Chinese culture?

I developed interest in Chinese language and culture when I was a teenager. At first, I wanted to learn Japanese. Unfortunately, there were no Japanese lessons offered where I lived. In my hometown, a Chinese night course opened up and I immediately registered. I then met some Chinese people, among them a professor from Beijing who shared his knowledge of Chinese culture with me. He encouraged me to register at his university, and 1 day, I left for China. I studied for 6 years there.

How did you develop an interest in Chinese language and culture when you were a teenager? Did your classmates and other teenage friend ridicule you for your interests in this area? Because even for many American- or Canadian-born Chinese children and teenagers, it was not considered a 'cool' thing to do. Many of their parents even have to force them to take classes on weekends. What were your own experiences? In addition, you said a professor from Beijing who shared his knowledge of Chinese culture with you – what kind of knowledge had he shared with you that had such a profound impact on you as a young European?

[5] Beijing International Studies University – Homepage. Available at: http://en.bisu.edu.cn.

I can't really explain. I remember being interested in maps, history and geography books. Somehow, Asia attracted me more than other parts of the world. I never had to face the kind of behaviour you described. With reference to this professor from Beijing, I remembered he used to compare France and China, pointing out many similarities. He was also very fond of Chinese history, especially the Ming dynasty. Another topic he liked was linguistics and translation. He contributed to a Chinese–French dictionary and was always trying to find the most appropriate French word for a Chinese one.

How many different languages have you mastered?

Three: French (mother tongue), Chinese and English.

Could you describe your typical day at work as the Chinese Librarian at the Lyon Public Library?[6]

This question is very difficult to answer since 1 day is usually very different from the other. The range of my activity is rather wide. Since our colleagues do not speak Chinese (there are two librarians in the Chinese department), we have to do things that are usually assigned to different working teams in a library: acquisitions, allotting the shelf marks, shelving, part of the delivery, etc. We also assist readers, researchers or project managers; organise exhibitions or presentations of documents; lend documents for exhibitions; take part in conferences; work on projects with our Chinese partners; etc. We have set project plans for each year. Still, these projects can be postponed according to our Library's general activity.

Could you provide a brief introduction to the Lyon Public Library? What were the aims of setting up the Chinese language collection in the Lyon Public Library? Was it meant to support the research needs of the nearby universities or to fulfil the needs of the Chinese immigrants in the city of Lyon?

The Collège de la Trinité's Library was founded in the 16th century. Originally administrated by Jesuits, this Library became a public library in 1765. Nowadays, Lyon Public Library's missions are based on the following five principles:

1. public reading (allowing easy access by the biggest number possible to the essentials of French and foreign publications);
2. information and education (facilitating access to information and knowledge);
3. reference and help (supplementing, by means of an offer, which is simultaneously encyclopaedic, consistent and retrospective, the facilities offered by the other smaller or highly specialised public and university libraries);
4. heritage conservation and appreciation (this mission concerns first and foremost the collections of manuscripts, incunabula, ancient books, artists' books, prints, photographs etc.,

[6] Lyon Public Library – Homepage. Available at: http://www.bm-lyon.fr/?lang=fr.

Figure 18.3 Lyon Public Library: Chinese collections.

which together form the largest collection in France, after that of the National Library of France); and

5. contribution to intellectual and cultural life (facilitating encounters between different publics, creators and bearers of knowledge).

The history of the Chinese collection in the Lyon Public Library began in 1974, with the transfer of the collections of the Franco-Chinese Institute in Lyon[7] (1921–46) passed to the brand new library at Part-Dieu by the Jean Moulin University of Lyon 3. Since that time, the Chinese collection continued to grow (see Fig. 18.3).

As the five mission statements emphasised, the setting up of the Chinese language collection in our Library was made to conserve and appreciate local heritage. Nevertheless, nowadays, this collection is supplementing facilities and resources offered by university libraries in Lyon, fulfilling our Library's reference and help mission. Since Chinese-language books are also available for loan in the literature and children sections, with a mind of public reading, our Library also facilitates access to knowledge and information for Chinese migrants and overseas Chinese.

What is the current size of the Chinese collection of the Lyon Public Library?

It is difficult to answer exactly your question since a lot of documents are still waiting to be catalogued. Nevertheless, the number of the documents we hold is usually estimated around 60,000 printed documents. We also hold 25 linear metres of archives from the former Franco-Chinese Institute in Lyon.

What best prepared you for the position as the Chinese Librarian at the Lyon Public Library?

[7] Franco-Chinese Institute in Lyon – Homepage. Available at: http://www.en.lyon-france.com/Guided-Tours-Excursions/Cultural-Places/The-Franco-Chinese-Institute.

I think my university curriculum best prepared me for my Chinese librarian position. On the one hand, I could acquire a good knowledge of Chinese language and culture and develop an interest in 20th century Chinese literature and history; on the other hand, it helped familiarise me with research methods and taught me strictness and precision.

What scholarly and professional associations are you a part of, and how do they assist you in your work?

I am a member of the European Association of Sinological Librarians[8] and DocAsie, a French network of librarians and documentalists (archivists) specialised in Asia. We share information via mailing lists and newsletters. These professional associations are very useful to share experiences, find solutions, locate documents, inform readers, etc.

Who are the majority of patrons and users at the Lyon Public Library? That is, who comes to see you about your collections? Are they mostly professors or students from higher education institutions? Or are they people from outside the postsecondary sector, that is, the general public?

Most of the users of our Library live in Lyon city or in the Lyon urban community. Regarding our Chinese collection, the situation is a bit different. Some of our readers are local people, while some come from the other parts of the world. In 2014, 41 readers of 8 different nationalities (Chinese, French, Americans, Canadians, New Zealanders, Germans, Koreans and British) asked for our Chinese documents within the Library (we also receive requests via email). Fourteen of them were living in Lyon. Some were researchers and students, while others were retirees, pupils, architects, designers, etc. In the past, we even introduced Chinese books to elementary school children.

Introducing Chinese books to elementary school children, what were the purposes of doing so? What benefits could you bring for your Library or for the City of Lyon?

Since teachers were teaching a unit about Asia, they contacted us to see if we could work together. Since our Library is meant to serve any public and provide access to knowledge and information, this presentation was surely meaningful.

Could you give examples of typical reference/research inquiries issued by the researchers or scholars at the Lyon Public Library?

Since we hold the archives and the library collections from the Franco-Chinese Institute in Lyon, a typical research enquiry would be about students who were registered there and studied in France between 1921 and 1946; for example, Chinese who studied fine arts in France in the 1920s. Since we serve also users who are not

[8] European Association of Sinological Librarians (EASL) – Homepage. Available at: http://www.easl.org.

Figure 18.4 Chinese magazines published by China during 1950–60s.

researchers or who do not read Chinese, another typical inquiry would be for pictorial books about traditional Chinese architecture.

As the Chinese Librarian at the Lyon Public Library, how do you acquire and evaluate your collection?

Our collection comes from three main sources: donations, exchanges, deposit and acquisition. More specifically:

1. Famous French sinologists donated their personal Chinese collection to our Library, among them: Jacques Guillermaz, Michelle Loi, Michel Soymié, Danielle Li and Li Tche-houa.
2. Every year, we send French books to our partners in China and Taiwan. In exchange, we yearly receive over 300 books.
3. The Franco-Chinese Institute collection and the Jesuit collection, including holdings in Chinese, are deposit collections.
4. We purchase new books from a bookstore in Paris and out-of-print books and periodicals from a bookstore in Hong Kong (Fig. 18.4).

Our Library holds a rich collection of Chinese documents from and about 20th century China's intellectual and political history: the Revolution of 1911, Republican era, May Fourth Movement, Civil War, Communist Party, Great Leap Forward, Cultural Revolution, Chinese economic reforms, etc. The value of this collection also lies in documents related to the Diligent Work-Frugal Study Movement and the Franco-Chinese Institute established in Lyon in 1921.

How does the collection catalogue and provide access for users? With a non-Roman script, what challenges does this present to cataloguing?

Considering that we are a public library at a city level, our LMS's functions and priorities are clearly defined according to a public reading politics. We do endeavour to catalogue and give access to our Chinese collection in both pinyin and Chinese characters with reserved success.

Still, if we compare the current situation with what it was decades ago, we improved a lot. At this stage, our main difficulty is not the cataloguing, but getting research results in our online public access catalogue. We try to overcome this difficulty buy joining union catalogues, such as [Online Computer Library Center (OCLC)] WorldCAT[9] or the Rare Books and Special Collections from Taiwan Central Library[10], in order to gain in visibility.

The themes and information needs of libraries, archives and museums (LAMs, as some have referred to them) have increasingly converged. What are your experiences and thoughts about these cultural institutions whose work and best practices now often overlap?

Since LAMs do not necessarily work with the same materials, their professional practices are different, even if they tend to overlap. Despite these differences, these institutions are devoted to knowledge accumulation and organisation; they aim to support education and research, but also to serve users' needs.

At this stage, I do not have much experience to share on this specific subject. Nevertheless, I think that digital curation, for example, can be seen as an opportunity to merge norms and standards, but also to be a source of innovation in knowledge management, with a view to support common goals across these three types of institutions.

The current refugee situation in Europe, has it caused any major impacts on the range and nature of services provided the cultural institutions in France, let's say, libraries in particular?

The current refugee situation in Europe does not have much impact on our Library. Our Library takes part in a programme called Students Welcome Desk, organised by Lyon City and Lyon University.[11] This programme was created to assist foreign students in Lyon. We also take part in Forum refugiés by introducing to migrants our resources and services. Unfortunately, no survey on these two actions has been done so far.

Which part(s) of your job as the Chinese Librarian at the Lyon Public Library do you find most rewarding?

I already mentioned the archives of the Franco-Chinese Institute in Lyon. Since I started working here, I had the opportunity to meet with some descendants of the Chinese students who were registered between 1921 and 1946. It is always a special moment to exchange with them while showing documents left behind by their ancestors. It can also be a very emotional moment. I remember showing to a grandson photographs of the grandfather he never saw.

[9] OCLC WorldCAT – Homepage. Available at: https://www.worldcat.org.

[10] Taiwan Central Library – Homepage. Available at: http://www.ncl.edu.tw/mp.asp?mp=5.

[11] University of Lyon – Homepage. Available at: http://lyon-university.org.

The Kingdom of Naxi Manuscript Collections at the French School of the Far East

19

Dat-Wei Lau
Library of the French School of Asian Studies, Paris, France

Introduction

Founded in 1900 in Saigon, École française d'Extrême-Orient (EFEO/French School of Asian Studies) is a public institution under the aegis of the French Ministry of Higher Education and Research with the mission to study the classical Asian civilisations through humanities and social sciences. Indeed, many of the interdisciplinary projects set up by the EFEO are meant to bring together leading scholars in the fields of anthropology, archaeology, history, philology, religion, history, etc. Managing the Chinese collections at the EFEO library is the Parisian-born Chinese Mr. Dat-Wei Lau (Fig. 19.2), who 'fell' into the librarian profession after failing to become a high school teacher in France. In the following interview, Dat-Wei discusses his experiences in handling the Naxi (Chinese minority group) manuscript collection at the EFEO library (see Fig. 19.1), as well as the minimum professional qualification required to practise as a librarian in France.

Could we begin this interview by first introducing yourself, for example, your training and background, and your major roles and duties at the librarian at the Bibliothèque de l'EFEO?

I was born in Paris, and my parents from came from Hong Kong originally. I entered a bilingual school (French–English), École Jeannine Manuel Dupleix,[1] at kindergarten level. After graduating from high school, I decided to learn Chinese because, in spite of my origins, I never learned Mandarin (Cantonese was spoken in my household), nor did I know how to read or write.

After obtaining a master's degree in classical Chinese linguistics at Institut National des Langues et Civilisations Orientales,[2] I decided to give teaching a try; I prepared for the national secondary school teaching degree in Chinese. The annual national exam is composed of one written exam (where a first selection is made) and an oral exam (where

[1] École Jeannine Manuel Dupleix – Homepage. Available at: http://www.ecolejeanninemanuel.org/fr/.
[2] Institut National des Langues et Civilisations (INALCO) – Homepage. Available at: http://www.inalco.fr/.

Inside the World's Major East Asian Collections. http://dx.doi.org/10.1016/B978-0-08-102145-3.00019-4

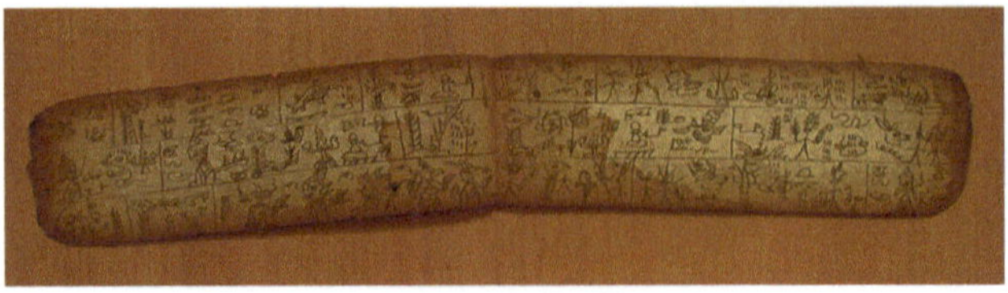

Figure 19.1 Mss Nashi 46.1; Naxi Dongba manuscript from the collections of the Bibliothèque de l'Ecole française d'Extrême Orient (EFEO).

Figure 19.2 Dat-Wei Lau. Librarian in charge of the Chinese collections of the EFEO library.

the final candidates are chosen). After failing two times at the oral exam, I decided to apply for a librarian position at the former *Bibliothèque InterUniversitaire des Langues Orientales*, the current Bibliothèque Universitaire des Langues et Civilisations (BULAC),[3] where there was an opening for the Chinese collections. I ended up working for this institution for a period of 5 years, during which I had the opportunity, by working on several projects, of learning multiple aspects of how a library works.

After this 5-year period, I heard of an opening for the Chinese collections at the library of the EFEO.[4] I applied for it and was chosen; I am now in my third year in this prestigious school.

My role at the EFEO library is to be responsible for its Chinese collections, from acquisition to cataloguing, without mentioning giving bibliographic information to readers and communicating with researchers and professors of our school in order to provide the best possible services to this key section of our readers. In addition to this, one of the most rewarding roles of my position is presenting and promoting our library and its collections towards foreign guests, outside colleagues or during conferences.

[3] BULAC – Homepage. Available at: http://www.bulac.fr/.
[4] École Française d'Extrême-Orient (EFEO) – Homepage. Available at: http://www.efeo.fr/index.php?l=EN.

For example, I have recently taken part in a conference concerning Naxi (纳西) culture, where I have given a presentation of our collection of Naxi manuscripts.

According to you, your family was originally from Hong Kong. Could you tell us more about the Hong Kong and mainland Chinese immigrant population and the situation in Paris, as well as France in general?

One of the last French censuses showed the number of Chinese (Chinese passport, or French passport with Chinese origins) was approximately 600,000. Chinese immigration in France can be summarised by three major communities: Chauzhou (潮州), Wenzhou (温州) and Northeast China (Dongbei/东北). The communities are, in majority, located in Paris, in Parisian suburbs, or in the north, around the city of Lille and in the city of Lyon. Hong Kong immigrants are not very numerous; the Cantonese-speaking community normally came from Vietnam, Laos and Cambodia in the 1970s, and these immigrants originally emigrated from Canton, the so-called 'boat-people'. From the 1980s to 2008, Chinese immigration came mostly from the region of Wenzhou. The last and most talked about immigrants are the illegal ones from Dongbei. Ironically, they are the least in numbers, but the most talked about in the media; I think this community comforts French people in their vision of the 'Chinese', meaning mysterious with its load of secrets, with a pinch of triads, of illegal immigrants.

In the student community, there are about 50,000 Chinese students in France, which make them one of the most important in terms of numbers. Their choice is based on the fact that studying in France is cheaper than in Anglo-Saxon countries, but still of good quality.

When you said the Chinese illegal immigrants from Dongbei 'comfort' French people in their vision of the 'Chinese', did you mean 'confronts' and not 'comforts'?

I did mean 'comforts', meaning the illegal immigrants satisfy the cliché that certain French people have of Chinese people; I wanted to point out that certain French people have some prejudice on foreigners, and in that event, though most Chinese people live in France abiding to French laws, the media prefers talking about those who cross the line.

For the new Chinese immigrants who have received a university or above education, after settling down in France, what kind of careers would they usually choose? In addition, what about the second generation of China immigrants who were born and raised in France (like you); would their choices and career opportunities be any different, given that they have a better master of the French language and the lifestyle in a foreign country?

To my knowledge, Chinese students do not necessarily stay in France at the end of their studies, but not knowing a lot on the subject, I will not speculate too much. Concerning the second-generation Chinese, I do not think that there are any restrictions regarding the line of work for a French-born Chinese, if we put aside those who need/want to take over the family business. But again, I will not hypothesise because I am no expert on the matter.

Do you have any statistical figures indicating the number of people at university who are interested in learning an East Asian language in France, for example, Chinese, Korean or Japanese?

Chinese is in the top five of the most taught foreign languages. The last census (2013, I think) counted 30,000 students of Chinese, and the previous one revealed 9000, so the next one should be interesting. Most importantly, Chinese is now an option in primary schools.

In North America and other British Commonwealth countries, as well as other former British colonies, one needs to have a master's degree in library and information science (LIS) as a minimum professional qualification requirement in order to practice in the field of LIS. I wonder if the situation is similar in France? Are there also the same/similar professional qualification requirements in France? If yes, would such LIS professional qualifications issued by a university in France also enable one to seek employments in other French-speaking countries in Europe and North America, for example, Canada, Switzerland, Belgium, etc.?

There are indeed different degrees for librarianship; it is not compulsory though, and in fields like mine, most librarians are chosen among linguistic specialists. Libraries consider that it is easier to teach librarianship to a language specialist than foreign civilisation to a librarian. French qualifications, in general, are recognised all over Europe and Western countries, so I would think it would be the same for LIS professional qualifications.

Which are the universities that offer LIS and archival science programmes in France?

Numerous universities have degrees in LIS, but the most renowned program of LIS is at the École nationale supérieure des sciences de l'information et des bibliothèques (National Superior School of Library and Information Sciences).[5] As for archival sciences, the most prestigious school is the École nationale des chartes,[6]which is one of the most prestigious schools in France.

Is that true that university education is totally free in France? One does not need to pay any tuition, and one could choose to study as long as one wishes? One could also

[5] École nationale supérieure des sciences de l'information et des bibliothèques (ENSSIB) – Homepage. Available at: http://www.enssib.fr/about-enssib-0.

[6] Ecole nationale des chartes – Homepage. Available at: http://www.enc-sorbonne.fr/.

choose to undertake the graduation examination whenever one wishes, as long as the student is read?

Education in France is not free, tuition exists, but it is indeed less expensive than in Anglo-Saxon countries. The amount of the tuition depends on the level of studies that one pursues; lower-level degrees are less expensive than higher ones. Tuition fees also vary; whether you attend a public institution or a private one, the difference is very important. One can put a stop to one's studies and resume whenever one chooses, if one has the requirements. The graduation examinations are decided by the school or by the thesis director.

Could you describe your typical day at work as the librarian at the library of the EFEO?

As the librarian for Chinese collections at the library of EFEO, an average day is occupied by acquisitions, cataloguing, answering to questions by readers, students, professors and researchers or collaboration projects with the photo library of the school, or the publications service. There is no typical day, and I never know when a Chinese delegation comes to visit or when one of our researchers comes to visit us.

Could you provide a brief introduction to the library of the EFEO and its current size of its collections?

Founded in Hanoi in 1903, the EFEO library bears witness to the manner in which the organisation's centres of interest have evolved over time. During the Indochinese period (1900–57), the School's mission was to collect all printed books and manuscripts relating to French Indochina and to acquire all the important publications on East Asia. The library added to its collections by means of regular purchases, gifts and exchanges, but it also acted as a depositary for books it printed itself. In 1944, the EFEO's Hanoi library contained approximately 80,000 volumes (including manuscripts), half of which were in European languages. At the end of the colonial period, agreements concerning the way in which the EFEO's collections should be shared between France and the three new nations of the former Indochina stipulated that works in European languages should be kept by the School, while works in local languages should go to the new countries. The most important local language manuscripts were then microfilmed. Later, several thousand books, most of them on Southeast Asia, were sent to France to form the core of the School's Parisian library, opened in 1968 at the same time as the Instituts d'Extrême Orient, which later became the Maison de l'Asie.

Today, the EFEO library (Fig. 19.3) contains approximately 100,000 monographs and over 1700 periodicals (700 of them current). Its collections also include several thousand rubbings and photographs. The library has evolved to keep abreast of the development of new fields of research, which now cover a large part of Asia. Historical collections covering Japan, China and South Asia have been added to those on Southeast Asia. While policy concerning the accumulation and study of documents has remained faithful to the School's core disciplines (archaeology, epigraphy, ethnology, religions, etc.), emerging fields have not been neglected, as is witnessed by joint research programmes run with institutions possessing similar collections (the Collège

Figure 19.3 Reading room of the EFEO library.

de France,[7] the Bibliothèque des langues orientales). The exchange of publications with Asian, European and American universities and research centres constitutes an important part of the acquisitions process. More specifically, Chinese collections have over 20,000 monographs and 450 periodical titles (175 of them current). The collections are 75% in Chinese. We are specialised in Daoism/Taoism and Buddhism studies, archaeology, folklore, religions (民间宗教), etc.

How did you library obtain such a significant collection of Naxi manuscripts? Was it via private donation? What kind of people would come to consult this Naxi collection?

Our Naxi manuscript collection was constituted at the beginning of the 1940s; it was acquired by the famous Dr. J.F. Rock, who, at that time, was a correspondent for our school in China. J.F. Rock was well known for being the father of the Naxi studies in the West. The manuscripts were bought by Dr. Rock directly in Lijiang, so the paper support was made by the Naxi; they have an important papermaking tradition. From what I understand, they used two types of trees, cut a very fine piece of bark and plunged it into different kinds of liquid and let it dry under sunlight.

What best prepared you for the position as the librarian at the library of EFEO?

My experience in working in libraries, my studies and my proficiency in foreign languages.

What scholarly and professional associations are you a part of, and how do they assist you in your work?

I am part of two professional associations, DocAsie and EASL. DocAsie[8] is a French association where librarians on Asian studies meet annually in order to share their

[7] Collège de France – Homepage. Available at: http://www.college-de-france.fr/site/college/index.htm.
[8] DocAsie – Homepage. Available at: http://docasie.cnrs.fr/?lang=fr.

experiences, their knowledge. EASL, as you might know, is the European Association of Sinological Librarians.[9] Being new to the trade, I found it really enriching to be able to talk about the profession with colleagues with more than 20 years of experience, for instance, our library has not yet switched to e-resources, for numerous reasons, such as institution not ready, no specific demand from readers, but I know who I can turn to when that will happen.

Who are the majority patrons and users at the library of EFEO? That is, who comes to see you about your collections? Are they mostly professors or students from higher education institutions? Or are they people from outside the postsecondary sector, that is, the general public?

Our patrons and users are researchers, professors and doctoral degree students.

As the librarian at the EFEO, how do you acquire and evaluate your collection?

Acquisition is made in different ways, such as suggestions by our professors, by our patrons or RSS feeds on websites of research centres, publishers or catalogues of our vendor China International Book Trading Corporation (CIBTC).[10] RSS refers to '**R**eally **S**imple **S**yndication'; once you have established an RSS feed with a webpage, you will receive a notification when new information is published on the webpage.

Once the books arrive, I generally check in the bibliography to see what we are missing. Evaluation is validated by the patrons, but apart from questioning our integrated library system, I do not have another solution.

How does the collection catalogue and provide access for users? With a non-Roman script, what challenges does this present to cataloguing? Is there any?

Our collections appear in two catalogues, SUDOC (Système universitaire de documentation),[11] a union catalogue of all university documentations in France, and Koha (integrated library system) catalogue of the BULAC library and its partners, which we are part of. Both catalogues are in Chinese in double scripture, Chinese characters and Pinyin. I personally do not know if this represents a challenge because I came to cataloguing when this was already put in place, and I've always been taught to catalogue this way, so to me, there is no real challenge.

Are there any Asian/Chinese–French history collections that document the experience of Asian migrants in France? Are there any that we should know about?

There are quite a few, but not being a specialist on the subject, I would not be the one to turn to.

[9] European Association of Sinological Librarians (EASL) – Homepage. Available at: http://www.easl.org/.

[10] China International Book Trading Corporation (CIBTC) (中国图书首页) – Homepage. Available at: http://www.cibtc.com.cn/gtweb/enaction.do.

[11] SUDOC (Système universitaire de documentation) – Homepage. Available at: http://www.sudoc.abes.fr/xslt/.

The themes and information needs of libraries, archives and museums (LAMs, as some have referred to them) have increasingly converged. What are your experiences and thoughts about these cultural institutions whose work and best practices now often overlap?

Our library has an archive section; a colleague has been hired in order to organise our archives, and we have more and more patrons coming to consult the school's archives. One of our institutional partners is the Guimet Museum,[12] a museum and library with which we have many professional exchanges. Being close to my colleagues in these fields, I never hesitate to question them on their work and vice versa. I do not necessarily have a lot of experience on those fields, but getting to talk with them has showed me the subtle differences in our professions.

The current refugee situation in Europe, has it caused any major impacts on the range and nature of services provided the cultural institutions in France, let's say, library in particular?

Being in the centre of Paris, in a research library on Asia, the refugee situation has no real impact on us or on our services.

Which part(s) of your job as the librarian do you find most rewarding?

I think that the most rewarding part of my job, also the one I most fear, is when I have to promote our collections in conferences. I fear it because I do not like talking in front of an audience, but there are no circumstances where I feel more useful in my job.

[12] Guimet Museum – Homepage. Available at: http://www.guimet.fr/en/.

A Library That Reflects the History of French Interest in China and East Asia

20

Soline Lau-Suchet
Bibliothèque universitaire des langues et civilisations (BULAC), Paris, France

Introduction

With part of the collection dating all the way back to the 17th century, Bibliothèque universitaire des langues et civilisations (BULAC; University Library for Languages and Civilizations Studies) was founded with a specific mission to bring together the holdings of around 20 libraries, aiming to create relevant and robust collections of books and documents, mainly in vernacular languages, with special emphasis on Oriental and African Studies. Parisian-born, French-educated Soline Lau-Suchet (Fig. 20.1) is currently serving as the Librarian of the premodern Chinese collection at the BULAC. In the following interview, Ms. Lau-Suchet discusses her joy in being able to combine her love of library work with her love of the Chinese language and culture.

Could we begin this interview by first introducing yourself, that is, your training and background and your major roles and duties at the BULAC[1]?

Born not far from Paris in 1980, I naturally went to the French capital to complete my studies. I attended three institutions: Paris-Sorbonne University[2] (1998–2002), where I studied history and Latin; École nationale des Chartes (ÉNC), where I graduated with a diploma of archivist-paleographer (2002–06) and the École des hautes études en sciences sociales (EHESS, or School of Advanced Studies in the Social Sciences),[3] where I graduated with a master's degree in history of Chinese civilization (2005–06).

In 2007, I moved to Lyon, where I graduated 1 year later from École nationale supérieure des sciences de l'information et des bibliothèques (ENSSIB, or National Superior School of Information Science and Libraries) as a library curator. After graduation, in September 2008, I was hired by the former Bibliothèque interuniversitaire

[1] Bibliothèque universitaire des langues et civilisations (BULAC) – Homepage. Available at: http://www.bulac.fr/.

[2] Paris-Sorbonne University – Homepage. Available at: http://www.english.paris-sorbonne.fr/?lang=en.

[3] École des hautes études en sciences sociales (EHESS or School of Advanced Studies in the Social Sciences) – Homepage. Available at: http://www.ehess.fr/en/.

Inside the World's Major East Asian Collections. http://dx.doi.org/10.1016/B978-0-08-102145-3.00020-0

Figure 20.1 Photograph of Soline Lau-Suchet (2014) © Grégoire Maisonneuve.

des langues orientales (BIULO, or University Library of Oriental Languages), where I was given charge of the Chinese language collections. My main tasks were to select, order and catalogue monographs and collections from China and Taiwan; help students and scholars with their bibliographic research; and build an open-shelf Chinese collection for the future reading rooms of the BULAC project (see as follows).

In 2011, BIULO merged with the BULAC project. The BULAC project began in 2000, aiming at gathering in one modern institution the non-Western collections scattered in 19 different prestigious Parisian research libraries. It opened in 2011, sharing the same building as the renovated Institut national des langues et civilisations orientales (INALCO, or National Institute for Oriental Languages and Civilizations).[4]

In France, library curators tend to be appointed to managerial more than scientific charges. That was how, in 2012, I was asked to take charge of a newly created position whose mission was to promote enhanced cooperation with the various teaching and research units in the area of non-Western studies. In curating the Chinese collections, I was helped by another librarian who took over the cataloguing part, while I focused on selecting Chinese prints, evaluating electronic resources, providing bibliographic information, training students and researchers as well as promoting the library's Chinese collections (publication and exhibitions).

At what age and how did you develop an interest in the Chinese language and culture?

[4] Institut national des langues et civilisations orientales (INALCO or National Institute for Oriental Languages and Civilizations) – Homepage. Available at: http://www.inalco.fr/.

Figure 20.2 Research reading room (Chinese collections) © Grégoire Maisonneuve.

This is a long story, but to put it briefly, while I was studying history, I was keenly interested by foreign countries' history, but hugely annoyed and taken aback by the underlying ethnocentrism of history teaching in France. I remember my medieval history teacher telling us in 1999 (I was 18 years old then): '*In 800, Charlemagne was crown emperor and thus founded the major empire of that time*', and I thought, '*What about the Chinese Empire!?*'. I was also very intrigued by the way East Asian countries (mostly China and Japan) had withstood imperialism and had not been acculturated to the monotheisms, which had slowly but surely overrun the whole world. I did not know a thing about these countries, but it seemed to me that these old civilizations, contrary to other colonised regions, had such a consistent cultural and philosophical system that they resisted assimilation. I wanted to know more about their history and philosophy to understand how, contrary to the rest of the world, they had resisted imperialism. Although this was a naïve and simplistic view of the situation, it nevertheless encouraged me to take a first step onto this path. The first step was to learn their language. As China was the oldest civilization of this part of the world, I decided to start with the Chinese language. While my studies destined me for curating work in French library or archive collections (ÉNC is specialized in medieval and modern French history, archives and materials), I decided to take on Chinese language lessons in 2003. When I had to decide on my dissertation thesis at ÉNC, I chose to study French imperialism in China, and in 2005, I asked for 6 months leave in order to travel to China and test my interest. I must confess I immediately fell in love with China and Chinese people, and decided my future job would have to do with China. Then, while studying at ENSSIB, I took the opportunity of a mandatory long-term training to spend 8 months in Fuzhou, working on a library project under sinologist Kristofer Schipper's direction.

Could you provide a brief introduction to the BULAC, particularly the Chinese collections that you are in charge of?

While the BULAC is a brand new library (see images of the library in Figs 20.2–20.4), its collections have a long history, and part of it started to be collected as early as the 17th

Figure 20.3 View of the study reading room from the mezzanine © Grégoire Maisonneuve.

Figure 20.4 Photo of the study reading room © Grégoire Maisonneuve.

century. Though the BULAC's holdings come from various libraries, the most important of them, in size and prestige, originate from the late BIULO, which started as the research and teaching library of the École des langues orientales vivantes (ÉLOV), opened in 1795 and ancestor of INALCO. Its library later integrated the collections of the École des 'Jeunes de langue', founded by Colbert in 1669 and closed in the first half of the 19th century.

BULAC now holds 1.5 million documents, mostly in vernacular languages, covering 180 countries and 350 languages written in 80 different scripts. The most important collections, in size and quality, are the Arabic, Persian and Turkish holdings (Near and Middle East section); the Russian holdings (European section); the Chinese and Japanese collections (Asian section) and the African collections. The old and precious collections are unique in size (around 90,000 vols.) and diversity: rare prints, manuscripts (around 4000), old periodicals, archives, photographs, etc.

Furthermore, because of its link with ÉLOV, BULAC's collections reflect closely the history of French interest towards non-Western countries.

The Chinese collections originate from the research and studies library of the ÉLOV. The Chinese chair was created in 1843, following the *Treaty of Nanking* (南京条约), and marked an important step for Chinese studies in France. But the first goal of this teaching was to train translators and diplomats in order to carry out French diplomatic and commercial ambitions in China. In order to do that, teachers and students needed Chinese documentation aside from the books published on China in Western countries. The needs were focused on linguistic tools (dictionaries, encyclopaedias), Chinese classics (in order to give the students the basics in Chinese literati culture of that time), books about contemporary China's organisation (laws, administrations, technics, customs, etc.) and literature.

In 1872, the school set up a network of providers in the Chinese Empire through the French missionaries, consuls and trained translators posted in China. The first Chinese collections arrived mainly from Guangzhou through the Consulate, Chongqing and Shanghai through the diocese and Beijing through the 'Collège des interprètes'. In the first part of the 20th century, the acquisition process came from the auction of private libraries, bibliographical missions sent to China conjointly by ÉLOV and the Institute of Chinese Studies (Collège de France)[5] and donations. The latter came mostly from explorers, missionaries and scholars who had travelled to China as well as previous students of ÉLOV who worked in China, for instance, Jean Joseph Beauvais, who gave his collection of classics, local monographs and literature to the library in 1928.

Between the 1920s and 1956, the flow of acquisitions ran almost dry due to the Chinese Civil War, but resumed after the recognition of the People's Republic of China by the French government in 1964.

Though the Chinese collections started with an encyclopaedic ambition, with time, they focused on three main areas: history, literature and language and linguistics. Since the end of the 1990s, an effort has been made in the social sciences area in order to take into account the new research trends. While it used to be a research collection, since the opening to BULAC next to INALCO (Fig. 20.5), our recent efforts have focused on acquiring the documentation needed for undergraduates.

According to Mr Dat-Wei Lau, the BULAC Library in Paris is one of the most important libraries about Asia in Paris as well as in France. Could you describe why the BULAC Library deserves such a high reputation?

The reason lies once again in the role of ÉLOV. In the 19th and 20th century, the School opened new languages chairs each time French ambitions abroad required it, often setting the first step of a new field of studies. Accordingly, the Library started to acquire books from the concerned areas. The specificity of BULAC's Asiatic collection is partly due to the number of languages it covers: Vietnamese, Burmese, Malay and Indonesian, Filipino, Laotian, Cambodian, Thai, Bengali, Hindi, Urdu, Pashto,

[5] Collège de France – Homepage. Available at: http://www.college-de-france.fr/site/college/index.htm.

Figure 20.5 BULAC and INALCO building from outside © Grégoire Maisonneuve.

Panjabi, Tamil, Nepali and Tibetan, Chinese, Korean, Mongolian and Japanese, including the numerous minority languages and dialects spoken in these countries. Furthermore, due to some of these countries' individual history, part of these collections are not available anywhere else, not even in their country of origin.

The Chinese/East Asian collections at the BULAC Library, compared to the collections at the National Library of France,[6] what are the differences in terms of collection size and coverage?

I must confess I have no idea of the exact size of the National Library of France's Chinese collections, and it depends on if you are asking about the Richelieu-Louvois Library[7] or the François-Mitterand Library.[8]

[6] National Library of France – Homepage. Available at: http://www.bnf.fr/en/tools/lsp.site_map.html.
[7] National Library of France, Richelieu-Louvois Library – Homepage. Available at: http://www.bnf.fr/en/bnf/sites_eng/a.richelieu-louvois_library.html.
[8] National Library of France, François-Mitterand Library – Homepage. Available at: http://www.bnf.fr/en/bnf/sites_eng/a.francois_mitterrand_library.html.

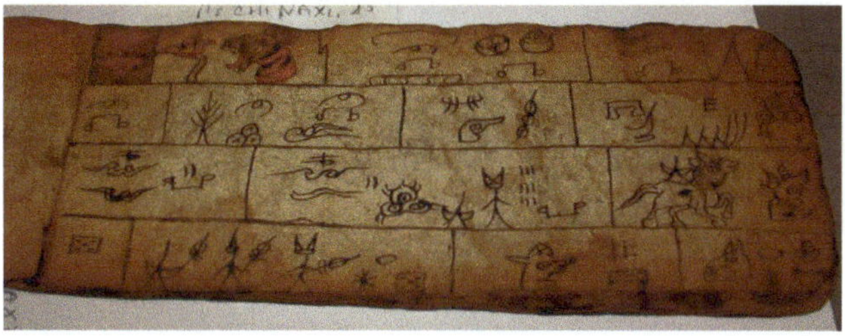

Figure 20.6 Naxi manuscript (ms.chi.naxi.10) CC BY-NC-SA 4.0 BULAC.

Regarding the latter (the François-Mitterand Library), its collections are mostly focused on Chinese contemporary literature and art. This is a small collection, which started in the second part of the 20th century, and cannot be compared in size with the BULAC's. Our collection is more complete on literature, but, contrary to the National Library of France, we do not specialise in contemporary art where we mostly buy reference books.

As for the Richelieu-Louvois Library, its collections are the earliest collected ones in terms of prints and, starting from Pelliot's discoveries, the most prestigious ones in terms of manuscripts. Therefore, our collections cannot compare to it when it comes to seniority and preciousness. Regarding disciplines, the Richelieu-Louvois Library focuses on classical China and book history. The BULAC's collection is more encyclopaedic (we cover all areas, except medicine and sciences, at least for the study level), while focusing on history, literature (both classical, modern and contemporary), language and social sciences. I must add that due to the number of sinological institutions in France, a kind of complementary acquisition plan is being implemented on the national level, and BULAC nowadays tends to focus on post-1911 China.

What is the size of the collections? Could you describe the highlights of the Chinese collections? How does this collection differ from the other Far East collections, that is, Japanese and Korean collections at the BULAC?

It is always difficult to give a precise figure, since Chinese publications have long been dominated by collections. It is easier for me to talk in terms of volumes. Including the Western books on China, it should be above 70,000 volumes (85% in Chinese language) and around 180 periodical current titles. The specificity of this collection lies in its historical, language and literary materials, especially literary and historical collections, including some rare local monographs. Another lies in its 'multilingualism', since the Chinese section holds various materials in other languages and dialects spoken in China. Most of the collection is made of prints, but the BULAC does hold some manuscripts from China, including Naxi (纳西) manuscripts (25) (Fig. 20.6), Yi (彝文) manuscripts (around 50) (Fig. 20.7), Chinese manuscripts and archives (not yet inventoried).

Some highlights (I only talk about Chinese-language materials) include:

- local monographs, originals and reprints
- periodicals from the late Qing dynasty

Figure 20.7 Stack where precious books and manuscripts are held (Yi manuscripts boxes) © Grégoire Maisonneuve.

- Qing Dynasty prints, including numerous xylographies (above 1000 vols.)
- Chinese Republican era (1912–49) prints (above 2500 vols.)
- 18th and 19th Chinese publications from the Jesuits

The Chinese collections are older than the Japanese and Korean ones, but the latter are more prestigious, since French libraries with Japanese and Korean holdings are rarer. The Japanese collections, collected from the 1870s, are the oldest and most important ones in France (above 60,000 volumes and 147 current periodical titles) and especially fine in literature and old periodicals. The Korean collections are smaller (15,000 volumes and a dozen periodicals) and focus on history and literature.

Could you describe the staffing structure at your department?

The Collections Department is divided in three sections, that is: Asia; Europe (excluding Western Europe) and Africa, Middle East and Central Asia.

In most cases, there is only one librarian or a part-time librarian in charge of one or various language collections (acquisition, cataloguing, promotion). There are currently 20 librarians working in the Collections Department, including nine librarians for the Asian section: four full-time librarians (Chinese/Japanese/Vietnamese/Urdu–Punjabi–Pashto) and five part-time librarians (Mongol–Korean/Indonesia/Tamil–Telugu/Bengali/Chinese retro-cataloguing).

Since we cover so many countries and languages, we sadly cannot hire a librarian for each of them, which explains why the department is organised around 'permanent' collections and 'rotating' collections. It means that some positions are permanent, according to the collection size and the number of students and scholars (for instance: Chinese, Japanese, Arabic, Persian, Russian), and some are short-term positions, usually 2 years (for instance, in the Asian section: Tibetan, Burmese, Nepalese, Malaysian, etc.)

What best prepared you for the position of librarian at the BULAC?

I feel that both my library training and my years of research on China helped me. They are very complementary.

What scholarly and professional associations are you a part of, and how do they assist you in your work?

I am a member of the board of the Association française des études chinoises (French Association of Chinese Studies)[9], publisher of the French academic journal *Etudes chinoises*. It is a way for me to stay close to French Chinese studies developments, scholars and PhD students. Moreover, as a librarian, it seems to me that working closely with researchers helps in my everyday job at the library.

I am also a member of EASL (European Association of Sinological Librarians).[10] Being a member of this association has proved very useful for me, especially when I started working, since I could benefit from the knowledge and expertise of my European colleagues. We exchange feedback on our book providers, on electronic resources and our collections, which helps in appraising Chinese resources in Europe and helping more efficiently our scholars and students. It is also a place where we can share our difficulties and the challenges special collections face in an evolving world.

Who are the majority of the patrons who use the BULAC? That is, who comes to see you about your collections? Are they mostly professors or students from higher education institutions? Or are they people from outside the postsecondary sector, that is, the general public?

While BULAC is an academic library, it is open to all and you do not need special credentials to use our collections. I would say that two-thirds of our readers are students, professors and scholars from various institutions around Paris, France and abroad, and one-third are people from outside the postsecondary sector.

Could you give examples of typical reference/research inquiries issued by the researchers or scholars at the BULAC?

The researchers and scholars are usually autonomous. Most of their requests concern books they want us to buy, books they cannot find and help for using electronic resources. Due to the encylopaedic nature of our collections, it is difficult for me to single out a specific example.

As the individual in charge of the Chinese collections, how do you acquire and evaluate your collection?

[9] Association française des études chinoises (French Association of Chinese Studies) – Homepage. Available at: http://www.chinesestudies.eu/.

[10] European Association of Sinological Librarians (EASL) – Homepage. Available at: http://www.easl.org/.

For students (meaning undergraduate), I use both their professors' bibliographies and reference works' bibliographies, while following which books are used and which are not.

For the research collections, I select books according to the following factors:

1. our original plan of acquisitions, based on the historical strengths of our Chinese collections: history, literature, linguistics and social sciences, etc.;
2. the complementary acquisition plan implemented by French Chinese Studies libraries (meaning that I will not buy huge collections on Buddhism or archaeology, which are the disciplines covered by the École française d'Extrême-Orient library);
3. requests from students, researchers and scholars, etc.;
4. the research projects of French scholars on Chinese studies in order to keep track of current research and the topics of PhD students;
5. the areas not covered by any library in order to build a reference collection in these areas to scholars who need it (for instance: Taiwan studies, history of education, law, etc.); and
6. I use the same basis to evaluate our collections, adding selective requests from our library system, bibliographical monitoring and studies on sinological libraries around the world.

In the past few years, the BULAC has been engaged in the digitisation of some of its collections. What are some of the projects of the BULAC and what future plans are there for its digital collections?

We are actually quite late in the digitisation process. During the past years, we mostly digitised small corpuses, which are exceptional and easy to digitise on-site, for instance, our Naxi manuscripts, some of our Arabic manuscripts, or illustrated Japanese periodicals. But we are currently engaged in a huge project, which would see the digitisation of our collections of Arabic, Persian and Ottoman manuscripts, the heart of our historical collections. We are also working on another project with other research libraries, which will focus on old prints' digitisation.

How does the collection catalogue and provide access for users? With a non-Roman script, what challenges does this present to cataloguing? Are there any?

We catalogue in the SUDOC (the Union Catalogue of French University Libraries).[11] For non-Roman scripts, we use bi-script cataloguing, meaning that we catalogue in transliteration and in the original script. For Chinese, there is one challenge we have not met yet: our catalogue system does not include a correspondence index between traditional and simplified characters, meaning that users have to type traditional characters if they want to find a book written in traditional characters, the same for simplified characters.

Which part(s) of your job as curator do you find most rewarding?

[11] SUDOC – Homepage. Available at: http://www.sudoc.abes.fr//DB=2.1/LNG=EN/?COOKIE=U10178,Klecteurweb,D2.1,E99ce0695-3b9,I250,B341720009+,SY,A%5C9008+1,,J,H2-26,,29,,34,,39,,44,,49-50,,53-78,,80-87,NLECTEUR+PSI,R133.51.6.189,FN.

There are so many of them! I would say that the times I feel the most rewarded are when I see the look of relief or gratitude on the face of a scholar or student I helped find what he needed, and also when they come back to me or recommend someone to me, because they feel they can count on me.

But I also love teaching students, some professors having asked me to take part in their teaching. And of course, it is always a pleasure to promote the Chinese collections by taking part in conferences or organising exhibitions.

Do you have any questions for me? Is there anything you would like to add before we finish this interview?

I look forward to reading your book! I am sure it will be most useful.

The Most Comprehensive Collection of Asian Art at the Guimet Museum (National Museum of Asian Art), Paris

21

Cristina Cramerotti
Musée national des arts asiatiques – Guimet, Paris, France

Introduction

Founded in Paris in 1879 by a French industrialist, Émile Étienne Guimet, the Guimet Museum is most notable for having one of the largest and most complete collections of Asian art outside Asia. From his many travels around the world, Emile Guimet brought back large collections of objects and works of art, which he first exhibited in his museum of Lyon, his hometown, in 1879. The Guimet Museum is internationally well-known for its fine collection of Chinese and Japanese porcelains, manuscripts and many artefacts relating not merely to the religions of the East, but also to those of Ancient Egypt, Greece, Rome, etc. In the following interview, in addition to sharing with our readers her valuable experiences as a library professional in the museum setting, multilingual Cristina Cramerotti (Fig. 21.1, curator of the Guimet Museum Library), discusses in detail the various professional training and career opportunities available for working as a librarian–curator in France.

Could we begin this interview by first introducing yourself, for example, your training and education background, and your major roles and duties at the Conservatrice de la bibliothèque, Musée national des arts asiatiques Guimet (The Guimet Museum)[1]?

I studied Asian languages at Institut national des langues et civilisations orientales[2] and history at the École des hautes études en sciences sociales[3] in Paris, then attended a special training school on information and communication sciences after passing a civil service examination to become a librarian–curator (conservateur in French).

[1] The Guimet Museum – Homepage. Available at: http://www.guimet.fr/en/.
[2] Institut nationale des langues et civilisations orientales (INALCO) – Homepage. Available at: http://www.inalco.fr/.
[3] Ecole des hautes études en sciences sociales (EHESS) – Homepage. Available at: http://www.ehess.fr/en/.

Inside the World's Major East Asian Collections. http://dx.doi.org/10.1016/B978-0-08-102145-3.00021-2

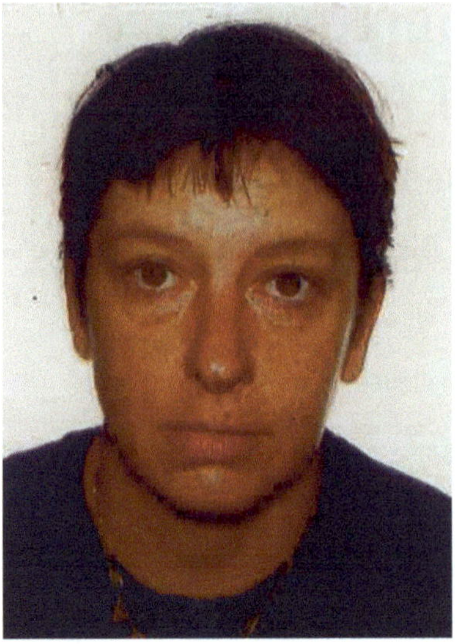

Figure 21.1 Cristina Cramerotti.

I worked at the Bibliothèque des langues orientales (Paris) as East Asian Department Curator for 7 years, then as director of the libraries of the École française d'Extrême-Orient[4] (Paris and seven locations in Asia) for 8 years. Since 2011, I have been serving as a curator of the library and archives of Musée national des arts asiatiques Guimet[5] (Figs 21.2 and 21.3).

Could you elaborate more on your education before becoming a curator? You mention you entered training school for information and communication sciences. What does that look like? What types of courses did you take, and what was the educational qualification that you obtained from this programme?

In France, you have to pass a nationwide examination if you want to become a civil servant (museum and libraries are mostly public services). Depending on the examination, you will enter a dedicated training school; for libraries, it is École nationale supérieure des sciences de l'information et des bibliothèques[6] in Lyon. The programme lasts for 1.5 years, during which we had theoretical courses and training sessions in different libraries (4 to 5 months). Courses included: history of libraries and librarianship, management, law, informatics (at that time, it was just beginning to enter libraries), etc. We also had some ideas on cataloguing (UNIMARC) and indexing, but an overview, since at that level (catégorie A), we

[4] Ecole française d'Extrême-Orient (EFEO) – Homepage. Available at: http://www.efeo.fr/index.php?l=EN.

[5] Musée national des arts asiatiques Guimet – Homepage. Available at: http://en.parismuseumpass.com/musee-musee-national-des-arts-asiatiques-guimet-10.htm.

[6] Ecole nationale des sciences de l'information et des bibliothèques (ENSSIB) – Homepage. Available at: http://www.enssib.fr/.

Figure 21.2 Musée national des arts asiatiques Guimet (exterior).

Figure 21.3 Musée national des arts asiatiques Guimet (interior).

were supposed to be managers. I must confess that many theoretical courses where quite boring.

The training sessions were much more interesting; one took me to the Library of Congress (US)[7] for 3 months, where I worked on the Chinese and Burmese retro-conversion project. At the end of the programme, you have to write a paper on a subject you choose.

With the diploma in my pocket, I applied for a job on a list. Being specialised in Asian studies, I had no difficulty finding a job at the Bibliothèque des langues orientales.

How many different languages have you mastered?

It depends on what you mean by 'mastering'. I am more or less fluent in eight languages, but can 'manage' some others related to some languages I know.

[7] Library of Congress (LC) – Homepage. Available at: http://www.loc.gov/.

At what age and how did you develop an interest in the Chinese language and culture?

Right after the secondary education, after passing the Baccalauréat,[8] I went to Paris to study Chinese, then Tibetan, Japanese and Burmese (languages).

Could you provide a brief introduction to the Guimet Museum and its relations to the library that you are working at?

The Library was created at the very same moment as the Museum was founded in 1889. From the beginning, the Library was intended to be the core of Emile Guimet's project, for museum curators, of course, but for the general public as well. It was and still is a public library open to all.

It is interesting to remember that Guimet's project was to create a museum devoted to the history of religions. It became more and more an Asian art museum after Guimet's disappearance in 1918, with his successors at the Head of the Museum. Then in 1945, the Museum officially became an Asian art museum, after an exchange of collections with the Louvre Museum.[9] But this exchange was not extended to the library, explaining why we still have a very important collection of books on religions, Egyptology, etc.

Nowadays, the Library is one section of the Conservation Department, together with other curatorial sections, which depend directly on the President of the Museum.

What is the size of the collections? Could you describe the highlights of the overall collection and the highlights of the Chinese collection?

The library maintains some 100,000 monographs and 1500 periodicals, some 600 living in Occidental and Asian languages (mainly Chinese, Japanese, Korean, Tibetan). Then there are some 500 manuscripts from all over Asia on all kind of materials, old maps, rubbings, drawings, etc. The Library manages also a collection of oil paintings on Asian subjects (Félix Régamey, Louis Dumoulin), together with drawings and pastels.

We have an important collection of sound recordings dating from the 1930s on various materials, dealing mainly with Asia.

The highlights of the overall collection are definitely an important collection of Japanese books illustrated by the best illustrators of their times (Hiroshige, Hokusai, etc.), a beautiful collection of old European editions dealing with Asia (for example, from the Jesuits). We received, as legacy from Alexandra David-Néel, her collection of books and manuscripts in Tibetan – a 13th-century manuscript.

As for the Chinese collection, the highlights are: imperial editions from the Qing Dynasty, sometimes bilingual; a Tangut (党項) Lotus Sutra (妙法蓮華經) on blue indigo paper inscribed in gold ink and old maps (Fonds Vissière).

[8] Baccalauréat is an academic qualification, which students in France take at the end of their high school education.

[9] Louvre Museum – Homepage. Available at: http://www.louvre.fr/en.

Could you describe the staffing structure at your Library?

The Library lost half of its staff in 3 years due to government policy of reducing public service employees. We are five persons: two receptionists storekeepers, one assistant for archives, one librarian for Japanese and the curator (myself). It's clearly understaffed, and this situation is not likely to improve in the future.

What best prepared you for the position as the Curator of the Guimet Museum Library?

First of all, I would say, my knowledge of Asian languages and cultures, thanks to years of research and travels in Asia. Second, having already been working in specialised libraries on Asia.

What scholarly and professional associations are you a part of, and how do they assist you in your work?

I'm a member of the European Association of Sinological Librarians[10], even if I had not many opportunities these past years to attend the annual meetings. I maintain ties with the European Association of Japanese Resources Specialists[11] and Southeast Asia Library Group.[12] In France, I am a member of the archivists network, Archives en musées.

I'd say that being part of these (professional library) associations is not a direct assistance, each library having its peculiarities. What is really important is exchanging ideas and opinions upon our work methods and exchanging information on developments elsewhere, not feeling alone sometimes in a competitive working environment.

Who are the majority of the patrons who use the Guimet Museum and at the Museum Library? That is, who comes to see you about your collections? Are they mostly professors or students from higher education institutions? Or are they people from outside the postsecondary sector, that is, the general public?

The main public is museum curators from Guimet and other museums, especially when preparing an exhibition, and Asian art students (Ecole du Louvre, universities). Many foreign scholars come from abroad in summer during their holidays.

The library and archives collection is much solicited for exhibitions, in-house and outside: iconographic research, loan of documents.

The general public is coming too in lesser numbers; usually museum visitors believe that the Library is restricted to scholars. We also have some journalists, art editors, etc.

[10] European Association of Sinological Librarians (EASL) – Homepage. Available at: http://www.easl.org/.

[11] European Association of Japanese Resources Specialists (EAJRS) – Homepage. Available at: http://eajrs.net/.

[12] Southeast Asia Library Group (SEALG) – Homepage. Available at: https://southeastasianlibrarygroup.wordpress.com/.

How do you acquire and evaluate your Library's collection?

I acquire research-level books on Asian arts and archaeology and exhibition catalogues, focussing on the needs of our museum curators. I exchange new acquisitions listings with other specialised libraries and try not to double important book series with other libraries in Paris.

How do I evaluate the Library's collection? I'd say that our collection is a kind of 'niche', being patrimonial as well as a living library. We have no electronic resources, for example, because of lack of budget, but very few patrons ask for these. In case they look for some electronics resources, we advise them where to go for it.

How does the collection catalogue and provide access for users? With a non-roman script, what challenges does this present to cataloguing? Is there any?

We have a collective catalogue shared by libraries of national museums: Catalogue collectif des bibliothèques des musées nationaux,[13] since 2010. Retrospective cataloguing was undertaken for Latin script catalogue cards only. Since 2010, we catalogue incoming documents in both Latin and vernacular scripts for much of them (Chinese, Japanese, Korean, Russian, Mongol, Thai, Khmer), but we still have problems with Tibetan, Tamil, Burmese, etc.

The themes and information needs of libraries, archives and museums (LAMs, as some have referred to them) have increasingly converged. What are your experiences and thoughts about these cultural institutions whose work and best practices now often overlap?

The three work together in our Museum. The Library is holding books, archives and documentation, participating actively in the Museum's life.

Which part(s) of your job as curator do you find most rewarding?

Many, that's the beautiful part of the job. I like being part of exhibition projects, searching for materials to enrich an exhibition, writing introductions or focuses on these documents. I enjoy working with scholars to draw their attention on specific manuscripts or documents, sometimes leading to a publication (last examples, L'épopée tibétaine de Gesar: manuscrit Alexandra David-Néel, Musée Guimet BG 54805: une version bon po inédite/par dBang chen nyi ma; présenté par Anne-Marie Blondeau et Anne Chayet; Illuminator, a light of gnosis: the great commentary on The single intention = dGongs gcig' grel chen snang mdzad ye shes sgron me: the manuscript at the Musée Guimet in Paris brought to France by Alexandra David-Néel/Dorje Sherab = rDo rje shes rab; foreword by Jan-Ulrich Sobisch).

[13] Catalogue collectif des bibliothèques des musées nationaux - Homepage. Available at: http://www.culture.gouv.fr/public/mistral/doclvr_fr?ACTION=RETOUR&USRNAME=nobody&USRPWD=%244P.

You mentioned the collaboration among your LAM. Could you elaborate on this collaboration? Can you give some examples of the type of collaboration?

The best examples concern exhibitions in-house or loans to exhibitions outside the Museum. When I receive the exhibition synopsis, I propose documents that could interest the exhibition curator. We participated to an important exhibition in Geneva, Switzerland, on Le japonisme bouddhique; I searched and discussed with the Geneva curator and we chose a set of books taken to France by Emile Guimet, our Museum founder, archives from the same person, together with drawings and paintings made by Felix Régamey, an artist who agreed to accompany Guimet on his trip to Asia. At the same time, our Japanese section curator in Guimet chose Japanese artefacts belonging to Guimet.

The interesting thing is that a Buddhist ceremony was held at the Museum in 1891, and the Geneva curator tried to recreate an idea of this ceremony with original archives, drawings and religious furniture used at the time still in our collection. Archives and drawings helped us to search for this furniture.

Old pictures of the Museum interiors, together with archives on the history of the permanent collection on display, are very useful to track some items missing in our storeroom, either because in the mass of artefacts (some 65,000 in the museum), the location was forgotten, or because it was deposited on loan to another institution long ago.

The archives are the memory of the museum for the long term; it is therefore crucial to our curators. The Library is a living study tool and the museum curators use it everyday.

Collecting the Orient and Eastern Collections at the Bibliothèque Nationale de France (National Library of France)

22

Jie Formoso
National Library of France, Paris, France

Introduction

With a long history that dates all the way back to the 1300s, the National Library of France is notable for being the largest book repository in France and also amongst the largest in the world. Held at both the Richelieu Library and the François Mitterrand Library in the National Library of France, the Eastern Collections are among the world's most important collections in terms of their diversity, quality and size, and are continuing to grow. With manuscripts in more than 100 ancient and modern languages, they are characterized by a variety of forms and media: codices, rolls, bone fragments, palm leaves, parchment, paper, etc. As a Chinese language major who graduated from Yunnan University (China), Jie Formosa (Fig. 22.1) (librarian, the Orient and eastern collections, National Library of France) explains how the library's heritage collection dates all the way back to the library's earliest origins and includes more than 20 languages spoken by more than half the world's population: Arabic, Armenian, Chinese, Korean, Greek, Hebrew, Japanese, Persian, Polish, Russian, Slovakian, Czech, Tibetan, Turkish and Vietnamese, as well as Finno-Ugric, Indian, South Slavic languages, etc.

Could we begin this interview by first introducing yourself, for example, your training and background, and your major roles and duties at the National Library of France?

My name is Jie Lucie Fu-Formoso. I graduated in spring 1982 from Yunnan University[1] with a major in Chinese language. From 1982 to 1987, I was the *Literary Review* editor of the *Dianchi* (滇池) magazine. In 1987, I went to France to study for a master's degree of social sciences in anthropology. In 1991, I started working in the National

[1] Yunnan University – Homepage. Available at: http://www.csc.edu.cn/studyinchina/universitydetailen.aspx?collegeId=5.

Inside the World's Major East Asian Collections. http://dx.doi.org/10.1016/B978-0-08-102145-3.00022-4

Figure 22.1 Jie Formoso.

Library of France (Figs 22.2 and 22.3)[2] and have been in charge of the Chinese section of the François-Mitterrand Library[3] since 1995. I set up a reading room for Chinese language and literature, open shelf for books on Chinese culture and the collection of Chinese book stacks (that is including the selection from international exchange and book donation). In addition, I oversee the cataloguing and other management information for Chinese books, organize promotional activities related to Chinese literature and provide reference services for readers.

How long have you been working for the National Library of France?

I started working for the National Library of France in 1991 and took part in the relocation of the library building to its new, present home. I was later transferred to the Department of Chinese Collections at the National Library of France.

What best prepared you for the position of librarian at National Library of France?

I do not have a professional librarianship diploma. But from 1973 to 1977, I worked independently in a school library in China and learnt some general knowledge about library management. After entering the National Library of France, I received a wide range of professional training and learnt much through practical working experience, especially on the information management systems for libraries. This is a disruptive era; electronic information changes library management so much. I am lucky to have the opportunity to witness this transition. As a special language information manager, I think my education and work experience in Chinese literature from mainland China

[2] National Library of France – Homepage. Available at: http://www.bnf.fr/en/tools/lsp.site_map.html.

[3] François-Mitterrand Library – Homepage. Available at: http://www.bnf.fr/en/bnf/sites_eng/a.francois_mitterrand_library.html.

Figure 22.2 National Library of France (exterior).

Figure 22.3 National Library of France (interior).

is an important foundation to accumulate current professional knowledge. French is also a very important (working) tool. Incidentally, in France I translated and published a Singaporean poet's poems, mainland writer Naiqian Cao's books and also the poems of Jian Yu.

You are a scholar in your own right, a Chinese literature specialist. How does your research and scholarship inform your work as librarian at the National Library of France?

A good librarian is not just an information processing technician. They should be an encyclopaedic learnt scholar, or at least a specialist in a certain field of knowledge. Chinese language and literature is my university educational background and also my interest focus. The foreign language collection of the François-Mitterrand Library focuses on contemporary literature. I can unabashedly say that our contemporary literary books are the most valuable special collection in France.

What scholarly and professional associations are you a part of, and how do they assist you in your work?

As for professional associations, I am a member of the European Association of Sinological Librarians (EASL),[4] but frankly, due to personal reasons, I seldom participate in their annual meetings. However, I am very concerned about their annual reports, which are an essential source of my professional information in the field of East Asian librarianship. Before 2000, the Association française des bibliothécaires et des documentalistes en sinology discussed many common library management issues. Although many issues never reached a consensus, such as Pinyin ligatures problem, such professional discussions of the special circumstances (Chinese library information management in the French cultural environment) in library management is absolutely essential. Since the Réseau national DocAsie established in France in 2007, I have been a founding member of this association. Though the association's annual meetings are not just focussing on Chinese, the broader Asian context continues to enrich my professional knowledge in all respects.

As for academic affiliations, I have a lot of close contact with sinology departments in French universities and social science research communities, but mostly personal contacts. We have a wide range of academic collaborations, such as co-organizing symposiums, bibliographic information exchange and so on.

Who are the majority of the Asian collection users? That is, who comes to see you about your collections? Are they mostly professors or students from higher education institutions? Or are they people from outside the postsecondary sector, that is, the general public?

Our library reading room has two parts. Firstly, for general readers (age 16 and above), with open-shelf books, about 1500 Chinese books, including dictionaries, books on general culture and more importantly, French translations of Chinese literature and masterpieces of representative Chinese writers. Here, readers are mostly students, especially those learning Chinese, those from mainland China and Taiwan, as well as general readers interested in Chinese literature.

[4] European Association of Sinological Librarians (EASL) – Homepage. Available at: http://www.easl.org.

Another part is the researchers' reading room, with some open-shelf reference books, but mostly closed stack books. Readers are mainly doctoral students, university teachers, translators, researchers, reporters, etc.

Could you give examples of typical reference/research inquiries issued by the researchers or scholars at National Library of France?

Needless to say, the National Library of France provides a fertile ground for the cultivation of sinology and Chinese literary translation. Many Chinese language workers, doctoral students and scholars are our readers. Their work results are closely related to our services. I refrain from giving examples to avoid missing other important cases.

As the manager of the Asian collection, how do you acquire and evaluate your collection? Do you proactively collect or do you accept gifts?

For Chinese books, we have a long-term purchase relationship with China International Book Trading Corporation[5] in mainland China and France, and Chinese bookshops in France, like Librairie le Phenix.[6] Our book selection not only refers to the electronic catalogues of the bookstores, but also takes full advantage of international networked catalogues. We also refer to various types of reader websites, blogs and social networks. We have long-term book exchange arrangements with the national libraries of Taiwan and mainland China. We also get a lot of donated books. For example, the mainland China Taoist Association donated their whole set of the precious publication, *Chinese Tao Sutra* (中華道藏目錄),[7] in 2013. We have been selective in international book exchange and donation acceptance.

In the past few years, the National Library of France has been engaged in the digitisation of some of its collections. What are some of the projects and what future plans are there for the digital collections? Could you tell us about the library's re-cataloguing and full-text digitisation of Chinese ancient books and manuscripts project?

The digital archive of the National Library of France, Gallica,[8] is now online with millions of digitized books. In Gallica, there is a Sinica collection, mainly related to the French sinology literature, with 1664 books online. In 2015, the National Library of France and the National Library of China (Beijing)[9] signed a Sinica cooperation agreement. Books in Chinese will soon be online.

In 2015, the National Library of France and Shandong University (China)[10] signed an agreement so that 10,000 Chinese books of the National Library of

[5] China International Book Trading Corporation – Homepage. Available at: http://www.cibtc.com.cn.
[6] Librairie le Phenix – Homepage. Available at: http://www.librairielephenix.fr/.
[7] 中華道藏目錄 – Homepage. Available at: http://www.byscrj.com/jmm/cnTaoSutra_contents.htm.
[8] National Library of France, Gallica – Homepage. Available at: http://gallica.bnf.fr/.
[9] National Library of China – Homepage. Available at: http://www.nlc.cn/newen/.
[10] Shandong University – Homepage. Available at: http://en.sdu.edu.cn/.

France (mostly ancient ones) will be entered into the catalogue, and a large amount of pages of books (ancient Chinese) will be entered into Gallica for online reading purposes.

In institutions with Asian collections, it is inevitable that there is a balancing act in terms of managing priorities between the various areas of language expertise/collections in regards to the other Asian language collections (i.e., Japanese, Korean, etc.). What are your experiences as librarian in terms of balancing and prioritizing? Do you need to?

In Asian languages, we have no particular preference policy. However, the international status of the Chinese language and brilliant achievements of Chinese studies in France determines the importance of the Chinese collections. This is obviously reflected in terms of the allocation of funds and in the number of open-shelf books.

How does the collection catalogue and provide access for users? With a non-roman script, what challenges does this present to cataloguing? Are there any?

Currently, readers can query our main library catalogue for Chinese titles entered since 1996. For contemporary titles and a portion of the ancient entered between 1986 and 1996, they are now available as an online card catalogue (for example, see Fig. 22.4). The National Library of France is gradually implementing a comprehensive unified catalogue. It is expected to be able to query all Chinese books in the near future.

Pinyin and Chinese double data entry are the key cataloguing principles for Chinese (same for non-Latin languages). A number of historical Chinese spelling problems can still be found in our old catalogues. However, with Chinese character input and display solutions in the modern information systems, cataloguing of Chinese books is no longer a big problem.

What are some of the technical challenges that you face in this position, particularly in terms of preservation and digitisation?

We have begun purchasing digitised books, though at a cautious pace. But some e-books are already online, such as the *Ricci Chinese-French Dictionary*.[11] We are extremely concerned about the existing digital library platforms. This is undoubtedly the future direction, which is a new opportunity rather than a challenge.

The themes and information needs of libraries, archives and museums (LAMs, as some have referred to them) have increasingly converged. What are your experiences

[11] *Ricci Chinese-French Dictionary* – Homepage. Available at: http://chinesereferenceshelf.brillonline.com/grand-ricci.

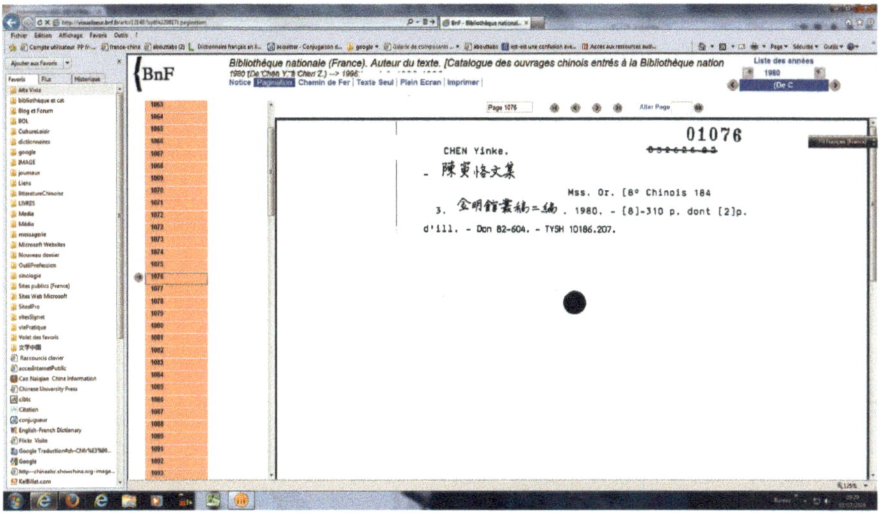

Figure 22.4 Scanned image of card catalogue of Chinese item.

and thoughts about these cultural institutions whose work and best practices now often overlap?

The National Library of France has actually been a cross-cultural institution, performing also archive and museum work. In 2004, an exhibition, *Chine: l'Empire du trait*, hosted by Ms. Nathalie Monnet, introduced our collection of Chinese calligraphy and painting. Particularly worth mentioning is the international Internet archive that retains the fast-changing information of websites (including blogs and social networks), not just those in France, but also those about France or in French overseas. This is a very visionary, important project.

Which part(s) of your job as the librarian at the Orient and eastern collections in the National Library of France do you find the most interesting and rewarding?

These are indeed very interesting work. Personally, I like selecting and purchasing books, especially some unique literary writers, scholars with independent thinking and good academic works. Including their books in our collection to satisfy learnt users is indeed a great pleasure. Organizing seminars to spread the achievement of Chinese literature is also encouraging work. For example, some of our activities in recent years include:

- 2011: Yu Jian's poem, *Flight*: song symposium;
- 2012: Mo Yan's novel, *Frog*: reading seminar; and
- 2014: Zhang Wei's novel, *The Old Boat*: book club.

These seminars attracted many participants and form the bridge between Chinese literature and French readers.

In France or in Europe, who do you think is the most prominent scholar in the field of Chinese or East Asian Studies? Please describe his/her contributions in the field.

French sinologists have had brilliant contribution worldwide, such as Jean-Pierre Abel-Rémusat (1788–1832), Stanislas Julien (1797–1873), Séraphin Couvreur (1835–1919), Édouard Chavannes (1865–1918), Henri Cordier (1849–1925), Paul Demiéville (1894–1979), Marcel Granet (1884–1940), Henri Maspero (1882–1945), Paul Pelliot (1878–1945), etc.

For contemporary sinologists, outstanding ones include Léon Vandermeersch and Anne Cheng on Chinese culture; Jean-Philippe Béja, Lucien Bianco and Jean-Luc Domenach on Chinese politics, society and modern history; François Julien on philosophy, Joël Bellassen on Chinese language, etc. You may see further in Wikipedia.[12]

There are so many of them; judging who are the best is out of the scope of my profession.

[12] https://fr.wikipedia.org/wiki/Cat%C3%A9gorie:Sinologue_fran%C3%A7ais.

The Knowledge of Digital Archives and History in Japan

23

Muneaki Hirano
Japan Center for Asian Historical Records, Tokyo, Japan

Introduction

Historical records are documents created in the course of political events that contain significant information about the past and/or present and are undeniably the basis for establishing a plurality of histories, as well as other contemporary trajectories. In addition to their immeasurable influence on the current, as well as future, course of world history, archives made up of historical records also play a vital role in bringing closer an increased international and mutual understanding of different conflicts among nations.

In the past, historical documents and the power of historical interpretation were monopolised by historians and politicians. However, digital archives, such as the JACAR (Japan Center for Asian Historical Records) now prevent historians and politicians from holding such unfair privileges. With the aim of promoting a deeper understanding of history and to improve international relationships, the JACAR makes as many historical documents as possible, not only for professional historians, but also for the general public, both within and outside of Japan. In the following interview, Muneaki Hirano, a researcher at the JACAR, discusses in detail how the centre's records have opened up new directions for historical study, as well as its valuable contribution in making historical research not only more democratised, but also more scientific, thereby making it possible to share an understanding of history between victims and victimisers.

Could we begin this interview by first introducing yourself, for example, your training and background, and your major roles and duties at the JACAR?[1]

My major at university was originally the history of the French Second Empire. So, at first, in the early period of constructing the JACAR's database, I was asked to read the historical documents written in French, such as the minutes of the League of Nations and the documents on French Indochina, and to collect information for the metadata from them. Today, with over 10 years of experience in JACAR, I'm working mainly on collaboration with similar organisations at home and abroad, as well as on publicity planning.

[1] Japan Center for Asian Historical Records (JACAR) – Homepage. Available at: http://www.jacar.go.jp/english/.

Inside the World's Major East Asian Collections. http://dx.doi.org/10.1016/B978-0-08-102145-3.00023-6

Publicity planning, why is publicity so important for the JACAR?

JACAR's establishment was based on the cabinet decision on 30 November 2001, which mentions that JACAR's aim is the mutual understanding between Japan and other countries, especially neighbouring Asian countries. Thus, we believe that publicity is one of our most important tasks. JACAR's raison d'etre is being used by both Japanese and foreign people and contributes to share these historical documents with many people.

Where did you study history of the French Second Empire? Did you go to university in France or Japan? Would you mind telling us which university you attended?

Until a few years ago, I enrolled in the doctoral programme at the Tokyo Metropolitan University[2] and was studying this theme. Although I had hoped to study in France, I unfortunately did not have the opportunity to study abroad.

How many different languages have you mastered? What language skills are necessary for performing your tasks at the JACAR?

I have not perfectly mastered any languages except Japanese! My English is not good enough, I think, because I have not got the academic or practical training. If my English texts are good as you said, I thank my benign boss. He is a good English speaker and improved original English texts. I can read and speak French for document searches in Paris to some extent.

Please provide a brief introduction to the collections at the JACAR.

JACAR is a digital archive offering online access to 'Asia-related historical documents'. 'Asia-related historical documents' are defined as documents possessed by Japanese national archival institutions concerning modern Japan and its relations with neighbouring Asian countries, etc. JACAR releases digitised document images supplied from three archival institutions as follows:

- from the National Archives of Japan,[3] which offers the documents once managed by the Council of State and the Cabinet, records transferred from Japanese government ministries and public records restituted from the US, as well as publications of the Korea Governor-General's Office and Taiwan Governor-General's Office;
- from the Diplomatic Archives of the Ministry of Foreign Affairs,[4] which offers the records from departments and bureaus of the Ministry of Foreign Affairs as well as the correspondence with its overseas diplomatic missions; and

[2] Tokyo Metropolitan University – Homepage. Available at: http://www.tmu.ac.jp/english/index.html.

[3] National Archives of Japan – Homepage. Available at: http://www.archives.go.jp/english/.

[4] Diplomatic Archives of the Ministry of Foreign Affairs of Japan – Homepage. Available at: http://www.mofa.go.jp/about/hq/record/.

- from the National Institute for Defense Studies of the Ministry of Defense,[5] which offers the Army Ministry and the Navy Ministry documents, such as 'Rikugunsho Dainikki' (陸軍省大日記) and 'Kaigunsho Kobun Biko' (海軍省公文備考), as well as combat records from the Army and Navy.

What is the size of the collections? Could you describe the highlights of the collection?

As of November 2015, JACAR has approximately 1.93 million documents (=30 million images).

Your job title is researcher at the JACAR? I take that there are also professional archivists working at the JACAR. So what are the functional differences between researchers and archivists working at the JACAR? In addition, could you describe the staffing structure at the JACAR? How many researchers and archivists are there in total working for the JACAR?

Yes, I am a researcher at JACAR. I think that it's so difficult to identify who is 'professional archivist' and who is not because there is no legal definition of archivist in Japan. At JACAR, there are three 'researchers', including me, who are taking care of the archivist job, but originally we are specialists of history. We are defined institutionally as part-time officials, while we work here full-time for 5 days a week. Other part-time officials, 12 inspectors, are working for 2, 3 or 4 days a week. They are also historians. The 'researchers' are working for management of database constructing, web content making, publicity planning, etc. The inspectors are working mainly for inspecting metadata and image data outsourced and for correcting their errors.

On the other hand, the full-time officials in JACAR are temporarily sent from the Ministry of Foreign Affairs[6] and the Ministry of Education, Culture, Sports, Science and Technology,[7] and they are management officials, not specialists of archives. As stated previously, there is no designation of professional archivist or any position named 'archivist' in JACAR, but some of the staff members are working as 'archivists'.

What scholarly and professional associations are you a part of, and how do they assist you in your work?

I am a part of the Japan Society for Archival Science (JSAS).[8] I have presented to my colleagues in annual conference meetings of the JSAS in 2008. Those were very important opportunities to introduce JACAR's service and our work to archivists and archival specialists. I also belong to the Société franco-japonaise des Sciences

[5] National Institute for Defense Studies of the Ministry of Defense – Homepage. Available at: http://www.nids.go.jp/english/.

[6] Ministry of Foreign Affairs of Japan – Homepage. Available at: http://www.mofa.go.jp/.

[7] Ministry of Education, Culture, Sports, Science and Technology (of Japan) – Homepage. Available at: http://www.mext.go.jp/english/.

[8] Japan Society for Archival Science (JSAS) – Homepage. Available at: http://www.jsas.info/modules/english09/.

historiques,[9] which gave me a chance to publish an article on the society's journal that introduces JACAR and its documents concerning French history.

Who are the majority of the JACAR's users? That is, who comes to see you about your collections? Are they mostly professors or students from higher education institutions? Or are they people from outside the postsecondary sector, that is, the general public?

We know that the majority of JACAR's users are academic/nonacademic historians of modern Japan, China, Korea or Southeast Asian countries. Of course, most of them are in Japan, but the users are also in China, Korea, the US and some other countries. In Japan, history teachers in high school seem to be frequent users of our service. We heard that many professors and teachers recommended JACAR to their students.

We often receive applications for secondary use of our documents from television production companies or publishers. We can have direct contact with our users only through the inquiries (phone call, email, postal mail) from them because JACAR is an online digital archive without original documents and reading rooms.

What are the highlights of the JACAR collections? Or which collections are most sought-after materials by the general users and the scholarly community?

As I wrote in the previous interview answer, JACAR possesses and makes public only digitised documents provided by three governmental institutions. So, it can be said that JACAR did not have its own collection. If I point out one of the most seen digital collections of JACAR, it is the digitised documents possessed by the National Institute for Defense Studies of the Ministry of Defense, specifically, the Japanese Imperial Army and Navy documents, which are frequently asked for inquiries from Japanese and foreign users.

Could you give examples of typical reference/research inquiries issued by the researchers or scholars at the JACAR?

Normally, most of the specialists search documents they need by themselves, and they give a call or send an email to us in the case of troubles in the searching interface of JACAR. A small amount of researchers and scholars ask us mainly whether the documents concerning their research exist in JACAR's database. We often receive requests from elderly persons to introduce them those documents relating to their fathers or grandfathers who served the Japanese Imperial Army or Navy in the Second World War.

There is a strong component of Korean–Japanese relations at JACAR, such as correspondence between the director of Tsushima-no-kami and the Korean Court in 1867, with many diplomatic records concerning the Ganghwa Island incident in 1875, the Imo Incident in 1882, the Gapsin Coup in 1884 and events dating until the outbreak of the Sino-Japanese War of 1884–85.

[9] Société franco-japonaise des Sciences historiques – Homepage. Available at: http://www.ambafrance-jp.org/Societes-savantes-franco.

What is the extent of promotion and outreach to East Asian institutions, particularly to Korea? How about the rest of the Western world?

We are offering many documents, including the records concerning to the important events on the history of relationship between Japan and other countries.

When we held some presentations of our service at some institutions in Korea in these years, we introduced some documents concerning the Korean–Japanese relationship, including the documents about the Imo Incident or the Gapsin Coup as examples. We offer the documents themselves, and we do not show any interpretation on the events. For outreach to introduce our database to the foreign countries, we have had some presentations and exhibitions, for example, in the Netherlands, Turkey, US and other countries.

Could you tell us more about an interesting project, which was a collaboration between the JACAR and the British Library (BL)[10] about the Sino-Japanese War (1894–95)?

We made a good relationship with staff members of the BL's Japanese section through using the occasion of the annual conferences of the European Association of Japanese Resource Specialists.[11]

In November 2012, when the BL's staff were preparing to display one of their 235 prints on the Sino-Japanese War of 1894–95 in an exhibition of the BL, they approached us to open to the world all the prints of this collection with the cooperation of JACAR, because they considered JACAR as an organisation with expertise of presenting historical records to the public. Soon, the collaboration between JACAR and BL was agreed to digitise the whole collection of prints and create a bilingual Japanese–English website, which presents the collection and also related archival documents from JACAR. That is the web exhibition, 'The Sino-Japanese War of 1894–95: as seen in prints and archives', opened in May 2014.

In this collaboration, JACAR was responsible for creating the Japanese text and constructing the website while the BL undertook to prepare the English text, the digital images and the bibliographic data. The most important point was that JACAR and the BL agreed to keep the exhibition simple and were to be careful that both institutions keep a neutral stance, as far as possible, through showing both Japanese and Chinese prints side by side when they treat the same subject or event, not putting any additional explanation to any text written on them.

In the past few years, the JACAR has been engaged in the digitisation of some of its collections. What are some of the projects and what future plans are there for the digital collections?

As mentioned previously, JACAR is a digital archive and its collections are digitised document images only. We receive digital images and metadata of the documents

[10] The British Library – Homepage. Available at: http://www.bl.uk.

[11] European Association of Japanese Resource Specialists (EAJRS) – Homepage. Available at: http://eajrs.net/.

from the National Archives, the Diplomatic Archives[12] and the National Institute for Defense Studies.[13] We convert the images received into the format suitable to our database and add more information to the metadata. These three institutions, not JACAR, select the documents to provide to JACAR. From its establishment in November 2001, JACAR had been advancing the project of database construction.

Could you talk more about the digital archive, particularly the DjVu system?

When JACAR was established in November 2001, many people were using dial-up Internet access. Therefore, it was the most important task for JACAR to introduce the image format of high compression ratio in order to smoothly provide high-quality images of documents to all users. The DjVu was the most suitable format to solve this problem at that time.

By now, 14 years after JACAR's establishment, the DjVu format has become inconvenient for many users, particularly because the format is not yet supported by Windows. In addition, downloading of any programmes, including the DjVu plug-in, are now broadly prohibited in most of public facilities for its security. So we have decided to adopt the PDF format on the next JACAR system, started in October 2016.

How does the collection catalogue and provide access for users? Could you tell us more about the 'layer search'? With a non-Roman script, what challenges does this present to cataloguing? Are there any?

In JACAR's database, all documents are organised according to their original order and layer of their supplier institutions. In brief, the metadata of each item (document) has information about the particular file. The metadata of each file has information, which is about its subseries. The metadata of each subseries has information that signifies which upper subseries or series contains them. The metadata of each series has information about the subfond that contains them. The metadata of each subfond has information, which signifies the fond that contains them.

These information layers construct the same hierarchy of their original documents in their original institutions and are arranged accordingly in our database. This hierarchy is shown on 'Layered Information', and on this interface, we can search documents by tracing the original order.

Most of the documents in JACAR's database are written in Japanese. Some of the documents include English, French, Germany, Chinese, Korean and other languages. We keep the information of which languages are included in a document within the metadata.

[12] Diplomatic Archives of the Ministry of Foreign Affairs of Japan – Homepage. Available at: http://www.mofa.go.jp/about/hq/record/.

[13] National Institute for Defense Studies – Homepage. Available at: http://www.nids.mod.go.jp/english/.

The themes and information needs of libraries, archives and museums (LAMs, as some have referred to them) have increasingly converged. What are your experiences and thoughts about these cultural institutions whose work and best practices now often overlap?

I think collaboration with other organisations is one way to overcome the limits of budget, persons and collection in each institution. In the case of the collaboration with the BL, a very good partnership was established between the BL's visual collection and JACAR's documental collection, as well as between the BL staff's knowhow as librarians and the JACAR staff's knowledge of digital archives and history.

JACAR often receives applications for secondary use of its documents from television production companies; could you name a few TV programmes, which the JACAR was responsible for providing documents for supporting their TV productions?

There is no TV programme, which JACAR is 'responsible' for making. We do not have this information because of a law regarding the release of government documents effective back in April 2011. As a result, there is no more need from our users to notify JACAR when they use information from our databases. It is only when we receive calls or emails from the users that have the opportunity to know which documents are used for research purposes. Based on my experience, I guess that at least about half of our resources have been for television news programmes and newspapers, particularly when events concern historical or territorial issues.

A Contemporary Russian Museum Combining the Traditions of Ethnography and Western Anthropology

24

Vladimir Davydov
Peter the Great Museum of Anthropology and Ethnography (Kunstkamera), Russian Academy of Sciences, St. Petersburg, Russia

Introduction

Similar to China, Russia is a multiethnic nation with over 180 ethnic minorities living throughout the whole country. More interestingly, a number of such indigenous groups still maintain very traditional lifestyles, often living in very cold and hazardous environments without expressing any desire to adapt to the modern world that is driven by technology and industrialism. UK-educated Dr. Vladimir Davydov (Figs 24.1 and 24.2), Head of the Siberian Ethnography Department at Peter the Great Museum of Anthropology and Ethnography (Kunstkamera) (Fig. 24.3), is the person who dedicates his entire professional life to researching the Tungus-speaking groups living in Russia and China. In the following interview, Dr. Davydov tells us how he became interested in anthropology at the age of 17 from listening to the music of northern indigenous peoples and how we could learn to research the political situations and cultural exchanges between Russia and other neighbouring countries by studying the lifestyles and migration patterns of these indigenous groups.

Could we begin this interview by first introducing yourself, for example, your training and background, and your major roles and duties at Peter the Great Museum of Anthropology and Ethnography (Kunstkamera)?[1]

My name is Vladimir Davydov; I have worked at the Kunstkamera for 4 years, beginning in 2012. Three years ago, I was elected by our collective to be the Head of the Siberian Ethnography Department. I was educated as a social anthropologist, and in 2007–11, I worked as a graduate research fellow on the Baikal Archaeology Project

[1] Kunstkamera Peter the Great Museum Anthropology and Ethnography – Homepage. Available at: http://www.kunstkamera.ru/en/history/the_museum_and_its_directors/.

Inside the World's Major East Asian Collections. http://dx.doi.org/10.1016/B978-0-08-102145-3.00024-8

Figure 24.1 Vladimir Davydov at the opening of photo exhibition in the University Museum, Inner Mongolia University, Hohhot, China, 2015.

Figure 24.2 Vladimir Davydov gives a lecture in Nord University, Bodø, Norway, 2016.

at the University of Aberdeen.[2] I was lucky to receive a full-time job in Kunstkamera just after finishing of my PhD. I am responsible for organisation of work with Siberian collections in the museum and ethnographic fieldwork in the region. Our duties in the museum are a combination of collections research and fieldwork in Siberia. There are seven persons in the Siberian Ethnography Department; everyone works with particular cultural groups. My research interests are connected with Tungus-speaking groups in Russia and China, and starting from 2012 I became involved into work with Ewenki (鄂温克族) and Orochen (鄂倫春族) collections.

[2] The University of Aberdeen – Homepage. Available at: http://www.abdn.ac.uk.

Figure 24.3 Peter the Great Museum of Anthropology and Ethnography (Kunstkamera), Russian Academy of Sciences (in the middle). University embankment, St. Petersburg, Russia.

At what age and how did you become interested in anthropology? Are your parents also anthropologists?

I became interested in anthropology at the age of 17 listening to the music of northern indigenous peoples. I was inspired by Siberian throat singing and the sound of *khomus* (*vargan*). This gave me a very strong inspiration, and I have chosen social anthropology as a field for graduate studies. There was a new educational programme on a base of Sociological Faculty of St. Petersburg (State) University.[3] I liked the romantic idea to go somewhere and spend a long period of time in the field. I read books of B. Malinowsky and James Frazer and understood that I wanted to be an anthropologist. My parents were very far from this field: my father is an engineer, and my mother is an artist. At the same time, my mother strongly supported my ideas of doing fieldwork with Siberian indigenous groups.

'Ethnology' and 'anthropology': for many of us who are not trained in the field, could you briefly describe the distinctions between these two disciplines, and how are they interrelated to each other?

Now this is more a question of self-definition of particular scientists, and the border between these disciplines is blurring. Both disciplines started their development in Russia in the 1990s. Before this period, Russian scientists used the term ethnography, and this discipline was based on historical faculties and was considered as a part of historical science. If we have a look into history of 'ethnology' and 'anthropology', we will see that these are two different traditions of the research of the same subject. Anthropology was historically connected with Anglo-Saxon tradition. Ethnology tends to be more theoretical science about ethnic processes. In the 1990s, many Russian institutions and their divisions, which had the word 'ethnography' in their official names, changed it to 'ethnology' or 'anthropology'. In this sense, contemporary Russian anthropology combines the traditions of ethnography and Western anthropology.

Anthropology and anthropologists: there are anthropologists who study the evolution of human physiology and human behaviour and the relation between hominids and nonhominids. For example, did human come from apes? How do we know 'Lucy' walked upright? Meanwhile, there are other anthropologists like Dr. Liza Dalby, who specialises in Japanese culture and performed extensive fieldwork of the geisha community in Kyoto. Since you are all carrying the title as 'anthropologists', how are the training and the kind of research skills and knowledge needed for carrying out the work you do different from each other?

I agree that the word 'anthropology' can mean absolutely different domains of knowledge, which imply different research skills and procedures. Even in the context of Kunstkamera, it may signify different approaches. For instance, we have a Department of Physical Anthropology in our Museum, which deals a lot with human remains from

[3] St. Petersburg State University – Homepage. Available at: http://eng.spbu.ru.

archaeological excavations and employs a number of measurement procedures. I work with communities in Siberia as a social scientist. We have many discussions in our Department concerning the proper anthropological investigation. I see that an anthropologist needs the skills connected with collection of own fieldwork data combined with the research of archival materials and museum collections. An anthropologist should be open to all kind of sources he may employ in his case. The most important skills for one involved in Siberian studies would be the ability to collect and organise his own field materials, including the information on oral history; kinship relations and economic, political and administrative contexts, to reveal and analyse historical documents, museum collections and published works on the topic, etc.

According to information I found on the Internet, Saint Petersburg was founded by Tsar Peter the Great in 1703 and later became the imperial capital of Russia in 1713. And the Kunstkamera Museum was founded in 1727. Could you tell me what was Peter the Great's vision behind establishing the Kunstkamera Museum in this newly founded imperial capital?

The document of the concrete date of the establishing of the Kunstkamera was not found. However, the published sources of the 18th century reference 1714 as a year when Kunstkamera and a library were established by Peter the Great. This date was mentioned in a book written by I.D. Shumakher (published in 1744), who participated in the creation of this first Russian public museum. Another reason for 1714 is that Peter the Great transported his library and private collections from Moscow to St. Petersburg in 1714. Thus, in 2014, we celebrated the 300-year anniversary of the Museum. The year 1727 was when the construction of the historical building of Kunstkamera, which became a symbol of the Russian Academy of Sciences, was finished on the Vasilyevsky Island. Before this time, Kunstkamera's collections and library were kept in other buildings. The purpose of the creation of this Museum by Peter the Great was the collection and research of rare objects created both by people and nature. The Museum received a European manner name, Kunstkamera, which translates from German as 'a collection of rare objects and miracles'.

All over the world, St. Petersburg is well known for its architecture and history, grandeur and beauty, and famous for its famous museums and churches, etc. As a Russian native and from a museum curator's viewpoint, could you describe the overall cultural scene in St. Petersburg? How is it when compared with Moscow and other European capital cities, such as London, Paris and Vienna? Has St. Petersburg's 'cultural scene' played any role in shaping the collection development, exhibitions, museum programmes and staffing situations of the Kunstkamera Museum?

Yes, from the very beginning, this Museum cannot be separated from the 'cultural scene' of St. Petersburg. For many years, St. Petersburg was a capital of Russia, and Kunstkamera always played a role of one of the central cultural institutions in our country. This Museum is known for everyone in St. Petersburg. Its central location is very important; the Museum is located in walking distance of other famous and important institutions, such as Hermitage, the Zoological Museum, Library of Academy of Sciences, St. Petersburg State University and Menshikov Palace. St. Petersburg is different from other Russian cities and is often referenced as a 'cultural capital' of Russia. In this sense, cultural life in our city is very rich and can be compared with other capital cities and Moscow. The idea to collect and preserve unique ethnographic objects from all corners of the world is a result of this 'cultural scene' of St. Petersburg. There are no such extensive ethnographic collections in any other Russian cities.

Could you give us a brief account of the history of the Kunstkamera Museum, as well as the highlights of the Museum's general collection?

The history of Kunstkamera starts more than 300 years ago when Peter the Great moved his collections of rare things from Moscow to St. Petersburg and decided to organise a museum in 1714. Five years later, in 1719, Kuntkamera's collections became open for the wide public. An interesting fact is that the visiting of this Museum was free of charge. In 1727, collections moved to a new building on Vasilyevsky Island. In 1747, a strong fire took place in Kunstkamera. Most of ethnographic collections were destroyed. Later on, the Museum was repaired and opened again in 1766. Kunstkamera is the museum of peoples and cultures of the world. It combines ethnographic collections from the cultures belonging to different continents. Many objects are unique and represent the earliest collections of particular cultures; some of Kunstkamera's collections were brought by famous researchers: Capitan J. Cook, L. Frobenius, I.F. Kruzenshtern and N.N. Miklukho-Maklai. At the same time, most people in Russia know Kunstkamera because of its anatomic collections and associate our Museum with monsters in jars. Overall, the collections of Kunstkamera combine more than one million objects collected in different corners of the world.

Could you provide a brief introduction (including the history of its setup) to the Siberian Department of Collections at Kunstkamera Museum?

Kunstkamera contains the oldest ethnographic Siberian objects in the collections of Russian museums (Fig. 24.4). They are one of the best and the most extensive collections of Northern Asian objects in the world. Siberian objects became a significant part of Kunstkamera's collections from the first years of its existence. However, most from the earliest Siberian collections were destroyed by the fire in 1747. By that time, Siberian collections included more than 200 objects. Even though the fire destroyed most objects, some drawings of them remained and are kept in the St. Petersburg branch of Russian Academy of Sciences Archive. An important role in collecting objects in the 18th century was played by G.F. Miller. The main problem of the earliest Siberian collections was incomplete documentation of the objects. In the 19th century, Siberian collections significantly increased due to objects brought by the members of numerous expeditions: F.P. Litke, M.A. Castren, A.F. Middendorf, et al. The collections of the second part of the 19th

Figure 24.4 Storage of Siberian photo collections, Department of Siberian Ethnography, Kunstkamera, St. Petersburg, Russia.

century and the beginning of the 20th century include more than 20,000 objects; that is the biggest collection of Northern Asian objects of this period in the world. The history of the Siberian Department is connected with the famous Jesup North Pacific Expedition, leaded by Franz Boas. The researchers from Kunstkamera, V.G. Bogoraz and V.I. Iohelson, made a significant contribution to the work of expedition.

The definition of the 'Siberian Ethnography Department', is it defined by the geographical region 'Siberia'? Or is it defined by the cultures and languages of the different ethnic groups who live within this region? As you understand, tribal groups migrate and mix with each other. Some tribal groups do not stay at one place for a long time. They keep on roaming from place to place for their livelihood for generations together. Hence, their religions and ways of living, as well as languages, tend to change when they need to adapt to a new environment.

At the first stage, the idea to have such a department in the Museum was geographical. At the same time, we are not limited in our research just by geographical definition of Siberia, which belongs to Asian part of Russia. Nenets and Saami reindeer herders live in the European part; however, the objects collected among these groups became a part of Siberian collections. The same happened with Chinese Orochen collections, which theoretically should be registered in the East and Southeast Asia department. In this sense, Siberia can be seen as a particular way of life of indigenous populations. In this sense, way of life and culture is more important than rough geographical classification. A good example is a contemporary collaborative project, conducted by our colleagues from the Caucasian Ethnography Department in Kunstkamera, on the research of migrants from Dagestan in Siberian cities. These people reproduce their religious patterns and cook ethnic food in the places that are several thousand kilometres from their home. At the same time, we understand the ethnography in a broad sense; we are not limited just by indigenous cultures. In this sense, the representatives of Siberian subcultures, political and religious movements and different processes and innovations are as well in the focus of Kunstkamera's researchers.

What is the size of the collections? Could you describe the highlights of the Siberian collections at Peter the Great Museum of Anthropology and Ethnography (Kunstkamera)?

It is very difficult to give the exact numbers because the collections have to be re-registered. Very often, the sets of objects are actually registered as one object. After the re-registration, the actual numbers may change. Moreover, colleagues continue registration of new objects. Therefore, I will give the numbers, which we know from the inventories. Siberian collections of Kunstkamera include more than 30,000 objects, which include more than 750 collections representing 42 different ethnic groups from Siberia (e.g., 68 collections of Evenkis, 53 of Chukchees, 45 of Yakuts, 41 of Nivkhs, 39 of Nanai, 37 of Khanty, 33 of Nenets, 32 of Koryaks). Moreover, we keep at the Department 593 collections of printed photographs with a whole number of pictures with more than 40,200 photos. Finally, 321 Siberian collections of glass negatives are kept in our Museum in a special archive for negatives.

How did you become the Head of the Siberian Department at such a young age? What best prepared you for the position of Head at the Siberian Department at Peter the Great Museum of Anthropology and Ethnography (Kunstkamera)?

I think the main thing that helped me a lot was my interest in Siberian anthropology and Evenki culture in particular. A significant advantage for me was that I was educated in two systems: Western European and Russian. I received my PhD degree at the University of Aberdeen (2012), which has a strong school of northern studies. My dissertation was based on 10 months field research of Evenki hunters, reindeer herders and fishermen in the Northern Baikal area in Buriatiia (see monograph in Fig. 24.5). At the same time, in 2001–05, I conducted research among the indigenous Siberian students in St. Petersburg that helped me to write a the dissertation submitted

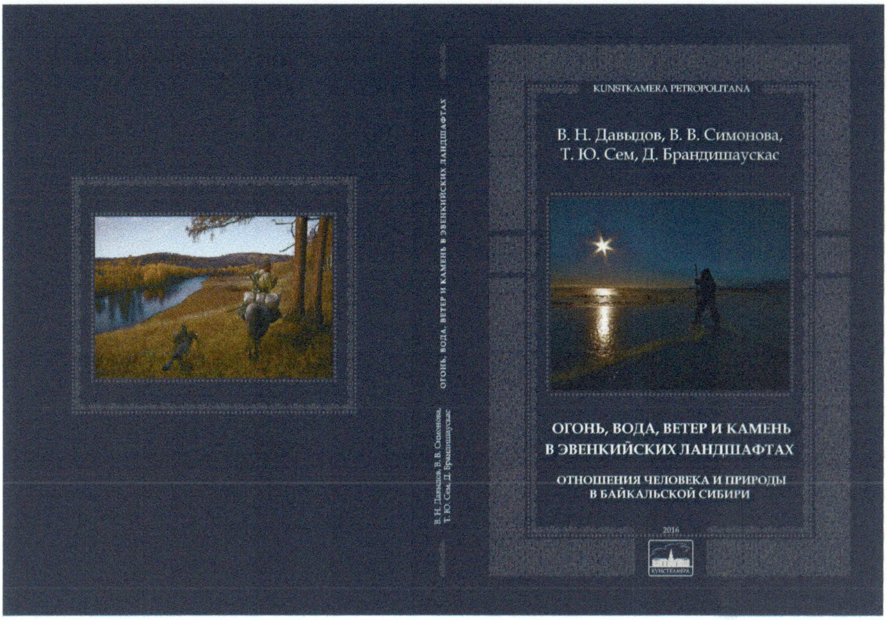

Figure 24.5 Cover of the collective monograph (edited by V. Davydov) published by the Kunstkamera. Fire, water, wind and stone in Evenki landscapes: Human-nature relations in Baikal Siberia. St. Petersburg: MAE RAS. (2016).

for a Candidate of Sciences degree (equivalent of PhD) in Sociology at Sociological Institute of the Russian Academy of Sciences in Moscow (2008).

What are the core working skills, language abilities, professional knowledge and personality traits that are necessary for taking up your job as the Head of the Siberian Department?

The main skill for the head of a department in the system of Academy of Sciences is probably an open mind and sensitivity to the research interests of other people at the Department. Of course, language and communicative skills are of great importance at this administrative position. At the same time, this work takes a lot of energy for writing official papers, reports, participation in working meetings and so on.

Could you describe the staffing structure under the Head of the Siberian Department?

In the system of the Russian Academy of Sciences, we have a multilevel system of different kinds of research fellows: junior research fellows, research fellows, senior research fellows, main research fellows and leading research fellows. We have other positions, such as research assistants, postgraduate students and scientific consultants. The task of the head of the department is planning research work of this collective of researchers. Our Department consists of seven research fellows of different kinds (including me), two postgraduate students and one research consultant. Now I am responsible for the supervision of one PhD student.

Could you describe Kunstkamera Museum's collaborations with academic institutions and museums around the world in general? What are the benefits of such collaborations with outside parties?

Our Museum collaborates with hundreds of institutions and museums in Russia and abroad. Kunstkamera has signed a number of agreements and memorandums of understanding with many institutions. These collaborations result in exhibitions, research projects, fieldwork research, publication of catalogues and archival materials, work on documental movies and organisation of conferences and seminars. In the context of northern and Siberian studies, we collaborate a lot with British, American, Canadian, Austrian, German, French, Lithuanian, Latvian, Estonian, Finnish, Norwegian, Chinese, Japanese and a number of Russian museums and research institutions, etc.

Why does the Kunstkamera Museum's collaborations have one of the most extensive ethnographic collections?

Kunstkamera itself is a kind of model or map of the world. Historically, this Museum collected the objects from numerous corners the world. Many of these objects are unique. It is not surprising that these collections attract researchers and exhibitions' curators from different Russian and foreign institutions.

What scholarly and professional associations are you a part of, and how do they assist you in your work?

I am a member of a number of professional associations, such as the International Union of Anthropological and Ethnological Sciences,[4] the International Arctic Social Sciences Association,[5] the International Society for Hunter Gatherer Research,[6] Russian Geographical Society,[7] the Kovalevskii Sociological Society and the Association of Russian Anthropologists and Ethnologists. Almost every year, I participate at the conferences organised by these professional associations. This helps me to be aware in contemporary tendencies in anthropology, to meet colleagues, to participate in project meetings, to plan future research and publication plans and to present results of my research.

Who are the majority of the Museum's patrons and users? That is, who comes to see you about your collections? Are they mostly professors or students from higher education institutions? Or are they people from outside the postsecondary sector, that is, the general public?

[4] International Union of Anthropological and Ethnological Sciences (IUAES) – Homepage. Available at: http://www.iuaes.org.

[5] International Arctic Social Sciences Association (IASSA) – Homepage. Available at: http://iassa.org.

[6] International Society for Hunter Gatherer Research (ISHGR) – Homepage. Available at: http://ishgr.org.

[7] Russian Geographical Society – Homepage. Available at: http://www.rgo.ru/en.

Museum exposure is visited by the general public, including all groups of the population. For instance, according to the data from the Excursion and Education Department, in 2014, our Museum had 558,568 visitors. At the same time, the Siberian collections' repository is open only for researchers. One needs a special letter to visit and work with our collections. The total number of external visitors of Siberian collections is usually less than 50 per year. We also have about the same number of visitors working with photographs in our Department. Most of them are professional museum workers and researchers. We also have a small number of visitors, mostly artists belonging to indigenous communities.

Could you give examples of typical reference/research enquiries issued by the researchers, scholars or the general public at the Siberian Ethnography Department at Kunstkamera, Peter the Great Museum of Ethnology and Anthropology?

We receive a number of requests for publication of our photographs and objects. Many requests are concerned with the identification of particular objects or with the information about particular personalities. Some researchers ask to give the information concerning particular ethnic groups in the collections of our Museum. One of the recent enquires was a letter from the Museum of Ethnology, Hamburg[8] (Germany), asking for an official cooperation between our two institutions for the exhibition 'Ice Ages' (2016). Our Department made a preliminary selection of 20 Nganasan objects brought from the Taimyr Peninsula. We usually receive one to three different requests per week. We are responsible for giving the recommendations for the requests of the federal authorities and the representatives of the regional administrative apparatus as well.

The Department of Ethnography of Siberian Russia organised the premiere of the documentary 'Tungus - the herders of Manchuria' and opening of a photo exhibition of the same name at the Headquarters of the Russian Geographical Society in St. Petersburg. Could you tell us its significance in terms of ethnography and collections related to the Tungusic peoples of Manchuria and Asia?

This was a very important event for our Museum since it was the first exhibition of unknown S.M. Shirokogoroff's pictures made exactly 100 years ago and the first exhibition of E.J. Lindgren's and Oscar Mamen's photos in Russia. The works of these researchers were not known to the wide public in Russia. This exhibition is a result of collaboration between the scholars of Kunstkamera, the University of Aberdeen and the University of Cambridge.[9] We started a scientific dialogue about the history of Manchurian ethnographic expeditions and compared the approaches of Russian and British anthropologists. This exhibition was followed by a series of exhibitions in the UK and China in 2015.

[8] Museum of Ethnology, Hamburg – Homepage. Available at: http://www.voelkerkundemuseum.com.

[9] University of Cambridge – Homepage. Available at: https://www.cam.ac.uk.

As Head of the Siberian Ethnography Department at Kunstkamera Museum, how do you acquire and evaluate your collection?

Siberian collections in Kunstkamera are among the biggest collections of Siberian ethnographic objects in the world. Our Museum continues acquiring new objects now. Three to four times per year, we have special meetings of Expert Fund Procurement Commission, which either accepts or rejects new objects. The members of this commission are responsible for evaluation of the objects. Our Department issues all necessary documentation and prepares recommendations for these meetings.

In the past few years, the Siberia Department at Kunstkamera Museum has been engaged in the digitisation of some of its collections. What are some of the projects of the Department and what future plans are there for its digital collections?

We collaborate a lot with the University of Aberdeen concerning Evenki and Orochen collections. Kunstkamera is a partner institution in 'Etnos and Minzu: Histories and Politics of Identity Governance in Eurasia' (Leverhulme International Network Grant IN-2012-138) and 'Etnos: A life history of the etnos concept among the Peoples of the North' (ESRC ES/K006428/1) projects, curated from our side by Dr. Dmitry Arzyutov, that helped us to digitalise S.M. Shirokogoroff's photo collections. We have a plan to exhibit scanned items and publish them both in a form of a book as well as prepare a web publication on Kunstkamera's official site and publication on CD to distribute among local communities, museums and educational institutions.

According to Hing Chao (founder of the Orochen Foundation), a major exhibition is to be co-hosted by him, together with the Kunstkamera Museum in 2017. This exhibition aims to feature a collection created by the eminent Russian ethnographer Sergei Shirokogoroff back in the early 20th century. It will be the first time many of his objects are exhibited for the first time about the Orochen society and culture in China. Could you describe in details your working relationship with Hing Chao; for example, how did you find each other? And what inspired you both to inspire you to start building this exhibition?

We met each other in Cambridge during the opening of 'River. Stars. Reindeer. Imaging Evenki and Orochen Communities of Inner Mongolia' photo exhibition. I was inspired by Hing Chao's talk about Chinese Orochens at the seminar. He visited St. Petersburg in November 2015, and we worked with the selection of objects for the proposed exhibition (Fig. 24.6). We were lucky to reveal other almost unknown Shirokogoroff collections, which were curated by the neighbouring department. One of these collections was received by Kunstkamera from Amour, a local lore museum in Blagoveshchensk, and Shirokogoroff's name was missing in the inventory. I think this exhibition is very important for Orochen communities. We expect that this relatively small in spatial measurements exhibition will make a significant step forward in preservation of Orochen cultural heritage and will increase the interest among Orochens to their culture. We hope this event will bring positive changes to local communities.

Figure 24.6 Bai Jing, Anna Sirina, Vladimir Davydov and Hing Chao select objects for the Orochen exhibition in Hong Kong. Siberian collection storages are in Kunstkamera. St. Petersburg, Russia, 2015.

Sergei Shirokogoroff: could you describe his fieldwork and his contributions to the field?

Sergei Mikhailovich Shirokogoroff worked as a head of the Anthropology Department at Kunstkamera. From 1912 to 1918, he worked in the field among Tungusic groups, both in Russia and in China, together with his wife, Elizaveta Nikolaevna Shirokogorova. These researchers brought unique collections of Tungusic objects (including shamanic objects, tools and clothes) and photographs to Kunstkamera. Their output to Tungusic studies is still needed to be comprehended. Sergei Shirokogoroff is famous for his ethnos theory. His main works were published in English that make him a well-known figure in anthropology. During Stalin's epoch, his works were prohibited in the USSR and were interpreted as anti-Soviet (Shirokogoroff emigrated to China after the revolution in Russia). At the same time, the researchers of Kunstkamera, for example, G.M. Vasilevich, continued working with his Evenki and Orochen collections.

For the general public, and for other nonethnographers, what can we possibly learn by looking at such exhibitions of the Orochen people?

Such exhibitions help us to track local history and to see the changes that happened during last century. They show the richness and importance of local cultures and teach visitors to respect these people.

By examining the Orochen people, their migration patterns and their ways of living, could we draw a picture depicting the political relations between China, Mongolia and Russia, as well as other neighbouring countries during the past few centuries?

Yes, the research of Orochen history will be helpful for comparative research of political, administrative, as well as administrative situations in these countries. This will also help us to see the connections and cultural exchanges that existed between these states.

The themes and information needs of libraries, archives and museums (LAMs, as some have referred to them) have increasingly converged. What are your experiences and thoughts about these cultural institutions whose work and best practices now often overlap?

These convergence processes significantly increase the ability of researchers to receive necessary information. This helps us to find large number of interesting sources. Generally, this helps to increase the quality of research. Moreover, the digitalisation of endangered archives, scanning books and digital cataloguing of museum collections will help people to save valuable information for the future generations. Close collaborations between these institutions will definitely encourage researchers to make new discoveries in their fields.

Which part(s) of your job as curator of the Kunstkamera Museum do you find most rewarding?

The most rewarding is, of course, working with people in the field. We are the members of the research institution and are involved in a number of projects, which imply intensive fieldwork in different regions of Siberia. Fieldwork is one of the main duties I have in Kunstkamera. Even though I am very busy with administrative work, I try spending 1–3 months per year working with local people. In recent years, I have participated in field trips to Yakutia, Zabaikal krai, Buriatiia, Taimyr Peninsula and Sakhalin Island. Work with local people gives inspiration in writing and helps with the research of collections and archival materials.

If politicians or budget holders ask you, instead of spending so much money and resources on setting up exhibitions documenting the Orochen people, why do not you spend it on buying more beds for the hospitals, hiring more qualified teachers for the local schools or buying better computers or iPads for the local students, what would be your answers to these questions?

Orochen culture is a part of worlds' cultural heritage. The loss of this part of the history and culture of humankind will impoverish our understanding of ourselves in the world. The exhibition itself may have the same healing effect on our society that has no less value than beds in hospitals and equipment in local schools. Exhibitions devoted to indigenous cultures help us to improve the spiritual sphere of our society and transmit humanistic values to younger generation.

Do you have any questions for me? Is there anything you would like to add before we finish this interview?

Dear Patrick, thank you very much for these interesting questions! I can add that this is a very inspiring idea to interview museum curators, librarians and archivists from different institutions. I am looking forward to reading the responses of my colleagues.

Imperial China's Collections at the National Palace Museum in Taiwan

25

Daniel Sung
National Palace Museum, Taipei, Taiwan, Republic of China

Introduction

The National Palace Museum in Taiwan is one of the national museums of the Republic of China and has a permanent collection of nearly 700,000 pieces of ancient Chinese imperial artefacts and artworks, making it one of the largest in the world. The collection encompasses over 10,000 years of Chinese history from the Neolithic Age to the late Qing Dynasty. Although most of the collection is high-quality pieces collected by China's ancient emperors, brought from mainland China during the Chinese Civil War, there has been collaboration between the two institutions, which highlights the importance of art and culture despite the political differences of the two countries. In the following interview, Daniel Sung (Fig. 25.1) tells us how he began his career as a librarian at the National Palace Museum (Taiwan), after obtaining his MLIS degree from the University of Wisconsin–Madison during the 1980s.

Could we begin this interview by first introducing yourself, for example, your training and education background? For example, your biography states that you earn your MLIS degree from University of Wisconsin–Madison in 1984. You then worked as an Assistant Librarian for Technical Services at Floyd Junior College in the US from 1985 to 1987. During the 1970s and 1980s, it was very common for Taiwanese MLIS graduates to start and further their careers as librarians in North America. Could you tell me why you chose to return to Taiwan to work for the National Palace Museum (Taiwan) instead?

I have a BA in English literature from Soochow University[1] (in Taipei, Taiwan), and my interest in library work began with the course 'Introduction to Library Science' that I took in the fourth year of college (1979–80), in which I was first exposed to the thinking of such library philosophers as Jesse H. Shera (1903–82) and Margaret E. Egan (1905–59), as well as their continued pursuit of an epistemological foundation for

[1] Soochow University (Taiwan) – Homepage. Available at: http://www-en.scu.edu.tw/.

Inside the World's Major East Asian Collections. http://dx.doi.org/10.1016/B978-0-08-102145-3.00025-X

Figure 25.1 Daniel Sung. Courtesy of the National Palace Museum Library.

librarianship. In 1984, I received an MA from the School of Library and Information Studies of the University of Wisconsin–Madison.[2]

My immediate plan at that time was to pursue a doctoral degree in librarianship. That, however, was not possible for my failure to fulfil one of the admission requirements stipulated by most library schools in the US: job experiences as a practicing librarian. Accepting the position of Assistant Librarian for Technical Services at the Floyd Junior College in Rome, Georgia, was my initial step to meet that requirement. While there, I was able to clear away, with the assistance of a hardworking library technician, a cataloguing backlog of approximately 5500 titles within the first 9 months of employment.

My aspiration to enrol in a doctoral programme in librarianship was never realised, though, on account of my return to Taiwan in 1987 for family-related reasons.

Could you tell us how you landed a job as Assistant Researcher and Cataloguing Librarian at the National Palace Museum (Taiwan) in 1987? Was it by chance and circumstance or was it an active decision based on personal interest?

I'm a trained librarian with a profound interest in the arts (by which I mean literature, fine art and music), and have always thought that working in the library of a cultural institution would suit my character and personality just fine.

[2] School of Library and Information Studies of the University of Wisconsin–Madison – Homepage. Available at: http://www.slis.wisc.edu.

Shortly after I returned to Taiwan, in the summer of 1987, I was approached by Dr. Chou Kung-shin, then head of the Museum's Department of Exhibition Services (at the National Palace Museum, Taiwan) who was to assume the Museum's directorship between 2008 and 2012 and was offered a job opportunity as a docent. However, the Museum's director, Dr. Chin Hsiao-yi (秦孝儀) (1921–2007), having reviewed my curriculum vitae and chatted with me in person, suggested that I take the post of Assistant Researcher and Cataloguing Librarian, and act as his secretary on the side attending to matters requiring the use of the English language.

Yes, landing that job at the National Palace Museum (Taiwan) was by chance, so to speak; yet, it was also an active decision on my part. As I look back today, it was a career move that I have not regretted a bit.

Could you describe in detail your major roles and duties at the Department of Rare Books and Historical Documents at the National Palace Museum (Taiwan)?

I am the Chief Curator of the Museum's Department of Rare Books and Historical Documents, responsible for all aspects of its administrative, curatorial and professional operation. Rare Books and Historical Documents is one of the Museum's three collection departments, the other two being Antiquities and Painting and Calligraphy. The Department's holdings include more than 210,000 volumes of Chinese rare and antiquarian books, approximately 400,000 pieces/volumes of Qing archival materials and over 230,000 volumes of contemporary monographic publications.

Could you describe the staffing structure within the Department of Rare Books and Historical Documents at the National Palace Museum (Taiwan)? For example, what is the total number of professional staff and supporting staff? What is the ratio between librarians and curators within your Department of Rare Books and Historical Documents?

Manned by 24 professionals and paraprofessionals, the Department is made up of three sections: collection management, exhibition planning and library services. Their functions are fairly self-explanatory, requiring no reiteration. One thing about exhibition planning, though, is that the Department runs a permanent exhibition entitled *Rare Books and Secret Archives: Treasures from the Collections of the National Palace Museum*, with materials on display rotated every 3 months for purpose of preservation. It also organises two thematic presentations every year, and examples of such exhibitions would include *The Dao of Book Protection: the Art of Traditional Chinese Book Binding and Decoration*, *The Bibliophile Yang Shoujing and His Guanhaitang Library of Rare Editions and Antiquarian Books* and *The Printmaker's Ingenuity and Craft: Ming and Qing Prints in the National Palace Museum.*

Librarians versus curators: I noticed that there are both librarians and curators working in your department. Could you describe the functional differences between these two groups of professionals?

Functionally, the two groups of professionals are identical, serving as caretakers of the holdings previously outlined, the only difference being the objects they take care of. Those who are responsible for the management, study, preservation and exhibition of rare and antiquarian books, as well as Qing archival materials, are termed 'curators', while those who deal with contemporary monographic publications are 'librarians'. The curators in my department are trained bibliographers and historians with advanced degrees, and the librarians have all received graduate training in library and information studies.

The National Palace Museum (Taiwan), Palace Museum in the Forbidden City (Beijing), and the British Museum and the Metropolitan Museum (NYC), when comparing the job scope, areas of responsibilities, expected job skills, professional knowledge and opportunities for professional developments amongst the librarians and curators (specialising in East Asian rare books) working for these four major museums, how are they different from each other?

I have worked closely with colleagues from the British Museum[3] on several loan projects, including *Treasures of the World's Cultures: the British Museum After 250 Years*, *The Body Beautiful in Ancient Greece* and *A History of the World in 100 Objects*. My own experiences and observations from these exhibitions suggest that the expertise, knowledge and responsibilities required of the professionals of both museums are more or less the same and that the approaches employed to organising presentations of cultural relics are similar as well.

Turning to the Palace Museum in Beijing, I myself have not noted any significant difference insofar as the previously mentioned requirements are concerned. In fact, many of my acquaintances from the Palace Museum in Beijing are accomplished scholars in their own areas of specialty. With these people on board, the Museum has been progressing at a tremendous speed on all fronts of museum operation.

Are there any professional sharing or collaborative projects being carried out amongst the librarians at the National Palace Museum (Taiwan) and the National Taiwan Library?

Presently, there is none. However, we did borrow a number of works from the National Taiwan Library[4] a couple of years ago when organising a thematic presentation of historical materials on Taiwan's indigenous peoples.

How and at what age did you develop an interest for Chinese rare books?

I do not recall when that interest took root. Suffice it to note that it comes from years of managing and handling. This may, as a matter of fact, serve to explain how on-the-job training and continuing education can be important to an individual's career

[3] The British Museum – Homepage. Available at: http://www.britishmuseum.org.

[4] The National Taiwan Library – Homepage. Available at: http://www.ntl.edu.tw/mp.asp?mp=2.

development. To this day, I still consider myself a student of Chinese bibliographical studies.

Please provide a brief introduction to the collections at the National Palace Museum Library. For example, collections housed at the National Palace Museum (Taiwan) versus the collections housed at the Palace Museum in the Forbidden City (Beijing), how are they different and in what ways are they related to each other?

The Library (Figs 25.2 and 25.4) was inaugurated in 1968 to support the research undertaken by the Museum's professionals. It is a very specialised collection of scholarly books and periodicals in many languages, and it is perhaps one of the finest art libraries in Taiwan today. Areas of collection emphasis include art, archaeology, aesthetics, conservation, museum studies, history, literature, philosophy and the like. The collection is separate from the rare (and antiquarian) books and Qing archival materials.

I have visited the Palace Museum Library (the Shouangong Palace) in Beijing a number of times. It appears to me that it is somewhat smaller in collection coverage and size, and its holdings of foreign language materials are rather limited.

Are there any collaborative projects between carried out between the National Palace Museum (Taiwan) and the Palace Museum in the Forbidden City (Beijing)? If yes, please give a list of highlights?

Yes, we have been collaborating with our colleagues in the Forbidden City for many years. Each October, the two palace museums jointly organise an international symposium on a theme mutually agreed upon, for one thing. On a more personal level, art historians, conservators and other professionals from both institutions are on very good terms, frequently sharing work experiences and research findings. The exchange of publications has become regular between the two museum libraries. Even their gift shop managers have come to study how we produce commodities of cultural creativity.

Figure 25.2 National Palace Museum (Taiwan) Library. Courtesy of the National Palace Museum Library.

Figure 25.3 Paging service (Qing Dynasty archives). Courtesy of the National Palace Museum Library.

Figure 25.4 Reading room of the National Palace Museum (Taiwan) Library. Courtesy of the National Palace Museum Library.

The Palace Museum in Beijing has also been generous enough to contribute their finest *objets d'art* to such well-received expositions launched by the National Palace Museum as *Harmony and Integrity: the Yongzheng Emperor and His Times*, *Emperor Kangxi and the Sun King Louis XIV: Sino-Franco Encounters in Arts and Culture*, *The All Complete Qianlong: a Special Exhibition on the Aesthetic Tastes of the Qing Emperor Gaozong* and *Portrayals from a Brush Divine: a Special Exhibition on the Tricentennial of Giuseppe Castiglione's Arrival in China*. Presently, our Department is working with the Palace Museum Library and the National Library of China in Beijing in the compilation of an illustrated *catalogue raisonné* of all existing titles in the second Tienlu Linlang Library formed by Emperor Qianlong (r. 1736–95) in 1798. The work is soon to be published.

The collections housed at the Department of Rare Books and Historical Documents at the National Palace Museum (Taiwan) and the collections housed at the National Taiwan Library, how are they different from each other?

The National Taiwan Library is different from our Department on several counts. First, the National Taiwan Library is supervised by the Ministry of Culture, while the National Palace Museum enjoys ministerial status. Second, the areas of collection emphasis are by no means similar. The National Taiwan Library, founded in 1914 when Taiwan was still under Japanese rule, is probably one of the oldest public libraries on the island and is known for its comprehensive collections of local literature and resources for Taiwan studies. Our Department, on the other hand, was established in 1968 to manage the collections of rare (and antiquarian) books and archival materials brought from the mainland, which originated in the inner court of the Qing dynasty (1644–1912). Third, the patrons served, or target audiences, are not identical. As a public library, the National Taiwan Library is geared towards delivering services to the populace at large. The users who come to consult our collections are mostly scholars, specialists, graduate students, etc.

The Department of Rare Books and Historical Documents at the National Palace Museum (Taiwan), what is the size of the collections? Could you describe the highlights of the collections?

In the collection of rare and antiquarian books, there are imprints dating from the Song (960–1279), Yuan (1279–1368), Ming (1368–1644) and Qing dynasties, volumes executed in movable type, editions annotated and commentated by renowned literati, manuscripts and hand-copied editions, as well as imprints and hand-copied works from historical Japan and Korea. Many of the volumes are extremely rare, being the sole extant copies that have survived the passage of time. Not only does the collection serve to illustrate the historical development of the book and the evolution of printing in China, but also provides authentic source materials against which later editions or imprints may be examined and compared. Here, it is important to note that while in most libraries, all Chinese language books printed before 1911, the year of the fall of the Qing dynasty, are kept in the rare books collection, our Department abides by a somewhat stricter definition. All books hand-copied or printed prior to the end of the Yuan Dynasty (1271–1368) are defined as rare, and those of the Ming (1368–1644) and Qing (1644–1912) dynasties are considered antiquarian.

The collection of historical documents, on the other hand, is largely made up of official documents created for the conduct and management of government affairs during the Qing Dynasty and is therefore a source of valuable materials for the study of the history of the empire and for research into the Chinese imperial archival system. Indeed, the rare books and historical documents in the Museum are regarded so highly by members of the Chinese studies community that they are consulted each year by many international scholars and researchers.

Royal and noble ranks of the Qing Dynasty were Manchurians. Members of the royal family (Qing Dynasty) also married princesses from Mongolian, Tibet and Xinjian. Does it mean that a large number of the books and other old documents housed in your Department are in other non-Chinese (non-Han) languages, e.g., Mongolian, Manchurian, Uyghur, Tibetan, etc.; in order to do your job well as a curator, how many different languages do you need to work with on a daily basis, and how many other non-Chinese character–based languages have you mastered?

A number of our curators working with Qing archival materials are fluent in Manchu, and others have fine Tibetan language skills. I myself work with Chinese and English on a daily basis, and I think I can read French and German with the help of a good dictionary, a skill developed over a very long period of time cataloguing and classifying Western-language books. As for those non-Chinese character–based scripts, I have mastered none.

Could you describe your topical day at work? Is there ever a typical day at work?

The word 'busy' describes it all. My typical day at work is packed with endless meetings and administrative tasks, as well as discussions with professionals on curatorial matters and exhibition planning. Since we have to deal with the 'publish or perish' pressure, I do my writing at home in the evening and on weekends.

What scholarly and professional associations are you a part of, and how do they assist you in your work?

In the 1980s, I was a member of the American Library Association[5] and the American Society for Information Science, and the periodicals I regularly received, the *American Libraries* and the *Journal of the American Society for Information Science*, were extremely helpful in terms of knowledge building and perspective broadening. My membership in these two associations ended after my return to Taiwan. Today, I am not a member of any professional association.

Our Library is affiliated with many professional associations, though, such as the Chinese Library Association, Interlibrary Cooperation Association, and the

[5] American Library Association – Homepage. Available at: http://www.ala.org/.

International Federation of Library Associations and Institutions,[6] and I get to read their publications quite regularly.

Who are the majority users of the Department of Rare Books and Historical Documents of the National Palace Museum (Taiwan)? Are the collections at your Department open to the general public?

Yes, our collections are open to the general public, and our users are largely scholars, specialists and graduate students, as I noted earlier. In general, anyone over 16 years of age with a valid identification is eligible to apply for a library card, with which he or she may freely consult the Library's resources in-house during its hours of operation. Paging services for the rare (and antiquarian) books and Qing archival materials are available at the Library (see Fig. 25.3). For purpose of preservation, however, those that have been published or microfilmed will not be paged, neither will those that have been made electronically accessible.

One thing worth noting here pertains to the Qing historical documents. In terms of size, ours are but a small fraction of the various types of official written materials created by Qing officials and administrative bodies. The bulk of these first-hand resource materials are now in the care of the First Historical Archives of China in Beijing. The two collections complement each other, and more often than not, a serious student of Qing history would have to travel between the two cities to consult both.

Do you use the same system for cataloguing your library materials and the Museum's 3-D objects? Or are separate systems being employed for handling the library and museum objects?

For library cataloguing and other functions such as acquisition, periodicals control and circulation, we use the Symphony Integrated System by SirsiDynix. For the management of rare (and antiquarian) books and Qing archival materials, a proprietary system developed by the Museum's Center of Information Services is employed.

Could you give examples of typical reference/research inquiries issued by the researchers or scholars at the National Palace Museum Library?

There are too many of them to list here. Yet, I can come up with two that I personally dealt with years ago:

> In what way was the Jesuit lay brother Giuseppe Castiglione (1688–1766) involved in the restoration of the Dongtang (St. Joseph's Church) and in the decoration of the Nantang (Cathedral of the Immaculate Conception) in 18th-century Beijing?
> What is this thing, 'Bulani Daliwon [Chinese characters Romanised]', in English, on the list of gifts presented to the Qianlong emperor by the McCartney Embassy in 1793?

[6] International Federation of Library Associations and Institutions (IFLA) – Homepage. Available at: http://www.ifla.org.

In the past few years, the National Palace Museum Library has been engaged in the digitisation of some of its collections. What are some of the projects, and what future plans are there for the digital collections?

We are still working on it, and it may take many, many more years before we can get the entire collections of rare (and antiquarian) books and historical documents digitised, considering their sheer sizes. However, I'm pleased to report that the palace memorials (158,614 pieces) and the Grand Council copies of palace memorials (190,889 pieces) in our collections have all been digitised and are available for online retrieval and browsing.

The themes and information needs of libraries, archives and museums (LAMs, as some have referred to them) have increasingly converged. What are your experiences and thoughts about these cultural institutions whose work and best practices now often overlap?

This is a very good question, indeed. I can certainly attest to what is described here, for I have work experiences in all three settings.

LAMs (and/or galleries) are all repositories created for the common good, and professionals of these institutions are all expected to organise their collections in an orderly and effective manner so that the holdings can be made efficiently accessible to the patrons they serve. While the three types of institutions have historically evolved and developed on their own paths, the identical missions are making them ideal collaborators in the 21st century, a prospect for offering integrated services with the help of advanced information and communications technologies. I have not given this much thought, to be frank; however, I suspect that the toughest challenge may be to get librarians, archivists and museum/gallery curators to cooperate across different disciplines.

I know an increasingly large number of cultural institutions in the US, Europe and other regions are collaborating to deliver such services. The professional literature in Taiwan's LAM communities, however, shows scarce research or investigation about LAM cooperation. I therefore do not think I'm in a position to report on what is going to happen in this part of the world.

Which part(s) of your job as researcher/librarian at the National Palace Museum Library do you find most rewarding?

This is the type of work I'm cut out for, I reckon, so I've been enjoying every part of it, except for the administrative tasks. Personally, though, I have to admit that assisting Dr. Chin Hsiao-yi (秦孝儀) (1921–2007) between 1987 and 2007, during his tenure as the Museum's Director and after his retirement, has been most rewarding, in terms of what I learned from him.

A scholar–gentleman, or litterateur, in the most traditional sense, Dr. Chin was schooled in Confucian and classical texts, calligraphy and poetry, and possessive of a superior standard of conduct coming from his self-respect and intellectual refinement manifested in unrestrained but delicate manners. Listening to him giving accounts of historical events and lessons to be learned, or striking up witty conversations of literary topics with him, was like enjoying a sweet, gentle breeze. I have all these years taken him as a role model. His passing in 2007 was one of the saddest moments in my life.

You have been working with such 'gems' and treasures from the Forbidden City for the past few decades. Have such experiences in any ways enriched your personal life or deepened your own understanding of traditional Chinese history or culture?

Indeed, they have. Previous to working at the Museum, my perception of the essence of Chinese culture or its elements was limited to what had been written in the textbooks. Today, as I have been exposed to the *crème de la crème* of China's cultural heritage for almost three decades, and as I have aged and matured, I have become more appreciative of the naturalistic view of life, the principles of simplicity and contentment and the aesthetic taste for elegance upheld by the Chinese literati.

Witnessing the Birth of Asian Hollywood Through the Hong Kong Film Archive*

26

Richie Lam
Hong Kong Film Archive, Hong Kong, China

Introduction

Hong Kong Chinese-language cinema has a century-old history. In comparison to cinema in China, Hong Kong enjoyed a greater degree of political expression. The Hong Kong cinema industry produced a greater variety of Chinese-language films without having to suffer from the constraints imposed by government censorship. For decades, Hong Kong reported to be the third largest motion picture industry in the world, after Bollywood and Hollywood, and the second largest exporter. However, Hong Kong cinema did not attract scholarly attention until the mid-1980s. The Hong Kong Film Archive (HKFA; Fig. 26.1) is the first research-based institution to be established for documenting the history and evolution of the region's cinema. This article is a direct face-to-face informational interview with Richie Lam, head of the HKFA, who discusses the film collection, expertise at the HKFA, strategic plans at the HKFA, as well as the Institute's contributions to the film industry and popular culture.

Could you begin this interview by introducing yourself, your past training and professional experiences? In addition, could you also explain your current role(s) and duties at the HKFA?

I am Richie Lam. I am currently serving as the head of the HKFA.[1] Technically speaking, I am an arts administrator, not a film expert, but I absolutely love movies. Anyways, I graduated from the Chinese University of Hong Kong,[2] and I majored in government and public administrations. Although my major at university was not film-related, I have always been a keen moviegoer, even when I was still a student. I have already been a big fan of the film festivals. Being able to work for the HKFA, I feel like I have won the lottery because I really love my job, and I feel most fortunate to be working here.

* *This article was originally published by the* International Academic Forum in the Asian Conference on Film and Documentary 2013 – Official Conference Proceedings.
[1] Hong Kong Film Archive – Homepage. Available at: http://www.lcsd.gov.hk/ce/CulturalService/HKFA/.
[2] The Chinese University of Hong Kong – Homepage. Available at: http://www.cuhk.edu.hk/english/index.html.

Inside the World's Major East Asian Collections. http://dx.doi.org/10.1016/B978-0-08-102145-3.00026-1

Figure 26.1 Hong Kong Film Archive premises.

As I remember, back in the mid-1980s, soon after I graduated from university, I started working as the Cultural Services Manager for the Hong Kong Government. In fact, I have worked in many different arts administration positions in the Government. For example, when I first entered the Government, I worked for the (Hong Kong) Space Museum[3] to manage the venue operation. After that, I worked for the Cultural Presentations section[4] to plan for the performing arts programmes for the Hong Kong public. After the Cultural Presentations aection, I worked briefly as the training officer for the museum curators in Hong Kong. And in 1993, I had a chance to be involved in the planning of the Film Archive. At that time, there were only three staff involved in the overall planning of the HKFA, and I was one of the team members. In 1997, I was transferred to the (Hong Kong) International Film Festival[5] to work as the Manager of the Festival. Then, 2 years later, I was transferred again to the Hong Kong Cultural Centre[6] to manage the venue. In 2000, I went to the (Hong Kong) Film Programmes Office[7] to arrange for the corporatisation of the Hong Kong International Film Festival, which was originally organised by the Government. Then in 2002, I worked for the

[3] (Hong Kong) Space Museum – Homepage. Available at: http://www.lcsd.gov.hk/CE/Museum/Space/en_US/web/spm/whatsnew.html.

[4] Hong Kong Cultural Presentations Section – Homepage. Available at: http://www.lcsd.gov.hk/CE/CulturalService/Programme/en/index.html.

[5] Hong Kong International Film Festival – Homepage. Available at: http://www.hkiff.org.hk/eng/main.html.

[6] Hong Kong Cultural Centre – Homepage. Available at: http://www.lcsd.gov.hk/CE/CulturalService/HKCC/en/about/intro.html.

[7] Hong Kong Film Programmes Office – Homepage. Available at: http://www.lcsd.gov.hk/ce/CulturalService/filmprog/english/programmes.html.

Hong Kong Antiquities and Monuments Office[8] doing something related to the protection and preservation of the local built heritage. In 2007, I returned again to the HKFA. So that was the summary of my career path and professional experiences up to now.

Can you tell me whose idea was it to establish this film archive in Hong Kong? In addition, what were the aims and purposes for establishing the HKFA? Was the HKFA a governmental initiative?

I would say only partially. Back in the late 1980s, some cultural persons, like Law Kar (羅卡) and Yu Mo-wan (余慕雲),[9] who cared very much about the preservation of the local film heritage, requested the Government to open a film library in Hong Kong. At the same time, the Government also expressed interest in doing something similar. As a result, the Government engaged an archive expert from Canada to conduct a feasibility study, and the study concluded that it was both feasible and possible to set up a film archive in Hong Kong. However, since film archive was new thing to Hong Kong, a lot of studies and research had to be conducted before making any final decisions on building the archive.

So in 1993, we had a small team to begin the actual research and planning work for the film archive. Concurrently, apart from doing the research, we also started to build the film collections. Because we understood well that if we could not start the acquisitions process as soon as possible, many of the valuable film collections would soon disappear. As you understand, old films are very fragile materials and they simply cannot wait. So at that time, apart from gathering the information from the overseas archives, we also collected some films and printed materials, mainly from individual collectors. During that time, we also approached many large film companies, like the Shaw Brothers (Studio)[10] and the Golden Princess,[11] to ask for donations of any film-related materials.

Unfortunately, we were still very much under the planning stage at that time, so the responses from these big film companies were, 'Only until I can really see the Film Archive has been fully established, or the storage facilities for films are readily available, then we could seriously consider donating something to the Archive…. But not until then'. As you can see, it was really challenging to begin building the collections for the Archive during the initial stage.

From your perspective or from the Hong Kong Government's perspective, why do they think the film industry in Hong Kong plays such an important role in our local heritage? Is it a recent concept or it has always been very important since the early days?

Films, in a sense, are really special cultural products, but in another sense, they are commercial products for the entertainment industry in Hong Kong. The film industry

[8] Hong Kong Antiquities and Monuments Office - Homepage. Available at: http://www.amo.gov.hk/en/main.php.

[9] Further information on Yu Mo-wan (余慕雲) is available at: https://zh.wikipedia.org/wiki/%E4%BD%99%E6%85%95%E9%9B%B2.

[10] Shaw Studio (邵氏兄弟(香港)有限公司) – Homepage. Available at: http://www.shawstudios.hk/.

[11] Golden Princess Film Production, Ltd. (金公主電影製作有限公司).

in Hong Kong has had a very long history, almost 100 years old. Especially during the 1950s or 1960s, we had a large quantity of films being produced in Hong Kong at that time, and we also carried the name, 'The Hollywood of the East/東方荷里活'[12] or something that was equally fancy. Hence, films are very important in Hong Kong in terms of both their cultural and commercial values. In addition, to me, films are also a kind of carrier of social images, as well as social messages. Through a film, one can retrieve a lot of old information that you cannot find from a regular printed book or even from a photo. So the film industry or the film culture is a very important part of our local heritage in this regard. In addition, films could also reflect how we see society at a particular period of time. Apart from the documentary aspects, films can also give us the real pictures of the society in which we live, for example, the so-called feature films, the drama films and the dramatic cinemas; they all reflect a kind of cultural values at that time. For example, during the 1960s, through films, you can find out about the way people lived in Hong Kong during that time. In fact, not only in Hong Kong, but all over the world, many people find this art form (film) to be really important throughout different societies. As a result, many regions and countries have their own film archives. In fact, there is an international association called The International Federation of Film Archives,[13] and according to the information provided, there are altogether over 150 archives for films over the world. As a result, this International Film Federation serves as an important platform for the people who work for film archives like us to share and exchange our expertise and professional experiences.

As one of the founding members of the HKFA, during the initial setup stage, did you need to develop a set of policies and the procedures for operating the Archive? While developing the procedures and policies for HKFA, did you adopt existing policies and procedures from other overseas institutions, that is, to borrow ideas and techniques from them on how to operate a film archive in Hong Kong?

Yes, we did take references from other overseas archives. The idea of setting up a film archive in Hong Kong was indeed very new during that time. During the initial setup stage, we took references mainly from the film archives in the UK and in Australia. Yes, we did try to model the HKFA after their establishments overseas. Of course, our Archive was comparatively much smaller and more compressed in terms of the whole structure.

Why did you choose to take references from film archives in the UK and Australia, instead of archives in other places, for example, the USA?

There was not really a special reason. It was simply because the UK's and Australia's governmental structures were very similar to that of Hong Kong's because Hong Kong was still a British colony then, and their structures were very similar to some of the

[12] 'The Hollywood of the East/東 方 荷 里 活' – for details, see *Cinema of Hong Kong* at: http://en.wikipedia.org/wiki/Cinema_of_Hong_Kong.

[13] International Federation of Film Archives – Homepage. Available at: http://www.fiafnet.org/uk/faq/default.html.

governmental offices in Hong Kong. Besides, it was before 1997, and there were not any political considerations at that time, just for very practical reasons. For the North American models, we also took them into consideration; however, at that time, we really needed to set up the HKFA as soon as possible, so we preferred to start with a medium- to a small-size archive that would be more manageable. Of course, ideally, we would want to have a large archive, as we had to consider the future developments, but you would need to take much longer time for the overall planning, as well as getting the money from the Government.

When you first tried to set up this HKFA, were there any legislations or rules that had to be followed, for example, the copyright issues for films?

In fact, at that time, or even now, we do not have any legal deposit legislations, NO legislation at all whatsoever. For Korea, they have this legal deposit legislation for films, but frankly speaking, not many regions or countries have this so-called legal deposit legislation because films are really special products, especially for those commercial films. Even now, we have to acquire the films actively ourselves, that is, not to wait passively for the film production companies to donate or deposit their films to the Archive. We really have to actively go out to acquire the films from them instead!

Of course, it would be ideal to have an archive law so that any films produced in Hong Kong will be deposited automatically to the HKFA, but in actual practice, it could be really complicated because when it touches upon the property rights and the copyrights of the film materials, to many people, they think these rights are very personal or even private because these rights are closely related to the commercial values of the actual film products. As a result, the film companies were reluctant to give out their film productions to the Film Archive in our early stage. However, I still think that we need to take time to educate people in order to change their mindset. I think it is very important for the HKFA to acquire, to preserve and to provide access to the movies for nonprofit-making purposes. So far, we have collected over 10,000 copies of film, including negatives and film prints. After eliminating the duplicate copies, we have collected around 4000–5000 titles of Hong Kong films. You have asked about the policies of the HKFA earlier; it is very simple: we collect Hong Kong movies, that is, all movies related to Hong Kong, produced in Hong Kong or produced by the Hong Kong filmmakers, and if we find any films belonging to these categories, we will collect them.

You mentioned earlier, you worked in many different departments within the Hong Kong Government, for example, the Cultural Presentations Office, the Culture Centre, the Space Museum, etc. Would you say that these experiences in some way have contributed to your current work at the HKFA?

Although I have previously worked in many different offices within the Government, many of them were somehow related to films. For example, I have previously worked for the Festival Office, which organised the annual Hong Kong International Film Festival, and then the Film Programmes Office, etc. As you can see, all these past experiences are somehow related to the film business. Even for some other nonfilm-related offices, which I previously worked for, I still believe the learned office procedures and practices could be adopted when running the HKFA.

Part of the training and the past experiences within the Government were certainly beneficial to my current work at the HKFA. In fact, the setup of the HKFA is very similar to other cultural-related offices in the Government, although we are very different in many technical aspects. For example, we have engaged quite a number of contract staff to work for the HKFA, as we need a wide variety of experts from various backgrounds. All those film and other technical experts are simply not available inside the Government. Hence, we need to open some contract positions to recruit them to work at the Archive.

Please highlight your collections here at the HKFA; for example, do you have any rare film items that you are very proud of or any unique film items that are only available at this Archive?

For example, we have a very valuable film of Bruce Lee (李小龍) entitled *The Orphan* (人海孤鴻). The story behind this film goes all the way back to 1994, when our HKFA colleagues were receiving training at a film laboratory in UK, the laboratory manager told us that they had gathered some Asian films, maybe from Hong Kong, and they were about to dispose it. Because they knew that we came from the HKFA, so they wanted us to handle this film, perhaps to return the film to the appropriate archives or organisations. So we went to the storeroom to inspect the film. Wow! As it turned out, it was a very important film of Bruce Lee! This film was commercially released in Hong Kong in 1960, just prior to Bruce Lee heading to the USA.

Okay! But since this film was released commercially, how come those people working at the rent laboratory did not recognise it?

Because those people who worked at that laboratory in the UK could not read any of the film's information in Chinese; it was all so foreign to them. In addition, they were only the negatives of the actual film, like the negative of a photo, so the laboratory staff in the UK could not watch the entire film either. It was indeed one of the most important films of Bruce Lee that was made in Hong Kong, in addition to four other films that he shot after he returned from the USA. So we felt so fortunate that we were able to retrieve the film. In addition, we only needed to conduct very minimal restoration on this film, because it has been so well kept over the years.

How did the negatives of a Hong Kong Chinese film end up in a film laboratory in the UK?

Have you heard about the Eastman colour film? Back in the 1960s, for the processing of such films, they had to do it in the UK, USA, Japan, etc. Once the processing of all the negatives was complete in the overseas laboratory, the prints would be sent to Hong Kong for screening while the negatives would be left in the film laboratories.

The HKFA would therefore have the opportunities of retrieving some of these negatives back to Hong Kong. We were indeed very lucky.

Who are the main HKFA users? Are they mostly from Hong Kong or overseas? Are they just regular moviegoers or they are serious scholars who are doing research on film studies at the HKFA?

In 2011, a user survey was conducted, and according to the survey results, the average age group of our users is over 50, that is, something between the age of 50–60. In other words, most of the local HKFA users are senior citizens or retired people. I think this could be related to HKFA's location because we are located in a residential area. Our user groups are very different from that of the other public museums in Hong Kong. Also, many of them are situated in the heart of the city, viz. Tsim Sha Tsui, where you could attract a more diverse group of audience, including tourists from mainland China and from other overseas countries. Anyhow, we still have younger audience group using the Archive, although the proportion is not really that large.

Would you say a majority of the users come to the HKFA for entertainment purposes?

Yes, a majority of them come for entertainment purposes. They come to see the exhibitions on the ground floor, to browse the magazines at the Resource Centre (Library) and also to attend the film screenings at the cinema inside the HKFA. Of course, we also get a lot of scholars and researchers from both local and overseas who come to the HKFA Resource Centre for research purposes.

For the local and overseas scholars, what kinds of inquiries or requests would they usually make? What kind of information would they want to obtain from the HKFA?

Normally, the researchers are interested in finding out information about the old movies, for instance, movies produced in Hong Kong during the 1950s and 1960s. Moreover, they want to find information on the major film studios in Hong Kong, for example, the Shaw Brothers and the Golden Harvest. The researchers could read our collection of old magazines in which much information on local film history could be found.

Am I to understand that the Resource Centre (Library) would be responsible for answering this kind of questions? In other words, within the Film Archive, you also have a library, which you call the Resource Centre, so what is the purpose and function of the Resource Centre?

The basic functions of the Resource Centre are to make our collections available for the public to access. You may say that the Resource Centre is a facility that the public or the researchers can come to conduct their searches and researches on the materials we hold. For the HKFA, in addition to collecting and keeping the film materials, the ultimate goal is to make these materials accessible to the researchers and to the general public for appreciation and even for entertainment purposes through which the general

Figure 26.2 Exhibition, Zen and Sensibility Legend in King Hu's Drawing.

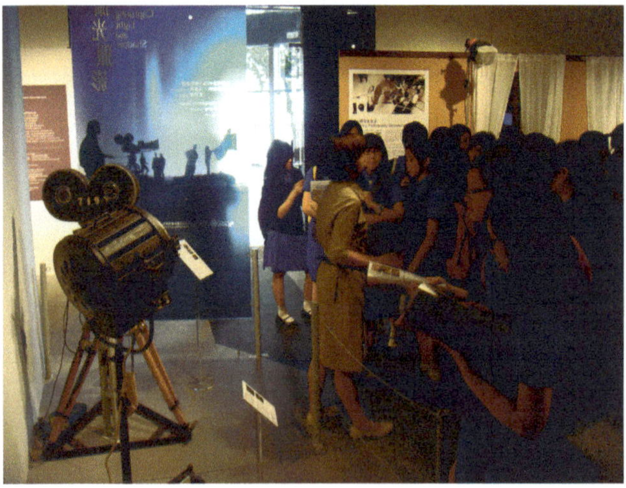

Figure 26.3 Guided tour of exhibition.

public can learn about the film history, film industry and film culture in Hong Kong. Of course, the HKFA also has a Programming Team, which is responsible for organising various public programmes including film screenings, exhibitions (Figs 26.2 and 26.3), talks, seminars, etc. (see Fig. 26.4 for an HKFA publication). That is another way to make our collection accessible to the public.

How far ahead do you need to plan your public or outreach programmes?

We usually have an annual programme plan for those film screening programmes and exhibitions. However, we also have initial ideas for more long-term programmes, say, for 3–5 years. For example, for the coming year, in April 2014, we will have an exhibition on the theme of 'Hong Kong gangster film'.

Figure 26.4 Publication: Mastering Virtue: The Cinematic Legend of a Martial Artist.

Could you please tell me how does the HKFA develop ideas and plans for public programmes and exhibitions? While developing these programmes, how could you ensure that they are corresponding to the public's needs and interests?

There is a really complicated workflow, but I try to make it simple for easy understanding. First of all, we have a panel of colleagues, who would discuss all the ideas first, and then we will develop more concrete proposals for the different film programmes (see Fig. 26.5 for a programme launched in 2012). In fact, we have already developed some ideas for our programmes for the next 5 years. But how do we develop them? Well, there are so many factors, which will affect our programming considerations and decisions. First of all, we have to look at our film collections, for example, if we have acquired or restored some representative collections, we will certainly develop a series of special programmes to promote them, and that is one way. The other way is that we are systematically doing research on different film studios, film companies, filmmakers and film genres in Hong Kong, etc., so we can organise special programmes on these major film studios, for instance, on the Shaw Brothers, on Cathay Organisation

Figure 26.5 Hong Kong Heritage Project co-sponsored and organised Voices and History: Oral History Seminar and Workshop with Hong Kong Archives Society and HKU-SPACE in 2012.

(HK) (國泰電 懋) and also on the Great Wall (長城電影製片有限公司), Feng Huang (Phoenix) (鳳凰影業公司) and Sun Luen (長鳳新電影公司).

We also launched programmes on important filmmakers, for example, on Li Han-hsiang (李翰祥),[14] Yi Wen (易文)[15] and King Hu (胡金銓)[16]; all these programmes were results of our research works and with a view to arouse the interest of the public and researchers on the Hong Kong film history.

The HKFA offers a variety of public programmes and exhibitions every year; how can you ensure that you have the adequate funding for them? What resources are needed to implement the programmes proposed for the forthcoming year?

Luckily, we have a rather stable budget from the Government every year, around 30–35 million Hong Kong dollars for the operational expenditure of the organisation. The budget would then be allocated to various functional units of the HKFA. Every year, we would come up with an annual programme plan for the approval of the Government.

Have there been situations that you and your colleagues both thought, 'Oh! This is such a great programme!'? And you knew that HKFA audiences would also love it. But after you have submitted your proposal or funding application to the Government, they told you that they did not like your proposal and did not give you the funding that you sought.

Frankly speaking, NO! Maybe because the Government has a lot of trust in our expertise and therefore gives the Archive a great deal of freedom to do our jobs. Not all

[14] Li Han-hsiang (李翰祥). Further information available at: http://en.wikipedia.org/wiki/Li_Han-hsiang.
[15] Yi Wen (易文). Further information in Chinese available at: http://zh.wikipedia.org/wiki/%E6%98%93%E6%96%87.
[16] Hu Jinquan (胡金銓). Further information available at: http://en.wikipedia.org/wiki/King_Hu 10.

our colleagues are civil servants; in fact, some of them are engaged on contract terms who are professional in film research, editorial and programming. We have a total of seven different functional units within the HKFA. One unit is mainly responsible for the acquisition of films. We have another team, which is responsible for the film conservation and preservation. As I mentioned earlier, we have a Programming Team, and they take care of all the film exhibitions and the screening, and for the Research Team, the colleagues make use of the collected materials for conducting research on various themes, for example, doing research on film studios like The Golden Harvest, on film directors such as King Hu (胡金銓), on Bruce Lee (李小龍), etc. Then we have the Resource Centre, which is staffed by the librarian colleagues who will take care of the printed and audio–visual collections and manage the Centre, and we also have the Systems Unit, which takes care of the computerised system for recording the information of the archive collection. Last but not least, we have the Venue and Administration Unit, looking after the daily administration and operation of the Archive.

Throughout the years, the HKFA has developed many interesting programmes for the Hong Kong public; could you name one or two programmes, which you thought were great successes? Maybe you could tell me about a programme that you are really proud of, the audience loved it, it was also well-received by the media, and also received a lot of support from the Government.

I think it has to be the project on the famous Hong Kong movie actress, Linda Lin Dai (林黛)[17]; it was, no doubt, an exhibition that we are really proud of. The experience from the whole event was hard for me to forget, even until these days. Lin Dai committed suicide in 1964, and her son approached us around 2008, as he generously offered to donate his mother's personal items to the Archive. It was my very first time to visit Lin Dai's residence. We could see that her family did not make any changes to the settings inside her bedroom since the day she passed away, and being able to witness that first-hand was definitely an unforgettable and sentimental experience for me. We then collected all the items and tried to recreate her bedroom in our Exhibition Hall. That particular exhibition on Lin Dai received overwhelming responses. It was so well-received by both the public and the media that it actually broke the attendance records of our previous programmes.

For those personal items taken from Lin Dai's bedroom, did you have to return them her family after the exhibition, or they were simply donated to the Archive?

No, all those items belonging to Lin Dai were donated to the Archive. In fact, for the HKFA, we also take up a minor role of a museum, that is, to keep some film-related artefacts, such as movie cameras, projectors, costumes, props, etc.

[17] Lin Dai (林黛), 1934–64, was a very famous Chinese actress of Hong Kong films in the Shaw Brothers Studio during the 1950–60s. Further information is available at: https://en.wikipedia.org/wiki/Lin_Dai.

In other words, this institute is not just an archive for films, but also a museum for personal items related to the film industry?

Yes, that is correct!

Could you give me another successful programme launched by the HKFA?

Another example I want to give is not an exhibition, but a film. You might have heard of a long-lost film entitled *Confucius* (孔夫子),[18] directed by famous director Fei Mu (費穆).[19] It is a black and white film made in 1940 in Shanghai during the Japanese occupation. This film was very meaningful in terms of its main message, as well as its overall aesthetics. Director Fei Mu tried to use the character of Kongfuzi to promote the awareness of Chinese people about our own national image, giving us a sense of national pride during the Japanese oppression.

How did you acquire this film, and when was it acquired?

As said, *Confucius* was a long-lost film. Originally, we thought that we would never discover this film again. Many people had tried to locate this film for over 50 years, but without success. This film was originally released in Shanghai in 1940, and it was then released again 8 years later in 1948. It then suddenly disappeared, and only the film's printed brochures were remaining. But in 2001 or 2002, a member of the public telephoned the Archive, saying that a relative had just passed away and left behind some reels of films. As usual, we went to the site to check out the collection without much expectation. As the donor handed the film cans to us, we found one of the cans was labelled *Confucius* (孔夫子) in Chinese. As we saw this, we were all totally shocked and amazed! Initially, we were very sceptical about the real content of the film reels being handed to us. But later on, we were able to verify that it was indeed the long-lost *Confucius* that we have been searching for so long (Fig. 26.6). This was another amazing experience for me.

Did you also organise another exhibition or special film screening for promoting this long-lost film?

We acquired that film at that time, and frankly speaking, we do not have the expertise to handle it. First of all, it was a flammable nitrate film, so we had to put it aside first. We spent quite a lot of time researching this film, including the details of its production background, copyright issues, condition of the film negatives, etc., to prepare for the restoration work. We had then collaborated with an overseas film laboratory in Italy to conduct the restoration work. That was the first large-scale restoration project of the Archive. Before that, we have conducted a number of restoration projects as well, but the scale was comparatively small.

[18] http://en.wikipedia.org/wiki/Confucius_(1940_film); http://www.cuhk.edu.hk/cuoaa/conficious%20add.pdf.

[19] Fei Mu (費穆). Further information available at: http://en.wikipedia.org/wiki/Fei_Mu.

Figure 26.6 Restored treasures: *Confucius* (1940).

Which part of your work at the HKFA do you find most satisfying?

In fact, when I first arrived at the HKFA many years ago, I worked as the Film Acquisitions Manager, and I absolutely loved my job then. I really did enjoy my job. For example, being able to collect, to rescue our film heritage, I have to say it was the most satisfying part of my job. Frankly speaking, I was happier and more satisfied when I worked as the Acquisition Manager during the old days. I truly enjoyed being the 'Acquisitions Person', namely building my film networks, approaching different people in the film industry and learning how to acquire films to expand the HKFA collections.

What about being able to see how the audiences' positive responses towards the programmes developed by the HKFA; do you find it to be satisfying?

Of course, most satisfying indeed! In addition, I have the chance to witness the developments of the HKFA in the past 20 years. When we first started the HKFA project in early 1990s, we only had a very small team for doing all the planning. Now, we have a team of 50 staff, although not of large scale; we still manage to organise many meaningful programmes for the public. The success of the HKFA is really a team effort; all our colleagues came from all sorts of professions, of very diverse training and backgrounds, etc. Without programming colleagues, we would not be able to develop any programmes to promote our unique film collections. Without our library colleagues, we would not be able to provide good public services to the public and to the film researchers. Without the conservation team, we would never be able to preserve the films and make them available to our Archive audience. Without the acquisitions colleagues, we would not be able to develop such a rich and diverse film collection as we now hold, so we really need all these different experts to work together in order to get the HKFA to work.

Would you prefer the HKFA to stay at where it is now, or would you prefer it to be somewhere around the Cultural Centre, for example, next to other museums in Hong Kong via which you could attract more visitors or tourists?

Yes, you may say that our present location in Sai Wan Ho is not that accessible. As I mentioned earlier, back in 1993, at that time, if we had not accepted this present site in Sai Wan Ho and if we had chosen to wait for a more centralised location, I seriously do not think we could not have begun the HKFA immediately. I was directly involved in this project since its planning stage; hence, I totally understand how difficult it was to build the whole Archive from scratch. Of course, every single archivist or librarian would want their archive or library in a more centralised area, but in actual practice, it is very difficult to. As a result, we decided to take up a location in Sai Wan Ho. Maybe now is the time for us to think about opening a branch for the Archive in a more centralised location.

Where would you prefer the new branch to be?

I do not have any preferences at the moment. In fact, even with our current location, we have been arranging some of our programmes to be organised in the more urban areas, for example, showing our films at the Broadway Cinematheque[20] in Yau Ma Tei, at the lecture halls of the Hong Kong Science Museum and Hong Kong Space Museum in Tsim Sha Tsui so as to allow our public to enjoy our film screenings without the need to come to the Archive premises. But of course, my ultimate goal is to find a place which is much more convenient for our patrons. Some patrons already told us that the Archive is too far away from where they live. In fact, I have already conveyed my idea of a new urban branch for the Archive to our senior management, and hopefully, such an idea can be materialised.

What are the major difficulties and challenges that you and your colleagues are currently facing at the HKFA?

I think the accommodation and storage issues are the challenges at the moment. Since our collection and staff size are growing, we are in great need of additional space for office and collection stores. In addition, the possible retirement of film stock (film celluloid) in the near future is probably another great challenge to us and, in fact, to the whole film archive community (see Fig. 26.7 regarding HKHP digitisation project). With the rapid development of digital technology, many films are now produced by digital means and screened by a digital projector in the cinema. It results in a sharp drop in the demand of film stock, which forces the production companies, such as Kodak, Fuji and Alfa, to stop the production of film stock. The diminishing demand also triggered the closing down of many film laboratories. With this trend developed, where can the film archive ultimately buy the film stock and process the film prints for screening? Will it be the end of 'film projection'? The impacts will become more salient in the coming few years, and a lot of discussion will be held among the film archives.

[20] Broadway Cinematheque – Homepage. Available at: http://bc.cinema.com.hk/.

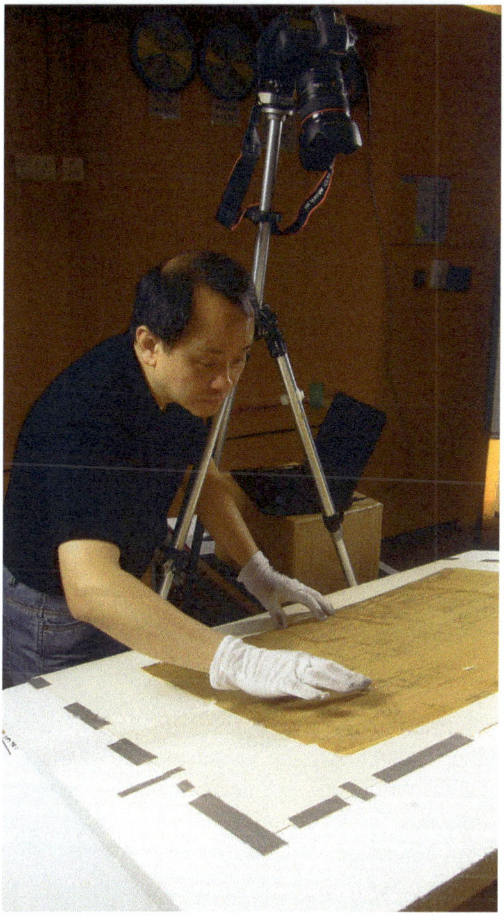

Figure 26.7 Hong Kong Heritage Project undertook a major digitisation programme in 2012 using professional photographers.

Do you have anything else that you would like to add before closing this interview?

I can easily talk about the HKFA for over 6 and even 10 hours. I really like to work in the Archive. I have previously worked in many different posts relating to cultural services and arts administration, but so far, this is the one that I enjoy working the most.

When watching a film, which cinematic elements do you enjoy most? Do you enjoy the aesthetics part, the visual part (for example, the graphic excitements), the drama itself, the narrative part or the other nostalgic elements? Which part of the film do you think is most important?

I can just say that I like watching movie in the cinema, not at home, because I can be enveloped in total darkness, being able to watch those moving images on the screen

Figure 26.8 Lord Lawrence and Sir Horace Kadoorie.

without any distractions; being able to be immersed 100% in the story and the drama, that is what I really enjoy.

To you, what elements are more important?

To me, it has to be the drama and the script. I really enjoy watching any films with good scripts. Of course, I also enjoy the visual aspects of the film. But I think the most important thing is the whole context; in other words, the actual script of the film should be the most important thing because you really need a good convincing script to bind all these different cinematic elements together. A film without a good script, to me, is not a good film (Fig. 26.8).

Documenting Traditional Chinese Medicine Library Collections at Hong Kong Baptist University

27

Lisa Song
Hong Kong Baptist University, Hong Kong, China

Introduction

According to the National Center for Complementary and Integrative Health, traditional Chinese medicine (CM) is a system of traditional Asian medicine that is built on a foundation of more than 2500 years of Chinese medical practice that includes various forms of herbal medicine, acupuncture, massage, dietary therapy and exercise (in particular, Qigong, a system of coordinated body posture and movement, breathing and meditation). As the first dedicated library with a focus on CM in the universities of Hong Kong established to meet the growing information demand in the development of CM and to provide quality information resources and services in support of the University's teaching, learning and research activities, the Chinese Medicine Library (CML) of Hong Kong Baptist University (HKBU) was officially opened to members of the university community in August 2001 (Fig. 27.1). With a floor space of 5000 square feet, 70 seats with computer, a multimedia room and group study rooms, the library collection has over 12,000 volumes of CM printed books and journals, and a growing collection of multimedia materials and e-books (Fig. 27.2). As librarian of the CML, Lisa Song (Fig. 27.3) manages one of the world's most unique collections and spaces that only caters to traditional CM. In the following interview, Lisa Song discusses her unparalleled path to becoming a third-career librarian, as well as sharing with us her personal stories of becoming a doctor of Western medicine during the peak of the Cultural Revolution in mainland China.

Could we begin this interview by first introducing yourself, for example, your training and educational background, your main roles and duties at the Head of the CML, HKBU?

My name is Lisa Song. I am originally from mainland China. I earned my bachelor's degree from Norman Bethune College of Medicine, Jilin University,[1] which is a university for studying Western medicine in mainland China. Usually, it would take

[1] Norman Bethune College of Medicine, Jilin University in Mainland China – Homepage. Available at: http://www.admissions.cn/bqeyxy/.

Inside the World's Major East Asian Collections. http://dx.doi.org/10.1016/B978-0-08-102145-3.00027-3

Figure 27.1 Naming ceremony of Hong Kong Baptist University Chinese Medicine Library.

Figure 27.2 Hong Kong Baptist University Chinese Medicine Library.

about 5 years to finish a bachelor's degree programme in medicine in China, but my case was kind of special. It was an English-language medical programme because all of the courses, teaching and workshops were carried out in English. During the late 1970s, China just opened its door to the West. During that time, not many people from mainland China could speak English because speaking in a foreign language and communicating with the outside world was strictly forbidden.

Later on in the mid-1980s, even in primary and middle school, we could learn English, but it was still not at the level to get to understand a native English speaker. At the Norman Bethune Medical College, our professors were natives from China. However, only a few of these Chinese professors of medicine, usually elderly, got excellent English training before the Cultural Revolution (1966–76), so their English ability was exceptionally good. The medical degree programme that I undertook at

Figure 27.3 Lisa Song.

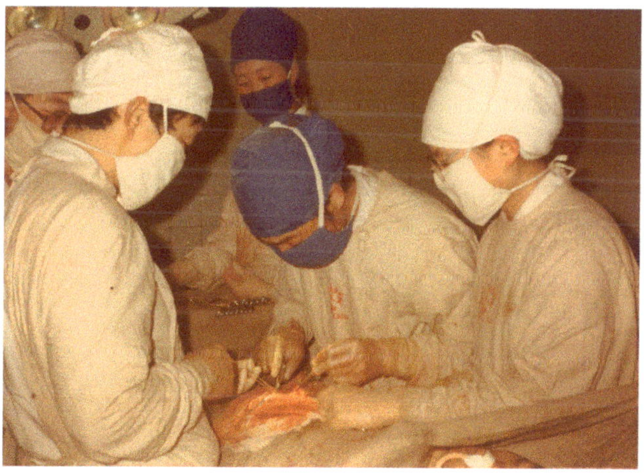

Figure 27.4 Lisa Song's internship as medical doctor in China 1.

Norman Bethune Medicine College lasted for 6 years. After earning my bachelor's degree in medicine, I began an internship practice under the guidance of a clinical doctor at a local hospital in the Jilin Province of China (Fig. 27.4).

Do you come from a family of medical doctors or healthcare practitioners? In addition, what was the social and professional status of traditional CM doctors during the Cultural Revolution?

Both of my parents are medical doctors specialised in internal medicine, so I thought I was destined to become a medical doctor since my childhood! With their medical influence, I do have a dream to become a real medical doctor.

During my childhood, I visited the hospital frequently, not as a patient, but as a visitor (observer). I witnessed many patients recovering from very serious, life-threatening illnesses and conditions and becoming healthy again. To me, it was absolutely a miracle to be able to witness that. The social status between the Western doctor and traditional CM doctors are relatively the same. Unfortunately, the salary and social benefits they received depended mostly on the number of years of practice (seniority), and not on their skills, competencies and professional qualifications.

Was it difficult to practise Western medicine during the Chinese Cultural Revolution?

My parents practiced medicine before the Chinese Cultural Revolution took place. Because they were medical doctors, whenever any of our family members got sick, especially my grandparents, they would give them medical treatments at home, even the IV treatment, instead of going to the local clinics or hospitals. Because of my parents, I often had chances to observe treatment practices. I would often observe the patients' stages of suffering and their levels of happiness during their recovery. Because I grew up in such an environment, I witnessed bloody situations and many happily recovered patients. These events jump-started my dream of being a medical doctor. I felt that I was born to become a medical doctor as well.

After a while, my dream came true, and I graduated from medical school. Afterwards, I had a 1-year internship in the different medical subject areas.

From 1976 and onwards, the People's Republic of China began to open up to the world and undertook a series of major economic and education reforms. As young university graduates with wide-open eyes, we were longing to see what was happening outside of China, and we were eager to go overseas to further our education. There was a group of 40 Chinese students who graduated from the same English medical programme with me. Eventually, a majority of my classmates went to the US to further their studies after 1987.

Your other classmates who graduated from medical school in mainland China around the same time as you (around 1987), are they now practising medicine in the US or they are now working in other nonmedical-related professions?

Only five or six of them stayed in the medical profession. Even though we received our medical degrees in mainland China, our degrees were not recognised in the US. In order to practise medicine in the US, one would need to do a lot of re-studying and passing many different types of US Medical Licensing Examinations (USMLE) that were set out for assessing a physician's abilities to apply knowledge, concepts and principles, and to demonstrate fundamental patient-centred skills, etc. Eventually, only five or six of my classmates who went to the US managed to pass the USMLE. Currently, they are practicing medicine outside of China, whereas for me, I got a

Figure 27.5 Lisa Song as MSc graduate in US.

scholarship to undertake a PhD programme in medical informatics (specialising in hospital information systems) at the University of Utah.[2]

So do you have a PhD in medical informatics?

No, I do not, despite that I managed to finish all the taught units and coursework of my PhD programme. This was because of my husband, who was 3 years ahead of me doing his PhD programme at the same university. By the time he got his PhD, he already got a job offer in another city of the US. I therefore decided to withdraw from my PhD programme and obtained a master's degree instead (Fig. 27.5). Eventually, I ended up working as an IT programmer and then a system analyst in the US.

What are the major differences between the treatments of electronic medical records and regular medical records in printed format?

Electronic medical records allow the patient's information to be transferred from one department to another in the most convenient fashion. It is undoubtedly a huge asset. Such a setup allows healthcare providers to finish their patient registration more speedily, thereby facilitating for the scheduling of more patients under a short period of time. Digital medical records also allow a new prescription to be transmitted electronically or facilitate the renewal authorisation to a community or to the pharmacy. Unquestionably, this type of medical records storage fosters more effective medical practices.

During the early years, what were the main challenges and difficulties when you first started to develop these electronic records?

[2] University of Utah – Homepage. Available at: http://www.utah.edu/.

Different hospitals selected their own favourite information system, such as SMS, PiMS, and CENER, etc. When I was a student in medical informatics, I needed to write programs and create individual modules. Each system module will then be linked up and integrated together so that they would function interactively and become the final automated hospital information system that would be used by the hospitals. In fact, the University of Utah[3] is a pioneer in this area.

In the middle of the 1990s, my husband decided to move to Hong Kong. When I first came to Hong Kong, I was working for a private hospital to install their hospital information system. After finishing the IT project, I started to work at HKBU. In my first year, I worked for the HKBU School of Chinese Medicine (SCM)[4] because I have a medical background. During the initial years, I had a chance to work with the HKBU Library staff to set up an electronic CML dedicated for serving the SCM at HKBU. At that time, we did not know what an electronic library was and how it should function, so what I did was identify a large number of relevant websites, evaluate the scope and quality of these websites' contents and group them logically together based on their subject contents. Basically, it was a website of digital pathfinders dedicated to the subject of CM.

At that time, the President of HKBU was a keen supporter of traditional CM and came up with a very ambitious idea, that is, to establish the very first SCM in Hong Kong under the HKBU. He managed to find a large donation for setting up the SCM. The SCM offers two different programmes, namely, the CM programme and the Chinese Pharmacy programme. Almost all of the SCM faculty members came from mainland China for the reason that they simply could not find any qualified experts locally from Hong Kong to fill the teaching positions of this newly established school. Before Hong Kong was handed over from the British to Communist China in 1997, the British colonial government did not encourage the development of CM in Hong Kong. The Hong Kong colonial government simply did not care about traditional CM and the professional developments and practices amongst its practitioners.

In 2000, HKBU managed to establish the very first SCM and a research institute in Hong Kong, despite still being relatively very small in comparison to their counterparts in mainland China.

The HKBU President also initiated the idea of establishing a professionally run CML to support the overall teaching, learning and research of the SCM. During the initial stage, none of us at the HKBU had the intention of building a separate physical library dedicated to CM. During that time, although I worked closely with the HKBU Library to develop their early version of an electronic library on CM, I was not a member of the Library staff.

Back in 2002, after spending 1 year working at the SCM, the HKBU Library finally decided to set up this subject branch library. At that time, I did not have any interest in becoming a librarian of any kind, despite having already developed a keen interest in working for the SCM. The HKBU Library tried many times to recruit a seasoned professional librarian, preferably someone with a medical background to manage this CML. Unfortunately, they could not find anyone who could fit the professional requirements on both sides, that is, an MLIS (master's degree in library science) degree, together with a

[3] University of Utah – Homepage. Available at: http://www.utah.edu/.

[4] School of Chinese Medicine, Hong Kong Baptist University – Homepage. Available at: http://scm.hkbu.edu.hk/en/home/index.php.

Figure 27.6 Lisa Song as MLIS graduate in Hong Kong.

background in medicine. My former supervisor at the SCM told me, 'I saw this Chinese Medicine Librarian job opening advertisement several times. Do you have any interest in applying?'. I said I never expected to work in a library, but I was happy to give it a try. Out of all the job applicants, I was the only person without an MLIS. Despite already having a master's degree in medical informatics, I would still need an American Library Association (ALA)–accredited MLIS degree in order to work as a professional librarian at academic libraries in Hong Kong. When I first started to work for the CML, although I had to perform all the functional duties as a professional librarian, I could only carry the job title and got paid as 'Library Coordinator' since I was not an MLIS degree holder (for a photo of Song later receiving the MLIS degree in Hong Kong, see Fig. 27.6).

During my time as the Library Coordinator, my first and most immediate task was to set up the core collections and other basic services for CML. A majority of our printed book collection of the CML came from mainland China. During the initial stage, we had to make several onsite professional visits to different CM libraries around Beijing, Guangzhou, etc., to familiarise ourselves the proper way to set up a CML.

You were originally trained in Western medicine and later switched to become a librarian of CM. Have you encountered any major challenges or difficulties during this critical period of your career transition? The concepts and practices of traditional CM, when compared with Western medicine, how are they different from each other?

In terms of medical concepts, treatments and practices, there are major differences. For Western medical practices, treatments are usually tailor-made to cater for each particular disease, meaning that the medical doctor will look for specific causes of diseases and focus on particular body components or organs to treat. For example, if you are coughing, they will treat your coughs only.

On the other hand, Taoism plays a major role in shaping the concepts and practices of CM. A person is seen as part of the holistic entity. For this reason, one should be analysed or interpreted with reference to the whole. As a result, the holistic concept of traditional CM includes integrity of the human body, as well as its relationship with the outer environment surrounding us. In other words, what a doctor of traditional CM deals with is not just the symptoms at all, but the actual root of the sickness. According to the CM practitioners, every symptom has a root (otherwise, there would not be a symptom). Furthermore, Western medicine is very good and effective for acute diseases, quick diagnosis, quick efficacy and fast cures, etc. On the other hand, CM is better for chronic diseases, but it would take much longer time to take effect.

When you first took up the position as the CM Librarian, did it take you a long time to master the basic terminologies in the discipline, for example, the long list of ingredient names of Chinese medical herbs and all the acupuncture points on human body?

I have to admit that I could not understand all the contents of CM at first because a majority of the training I had previously was in Western medicine. I only had two semesters of CM courses back in my student days at Norman Bethune College. Although my major is in Western medicine, we needed to master some general concepts about CM, such as acupuncture points, and common ingredients of Chinese herbs. During the CM clinical practice, most of time we had to follow the CM doctors and nurses to observe how they carry out their medical consultations and their daily ward rounds to check on their patients' conditions in order to understand the basic concepts and treatments of CM.

How long is the history of traditional CM?

It is really hard to say. According to legend, Chinese *materia medica* was first compiled by the Emperor Shen Nong over 5000 years ago. Emperor Shen was said to have been so moved by disease suffering that he went off to mountain forests in search for cures.

However, many people say that traditional CM is built on a foundation of close to 3000 years of practices, which include various forms of herbal medicine, acupuncture and dietary therapy, etc. The Ming Dynasty (1368–1644) was considered the peak of CM because it was the period when the Chinese medical doctors were able to access many different schools of medical thoughts and treatments, partly due to the easy access to medical literature facilitated by moveable type and block printing. Because of the Chinese block printing techniques, people no longer needed to copy books manually by hand. New sheets, as well as books, could therefore be produced in a much speedier fashion, thereby keeping the Chinese medical practitioners up to date with the latest information, in that way enabling a wide variety of people to share their ideas

Figure 27.7 Exhibition inside Hong Kong Baptist University Chinese Medicine Library.

with a large number of other people in the CM community. In other words, the block printing techniques played major roles in speeding up the spread of new thoughts, ideas and treatments.

Could you tell us about the collection highlights of the CML?

CML has a set of 400 volumes of books, which is called the *Complete Collection of Traditional Texts on Chinese Materia Medica*. This set includes more than 800 classical works and 10,000 articles on Chinese materia medica. The Library is honoured to have received a special serial designation as No. 1 for acquiring this collection. This set of collections helps us to supplement the shortage of ancient CM literature (see also an exhibition at the CML in Fig. 27.7).

What are your duties and responsibilities as a librarian for traditional CM?

My duties and responsibilities as the CM Librarian (Figs 27.8 and 27.9) include the following:

- oversee the daily operations of the CML, including services in areas of circulation, course reserves, interlibrary loan, printing and photocopying, book drop, lost and found, shelf and equipment maintenance, room reservation, etc.;
- provide CML reference services, conduct library orientation and tours, bibliographic instruction workshops to enhance the information literacy of CML users; answer questions; locate library materials and search electronic databases in response to patron inquiries;
- develop and maintain the CM collection in consultation with SCM faculties and the collection development and management guidelines of the Library, and to monitor the usage of CML collection and facilities;
- serve as a Liaison Librarian and work closely and collaboratively with SCM faculty and users in matters pertaining to the improvement of Library services; and
- initiate and develop interrelated digital CM database series.

Figure 27.8 Lisa Song and her library colleagues.

Figure 27.9 Lisa Song at reference desk at Chinese Medicine Library.

Which part of your job do you find most challenging?

Physical space for our printed collections. You can see that our Library is indeed very small. When the Library was first established, we had a lot of empty space inside the Library. As years go by, the Library's collection simply keeps growing and changing at such a rapid speed. The current collection of around 40,000 items includes books, journals, magazines, videos and CD-ROMs, as well as workstations for online access to a wide variety of databases, etc. In fact, our Library has been undertaking major weeding exercises, as well as trying our very best to replace our existing printed collection with electronic copies as a way to create more space for new items in our Library.

Are you the only library professional who specialises in CM in Hong Kong?

Amongst all eight universities in Hong Kong, I am the one and only CM librarian. In order to keep myself up to date in the field, I attend the annual meetings of the Mainland Chinese Medical Librarians Association. But, to my knowledge, a majority of these CM librarians practising in mainland China are not MLIS holders. For this reason, despite being considered subject experts in the field of CM, many of them do not have profound knowledge and practical skills in terms of how to manage the daily operations of a library.

For a CML to be managed by a subject expert without an MLIS degree, what kinds of disadvantages would that lead to?

For example, these 'subject experts' in mainland China would not know about the latest developments of digital libraries, how to manage library collections in electronic formats or how to provide information literacy instruction classes to students and teaching staff. Many of them do not even think that creating new data or knowledge in the relevant field via digital means is important. When I go to mainland China for professional visits, I would very much prefer to talk with and learn from their reference services colleagues instead because, for example, during their conference presentations, they are always talking about those classical works of CM and clinical practices [e.g., *The Medical Classic of the Yellow Emperor* (黄帝内经)], discussing classical formulae of remedies or treatments, etc. They are always talking about how to conserve and preserve these classics. Year after year, they talk about the same topics, whereas for me, I want to learn about new things, new professional developments, new services and new resources available in CM librarianship.

You kind of stumbled into this profession of librarianship by circumstance; are you totally happy with how your career has turned out to be? Do you have any regrets or second thoughts?

I spent many years studying to become a medical doctor. When I first started working in the library field, I would not say that I really liked the job nature and the working environment inside a library because I did not know I had other options or alternatives at that time. Surprisingly, my career as the CM Librarian at HKBU turned out to be very fulfilling and rewarding. I enjoyed communicating with people (our library end users). Through the communications, I learned new things from the others. I am very happy that I have built up close relationships with faculty members and colleagues and established several projects with them. I have absolutely no regrets.

If you had the choice, would you still want to become a librarian or would you want to go back to being a medical doctor?

Being a medical doctor is impossible now. I have been working as a librarian for over 15 years. I feel like I have accomplished a lot and have achieved a certain status in the field of academic librarianship. I really enjoy my work as the CM Librarian at HKBU, and I have no regrets.

What part of your job as the CM Librarian at HKBU gives you the most satisfaction?

When I saw that question, I suddenly remembered this case: there was a final-year student, and she may not be a very smart student. She came to me and said, 'This is my topic, I need to do a final project and I can't find anything'. So, I gave her a research consultation session and showed her different types of databases that she could use for her research. Every time I worked with her, it would take at least 1 h. At the end of each session, she would say, 'I will try to do it by myself'. The next time she would come back again, she would ask the same question. I repeated the same process five times with her. But one day, she brought her final-year project report and showed me a paragraph in her acknowledgement section, where she wrote, 'Thanks to the librarians (at HKBU Chinese Medicine Library)… You have made me realise that your job is extraordinary in such an ordinary place. You enabled me to learn things and other important knowledge that could not be acquired within the regular classroom environment. Your contributions to my learning are no less valuable than my professor!'.

Another example that gave me great satisfaction was the collaboration between librarians and faculty members from the School of Medicine. Through our joint efforts and interests, we collaborated to establish the first CM digital project in Hong Kong. At this time, we have set up five open-access databases that are available worldwide. The project team received a Reward and Recognition Scheme for Non-teaching Staff award from HKBU. Our CM Digital Project also received the 2012 ALA Presidential Citations for Innovative International Library Projects Award (Fig. 27.10). The ALA press release stated, 'While the (Chinese Medicine) databases were designed to improve teaching methods and effective use of these plants and herbs, making this information available for free via the Internet has historic and limitless benefits for medical providers and researchers across the globe'.

What is the role of traditional CM in Hong Kong?

In Hong Kong, actually, the professional environment and career prospects are rather bright and promising for traditional CM practitioners because the demand for holistic healing has been growing rapidly both in and outside of Hong Kong. Furthermore, there has been a long history and tradition of Chinese people using ingredients of traditional CM for home cooking and other domestic remedies. Surprisingly, when the clinic for traditional CM at HKBU was first opened, they received a large number of patients. Furthermore, there is an increasing number of the general public who hold equal respect for the Western physicians and traditional Chinese medical doctors in Hong Kong. In fact, mainland China did a very good job in terms of combining both Western and Chinese practices at many public hospitals and clinics. As a result, there is equal availability of traditional CM and Western medicine in hospitals and clinics in

Figure 27.10 American Library Association awards.

many large cities in China, whereas in Hong Kong, they still separate both practices, meaning that you need to go to different clinics and hospitals for treatments.

To conclude this interview, I would like to highlight that no matter what profession you are in, you will always find the interests if you set your heart to it.

The Politics Behind the Olympics and Sports Intelligence

28

Raymond So
Hong Kong Sports Institute, Hong Kong (SAR), China

Introduction

Sports, and the Olympics in particular, are seen as transcending politics. Unfortunately, professional sports communities worldwide have never been, and never will be, free from politics. With the advancement of modern sports science and communication technologies, competitive sports intelligence, a new concept that combines both theory and practice for understanding specific conditions of the sports scene, has become a natural extension of the professional sporting world. In the following interview, Dr. Raymond So (Director of Elite Training Science and Technology of the Hong Kong Sports Institute) (Fig. 28.1) discusses the current professional sporting scene in Hong Kong, as well as his vision and the need for converting a traditional library into a cutting-edge centre of sports intelligence of the future.

Could you please introduce yourself and also describe your job scope and areas of responsibility at the Hong Kong Sports Institute (HKSI) (香港體育學院)[1]?

Let me first give a brief introduction about the HKSI (see Fig. 28.2). The HKSI is the Hong Kong Special Administrative Region Government's elite sport training systems delivery agent. The HKSI is committed to working in partnership with the Government, the Sports Federation and Olympic Committee of Hong Kong, China and the National Sports Associations to provide an environment in which sports talent can be identified, nurtured and developed to pursue excellence in the international sporting arena. In other words, the HKSI supports elite athletes and trains them on full-time and part-time bases, based on their individual talents and potentials. The training base provides centralised support to athletes. Other than sports facilities, the support given to athletes includes elite coaching, sports science, sports medicine, strength and conditioning, athlete affairs and education, applied research and sports information. In 2015–16, the HKSI provides service to around 1000 athletes in 17 Tier A sports.

[1] Hong Kong Sports Institute – Homepage. Available at: http://www.hksi.org.hk/.

Inside the World's Major East Asian Collections. http://dx.doi.org/10.1016/B978-0-08-102145-3.00028-5

Figure 28.1 Dr Raymond So.

Figure 28.2 Sports Information Centre, Hong Kong Sports Institute.

Figure 28.2 Continued.

The HKSI uses the multidisciplinary biopsychosocial model to formulate its support strategy in order to provide science-based, athlete-centred support for elite training. The six centres in the Elite Training Science and Technology Division, namely the (1) Scientific Conditioning Centre, (2) Sport Biomechanics and Technology Centre, (3) Sport Nutrition Monitoring Centre, (4) Sport Psychology Centre, (5) Sports Medicine Centre and (6) Sports Information Centre (SIC), work as a team to identify the various training problems and concerns, and develop evidence-based solutions with the coaches. The support procedures are regularly updated through continuous monitoring, discussion and benchmarking against the latest research data.

I am currently the Director of the Elite Training Science and Technology Division of the HKSI. I have been serving the Institute since the mid-1900s, for over 20 years. I hold a doctoral degree in sports science, and my PhD dissertation was on human muscles in the context of modern sports science. I have been involved in sports training and sports science research for many years, particular research for windsurfing and cycling. My major responsibility at the HKSI is to drive innovation and scientific, medical and technological support to coaches to systematically and positively impact athletes' high-performance results. My role as sports scientist is to explore different training methods to improve the efficiency and effectiveness of training, such as to provide advice on design of training programmes, training venues and equipment. For instance, I provide professional advice on performance fitness evaluations. Such evaluation provides an overview of an athlete's physical condition for coaches to design individualised training plans and programmes.

Would you give me a brief account of the history and develpment of SIC? In addition, could you tell me what roles the SIC plays within the whole HKSI organisation?

The SIC was founded in 1986 and was named as Resource Centre at that time. As the volume of materials in the Resource Centre expanded steadily until saturation point, the Centre realized a larger working area was critical to future development, and it also recognised the need for a comprehensive sports information and resource centre; therefore, a decision to provide a new facility to be based at the Institute was made. The facility was officially opened in October 1991 and named as Hong Kong SIC.[2,3] The Centre moved to the new HKSI main building, the present premise, in September 2013 and was officially opened in October 2013. The Centre was also renamed as SIC. With its relocation to the new HKSI main building, the Centre boasts a spacious environment to cater for users' training and research needs.

The Centre is the only library in Hong Kong that specialises in providing the most up-to-date sports information services and resources to the local communities in a timely fashion. Such communities include local academic institutes that offer sports-related programmes, local secondary schools and sports associations, as well as the general public.

In terms of information service related to sports, the SIC plays an important role in supporting the work of the sports practitioners at the HKSI at all levels. The SIC functions more than just a traditional library, as it aims to contribute to the overall achievement and development of the HKSI's objectives by enabling access to a wide range of sports-related information resources and services.

In recent years, the Centre has gradually transformed itself into a versatile, multifunctional, multipurpose information centre in order to keep pace with the new developments in different information technologies as well as in sports science. For these reasons, our Centre could no longer stick to its traditional mode of operations and end-user services. In fact, the SIC is expected to play an important role in supporting athletes and their coaches at the HKSI by providing them the most up-to-date information on both local and overseas competitors, such as established rules and regulations for particular events

[2] Hong Kong Sports Institute (1991/92), *Annual Report*. Hong Kong: Hong Kong Sports Institute.
[3] Chan, Julia L.Y., Angela S.W. Yan, Lai-bing Kan. (1996). *Libraries and Information Centres in Hong Kong*. Hong Kong: Hong Kong University Press.

or competitive sports, funding situations of the home countries of overseas competitors, as well as competitors' signature events and their track records, etc. All this information is important for any athletes and coaches to learn about their opponents' tendencies and weaknesses so as to gain a competitive advantage.

In the past, repetitive hard and strenuous training exercises combined with postexercise nutritional strategies were the only solution to strive for top-flight performances amongst athletes. Nowadays, most sports practitioners recognise the importance of supporting their training by providing them with the most up-to-date information on a regular basis, thereby enabling them to be better prepared to participate in different competitions throughout the year. For instance, athletes, coaches, trainers and sports organisations, all these people working in the sporting world are constantly looking for new ways to improve performance, as well as strategies to improve self-awareness skills for athletes. Self-awareness is a quality associated with both developing and performance excellence. Thus, in order to determine an accurate response to questions, such as 'How is the athlete?', 'How is the team?' or 'How would the athlete perform in the next major game?', we continuously need to ask ourselves:

1. What if new workout options are to be introduced to the existing training programmes; would it enhance athletic performance?
2. How to define new goals for individual athletes, and the whole team, as well as the whole organisation?
3. Would it be possible to extend a certain skill training session?
4. What were the results of game day performance?
5. How to analyse the win/loss or success/failure of the sports events?

With reference to collection size, as of September 2014, the SIC holds a collection of approximately 18,000 items, including monographs, journals, magazines and audio–visual materials, as well as other digital resources. During the 1990s, before the widespread use of Internet technology, people had to consult different printed sources and a variety of nonprint resources held in different locations to compile, consolidate and then analyse the gathered information on their own. For this reason, the SIC is considered a pioneer in the field, as it aims to serve as a convenient one-stop, centralised information hub for anyone practicing in the field of sports, that is, including coaches, athletes, sports administrators, policymakers, researchers, physical activity educators, sports scientists, medical staff and many others.

The subject areas currently covered by the SIC include the following:

1. advanced training and coaching approaches for major sports played in Hong Kong and other overseas countries;
2. personal physical and fitness training, for example, psychology, biomechanics, exercise physiology, nutrition, injuries and injury prevention;
3. sports administration and management, such as sponsorship, governance, club management, law and legislations, funding and scholarship situations and so on;
4. information and latest developments on major sporting events, such as the Olympics and Asian Games, and so on;
5. sports policies or government policies related to the sporting world in Hong Kong; and
6. past sports competition results, records, statistics and so on.

In the past decade, the SIC has undergone major changes in terms of its functions and services as a result of the rapidly expanding sporting events in Hong Kong, as other neighbouring cities in Asia. As you may know, an increasing number of developing countries have become more willing to invest a lot more money and other resources into sports with the aim to win medals at the Olympics and other major games. In fact, ever since the 'Nazi Olympics', the Olympics have always been way to demonstrate a country's independence, its political values, economic power, ideological superiority and so on. It could also be used as a powerful tool for a government to build pride and a collective identity for its nation. In other words, hosting the Olympics could be seen as a way to unify the national spirits and enhance patriotism amongst its fellow citizens. For these reasons, like it or not, every country taking part in the Olympic Games attaches great importance to winning medals. It is a simple logic that the greater the importance placed on the Olympics medals, more funding and resources would be invested into training the athletes. Meanwhile, providing top-quality and speedy information services for supporting such sports training is comparatively a new phenomenon and yet a vital component of the library. As a result, the provision of information services and performance of library tasks have undergone significant changes, causing the former HKSI Library to gradually evolve into the current SIC.

Modern science and sports have become increasingly interrelated. As the modern sporting world has become increasingly science-oriented, training and research practices in sports also need to change in order to accommodate this shift in emphasis. My question is whether the SIC has also undergone major changes in terms of its research activities, collection development practices, as well as its core library services/operations, in order to cope with such shift in emphasis

It is not the SIC's role to do research. Despite of that, the SIC colleagues need to be fully aware of the latest developments and trends in the sporting world to ensure that the SIC will stay always relevant to the missions, as well as the needs of the HKSI. In terms of the SIC's resources, our sports journal and audio–visual collections play an important part in the training programmes carried out at the HKSI. In fact, the SIC holds a large collection of video clips that have been edited into footage of various athletes training at the HKSI. For instance, athletes need to view videotapes to critique their own performances and techniques, as well as performances of their opponents'. As a result, this footage collection is absolutely essential, especially for the athletes who are being prepared to participate in competitions, and they need such (visual) information to help them enhance the level of performance, physically and psychologically, as well as strategically. Other than the journals and AV materials, electronic resources have become increasingly important and much needed amongst the HKSI community, simply because of the global digital trend.

Secondly, the emergence of new, digital technologies has greatly influenced the way we (SIC colleagues) communicate with other overseas sports organisations. Because of the convenience brought by Internet connectivity, in an age where information is increasingly being transmitted from different sources at such an overwhelmingly rapid speed, information flow has therefore become increasingly important and absolutely vital for the successful exchange of information between different sports organisations. The information exchanged between us (SIC) and other sports institutes information include: new areas in sports trainings; sports policies in different countries; general athletes' conditions, situations and characteristics; activities and movements of other sports institutes (located overseas and in mainland China) and their training facilities, as well as the latest research focus on sports science. We sometimes need to create/compile our own in-house portfolios, based on the results of the current/past sports events, sports competition schedules, individual athletes' or teams' performances and so on to be exchanged with other sports institutes, as well as for use by our local HKSI athletes and coaches. From time to time, we work closely with the Japan Sport Council[4] on different sports information exchange programmes with the aims of keeping ourselves up-to-date on the latest development in the international sporting world.

Do you have any strategic plans worked out for the SIC for the next 5–10 years?

Electronic journals and other digital resources will certainly be the future and will be used to advance the SIC's roles and services. Digital resources will undoubtedly be the main focus of the SIC's collection development exercises for now, as well as for the foreseeable future. We are also planning to broaden the scope of information sources to be provided at the SIC, in addition to enhancing both the depth and quality of information collected. Meanwhile, enhancing the reliability and delivery speed of information is also crucial for the success of the SIC, as well as for the satisfaction amongst our HKSI users.

Currently, in terms of scope of information, owing to the limited manpower, resources and data sources available, the SIC can only afford to create a few competitor profiles to be used as reference for our local HKSI athletes. My target in the near future is to create 10 competitor profiles against one local key athlete. With such competitive information as reference, trainers and athletes would have a much more accurate picture of their opponents and the actual (competition) situations that they would be facing.

We are still at the learning stage in terms of creating sports profiles as part of SIC's core function and service for our HKSI users. Indeed, it takes time, skills, knowledge and experience for the SIC staff to function similar to a sports information specialist, that is, to harvest and consolidate the needed information from a variety of sources, identify the key points/elements, analyse the potential impacts of each piece of information and then identify its relevance to the training programmes carried out at the HKSI. For the SIC, our ultimate goal is to provide appropriate, relevant, comprehensive and up-to-date information for the relevant practitioners to design new training programmes or facilities under the HKSI organisation.

As far as I know, Japan is the leading country in creating 'intelligence gathering' in the international sporting world, that is, providing effective strategic solutions and

[4] Japan Sport Council – Homepage. Available at: http://www.jpnsport.go.jp/.

implementing them successfully, in addition to performing in-depth analysis on the (sports) intelligence gathered. In a newspaper article, it was reported that '*Olympic superpowers are turning to Japan's meticulous techniques for the analysing world-class athletes*'.[5] Following Japan, the UK and Germany are the two countries that have made a reputation out of their extremely high level of sports intelligence services. The Japan Sport Council manages the sports intelligence very well, as they could afford to allocate up to 10 or sometimes even 20 top-level information specialists/professionals to conduct onsite investigation, gathering data for just a single sport event. Information gathered will then be consolidated and immediately sent back to Japan for further analysis so that coaches and instructors in Japan could identify possible solutions for the athletes competing in a timely manner. Although the final results of a game could depend on a variety of factors, such as athletes' physical conditions on that particular day, with speedy and high-quality sports intelligence as reference, athletes would have a much higher chance of winning.

The major challenges currently faced by the HKSI is the lack of very experienced sports information professionals with the skills to compile and create sports intelligence, as well as the necessary knowledge to analyse the gathered intelligence afterwards. There is not a fixed or single source/channel that could provide all the information we need. Hence, we have to create our own pathfinders during the data collection/harvesting process. For the vast amount of harvested data that needs to be processed, it first needs to be organised and fed into a coherent order for analysis and then distributed for relevant sports units for further use.

Could you tell me, what are the major functional differences between an experienced sports information professional/specialist and a regular librarian working at a SIC?

An experienced sports information professional/analyst would have the knowledge and skills to harvest relevant data from a wide range of sources, organise the collected data and feed it in a well structured and coherent manner, analyse and interpret it and finally, convert the data into meaningful information that would be useful for the athletes, trainers and coaches training here at the HKSI. In other words, a sports intelligence specialist should also have in-depth subject knowledge, research skills and people skills, that is, including being able to establish good communications with the athletes and their coaches, as well as the talent for understanding and anticipating their needs, on top of being able to offer effective solutions that address those needs. Finally, with all the skills and knowledge previously mentioned, a successful sports intelligence specialist should also be able to provide an overview of the issues and trends that may affect the outcome of a game and to provide expert predictions on the results of sporting events under different situations and circumstances. On the contrary, an experienced librarian could be great at overseeing the circulation services and managing the physical collection, but may not understand the general regulations

[5] Akita, Hiroyuki. (5 July 2014). 'Japan's sports intelligence can help national-level gathering capabilities.' *Nikkei Asian Review*. Available at: http://asia.nikkei.com/Viewpoints/Perspectives/Japan-s-sports-intelligence-can-help-national-level-gathering-capabilities.

and rules of a variety of sports played at the Olympics, and such understanding is absolutely essential for preparing high-quality and useful sports intelligence to the athletes.

In short, sports intelligence specialists must be skilled and versatile information professionals who excel in capturing, analysing and managing the performance and participation data amongst athletes, as well as being able to work closely with them to realise their full potentials of such insights. In order to do the job well, sports intelligence specialists also need to stay fresh and current with the new trends taking place in the international sporting world, sports science and performance amongst athletes. He/she must be able to identify the value and relevance behind every piece of information collected and then convert it into knowledge that is useful for the athletes and the sports community that he/she serves. Such useful knowledge is what we sports practitioners call 'sports intelligence', and this is one of the many important elements that would determine winning or losing a game.

It is a simple equation! The more information that the SIC holds, the better prepared the athletes will be for the next game, being better not just physically, but also mentally as well as strategically. Being better prepared would also mean a higher chance for winning the game and lower chance of being injured.

Based on your experiences, are there particular individuals, departments or sports units that would frequently seek information services from the SIC? And what is the nature of these information service requests?

Yes, individual athletes, their coaches or their belonging units would request for information from the SIC on a regular basis, with topics ranging from sports injury recovery to identification and development programmes for young local talents. Indeed, such information is most useful and popular amongst our HKSI users for any phase of their sports training, as well as for the cultivation of young local talents all year round.

Would you briefly introduce the different sports programmes that are currently being supported by the HKSI?

The HKSI is the Government's agent responsible for providing a high-quality training environment and support services for high-performance athletes with the aim of grooming athletes to achieve good results at international sporting events. Under the HKSAR Government's Elite Vote Support Scheme (EVSS), achievements of both senior and junior athletes at major international competitions will be used as the selection criterion to identify high-performance sports to be supported by the HKSI for a period of 4 years. Review will be conducted every 2 years, which is aligned with the Asian Games and Olympic Games cycles, to provide stable support for sports within the 4-year support cycle. The EVSS provides for a tiered structure, and the tiers are Tier A*, Tier A and Tier B.

As on February 2016, badminton, cycling, table tennis and windsurfing, whose athletes have consistently performed at the highest level and have the potential to achieve medals at the Olympic Games, are Tier A* sports and receive additional resources for enhancing preparedness for major games in addition to full support. The high-performance sports in Tier A are athletics, billiard sports, fencing, gymnastics, karatedo, rowing, rugby sevens, sailing, squash, swimming, tennis, tenpin bowling and wushu, where athletes receive funding for training programmes, dedicated coaching led by a head coach and full sports science and medicine support. The high-performance sports in Tier B are equestrian, golf, judo, figure skating and triathlon, where funding and support level for athletes will be reviewed with the respective National Sports Associations. The HKSI also supports outstanding individual athletes in sports under the Individual Athletes Support Scheme and sports for athletes with disabilities.

Recently, we have witnessed an increasing number of Hong Kong athletes competing in the international sporting arena, winning medals, achieving awards, breaking new records, receiving both respect and recognitions on both regional and international levels. Do you think the Hong Kong athletes consistently achieving good results in different competitive sports at an international level has in any way altered the social attitudes towards **'sports'** or **'local athletes'** in Hong Kong?

Female windsurfer Lee Lai Shan (李麗珊) won Hong Kong's first ever Olympic gold medal in the 1996 Atlanta Olympics. Her achievement was undoubtedly monumental for Hong Kong, not just for bringing respect and recognitions to the local professional sporting community, but also helped establish a sense of pride and a stronger collective identity for the city of Hong Kong. In the media frenzy, she famously proclaimed, '*Hong Kong athletes are not rubbish*!'. Indeed, funding, sponsorship and other supports for particular competitive sports (from the local Government and society) will depend entirely on to the delivery of good results.

In the recent 10 years, we have witnessed an obvious increase in the number of local athletes receiving support (financial or nonfinancial) from different public and private sources. An athlete's increasing fame and popularity would automatically attract more funding and other resources to support their training. Better funding will bring in better resources. Having better resources is the key to optimising the athletic performance level of an athlete. Top-flight performances would automatically lead to better competitive results. All these different intrinsic and extrinsic factors simply go hand in hand.

In my opinion, social attitudes amongst the general public in Hong Kong towards choosing a career as a professional athlete only changed slightly. Parents, in general, do not prefer their children to become professional athletes because they often have very short careers with little or no job security. Despite of that, an increasing number of local young people excelling in sports are beginning to explore the opportunity of being a full-time professional sportsman as a possible career choice, especially after witnessing the recent achievements of the locally discovered and groomed talents like Sarah Lee Wai-sze (李慧詩) (racing cyclist) and Lee Lai-shan (李麗珊) (windsurfer) rising to the top in the international sporting arena.

As the Director of Elite Training Science and Technology at the HKSI, have you witnessed any significant changes in the development of sports science in the last 10 years?

In summary, sports science is a relatively new discipline. The study of sport science incorporates different areas of physiology, sports psychology, anatomy, biomechanics, biochemistry and so on. Higher education degrees in sports science, human physiology or sports psychology are also becoming increasingly popular, with many universities now offering degree programmes in the discipline at both undergraduate as well as postgraduate levels. For this reason, sport scientists, performance consultants and sports coaches/instructors (with proper qualifications in sports science) are all growing in demand, with the ever-increasing focus within the sporting world on achieving the best results possible. Through the systematic study of science and sport, both researchers and practitioners working in the field have developed a better understanding on how the human body works and how it reacts to exercise or training programmes. Such an understanding would no doubt enable us to analyse an athlete's techniques and optimise their level of performance under different competitive environments and many other stimuli, and so on. The recent developments in sports science and other related fields, such as biomechanics or physiology, have become increasingly interrelated.

By comparison, today's sports psychology has become an interdisciplinary science that draws upon knowledge from a variety of related fields, including biomechanics, physiology, kinesiology, psychology and so on. It also involves the study of a wide range of different psychological (intrinsic and extrinsic) factors that could affect an athlete's performance, as well as the interrelationships between different psychological and physical factors.

Asia Art Archive: Archiving Contemporary Art in Asia as Practice

29

Chantal Wong
Asia Art Archive, Hong Kong, China

Introduction

Described as young, dynamic and inspiring, Asia Art Archive (AAA) is a nonprofit organisation established in Hong Kong in 2000 with the core mission of documenting the recent history and developments of contemporary visual arts in Asia within an international context. After close to two decades of hard work from a team of devoted young talents, AAA is now well known worldwide for being the most comprehensive publicly accessible collection of physical and digital materials in the field. Instead of serving as a repository of material waiting to be discovered, AAA endeavours to take a very proactive approach, that is, instigating critical thinking amongst the general public by establishing dialogues through a variety of public forums, panel discussions, research, residency and educational programmes for engaging audiences that are as wide of range as possible (see Figs 29.2–29.4). Chantal Wong (Fig. 29.1) is currently serving as the Head of Strategy and Special Projects at AAA (Hong Kong), as well as the co-editor of the organisation's journal, *Field Notes*. She was also the Director of Development at Outset Contemporary Art Fund (London) from 2009 to 2012 and Head of Development at AAA from 2006 to 2009. In the following interview, Wong shares with us the operations of AAA from behind the scenes, and in her excitement, tells us how Hong Kong artists are slowly forging their ways into the international art market.

Could you begin this interview by giving us information about your background, for example, your training, educational background, and your major roles and duties at the AAA?

My name is Chantal Wong. I am currently working as the Head of Strategy and Special Projects at the AAA.[1] I earned my bachelor's degree at Concordia University[2] in Montreal and majored in art history. I then did my master's degree at Goldsmiths, University of London,[3] in cultural studies.

[1] Asia Art Archive (AAA) – Homepage. Available at: http://www.aaa.org.hk/.
[2] Concordia University – Homepage. Available at: https://www.concordia.ca/.
[3] Goldsmiths, University of London – Homepage. Available at: http://www.gold.ac.uk/.

Inside the World's Major East Asian Collections. http://dx.doi.org/10.1016/B978-0-08-102145-3.00029-7

Figure 29.1 Asia Art Archive (AAA) Head of Strategic development, Chantal Wong.
Photo: Stephen Lam.

Figure 29.2 View of A Space, event space of AAA.
Courtesy of Asia Art Archive.

Before you started working for the AAA, where did you work? Did you work for any other arts or cultural institutions?

I first worked for the AAA for 3 consecutive years from 2006 until 2009, focusing on communications and development (fundraising). I left (AAA) in 2009 to pursue my master's degree in London (UK). While I was studying for my postgraduate degree, I was also working for an organisation called Outset Contemporary Art Fund (Outset).[4] Outset is a nonprofit funding body founded in England in 2003, dedicated

[4] Outset Contemporary Art Fund – Homepage. Available at: http://www.outset.org.uk/.

Figure 29.3 Exhibition view of Toko Pura–Pura (Quasi-shop), ruangrupa, 29 August–30 September 2016.
Photo: Kitmin Lee 2016.

Figure 29.4 Entrance view of Excessive Enthusiasm: Ha Bik Chuen and the Archive as Practice, 11 March–30 May 2015.
Courtesy of Asia Art Archive.

to providing financial support to public contemporary arts projects and organisations. After finishing my studies in the UK, I returned to Hong Kong, re-joined AAA in 2011 and took up a different position as Head of Strategy and Special Projects.

Is art or contemporary art in particular something that you have always wanted to do since early childhood?

Originally, I wanted to go into management. Unfortunately, I failed calculus! Maybe this was a sign that I was not actually meant to 'do' management for the rest of my life. Then I thought about other areas I was interested in. I started experimenting by taking various classes at university. I remembered really enjoying my visits to the museum, so I gave art history a try. It is interesting how one small failure turns out to have a lot of meaning in life later. Doing art history was definitely the much better and wiser career choice. Otherwise, I think I may have been very miserable.

How does contemporary art speak to you on an emotional or spiritual level?

Well, it completely changed the way I saw the world. I think it made me more empathetic as a person. It has the potential to draw out one's 'humanist' side. It can inspire care and sympathy about different issues, as you are always seeing the world through others' eyes. Working in the art field, you constantly have to relate to other people, particularly artistic people who are creative and love to explore. In other words, working in the field of contemporary art has definitely reshaped my mindset and my attitude towards life in many respects. Honestly, I have discovered other aspects about myself that I never knew existed.

Could you tell us more about the AAA, for example, the missions and the objectives of establishing this Archive?

Originally, the AAA organisation was meant to serve as a place where ideas and knowledge around contemporary art from Asia could be collated, brought together and researched, etc. In the beginning, around 2000, there was a lot of speculation around contemporary art in Asia, and this interest would not be sustainable without research activities or discourse in the field. As stated on the AAA homepage, 'Through collecting, preserving, and making information on the recent history of contemporary art in Asia easily accessible, AAA aims to facilitate understanding, research, and writing in the field. AAA is a proactive platform, instigating critical thinking and dialogue, bringing people together, and organising diverse public, educational, and residential programmes for a wide range of audiences. At the core of its mission is AAA's commitment to create a collection belonging to the public, a collection that exists not in an enclosed space, but in a space that is open and productive, generating new ideas and works that continually reshape the Archive itself'. In other words, AAA was established with the mission of building anchors and pillars of knowledge around recent art in Asia to sustain the developments in visual art in the region.

Is the AAA the very first of its kind of art archive established in the world or in this part of the world (Asia)?

While there are already many galleries, museums, archives and art and design libraries, AAA is definitely a very unique model in many respects. Most libraries, archives and museums are governmental institutions, administrated by public officials, or are associated with universities and are therefore not easily accessible to the wider public. However, the AAA is a totally independent organisation and open to the public for free. Another unique aspect of AAA is that it is not a dusty archive located in a dark basement that one has to make advanced booking in order to use. We adopt a new approach at the AAA by trying the best we can to make all our materials accessible to the general public, that is, via both online and in person. In other words, AAA is not only about safeguarding the materials we collected. It is really about actively making sure that our materials will keep living and continue to grow and continue to be used, enjoyed and researched by the current, as well as future generations (Figs 29.5 and 29.6). Undoubtedly, all these new operational ideas are very new practices and indisputably a new model for any local and overseas archives.

Who are the majority of users of the AAA?

We have different types of users. I would say the people who go really in-depth into using our collections are academics or researchers. We also host a lot of art professionals from all over the world, with Asia becoming increasingly interesting to the international contemporary art community. Because of that, we have an increasing number of museum professionals, gallerists, artists or auction house professionals travelling through Hong Kong who make deliberate stopovers at AAA to visit and research our collections.

In addition, AAA offers a variety of educational and outreach programmes with the aim of nurturing an interest amongst wider cross-sections of the community in Hong Kong and, in particular, young people (secondary and university students) in our recent art histories. In summary, there are so many different ways of using AAA. Obviously, the way an art history professor uses AAA is very different from that of a gallery, museum, auction house professional or a local high school student, but they all are our AAA users.

Figure 29.5 Special collections room. Courtesy of Asia Art Archive.

Figure 29.6 Asia Art Archive collection.
Courtesy of Going Merry Design co.

Figure 29.6 Continued.

As the Head of Strategy and Special Projects at the AAA, what are your main roles and responsibilities?

My current role and responsibilities focus more on the infrastructural developments of the organisation. I work closely with AAA's Director and senior staff to ensure that as an organisation, we are aligned on AAA's mission and have the resources and capacity to achieve our medium- to long-term goals. In order to do so, we have to ensure that the AAA has the right infrastructural supports, as well as the necessary resources to achieve and sustain them in the long run. It comes down to having the right organisational structure (human resources), a versatile and effective digital platform that would allow our users to access our materials actively, etc. Very soon, AAA needs to move to a permanent home because you cannot have a collection that keeps growing while you are constantly vulnerable to rent increases. Right now, AAA's current physical space is sponsored, and we cannot rely on that forever. So these are different infrastructural things that I have to deal with as the Head of Strategy and Special Projects.

In Hong Kong, it is not uncommon to see librarians with no interest in music or visual arts taking up positions as heads and directors of music and visual arts libraries. They're hired because they are effective administrators, good managers and good at IT, and not because of their knowledge or research skills in related fields. Now there are also librarians who are hired to manage an art or music collection only because they are effective administrators, and not because they have an active scholarly or cultural interest in the materials themselves. So my question is, why is it important for someone like you to have the knowledge of art and art history in order to manage the AAA? Why can't they just find someone with an MBA or EMBA to work manage the AAA instead?

That is a very good question. I am not sure whether it is a 'must'. I am not sure whether everybody in this organisation needs to have a 'passion' or genuine interest for visual arts, but the mindset and expectations of skills needed at AAA are different in so many ways. It depends on the nature of the job at the end. But taking effective internal communications as an example, if we do not have someone who has grounded knowledge of the field, there will inevitably be communication gaps between this person and the rest of the 'art-minded' colleagues. Let's say you have someone who is great at business communications, could work as a brilliant PR manager and could do a great job in putting a brand out. But a competent PR manager with no training and interests in art could only go so far because at some point, one would have to speak eloquently about AAA's missions, that is, including explaining to the outsiders and the public about our priorities and many other art-related issues, for example, the relationships between the materials and the stories behind these collections. Without this kind of knowledge or interest, one could only go so far, and you would then end up relying a lot on other members at the AAA to feed you the contents.

In summary, you could always have someone who can do a great job with marketing and manage our finances really well, but if this person has no genuine interest or knowledge in art, there would definitely be communication gaps. What we really need is a person who could help our Director, Claire Hsu, to strive for a balance for the whole AAA organisation and its operations in the long run. As the Head of Strategy and Special Projects at the AAA, that is part of my main role. Because a lot is about the alignments with AAA's operations, especially when we are rapidly growing as an organisation. It is absolutely wonderful for everybody at AAA to be so passionate about what they are doing. I also think that it is this collective 'passion' that has really contributed to the overall success of the AAA. I also think that is what Claire (Hsu), AAA's Director, has managed to nurture throughout the years. On the other hand, when everyone has his or her own ideas and passion for their projects, it could also be an obstacle for the AAA because everyone simply wants to develop their own ideas, prioritise their own projects, as well as wanting others to support what they are doing, etc. As you can see, a major part of my job is constantly trying to strike that balance for the organisation.

How would you describe having 'passion' towards the work that one is doing, particularly in the AAA context?

No one in the team doubts the importance of the work. We all have strong work ethics and a never-ending desire to strive for excellence. Also many of AAA's team members have been committed to AAA for many years. For instance, I started here in 2006. This is a sign of strong commitments and devotions that stand in accordance with beliefs in the importance of what they are doing in the field.

Based on your experience, do you think it is rather difficult to find the right person who has all the matching knowledge, skills, mindset, genuine interest and passion from all sides to work for the AAA, especially when Hong Kong is never seen as one of the world's major centres of contemporary art?

I think this is still difficult in Hong Kong because contemporary art is a rather new field in the city, but definitely gradually growing. In Hong Kong, there have always been smaller art galleries and museums, but many face difficulties in employing people with the right skills and experiences. On the contrary, in other overseas places where they have a much larger ecology of contemporary art or artists and a much longer institutional history, it is relatively easier to find the right people to work for them. As a result, arts and cultural institutions in Hong Kong end up having to hire them from overseas. In addition to hiring people from outside of Hong Kong, you also want to nurture local talents within Hong Kong, and this is part the reason why many of our AAA team members are still young by comparison.

What are the major projects that are currently being implemented by the AAA, and how many of these new projects are currently under your direct supervision?

There are many! To continue to expand our collections in all possible formats in a way that could enrich different understandings of Asian modern/contemporary art in an international context. For instance, making our collections available online is undoubtedly one of our many priorities. Another priority is to identify a list of potential external partners that we want to collaborate with on an ongoing basis. For example, the AAA is currently working with the Fine Arts Department of the University of Hong Kong[5] to develop a course on recent art history of Hong Kong. We aim to reach out to wider audiences by enabling our collections to tell more stories through our website and programmes.

As you can see, the AAA is aiming in different directions. On one hand, we are actively acquiring more materials to enrich our collections as well as creating digital platforms that would facilitate open access of these materials. On the other hand, we are constantly exploring opportunities for future collaborations with different external partners, ranging from local high schools to universities to art initiatives. For example, the AAA is currently working with different high school students and educators from Hong Kong to organise a variety of workshops for local teachers during the summertime as a way to empower them to teach art writing to local students.

In 2008, the Hong Kong Education Bureau[6] introduced a new policy by making liberal studies one of four compulsory subjects in the New Senior Secondary Curriculum. Surprisingly, a large number of students chose to write about contemporary art, art history or the developments of visual arts in Hong Kong for their liberal studies school projects. The results were that sometimes students could not find necessary materials from the Internet or from the public libraries, and they would then come to consult the AAA collections instead. Local public libraries simply do not have the kind of materials that we do. Because of the success of the outreach and educational programmes launched by AAA, in the past years, we saw a number of teachers returning to our programmes. It is indeed encouraging that these local teachers are taking time to bring themselves and their students to come to take part in our educational programmes. All these are unquestionably clear signs that AAA is making positive contributions to the education of young people in Hong Kong.

I guess there is no one simple solution or a straightforward answer for our 'priorities'!

Since the AAA is already an archive with functions and services that are similar to a library, why do you still need a professional librarian to be working inside the AAA to manage its collection?

The AAA is not just a warehouse or a static archive! The AAA is about really trying to make information in the field of contemporary art accessible to everyone, that is, including allowing the users to visit and reference our regular library and reference materials (see Fig. 29.7). Since the AAA comprises a large number of activities around the lending of books and other printed materials, we also need a professional librarian to manage our daily services and respond to the inquiries of our users.

[5] History Department of the University of Hong Kong – Homepage. Available at: http://www.history.hku.hk/.

[6] Education Bureau of the Hong Kong (SAR) Government – Homepage. Available at: http://www.edb.gov.hk/en/.

Figure 29.7 View of Asia Art Archive (AAA) Library.
Courtesy of Asia Art Archive.

Which parts of your job at the Head of Strategy and Special Projects at the AAA do you find most rewarding?

Being able to see AAA grow and overcome philosophical and also operational challenges.

When you start merging things together, like 'art' and 'archive' under the 'Asia' framework, and then you link them all together in the library context, when you need to bring all these elements together, it is already a major challenge on its own. You cannot think or handle any one of the three individually or separately. As a matter of fact, just putting both 'art' and 'archive' together is already a big challenge in itself because art is all about freedom, that is, freedom of expression, freedom to experiment and imagine things outside reality, freedom of everything. On the other hand, in order for any archive to function, it has to be well structured. It is about good organisation and effective, long-term management of the materials that would simply include restricted access and organising the files and other related documents in a strictly controlled and logical manner. In order to do my job well, I need to be flexible.

But I also respect that certain members in our AAA team cannot afford to be as flexible as others. Taking our Librarian as an example, despite the fact that she really tries her best to accommodate everyone's wishes and needs, every day for her is a constant struggle. Because if she were to make everything flexible, that would also create other problems for the AAA's daily operations in the long run. The consistent struggle is having to create boundaries while maintaining a certain level of flexibility for our users, and making our clients understand and respect those boundaries is another challenge upon itself.

Another fascinating thing about AAA is that we never let ourselves get comfortable for too long. Otherwise, we risk being outdated and inadequate for our users' changing needs and demands. We can't take the way we work for granted. As you can see, all these different programmes and activities constantly make us think creatively about what we are doing. Artists love to challenge us, so change is a constant, but it is also part of the creative process.

What are the major challenges and difficulties that you and your other AAA colleagues are currently facing?

The difficulty AAA has been facing is the organisation itself has undergone rapid developments in so many different directions over the past 15 years. I am working with an amazing team where everyone is very committed, and interestingly, most of us come from the art world, but we have also started to realise we do not always have the business and managerial skills that we need to ensure the successful growth of this organisation. AAA is really becoming a medium-size organisation or a small institution. Initially, we began building this archive with a team of three only, whereas now, we have a team of 35 full-time staff members working here, not including our offsite researchers stationed in different countries who are collecting materials for the AAA.

As you mentioned earlier, AAA also has researchers or branch offices stationing in different parts of Asia, set up with the purpose of acquiring materials via different channels outside of Hong Kong. Could you please elaborate more on this for us?

We used to have individuals researchers based in different cities in Asia. At one point, we had researchers stationed in nine different cities. When the new head researcher joined AAA in 2012, he questioned this structure because there are so many cities in Asia; how many cities could AAA cover? The AAA researchers work for AAA and receive salaries from us. Their main roles and responsibilities are to collect materials or document events and exhibitions relating to the contemporary art activities/scenes taking places in different Asian cities, and they would then send them back to the AAA regularly, and this is how we built most of our physical collections at the AAA up until 2012.

We also have an office in Delhi, India, where we run a number of research projects and host programmes. We have a programming office and resource centre in New York City, US, run by our chairperson.

Do these overseas offsite researchers also analyse and interpret the materials they collected before sending them to the AAA?

Well, I think some of them do, while some of them do not! Eventually, it became a kind of subjective issue. For these overseas researchers, because of this 'satellite setup', they actually struggle to keep in touch with the AAA, and this is a real commitment issue for all parties involved. As a result, in 2012, we decided to shift from this 'satellite arrangement' to a project-based setup instead. Under this new setup, someone would first identify a potential project, and the research team would make the necessary arrangements for such collaborations. Such a project-based setup has proven to be more beneficial for both parties; not only has it allowed more flexibility on both sides, it also enabled the AAA to save more costs in the long run and to put more focus and energy on specific projects that we identify as important for the collection.

How would you describe the AAA organisation in terms of serving its user community?

AAA is responsive to the needs and demands of the community that we serve. In addition, we have a good understanding of what is going on in the outside world, and we are trying our very best to respond to our users' fast-changing needs. Another major challenge we face is that in much of the work we do, our performance is not easily measured through numbers or in financial terms. It takes a long time for benefits of our projects to become self-evident, so we really need to look at things in a more long-term perspective.

As mentioned earlier, we are launching a series of outreach and educational programmes catered for young people in Hong Kong with the aim of building a long-lasting and yet mutually beneficial relationship with these young people, so after completing the initial educational programmes with us, hopefully they will return and work for the AAA as interns. At some point, they might want to choose to study art history at university because they were once inspired by what we did at the AAA.

Are there skills that you wish you had acquired or knowledge that you should have acquired before taking up the current position at the AAA?

I wish I had forced myself to write more often so that I could be a better writer. Generally speaking, if one knows how to write a clear and coherent essay, it is definitely a very useful skill in terms of effective communications for any organisation, regardless of whether it is a profit or nonprofit organisation.

In terms of acquiring new materials to enrich AAA's collections, since there are so many different forms of contemporary art, such as installation art, conceptual art, performance arts, etc., is there a particular type of contemporary art or medium that the AAA is focusing on?

That's a good question. We have three main focuses. One is 'practice', which is what kind of art an artist makes. So we look at different practices, for instance, and we think performance art is the most urgent of all and is definitely at the top of AAA's priority list because of its flux and temporary nature. Once you have finished performing it, it can disappear forever, unless you have it well documented. AAA is fundamentally a documentation and archival-based institution, so I would say performance arts are an area that AAA is interested in preserving or documenting, and the major challenge is how we should go about to document them.

We then also look at different types of infrastructure. What we call infrastructure is the structures for circulating knowledge surrounding the field of art, so we look at art writings on many different types of visual arts, for example, magazines and newspapers, because these are the structures within which knowledge can be circulated. We look at who is teaching what and in what kinds of art institutions. Furthermore, we will try to archive as much art writing as possible from different regions, and we will try to translate aspects into English so that they can be widely researched. The third agenda is to look at how geography has also played a role in shaping the developments of contemporary arts. Taking India and Pakistan as an example, because of their partition history, the geopolitical realities have definitely played an important role in the way visual arts has been developed in these two countries that are next to each other. In short, we try to look at a phenomenon, ideas and paradigms instead of the work of an individual artist.

Is it difficult to identify this cultural or artistic phenomenon in contemporary art since everything is still growing, for example, recognitions for a particular new school of art still waiting to be earned, and a market for this particular style still being developed?

That is why we would prefer to look at the different (art) schools, that is, what an art school is actually teaching, rather than looking at one particular artist. Of course, there are times you see a well-known artist teaching at an art college/school. But we will look at what they are teaching, lecturing, like school of thoughts, styles or techniques, concepts or philosophies in aesthetics, etc., as being really seminal to change the way art is understood from that point onwards.

Archiving and Annotating Hong Kong Chinese Martial Arts as a Living Archive

30

Hing Chao
International Guoshu Association, Hong Kong, China

Introduction

China has an exceptionally long history of martial arts traditions, including countless numbers of different schools, sects and families, each of which comes with its own set of philosophies, concepts, techniques and training systems. In fact, Hong Kong once became internationally famous for its unparalleled kung fu (that is, martial arts) action movie industry, which flourished in the 1970s and 1980s. Unfortunately, in recent years, many masters are lamenting that the number of young people interested in learning this traditional art form is diminishing on a large scale. The Hong Kong Martial Arts Living Archive (HKMALA) is the first-ever comprehensive digital strategy of archiving and annotating Hong Kong's diverse and rich kung fu styles and traditions, using state-of-the-art data capture tools. In addition, this digital archive will become the wellspring of exhibitions and installations that promulgate rich cultural traditions, as well as mobile apps and other digital learning tools. The archive, with comprehensive metadata, descriptions and physical annotations, will also be a vital source of ongoing research. As a ground-breaking project to develop a sophisticated methodology for the complete four-dimensional analysis of Hong Kong martial arts applicable to numerous other performance-based activities (e.g., all marital arts and performing arts), the project builds upon extensive work done in dance annotations. Hong Kong native, Hing Chao, CEO of the International Guoshu Association and founder of the project, explains how the HKMALA will provide benchmarks in the formation of extensive analytics tools and intangible heritage documentation.

Could you begin this interview by first introducing yourself? What did you study at university?

I read philosophy at Durham University,[1] England. Subsequently, I pursued further studies in Chinese aesthetics, anthropology and frontier Chinese history. I now have

[1] Durham University – Homepage. Available at: https://www.dur.ac.uk/.

Inside the World's Major East Asian Collections. http://dx.doi.org/10.1016/B978-0-08-102145-3.00030-3

part-time teaching positions at the University of Hong Kong[2] and the Hong Kong Polytechnic University.

What age did you start training in traditional Chinese martial arts, and how did you develop a passion for martial arts over the years?

I started learning martial arts at the age of eight. Initially, it was karate. My first teacher Master Chan Cheuk Sam (陳卓森) was something of a polymath in the martial arts, being also versed in kick boxing, Muay Thai, taekwondo and, of course, Chinese kung fu. I trained exclusively in karate from 8 to 12 years old. I stopped training when I went abroad to study and had a break of 4 years. At the age of 16 I went back to training, and this is when I started to develop a deep interest in the martial arts. Chan Sifu started teaching me his family style of Chinese martial arts (Shaolin double dragon style Jin Wu Koon) during my gap year in Hong Kong when I was 18, and I have not looked back since.

Martial arts have been a constant guiding light in my life. I was an angry teenager once. Martial arts gave me balance and taught me the virtues of fortitude, courage and perseverance. It made me a calmer person and adversarial training – sparring so to speak – taught me the importance of having clarity of mind at all times. The lesson of hard work, essential for mastery of martial arts, was also imparted to me through assiduous practice. As I grew older, martial arts became more than a means for self-cultivation, but became a way of being and provided a unique window into Chinese culture and history.

My path as a martial arts researcher began when I was in my mid-twenties. At the time I was invited to read a master's degree in anthropology at the Chinese University of Hong Kong,[3] and I made the study of martial arts the focus of my research. Unfortunately, I did not get to complete my degree but training in social and cultural anthropology gave me valuable heuristic tools for understanding martial arts, which have enabled me to take a fresh approach to Chinese martial studies. I met Professor Ma Mingda and Lam Chun Fai Sifu during this time, and soon started to study under these two contemporary giants of Chinese martial arts.

Professor Ma Mingda introduced to me the discipline of Chinese martial studies and gave me a thorough academic training in the history and theories of Chinese martial arts. I also began training in Ma's Tongbei system of martial studies, which completely transformed the way I look at Chinese martial arts and what they represent. More importantly, Professor Ma gave me a vision, a sense of responsibility as well as empowerment to make martial arts a life-long career; not merely to 'preserve' traditional martial arts as many people erroneously interpret my work, but to construct a rigorous system of knowledge and practice under the dual streams of Chinese martial studies *qua* an academic discipline and Guoshu *qua* a system of Chinese physical education. Under Professor Ma's guidance and supervision, I started the International

[2] The University of Hong Kong – Homepage. Available at: http://www.hku.hk.

[3] The Chinese University of Hong Kong – Homepage. Available at: http://www.cuhk.edu.hk/english/index.html.

Figure 30.1 Hing Chao and Master Lam Chun-Fai (Lam Family Hung Kuen).

Guoshu Association (IGA) together with him and his son, Dr Ma Lianzhen. We formed a small research unit with Professor Ma Lianzhen and myself at the core, which formed the nucleus not only for the IGA, but for an ongoing series of books and research publications as well as cultural and sport events such as the International Kung Fu Festival.[4]

Lam Chun Fai Sifu also exerted a profound influence on how I perceive and practice martial arts. Since 2006 I have been training in Lam Family Hung Kuen, one of the most influential forms of martial art in southern China in the 20th century (Fig. 30.1). As a form of embodied knowledge, Hung Kuen forms the basis for my understanding of Southern Chinese martial arts, and continues to shed light on the emergence of a distinctive Cantonese martial art tradition in the early 20th century. Much of my recent work on Southern Chinese martial arts would not have been possible without this training, and in many ways I consider Hung Kuen most 'native' to my own practice.

Over the past 2 to 3 years, I started to have more autonomy in my research and have been greatly assisted in my efforts by several masters in Hong Kong. Chief among them are Masters Lee Kong of Fujian Yongchun (White Crane) and Li Tin Loy of Chow Family Southern Praying Mantis, but I have benefitted from the warm friendship and support of many others, whom I cannot name one by one here. They have given me valuable insights into the technical structure and cultural underpinnings of Southern Chinese martial arts (Southern Shaolin), and opened doors for research both in Hong Kong and China.

I have now reached a stage where I take an active role in promoting and developing Chinese martial arts in Hong Kong, not merely as a researcher, but engaging the public for deeper understanding and appreciation for Chinese martial arts as a unique and valuable cultural heritage. In this way, one might say that my involvement and interest in Chinese martial arts has evolved from a private 'passion' as you described, into a public campaign.

[4] International Kung Fu Festival – Homepage. Available at: http://www.kungfufestival.com/.

You are the current CEO of the International Guoshu Association (中華國術總會). Could you describe in detail the missions of the International Goushu Association?

The IGA is a nonprofit organisation dedicated to the research and revival of Guoshu, China's indigenous sports system. To achieve these aims, the IGA has organised multiple cultural and educational events in Hong Kong to generate greater awareness and understanding of Guoshu and Chinese martial culture. These include numerous talks, exhibitions and large scale public events such as the inaugural Hong Kong International Kung Fu Festival (2009) and the Hong Kong dragon and lion dance fiesta (2015). The IGA is also active in research and publishing: Firstly by being a research partner for *Journal of Chinese Martial Studies* 「武學 (founded 2009), to date the only academic periodical for Chinese martial studies. Secondly through publication of Hong Kong Martial Arts Community 「香港武林」 with Ming Pao Weekly, which is the first, albeit incomplete, study of Hong Kong martial arts. The IGA has also launched a book series in partnership with Lam Sai Wing Hung Kuen Research Society, having published *Hung Kuen Fundamentals: Gung Gee Fok Fu Kuen* (2013) and *Hung Kuen Training: Chin Cheung & Fok Fu Kuen Deui Chak* (2014). In 2013, the IGA initiated a research project with the School of Creative Media, the City University of Hong Kong,[5] to create a digital archive for Chinese martial arts in Hong Kong, 'Hong Kong martial arts living archive (HKMALA)'.

Could you describe the relationship between the International Guoshu Association, the Hong Kong International Kung Fu Festival, and the setup of the HKMALA?

The IGA is the official entity I use for most of my martial arts related activities, including the Hong Kong International Kung Fu Festival and the HKMALA. I have also been involved with setting up more focused research organisations over the past 3 to 4 years, including the Lam Sai Wing Hung Kuen Research Society, Hakka Kung Fu Culture Research Society and the Institute of Chinese Martial Studies. Going forward I would like to separate purely research-based activities such as the HKMALA, from publishing and public events such as competitions, exhibitions and festivals, which will continue to be organised by or through the IGA.

What inspired you to take up founding the HKMALA?

Since 2009 I have been thinking of organising a centralised digital resource hub for Chinese martial arts. I was uncertain what form it might take but the idea has been brewing since then. My initial thinking was that there is a lot of interest globally in Chinese martial arts, but information tends to be fragmented, of uneven quality and frequently biased or unreliable. This concept continued to develop as my own thinking and knowledge of Chinese martial arts deepened. During the writing of *Hong Kong Martial Arts Community* 「香港武林」 in 2013–14, I was

[5] School of Creative Media, the City University of Hong Kong – Homepage. Available at: http://www.scm.cityu.edu.hk/.

made aware of the multitude of martial art styles in Hong Kong which are slowly becoming endangered due to lack of interest from younger generations. In some ways this also applies to larger styles or schools such as Hung Kuen for, despite their popularity and widespread following, social changes have gradually removed martial art practice from real-life situations (such as the need for self-defence), so applications that lie behind the movements are increasingly being forgotten. In the same way, traditional martial arts are a form of embodied knowledge that goes beyond combat, but involves a referential totality of cultural symbols rooted in village life and popular culture of late imperial China. Even where technical knowledge is being passed down, the cultural system/meanings that lies behind the practice is often the first to go. Therefore, the HKMALA was set up with a sense of utmost urgency with support from the School of Creative Media, the City University of Hong Kong.

Please provide a brief introduction to the HKMALA.

Initially, the HKMALA was conceived as a centralised archive for motion capture data that we record at the City University of Hong Kong. Motion capture is the most advanced technology available right now to record movement in three-dimensional (3-D) space (Figs 30.2 and 30.3). As Chinese martial arts are highly complex in nature, we see motion capture as the only adequate tool for documentation. However, motion capture also has significant flaws and is unable to entirely replace conventional tools for visual documentation, such as photography and video. As a result, we began to think the HKMALA should contain all the other data formats, as well as other aspects of knowledge/formats including oral interviews, texts, live performances etc.

What is the overall scope and content coverage of the HKMALA?

The HKMALA is very much still a project in progress. We are yet to delimit what should go into the archive so in a sense it is open-ended and will remain so, hence a ‘living’ archive which evolves and has no terminal point. How we structure the archive now will determine its usability in the future, so we are approaching this with trepidation and the utmost caution. In very general terms, we see the HKMALA as a comprehensive data hub for traditional Chinese martial arts in Hong Kong encompassing: technical data recorded and represented in diverse formats (such as 3-D models from motion capture, video, photography, books and manuscripts with or without illustrations/images etc.); oral interviews with masters (again in various data formats from sound bites to transcripts and videos); and documentation of the cultural phenomena/contexts related to martial arts application or performance (such as recordings of rituals and temple festivals that frame and give cultural meaning to performance). While it may not be possible to literally record ‘everything’, we aim to reach out to as many styles/schools in Hong Kong as possible, inviting representatives from each of them to participate in this project.

Figure 30.2 Kung fu masters in motion capture sessions.

The HKMALA is described as 'a comprehensive digital archival strategy for intangible heritage'. What are the objectives of the archive? What benefits would this archive ultimately bring to the martial arts community and Hong Kong society as a whole?

The archive is a permanent repository of knowledge for traditional Chinese martial arts. In this sense it functions the same way as a library or any other special purpose archive, but focusing on China's – and more specifically, Hong Kong's – martial arts heritage. I hope the cultural and social value of such an archive is self-evident, given the fact Chinese martial art culture is considered one of the

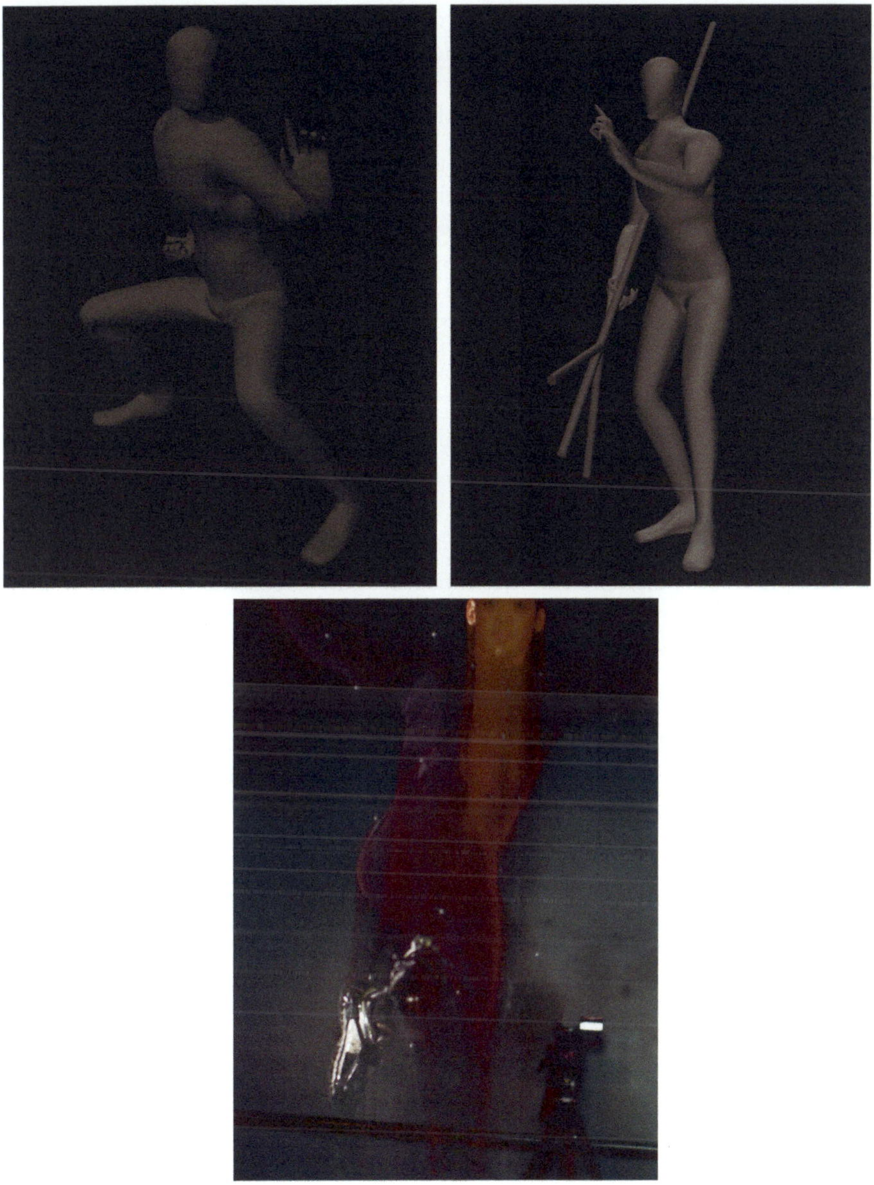

Figure 30.3 Motion capture data of kung fu masters turned into digital visual representations.

twin pillars of Chinese civilisation. However, rather than being an archive that stores information in a passive sense, we also hope to use the archive in a more constructive manner, using the information to generate knowledge through diverse media, such as books, publications and exhibitions that will proactively engage the public.

The HKMALA encompasses the first-ever comprehensive digital strategy of archiving and annotating Hong Kong's diverse and rich kung fu styles and traditions using state-of-the-art data capture tools, as well as for the development of mobile apps and other digital learning tools. What types of technologies will the HKMALA use in particular?

We use motion capture, which is perhaps the most eye-catching technology that distinguishes our archive from more conventional martial arts archives already existing in China and elsewhere. However in addition to motion capture, we also use a range of conventional technologies for visual representation, including different types of video recordings and photography. As I said, we do not set down a priori the range of cameras we use for documentation, depending on our needs and responding to advances in technology as they arise.

While the HKMALA digitally captures different styles of martial arts, how does it provide records on how these forms and techniques could be applied in actual combat situations?

At the moment, our focus is to record the routines for training and performance, as these are more easily organised and quantified. We have documented two-person training and application as trials, but as there are still a lot of routines to record, documenting the applied aspect of different martial art styles will have to come at a later stage. To be honest, as interpretations and applications of techniques differ considerably from master to master within a given style, I do not think it is possible to document the applications of every technique for all the styles. Moreover, given the labour-intensive nature of the data clean-up in motion capture, it may be more effective to record technical applications using more conventional equipment.

Who are the majority of the HKMALA collection users? Are they mostly professors or students from higher education institutions? Or are they people from outside the postsecondary sector?

The archive is currently under construction and cannot be accessed publicly. Fundamental issues concerning the process of data capture and clean-up are still under review as motion capture technologies continue to develop, and until these are properly addressed most of the motion capture data will remain unavailable or unusable, even after we launch the archive. At the moment, people who are regularly working on, and making use of, the archive are our immediate team, which composes of our own and university researchers. On a more positive note, we do intend to present our work to the public as soon as possible. It seems to us that the best way to do this is through exhibitions and publications, which are already scheduled for the second half of 2016.

The HKMALA used crowdfunding as a source of support in building the initiative. How successful was it and what will funders of this project receive upon its completion?

I should emphasise that we used crowdfunding as one of many sources of funding. The funds raised through crowdfunding were enough only to pay for the salary of one motion capture specialist for the period of one year. Crowdfunding typically functions on the basis of advanced payment for a desirable service or product which is not yet available on the market, often at discounted rates. While we also have a remuneration scheme the archive project differs from these crowdfunding projects in so far as it operated on a donation basis. If we choose to use crowdfunding again in the future, we will likely modify our approach to focus on delivery of a specific product (such as an app) which may be more effective.

Unlike a traditional archive of physical objects, the HKMALA is one which captures movements and techniques of martial arts practitioners, almost trade secrets that are not normally let out into the open. What strategies have you used in building this special archive to capture such sensitive information?

No particular strategy was employed. We have a wide network within the Hong Kong martial arts community. The IGA and I have a certain reputation within the field. We know, and have a personal relationship, with many masters who have participated in this project, and are able to reach out to more through their connections. This project is based on trust and a mutual desire to safeguard the legacy of Chinese martial arts.

What do you hope the martial arts community of practitioners could learn from the HKMALA? How about the general public?

The HKMALA will be a centralised hub for serious martial arts practitioners and researchers. It is a knowledge centre where one would find information on different types of Chinese martial arts, including interviews, live performances and artistic and detailed 3-D representations of movement. To make this information more accessible and interesting to the public, we anticipate creating a user-friendly website that either runs parallel to the archive or as a portal. This is technical question we have yet to decide on.

As someone who oversees the building of this collection, how do you acquire and evaluate your collection? Is it a proactive process where you seek out practitioners to donate their knowledge?

We take a multipronged approach to building up our data mass/collection. The starting point of this project is motion capture, which is the main technology we have been using to steadily build up our collection. At the same time, we employ conventional photography, videography and in-depth interviews to document the knowledge pertaining to representative masters. As the volume of work is vast, we approach this latter part thematically. At the moment we are focusing on the Hakka martial arts system, and have conducted in-depth interview with around 20 masters. This process is recorded with voice recording, video and photography. After we conclude this phase of work, which focuses on capturing information in situ, we intend to arrange studio shoots with the Hakka masters where their movements will be documented in studio conditions. This process will be repeated with other major martial art systems in Hong Kong.

The evaluation process is constant. For the motion capture part, we have Professor Matt Delbridge from the Tasmanian College of the Arts, Australia, as project consultant, who regularly comes to Hong Kong to review and comment on our work. We are currently reviewing our motion capture set up to try and (1) optimise the quality of the raw data by upgrading our equipment, and (2) enhance the quality of the performance by creating a more comfortable space for movement. Likewise, documentation of the more 'ethnographic', 'cultural' and 'cognitive' aspects of martial arts is constantly under review. I am personally responsible for supervising this second part.

You also conducted interviews with the individual masters. In what ways could these interviews complement or support the HKMALA project?

Interviews are extremely important. Without them we have an assemblage of important visual data in various 2-D and 3-D formats, but they are taken out of the cultural context. The interviews – but also documenting the sites where the masters practice and teach – help flesh out the social and cultural framework for performance, and endow the movements with cultural meaning. Interviews cover many dimensions beyond the technical aspects, including how martial arts transform through time both in terms of practice and sociocultural context, so it offers a temporal view of Chinese martial arts. They are an integral part of our archive and without them, this archive would be reduced to merely an archive of decontextualised body movements.

When interviewing these Chinese martial arts masters, or during your data collection process, were there any interesting anecdotes that you wish to share with the readers?

The interview process, which is always taken in situ, has taken us to different areas of Hong Kong. It opened our eyes to the deep connection martial arts once had with local communities, particularly in the New Territories, which is even more profound than we anticipated.

Can you tell us about the major challenges and difficulties faced by you and your project partners during the course of creating the HKMALA?

The greatest obstacles when we started were funding, technology and human resources, and they remain the biggest challenges going forward.

How does the HKMALA provide access to the public who want to search through the collections? Is there an online catalogue that provides access for users?

As I said earlier, the archive as such is yet to be launched. Right now public access is limited to publications and public events we organise, where we make use of selected materials from the archive. However, it is certainly our wish to open the archive to the public in the near future, and my team is brainstorming on the best strategy to achieve this.

The HKMALA will have comprehensive metadata, descriptions and physical annotations in order to be a vital source of ongoing research. Do you have librarians or archivists on your team? If not, whom do you have, or plan to have, to do some of this work at the HKMALA?

Yes, Dr Harald Kraemer at the School of Creative Media, City University of Hong Kong, is a key member of the team and is an experienced curator and archivist.

As the founder and project lead of the HKMALA, which part(s) of the project do you find most rewarding?

It is personally very rewarding to get to know some of the masters through this process. Their dedication to the arts is humbling to witness (Fig. 30.4). HKMALA has helped us build not only a network with individuals, but in an important way also to rebuild and strengthen the bonds of a community, which is deeply satisfying. And of course, with each step along the way, whether a single motion capture, a photo session or an interview, we get a sense that we have documented something of lasting value which might otherwise be lost, so the process itself is profoundly gratifying.

The HKMALA, the International Goushu Association and the Hong Kong International Kung Fu Festival. Do you think they contribute to the development of the design and creative industry in Hong Kong, as well as help to build a collective identity of Hong Kong in the long run?

Absolutely, we work closely with artists, designers and other creative talents such as photographers, cinematographers/film-makers, fashion designers, architects and dancers. Their participation is essential to helping us present our materials in an attractive manner and reach the public. I have no doubt that our work together will, in the long run, help foster a stronger collective identity for Hong Kong.

How would you measure the success of the HKMALA and the other activities launched by the International Goushu Association and the Hong Kong International Kung Fu Festival?

I see the IGA's work including HKMALA as part of a social movement. We do not take a quantified approach to measurement, but at the end of the day the most important thing for us is to change people's perception of Chinese martial arts, to make them understanding their value and position as an essential aspect of our intangible cultural heritage. We may measure the short-term success of a single exhibition by the number of attendees etc., which we use to evaluate our work on a project basis, but the greater project has a far more ambitious goal, which cannot be measured in these terms. At the end of the day, it is not just the number of people we engage that matters but the value of what we deliver. It is fair to say we take both a quantitative and qualitative approach to our work, the former tending towards raising general awareness and greater public participation, and the latter towards high-level research and cultural preservation. The

Figure 30.4 Masters of traditional Chinese martial arts in Hong Kong.

two are equally important but incommensurable. It would be simplistic to take one standard of measurement to judge our work.

In your opinion, why do you think it is so important to preserve the traditional Chinese cultural values via the various activities and projects launched by the International Goushu Association and the Hong Kong International Kung Fu Festival, i.e., the HKMALA?

Chinese martial culture is one of the twin pillars of Chinese civilisation. As Confucius said, 'a benevolent man must be courageous'. Since ancient times, martial arts training was a fundamental aspect of our education system, which tends towards moral cultivation. The loss of moral courage and thus the ability to properly align proper action with thinking, is down to the loss of martial valor among the general Chinese population in the past centuries.

If that is the case, in your opinion, what are the values and significance of building a collective identity for the Hong Kong society?

The significance of this project goes far beyond collective identity in Hong Kong.

Establishing a Permanent Kung Fu Museum in Hong Kong

31

Jeffrey Shaw[1], Sarah Kenderdine[1], Hing Chao[2]
[1]City University of Hong Kong, Hong Kong, China; [2]International Guoshu Association, Hong Kong, China

Introduction

The Hong Kong Martial Arts Living Archive is a collaboration between the International Guoshu Association and the City University of Hong Hong (CityU). The project encompasses the first-ever comprehensive digital strategy of archiving and annotating Hong Kong's diverse and rich kung fu styles and traditions using state-of-the-art data capture tools. In addition, the archive offers a wellspring of exhibitions and installations that promulgate rich cultural traditions, as well as mobile apps and other digital learning tools. The archive, with comprehensive metadata, descriptions and physical annotations, is a vital source of ongoing research. The Hong Kong Martial Arts Archive is thus a ground-breaking project aimed at developing a sophisticated methodology for the complete four-dimensional analysis of Hong Kong martial arts, applicable to numerous other performance-based activities (e.g., all marital arts and performing arts). It builds upon extensive work done in dance annotations. CityU professor Jeffrey Shaw (Fig. 31.1) and Hing Chao, CEO, of International Guoshu Association offer important insights into the intellectual and technological perspective into this initiative.

Would you please take time to introduce yourself, and your affiliation or association with the Chinese martial arts digital living archive?

Jeffrey Shaw (JS): I am a new media artist and dean of the School of Creative Media at CityU.[1] Professor Sarah Kenderdine and I have initiated a number of cultural heritage–related projects over the last years, many of which involve the documentation and artistic re-embodiment of tangible and intangible heritage. At our school, we have very good facilities for motion capture, so this has become an important aspect of our research.

After Sarah's first meetings with Hing Chao, CEO of the International Guoshu Association, it became clear that we could do some groundbreaking work together

[1] School of Creative Media, City University of Hong Kong – Homepage. Available at: http://www.scm.cityu.edu.hk.

Inside the World's Major East Asian Collections. http://dx.doi.org/10.1016/B978-0-08-102145-3.00031-5

Figure 31.1 Professor Jeffrey Shaw.

by combining his passion for the traditions of kung fu with the special capabilities and technical resources we have here at CityU.[2]

What kind of intangible heritage? Could you give some examples?

JS: Sarah and I have created projects at various UNESCO World Heritage Sites,[3] including Angkor Wat, Vijayanagara (Hampi) in South India and the Mogao Grottoes at Dunhuang, China. We have also done work in Turkey, encompassing most of the important heritage sites throughout the country.

Regarding the topic of intangible heritage, one of the earliest projects we did was in 1999 with William Forsythe (choreographer) of the Frankfurt Ballet. He wanted to document not only his performances, but also his dance philosophy and techniques, using an interactive analytical approach. The result of our cooperation was published as a best-selling CD titled 'Improvisation Technologies'. Following this was a project on Kyogen (狂言), a particular tradition of Japanese Noh theatre. We developed a new audio–visual method to better document and analyse this form of theatre in which its aesthetic appreciation is conjoined with a detailed academic explication of all its aspects, including the actor's movements, their costume, the stage architecture and the props.

Why did the ballet company need this kind of motion capture technology?

JS: William Forsythe's challenge was that each time a new dancer joined his company, that person would need to be trained in his dance theory. Doing this himself was very time-consuming, so he wanted to find an alternative. Before our project, all he could do was to instruct the dancer to study his archive of hundreds of videotapes of performances.

Why can't the ballet dancers just look at the videotapes, and learn from the video recordings instead?

JS: The videotapes documented performances, but did not explain the theory behind the movements. So we developed a format whereby Forsyth would stand in front of

[2] City University of Hong Kong – Homepage. Available at: http://www.cityu.edu.hk.

[3] UNESCO World Heritage Sites – World Heritage List – Homepage. Available at: http://whc.unesco.org/en/list/.

the camera and physically demonstrate and verbally describe the vocabulary of his 'dance language'. He went through it step by step like chapters in a book. These demonstrations could then be interactively cross-referenced to videos of actual performances where these techniques were applied.

So there were pieces of information, or elements, which could not be replicated by basic video recording?

JS: The information was presented on three levels: one was purely explanatory, another concentrated on the analytical demonstrations and the third showed their integration into performances. I can give you an example. One aspect of his 'dance language' is that he asks the dancers to imagine that they are working with items of furniture, such as a table or chair, that are not physically present. In the videos of the performances, we see the dancers dealing with objects that are invisible, but in the demonstrations done by Forsyth, the chair or table is drawn in with white lines so the viewers can understand and appreciate the dance expressions that emerge from this interaction with these imagined objects.

Forsyth also asks his dancers to imagine that as they are dancing, they are drawing circles or making lines in space. The dancer then use these imaginary shapes to affect their dance movements. In the DVD, we created a graphically augmented reality where you can actually see these virtual shapes that the dancers are creating and dancing with. This layering of analytical explanation and visual augmentation can then be cross-referenced to their actual stage performances, creating an overarching and powerful tool to educate his dancers, as well as anyone else interested in his universally acclaimed dance techniques.

So this (new motion capture technology) would be used as an educational training tool for the ballet dancers?

JS: We found that not only his own dancers, but everyone in the dance world was interested in this project, especially other dance schools. Initially, we presented the project on a computer in the foyer of the theatres where Forsyth was giving performances. However, this turned out to be insufficient because people wanted to take it with them, so we published it as an interactive DVD, and it's now in its fourth edition, including one translated into Japanese. This DVD also offers a paradigm for any multimedia approach to the 'intangible heritage' of performance codes.

What about people from the sporting world i.e., professional athletes? Do they also need technologies of a similar nature?

JS: Certainly, and there is an enormous amount of research going on in that field. We have been working with David Pledger, a theatre director in Melbourne, who is making a performance by connecting the movements of sports people, such as runners and cyclists, to image projections and sound.

So how did you and Hing Chao meet each other? What did you go through to initiate this project?

Hing Chao (HC): It must have been the end of 2012 or the beginning of 2013. I know for sure that by mid-2013, we had already started experimentation, and in November 2013, I did a joint presentation with Sarah at CityU.

JS: Before setting up the motion capture studio at CityU, Sarah and I had been experimenting with motion capture techniques at Deakin University[4] in Melbourne. We made a project together based on a text written by Samuel Beckett called *The Lost Ones*. We wanted to use the Beckett text as a set of instructions for a community of virtual computer-generated characters, so we went into a motion capture studio to digitise all the specific movements that were required of these characters, for example, people standing, squatting, walking around in circles and having various physical interactions with each other. We created a motion capture library of these movements that could then be freely joined together into meaningful sequences by a video game engine. The result is a theatre of automated characters controlled by a computer program, and that program embodies the narrative prescriptions of Beckett's script.

This project prompted us to build a motion capture studio here at CityU. Besides its important educational value for students, we also saw the opportunity to do innovative intangible heritage work with this system, as this technology is a great tool for digitally recording all aspects of human movement, and once you have that data, there are numerous ways in which you can represent it.

There are lots of professional studios out there that specialise in this kind of three-dimensional (3-D) technology, so why did a professional dance company approach an academic institution like you rather than find someone to commission a project?

JS: A commercial motion capture studio is a significant investment, so usually they are reserved for big-budget film and game productions. Comparatively, in the fields of art and cultural heritage, budgets are modest and it's difficult to get access to these resources, so the education and research–based context of a university offer an alternative way. This has been our experience working at universities in Germany, Australia and now here in Hong Kong.

Why would the School of Creative Media (CityU) be interested in taking on this project? Previously, we were talking about a professional dance technology, so this project would be paid for and used by the dance company as an educational tool. But with the Chinese martial arts digital archive, you still do not know who will use this database and for what educational purposes in the future. Why would you take on and trial this project with the staff, time and manpower at the School of Creative Media?

[4] Deakin University – Homepage. Available at: http://www.deakin.edu.au.

JS: There is immense value in the educational impact and innovative research that goes into its motion capture and digital visualisation. As these are the core missions of CityU, we are able to have university support for this. However, this is largely in kind support—facilities and people—rather than research funding, which every university expects its faculty to secure externally, so there are still financial challenges that need to be met to bring everything together.

HC: To follow up on what Jeffrey just said, I think it was very important for the collaborators to believe in the intrinsic cultural value and significance of this project. There is also a certain amount of faith involved; otherwise, a significant part of Chinese heritage would be lost. Sarah invested a portion of her personal research funding to get this project started, while my organisation, the International Guoshu Association, made a donation to CityU to enable it to continue. At the same time, both parties (CityU and myself) continue to pursue potential donors and funding possibilities. Thankfully, while we're devising our long-term strategy to develop this project in the fullness that we hope to achieve, the funding sources are beginning to fall into place. You set your ambition, make a leap of faith and then you go and look for funding.

How do you build a project like this from scratch? Do you look for the right technology first? Or do you say, 'I have certain people who would like to have the things we call good'? Or do you do multiple things at the same time? Do you start draughting a proposal first? How did you build it from scratch?

JS: All three of us have respective histories of research and production that gave this project a clear vision from the outset. We adopted certain resources, like the motion capture studio at CityU, to start making test recordings of the kung fu masters (Figs 31.2 and 31.3). In doing so, we discovered that we still had hurdles to overcome. For example, in kung fu, there are a lot of very fast and complex movements of hands and fingers, and our recordings using optical markers turned out to be problematic in postproduction.

How come the same problems did not happen when you were motion capturing the ballet dancers?

JS: Ballet dancers' hand and finger movements are less complex, and actually, with (William) Forsythe, we were mainly doing graphically augmented video documentation. We are now looking at a new generation of motion capture gloves that will solve these problems, but these gloves are quite costly.

Do you have the gloves now?

JS: We have an older generation of motion capture gloves that, for a number of reasons, are not up to the job. We require the newer technology that has just come on the market. We benefit from the fact that technology in all fields is evolving so fast these days, and motion capture has matured a lot over the last few years.

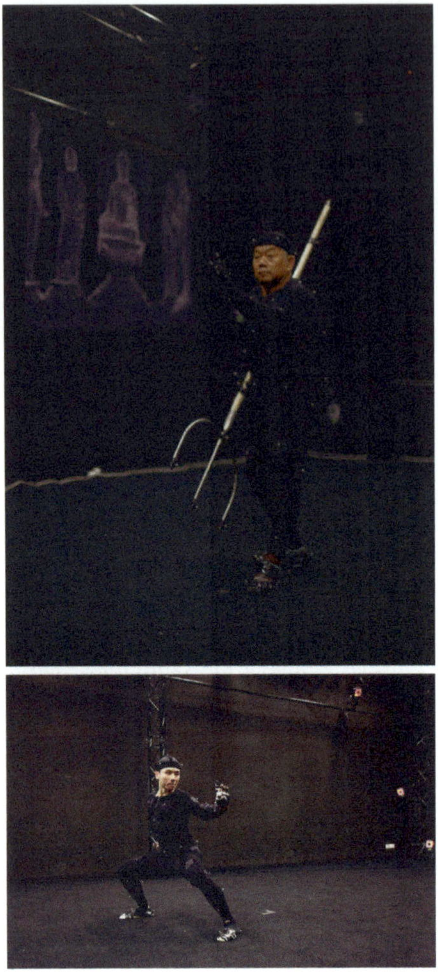

Figure 31.2 Kung fu masters in motion capture sessions.

You have just described your prototype experience. So now, can you talk more about your post-prototype experience? Specifically, what is going on now and what you plan to do in the next 2 years?

HC: As Jeffrey said, there is a great ambition with this project, which is to document the entire martial arts tradition preserved in Hong Kong. Motion capture is a starting point, but it is not everything. We also aspire to document the masters in different settings (outside of the studio), and we are talking about using high-definition, high-speed cameras and other tools to document the movements of the masters. While motion capture provides accurate 3-D data, there are also deficiencies. For example, we do not get facial expressions, and we lose the texture of the human body; this is something that you can't completely recreate.

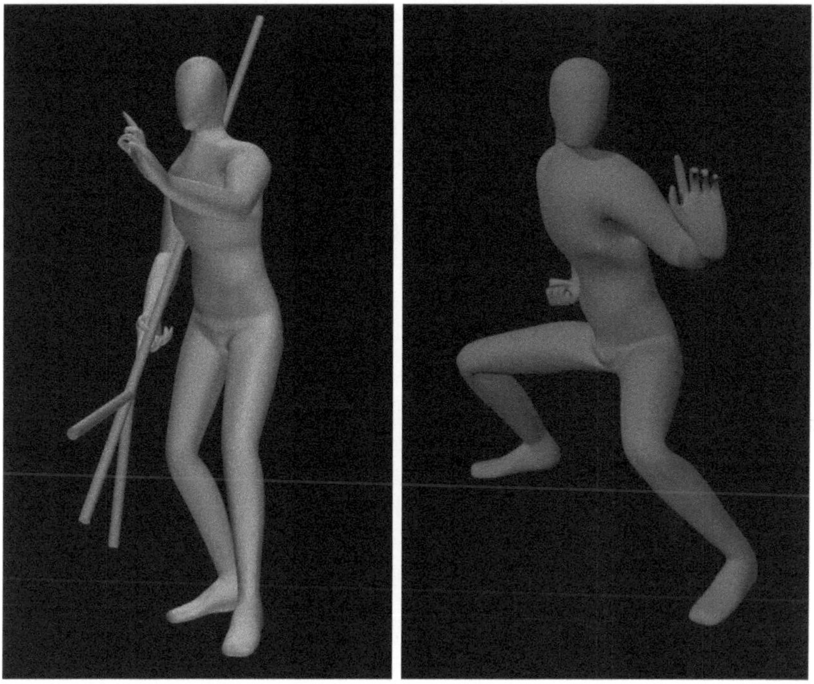

Figure 31.3 Motion capture data of kung fu masters turned into digital visual representations.

What do you mean by the 'texture of the human body'?

HC: Motion capture basically functions with a series of markers, which are placed on strategic and important places on the body. However, when the data is being recorded, all you see are these dots; we do not see faces or the particular features of each master's body.
JS: You could say it's just a skeletal recording of body shape and movement.
HC: So there are many steps towards completing this archive. Motion capture for us is a critical starting point together with the more traditional video and photographic documentation techniques. However, a lot of these masters are getting old, and the way they perform with their body is an entire system of knowledge, which is in danger of being lost. Therefore, the most critical thing is to capture this knowledge and these movements in a 3-D space. That is what motion capture offers, and therefore, it is a great starting point. But as Jeffrey said, motion capture itself is a developing technology. When I started looking at motion capture 4 or 5 years ago, the technology was not where it is today. Even 2 years ago, when we began recording at CityU, the motion capture gloves we had were insufficient for our needs. Therefore, our motion capture technician, Ricky, decided that it was best to place optical markers, about 18 points, on each hand. It was the best solution there was at the time. But 2 years down the road, there is something a lot better on the market, and therefore, we can revise our digitizing methodology. And as with all data capture procedures, this will continue to be refined in the future as the technology improves.

What was the most challenging part in implementing this motion capture project?

JS: As motion capture requires a lot of expertise, we decided that our motion capture technician, Ricky, would benefit from an advanced workshop with the Los Angeles–based company that manufactured our motion capture system. The company has a big studio that is doing production for the Hollywood movie industry, and this professional exposure will be an invaluable learning experience for him. While we have got the best motion capture studio in Hong Kong, we also want to hone the best skill sets to operate it.

What were the initial responses from the (Chinese martial arts) masters?

HC: The masters did not initially understand what motion capture really represents. Thankfully, however, they were willing to give it a go. For many of them, it's a quite exhausting experience; motion capture suits are uncomfortable, and it's difficult to perform strenuous exercises for a lengthy period of time. However, the feedback we had in general was very positive. They could see that 3-D motion capture goes beyond the conventional tools that they're used to, such as videos and photography. They can also see the benefits of using motion capture in the long term as a tool for documenting heritage and passing on this knowledge. So through word of mouth, these masters have told their friends to participate and told them that this is a worthy cause. So the general feedback we have from the martial arts community has been very positive.

What about the academic and scholarly communities?

JS: Sarah and I do a lot of presentations and keynotes at academic conferences around the world, and whenever we show examples of what we are doing, people are interested and excited.

What kind of comments or suggestions would they give to you about your project?

JS: In the digital humanities and creative media community, there is a good understanding of what we are trying to achieve. People want to see the new media technologies brought to bear on intangible cultural heritage in a meaningful and illuminating way. It's a community that is devoted to topics like the hybridisation of new media and the conservation and preservation of cultural memory. Hing, Sarah and I come at this project intending to make it culturally expressive and aesthetically satisfying. This brings a special quality to our work that is appreciated both by experts in the field and the general public.

You mentioned before that the gloves are inadequate. Are they technically not fast enough or is the resolution not high enough? What are the technical problems with this technology?

JS: One of the big challenges in technology is to register and make sense of human–machine interaction. The question is: how can we richly communicate with and via machines? An early breakthrough was the invention of the mouse interface. Yet try to imagine humans communicating with each other by just pushing this mouse around; there would not be much to say. Today's challenge is to find better ways of tracking the human body and interpreting its movements and gestures. The film industry, when making animated movies, has come to realise that rather than try to animate something by hand, it's better to motion capture a human actor and then use that data to drive whatever fictional character (or creature) they want to create. We see the effectiveness of this method in films like *The Lord of the Rings*.

There has been an important evolution of those technologies that digitise the subtleties of human behaviour and appearance. At first, it was just about tracking simple things like walking or climbing a ladder. Then, with optical markers attached all over the performer's body and lots of cameras to track them (there are hundreds in a big Hollywood-size studio), complex bodily actions could be recorded. Then came specialized apparatus to digitize facial expressions and, more recently, the development of gloves to capture rapid and complex hand and finger movements. The latter use numerous tiny position and velocity sensors (similar to the sensors we now have in smartphones) as well as fibre optics that measure the bending of light through optical 'veins' placed along each finger of the glove.

Do you use those technologies to record Grandmasters of music?

JS: One of the pioneering examples of motion capture was done in the early 1990s at MIT[5] by Tod Machover, working together with the famous cellist Yo-Yo Ma. He wired Yo-Yo Ma's hands and arms to an exoskeleton type of motion capture system and recorded this data while Yo-Yo Ma was playing his cello, capturing both the bowing and the finger movements on the strings.

Was it to capture the finger movements of the musicians? Is it important for their music playing, interpretation or for other educational purposes?

JS: Maybe soon, when there are robots that can play cellos, we will be able to give this MIT data set to such a robot, and it will replicate Yo-Yo Ma's performance! In any case, such a motion capture recording has enormous academic value for present and future generations of music students as a tool for study and analysis.

Sarah and I recently presented a keynote at a conference in San Francisco. The conference is called REAL, and its theme this year was *Capture, Compute, Create*.[6] First, you capture something in the real world, then you use computing processes to organise this data and then you do something creative with it. The conference presented a 'making of' movie of the recent (2013) Hollywood hit *Gravity*. To create this utterly convincing representation of human bodies suspended in space, a new paradigm for filmmaking was crafted using cutting edge technology. Looking back, one can say that the entire history of filmmaking is predicated on the evolution of the technologies

[5] MIT (Massachusetts Institute of Technology) – Homepage. Available at: http://web.mit.edu.

[6] REAL 2016 – Conference Homepage. Available at: http://real2015.com.

of film production and presentation, and our kung fu project is certainly part of this tradition and its development.

So with this motion capture technology, what are the potentials within these Chinese martial arts and their communities?

JS: In the first place, it will constitute a very complete record, one that can be used as an archival reference for all time. If 100 years from now, someone wants to see and understand what the Hong Kong kung fu masters are doing today, they should be able to get all the information they need from our project. Our ambition is to produce a body of documentation that will effectively encompass the intangible heritage of kung fu for present and future generations.

Another key aspect is that our recordings provide opportunities for interpretation and analysis so we can augment the performance with various types of analytical representation. For instance, as a certain action is being executed, we can follow the line of movement of the hands and the feet and then extract this information and represent it on a screen. It's like an MRI or CT scan of the kung fu movements. Such a high level of analysis—time motion studies of every detail of a kung fu master's craft—is very revealing and informative.

A further aspect is the creative extension of these recordings so that they become a resource for new forms of artistic expression. For example, Professor Tamas Waliczky at CityU did a project where he filmed a human figure in motion and then took all the frames from that movie and joined them together like a pack of cards. The result was a singular sculptural representation that contained the space–time information of the entire movement sequence, and this could then be given to a 3-D printer to print as a sculptural object. So today we have arrived at a whole new 'capture, compute and create' paradigm, whereby the kung fu masters can also become sculptors!

So could these Chinese kung fu masters download certain parts or data for use?

JS: Its popular dissemination and possible commercialisation could be done via the development of apps. In any situation, the public could get immediate instruction from a kung fu master directly on their smartphones.

When you have devices tracking the movements of this one master, do you also use other methods to collect additional information to support the motions that you have captured?

JS: In the next phase of this project, we will do both motion capture and new forms of video recording. For instance, multiple cameras can record the performers from different points of view, from all four sides, from above and even from below. These video recordings can also be done in 3-D and/or ultra-high resolution, the latter allowing the viewer to interactively zoom in on very fine detail. We will also film important kung fu stances on a turntable to create interactive 360-degree 'object movies' that the viewer can rotate to examine the kung fu master from every angle.

One of the video frontiers at the moment is cameras mounted on drones. Google's 'street view' is switching from car-mounted cameras to drones so as to more efficiently capture the whole urban environment. I can foresee that in the near future, we will be video recording a kung fu master with tiny drone cameras flying all around him/her. This kind of 'total' video recording is also being done at the University of Southern California[7] by Steven Spielberg's Shoah Foundation.[8] They are making audio–visual interviews with survivors and witnesses of the Holocaust while filming them with hundreds of cameras from every possible angle so as to be able to later recreate 3-D holograms of these people.

Your aim is to capture all the masters practicing in Hong Kong. How far have you gotten in terms of inviting these masters to take part in this project?

HC: It's a selection process. In Hong Kong, there are many, many martial artists of different styles. We have to consider if it is worthwhile to bring everyone in, and the answer to that is probably no. So it's a selective process that depends on time, who's available, whether they're willing, if we have the funding to sustain this project and whether we have the human resources to do the postproduction. From our perspective, our target is to document at least 200–300 sets, based on the fact that there are probably around 60 different styles of martial arts in Hong Kong. If we take 40 of them as representatives of Hong Kong, each of them have about 5 or 6 sets; that brings you about 200–300, which is a reasonable number for estimation's sake. We are about halfway, and, as Jeffrey said, we will continue to improve and diversify the ways in which we have been documenting movement with motion capture. While it may be hard to ask some of the older masters to do repeat performances, the younger masters who are available and willing can participate in these digitisation improvements.

So how large is your team at CityU for motion capturing these Chinese kung fu masters?

JS: We are a small but efficient team; besides the kung fu masters and their many colleagues, Ricky is our motion capture technician, and we have graduate students who help with the data postproduction. Another technician maintains the motion capture studio and its equipment, and my research centre administrator does project coordination, as does the staff of the International Guoshu Association. For any exhibition activities, we bring in creative, such as CityU School of Creative Media alumni. Our starting point for this project has been to maximise our existing resources and produce good results so we can grow from there.

Would you like to say something to conclude this interview?

JS: Hing Chao's ambition, shared by us all, is to establish a permanent kung fu museum in Hong Kong as a home for all these materials we are creating. This would

[7] University of Southern California – Homepage. Available at: http://www.usc.edu/.
[8] USC Shoah Foundation – Homepage. Available at: http://sfi.usc.edu/.

be a marvellous outcome because it would be a major enrichment of Hong Kong's cultural landscape. Such a museum could encompass everything related to Chinese martial arts and include spectacular use of new technologies, such as life-size 3-D holograms, to create vivid experiences for the general public as well as for martial arts specialists.

Countries like India, Korea and Japan also have a rich heritage and tradition in martial arts. Do you think they would also need similar motion capturing technologies?

JS: Yes, certainly. I already mentioned our earlier Japanese Noh theatre project, and an associate has recently done documentation of martial arts traditions in India. A few years ago, we finished a major work of immersive interactive visualisation of the Dunhuang caves, and we are currently working on another project that concerns the remaking of the Confucian Rites. Here, CityU is partnering with Jai Li Hall in Hong Kong and Tsinghua University[9] in Beijing to reconstruct and re-enact performances of the 14 Rites in the Book of Li (禮記). Similar to the kung fu project, we are using innovative technologies such as motion capture, panoramic video and virtual reality to create popular and academically rigorous documentations that can be used in the years to come as a definitive reference.

[9] Tsinghua University – Homepage. Available at: http://www.tsinghua.edu.cn/publish/newthu/index.html.

There Is No Truth: There Are Only Stories

32

Harald Kraemer
City University of Hong Kong, Hong Kong, China

Introduction

Dr Harald Kraemer is a 'wanderer' between the worlds. He is a media-design-art historian who is working as a 'Gestalter' (designer) of online and offline hypermedia applications, a system analyst for collection management systems and museums whilst also acting as Associate Professor of the School of Creative Media City University of Hong Kong (CityU). Kraemer has studied art History (PhD), classical archaeology and history at the universities of Trier, Vienna and Witten/Herdecke as well as museum studies and curatorship (Diploma) at the Institute of Cultural Sciences in Vienna. As Associate Professor at the School of Creative Media at CityU of Hong Kong, he is teaching 'arts management and curatorship', and he is currently working on the research project 'multimedia classics–hypermedia hermeneutics'. In discussing his thoughts about designing museum experiences, Kraemer recounts his collaborative projects with curators and experts from around the world, and that museum experiences require different expectations from audiences.

Could you please introduce yourself?

My name is Harald Kraemer. I was born in Trier, the oldest town in Germany founded by the Romans and located in the Mosel valley next to Luxembourg and France. First I studied art history, classical archaeology and history at the Universities of Trier[1] and Vienna, and I then became a PhD student at the private University of Witten/Herdecke.[2] After an internship in the City Museum of Trier in 1986, and some more or less successful experiences running an art gallery with friends, I decided to take the first programme for museum and curatorial studies offered by the Institute for Cultural Sciences in Vienna (1990). During the early 1990s my interest was focused on documentation and archiving with digital technologies. Since then I have worked in different fields including as a consultant in museum documentation, as a systems analyst in museum informatics and also as a creative director and producer of multimedia applications for museums. On the other hand, I have a strong relationship with contemporary art, museums and exhibition-making.

[1] Universities of Trier – Homepage. Available at: https://www.uni-trier.de/index.php?id=58392&L=2.
[2] University of Witten – Homepage. Available at: http://www.uni-wh.de/en/.

Inside the World's Major East Asian Collections. http://dx.doi.org/10.1016/B978-0-08-102145-3.00032-7

It seems that you have a wide range of interests?

You could say I am a wanderer between different worlds. On one hand I am a connoisseur, collecting rare moments with works of art in museums and exhibitions whilst on the other hand I am a raconteur, a narrator designing exhibitions, multimedia applications and books to tell my stories. And there is a third point: I am also a passionate teacher.

Did you start going to museums and art galleries at a very young age? Was that a special talent or interest nurtured by your parents?

No, absolutely not. My father was a police commissioner at the homicide unit, and my mother was more interested in opera and theatre. However, as a kid I liked to read stories about Greek and Roman gods, and I had a sparkling imagination; so much so that my religion teacher had forbidden me to make full-size drawings in my exercise book to illustrate stories of the Bible. When I was about 9 or 10, I found some fragments of antique pottery not far from the Roman aqueduct next to our village. In our local archaeological museum a registrar helped me to identify the clay pot that I had found. I remember being really impressed by the storage facilities, the artifacts and his knowledge.

One or two years later, I cut out all the pieces of works of art from my German schoolbooks and arranged them on the wall of my room. My teacher was not enthusiastic about this action, and so, I had to buy a new schoolbook with my own money. After the end of the school year, I cut the pieces again from the second book and used their reverse. That was how I 'curated' my first exhibition with illustrations of famous works of art.

After my high school graduation, and before I started my military service in the Air Force, I visited the registrar of the archaeology museum to ask him what I could study. He remembered me and said that the classical combination would be art history, classical archaeology and history. I asked him why and he explained that in art history, you become a specialist in perceiving and analysing; in Archaeology, a specialist in describing and deriving conclusions; and History is perfect for training in bibliographic searching and scientific writing. So I started my studies in my hometown, because Trier is well-known for art history, classical archaeology and history. I carried on my studies in Vienna.

There are so many good universities in Germany. Why did you choose to study in Trier and Vienna?

In German-speaking countries, we have different schools for art history. The institute of art history in Trier followed the Hamburg school with Aby Warburg and Erwin Panofsky as they helped to create the Hamburg school, which has a long tradition in iconography and iconology, as well as the formalism developed by Heinrich Wölfflin in Munich. To complete my knowledge in methods, I decided to study the formalistic, idealistic and structuralistic approaches at the Wiener Schule.

However, Vienna was a nightmare because it was common practice under their lecturers that art history stopped at 1925, so there were no courses on modern or contemporary art at this university. Together with a few interested colleagues we founded the student task force 'Save Modern Art' in 1987. Dieter Ronte, the former director of the Museum of the 20th century, allowed us to give lessons for our fellow students.

There are hundreds of museums and art galleries in Vienna. Which particular museum in Vienna did you like visiting the best?

This is a difficult question. I think that museums are not comparable. All have strengths and weaknesses in their collections. They are too different. It would be arrogant to compare them. However, I can say something about atmosphere. Museums offer special moments like the moment of joyful anticipation when you enter the staircase of the Kunsthistorische Museum, [3] because you are excited to meet again Vermeer's allegory of paintings or the paintings of Bruegel, or the remembrance of a wonderful childhood in front of Gerard ter Borch's painting of a mother peeling an apple for her daughter.

Not to forget the nostalgic feeling provoked by the drawings of Gustav Klimt, the Palais Stoclet Frieze at the Museum für angewandte Kunst (MAK) in Vienna, Austria or the moment of humbleness in light of the Beethoven Frieze at the Secession. If you are familiar with these works, then you can find the best places for different emotional states. In Vienna, I fell in love with the museums, with teaching art history and with an architecture student who introduced me to Michael Bockemühl, who fundamentally changed my way of perceiving works of art.

How did that happen?

In 1989 I met Michael Bockemühl in Stuttgart. He gave a summer course about William Turner, and he was a true eye-opener for me. He taught me that ideas spring from open-minded people, not from perfect ones or from those who are following the system. His training focused on the immanent power and the core energy of each individual work of art, as well as the practice of immediate perception or direct contemplation. The overall focus lies in the work of art itself and not in reading knowledge about it. At the Museum Ludwig[4] in Cologne, we spent the whole weekend in front of one painting. I mean, a bunch of young people looking at just one painting of Mark Rothko for 3 days. Here, you can see what a charismatic instructor Bockemühl had been. He taught me to look at works of art with tolerance, patience and a certain degree of humility. In 1990, he asked me to help him prepare another summer course with works of art of the Staatsgalerie Stuttgart. So, I became his first PhD student.

[3] Kunsthistorische Museum – Homepage. Available at: https://www.khm.at/en/.

[4] Museum Ludwig – Homepage. Available at: http://www.museum-ludwig.de/en.html.

What happened then?

In the same year, I made the decision to take the postgraduate programme, curator for museums and exhibitions at the Institute for Cultural Sciences, Vienna. After 3 years of gallery business with some friends in Trier, I understood that my hometown had a lot of culture to offer, but that contemporary art in Trier is a small fish compared with the big plantations Vienna. Trier is a small town with around 100,000 inhabitants. It is not the best town for contemporary art. In every exhibition we made, we had to explain why we were showing this painting and why this is art and so on. I have learned how to argue and fight for my shows. It was a nice training field but nothing for the future. So, I returned back to Vienna to start this programme for curators.

Over the next 2 years I learned a lot about the museum as a system and as a factory to produce educational value, as well as how to plan and produce exhibitions. As teachers I had some big names like the exhibition makers Harald Szeemann, Jan Hoet, Kasper König and Marie Louise von Plessen as well as the museum consultants Dieter Bogner and Gail and Barry Lord.

Before you graduated from university, did you think about what kind of career you would have in the next 5 or 10 years' time?

No. I have always been open-minded, flexible and prepared to take risks for my hunger for knowledge and creativity.

What was your PhD dissertation about?

Museum informatics and digital collections.

Why did you choose this topic for your PhD dissertation?

In 1986 Lutz Heusinger, former director of Bildarchiv Foto Marburg, gave a talk at the University of Trier. He invited us young students to embrace the upcoming digital technologies and to start to define strategies for the sensible use of computers in the humanities, otherwise we would follow technological developments like slaves. I was so impressed that the next day I bought my first computer, an Amstrad PCW8256 Joyce, and a few months later, I used Apple Macintosh Plus.

When I started my curatorial studies in 1990, I moved to Vienna. To earn some money, and as a project for my final study, I made an inventory of the inhomogeneous collections of Schloss Lengenfeld. Thereafter I built the archive of the Gallery in the Griechenbeisl, a famous Viennese art gallery in the 1960s. I learned how to use FileMaker as a tool to create inventories and archives, and I understood how the skills I learned in my studies could help me to deconstruct complex systems, analyse workflows and group information in a way that databases could make use of. In the 1990s, there was a need for museums to get in touch with collection management systems, and so I started to work as a system analyst for museums and archives in German-speaking countries.

The decision to make my PhD about museum informatics and digital collections was the result of the forward-looking advice of my 'Doktorfather' (mentor) Michael Bockemühl, and from the University Witten/Herdecke to bring art, museum and computer technology together. So, my PhD was a consequence of the projects I had realised in the field of museum documentation and digital collection management.

So your dissertation was about creating a prototype?

No. My dissertation was about how you can plan, manage, organise and design a collection or museum management system. I explained everything you should know if you would like to implement a database management system in your museum. At the end, I reduced over 600 pages of the thesis, with numerous case studies, to a very practical and successful handbook.

After you graduated with your PhD, where did you go, and what did you do with all of your skills?

I stayed in Vienna and worked with Dieter Bogner at the Institute for Cultural Sciences. Then, together with Norbert Kanter, I founded 'die lockere gesellschaft – Transfusionen', a consulting company for museum informatics and media in museums. We took over the title 'die lockere gesellschaft' from a painting by Jan Steen that we had seen at the Gemäldegalerie Berlin. It is not easy to translate the title, 'die lockere gesellschaft', which means the laid-back, easy going, relaxed, smart society. The idea was to create a network of people from different disciplines to come together to realise stimulating projects and inspiring products.

In the following years I worked for museums and archives, I produced several multimedia applications and I also organised conferences like 'Digital Euphoria' in 2001 or 'ICHIM04–Digital Cultural Heritage' in Berlin 2004.

Could you give me a list of projects that were initiated by you?

Seen from today's perspective, at the time I was really interested in the development of different strategies to transfer cultural knowledge using different forms of storytelling. My motto was 'there is no truth: there are only stories' (see Fig. 32.1). I used the artifacts as storytellers like in 'Virtual Transfer Musee Suisse', or I used different kinds of navigations to show that history can be a flow of chronological events as well as being part of simultaneity in dissimultaneity like in the CD 'Art and Industry' (see Fig. 32.2). We also experimented with real interaction like in 'Vienna Walk', the prototype of an interactive film. To show this potential for storytelling, I gave a talk at the International Conference on Hypermedia and Interactivity in Museums (ICHIM) in Toronto 2007 titled: 'Simplicity, slowness and good old stories as strategies and perspectives of design in hypermedia and media'.

You have argued about the simplicity, and narration-heavy strategies of how museum interactions and the attention can simplify the complexity of the narration. Can you elaborate on that?

In 1998 I worked with Science Wonder Productions, and we produced 'Vienna Walk Demo', a prototype of an interactive film on DVD. It gives a futuristic vision of real

Figure 32.1 'There is no truth. There are only stories', poster for transfusionen (2005). © Harald Kraemer, Hong Kong.

Figure 32.2 Screenshot from art and industry (2000). Transfusionen for museum of applied arts Vienna (CD).

interactivity and intelligent knowledge transfer in the field of cultural heritage, tourism and E-commerce. Originally presented at the 1999 Museum and the Web conference in New Orleans, 'Vienna Walk' has the distinction of being one of the first DVDs on MPEG2 with a total length of more than 4 h. The theme is that of a virtual institution planning to get an encyclopaedia of the values (economic, cultural and energy) of the city of Vienna. Three agents (Tatjana, Pauline and Tomo) have to fulfill their missions. They have 24 h each and they lead the viewer—their accomplice in the real world—to specific locations in Vienna. Through interactive crossings the user can leave the main story by following a skateboarding avatar to meet other people, or follow a subline of the story.

So the user can go shopping with Tatjana and purchase actual goods online, have a look at the current programme of the opera and buy tickets during the viewing of the CD. Pauline, who is responsible for art and culture, is meanwhile strolling in the Museum of applied Arts. When she meets another visitor, the user can start a discussion about the purpose of art by clicking on her (see Fig. 32.3). And, if the users do not agree with the statements, they can send the virtual visitor an email. By sending a real email to someone in the film without actually leaving the film, the gap between reality and virtuality is thus overcome. In this way, 'Vienna Walk' has shown that the relationship between navigation and content has significantly changed. Intelligent

Figure 32.3 Screenshot from Vienna walk (1998). Science Wonder Productions, Vienna (DVD).
© Harald Kraemer, Hong Kong.

navigation leads us through the world of facts and is part of the content at the same time.

I next worked for the Swiss National Museum.[5] During 2002–04, the project 'Virtual Transfer Musée Suisse' was produced as a new vision of interaction and communication with the museum visitors. All in all around 30 stories were being told, involving over 600 museum objects from eight different collections in five languages (German, French, Italian, Romansh and English). The artifacts, thus, become the narrators: the 'chamber of marvels', e.g., is divided into 'masterpieces', 'favorite items' and 'curiosities'. By using the manifold capabilities of an artifact, a message can also be a political and critical statement, as was realised with the 'Notzimmer' (a set of knockdown furniture) of Mauritius Ehrlich, a social politician and Jew who fled from Vienna to Zurich after Richskristallnacht (Crystal Night) (see Fig. 32.4). I have used the Notzimmer as an example to develop a way for the deconstruction of complex hypermedia applications and published this analytical method in the museum journal Curator in January 2014.

Another example to show my interest in quality-oriented storytelling is the fictive TV talk show 'Knowledge without Limits', which is part of the CD Museum Schloss Kyburg, a museum full of Swiss history not far from Zurich. Here, none other than the fictive Dr Gugel (the personification of Google) himself has invited Johann Jakob Leu, the famous historic Swiss encyclopaedist of the 18th century, to discuss the different methods of attaining knowledge in this work (see Fig. 32.5). Installed in the

[5] Swiss National Museum – Homepage. Available at: https://www.nationalmuseum.ch/e/.

Figure 32.4 Screenshot from Das Notzimmer des Mauritius Ehrlich (2002). Transfusionen for Swiss National Museum, Zurich (CD, Web).
© Harald Kraemer, Hong Kong.

Figure 32.5 Screenshot from museum Schloss Kyburg (2004). Transfusionen for museum Schloss Kyburg (CD).
© Harald Kraemer, Hong Kong.

former workroom of the bailiff at Schloss Kyburg, the discussion takes up the controversial question: Do pupils still need a classical education considering the wealth of downloadable knowledge available on the Internet? In a special competition the knowledge-based method of Leu's lexicon is competing against the search engine of Dr Gugel.

During the competition, the system simulates the search, analysis and creation of knowledge of three items: the Roman goddess 'Minerva', 'potato' and a special kind of Swiss toad named 'Geburtshelferkröte'. In the second part of the TV talk show, Leu and Dr Gugel are discussing the pros and cons. By following Leu and Dr Gugel, the users learn that both systems of knowledge-based methods have their positive and negative aspects.

Let's talk about museum experiences. You have previously worked with different curators and experts from different countries and cultures. The audiences' expectations versus their actual museum experiences — do they always measure up to visitors' expectations and interests?

Falk and Dierking have shown in 'the museum as Gestalt' the complexity of personal, social, and physical context concerning the visitor experience. By testing diverse types for classification of multimedia applications, I have found that there is a complex interplay between information architecture, interface design, navigation and dramaturgy as well as the behavior of museum visitors and the user of hypermedia applications. Even the philosophical background or the motto behind the motivation is part of this structure. Thus the visitors, as well as the users, are differentiated into groups of interested observers, playful discoverers, and encyclopaedists deliberately searching for information. This typology of user attitudes can also be applied to the form, the function and the content. Museums have yet to start understanding how their audiences are influencing and manipulating the museums experiences by their demands for the latest communication technology.

With this new kind of technology, do you think it will help you and the museum reach out to a much wider audience?

Yes, of course, but there is also a danger. Not every museum educator has welcomed this new rival in museum communication, and not every curator has been happy about presenting media in exhibiting spaces. Krzysztof Pomian, one of the pioneers in museology, declared to me in 2009 'Objects are for perception, works of art for emotion and media for fun. Media are—first of all—for fun'. Pomian identified one of the fundamental dilemmas in using multimedia in museums.

In contrast to the serious form of silent appreciation and admiration in front of the works of art, applications of new media mean to him entertainment, fun and amusement. Today, online and offline applications are omnipresent in museums. The danger is that museums could not avoid these developments and a few followed technology in a lemming-like fashion, creating a tail-devouring snake (an Ouroboros): to attract their visitors, museums need the latest technology, to attract their visitors.

How has your background helped lead you to a career in researching the subject of media in museums, media design and digital documentation?

My interest in analysing, designing and archiving digital cultural heritage is central for me, and has influenced and enriched my life in many ways. With my studies of art history, classical archaeology and history, I developed an excellent basis on which to become a critical and analytical thinker. To prepare my PhD about museum documentation, I worked as a systems analyst for over 40 museums, analysing and planning complex museum management systems, and through my education as a curator and in museology I have been trained in perception, communication and the making of exhibitions. Since 1998, I have been involved in the design and production of several multimedia applications.

Multimedia gave me the chance to learn how interactive technology can create pathways to knowledge, to cultural heritage and for the Humanities. In the recently I have started to analyse the reasons for the growing loss of the first multimedia masterpieces. I gave talks about the future of our digital cultural heritage, and I have published articles about these problems. With 'HyperHerald', I have designed a fictive journal of the future with articles about the lack of understanding we had in the past by not defining guidelines for the archiving of multimedia (see Fig. 32.6).

What did you do after that? How did you end up coming to Hong Kong to teach at the School of Creative Media, City University of Hong Kong?

I was invited to the NODEM conference 2012 at the School of Creative Media to give a talk about 'Multimedia classics–hypermedia hermeneutics'. I had a terrible jetlag, and because I lost my PowerPoint presentation, I had to work two nights to restore my talk. I was very tired and therefore I had to concentrate fully on my talk. I spoke slowly and carefully compared to the previous American speakers. As far as I can remember, I closed my talk by answering to a question of a colleague about the future of archiving multimedia with a proverb by Chuang Tzu: 'No great exploits. No plans. If they failed, no sorrow. No self-congratulation in success'.

After the talk, a few CityU[6] students came and said to me: 'You are a funny teacher. You have a lot of wisdom. Please come to Hong Kong and teach us'. I really was touched by the friendliness, openheartedness and the hunger for knowledge of these students. This had never happened to me, and after consultation with my partner in Switzerland and with Jeffrey Shaw, the dean of the School of Creative Media, I decided to come to Hong Kong to teach multimedia.

Are you teaching arts management and not multimedia? Is my understanding correct?

That's right. During the job interview, the committee asked me if I would be interested in the creation of a new MA programme for curating. Together with my colleague Zheng Bo, we have written a proposal for this new programme and in January 2014 I started with the restructuring of the course 'arts management & curatorship'. To make this course more successful and to reach the aims, I combined the theoretical background with practical implementations related to cultural institutions in Hong Kong. Firstly, I have met some of the key players in arts management in Hong Kong.

[6] City University of Hong Kong Library – Homepage. Available at: http://www.cityu.edu.hk/lib/index.htm.

HYPERHERALD

Vol. 01 No. 01
Jan 6th, 2113
Special Issue

Forget f.
Follow NMC in Austin!

Independent – Up to date – Reckless – Our motto: Past creates Future. And the Future is now.

MULTIMEDIA CLASSICS - HYPERMEDIA HERMENEUTICS

continue quit
quit continue

A SELECTION OF MULTIMEDIA CLASSICS OF THE NEOLITHIC AGE OF MULTIMEDIA. UNFORTUNATELY THEY ARE ALL LOST.

One CD-ROM saved.
A big success!
With Open Eyes. Images from the Art Institue of Chicago. Great Art for kids (and their grownups).

WITH OPEN EYES

All data of Multimedia lost. No hope for e-culture! Media archeologists are not able to open the files.

W. McCay / Jan. 6th, 2113 / Texas-City

„All the data on the silver discs of the hidden CD-ROM archive of Bill Gates have been lost," said Dennis W. Diderot, world leading Media archeologist and last librarian of the Library of Congress on the NMC Horizon Project Summit this morning.

„We are not able to open the files. With one exception: A CD-ROM from the Art Institute of Chicago. The title is: „With Open Eyes. Great Art for Kids (and their Grownups)." Probably produced at the last decade of the 20th century. The games about works of art are very simple, the navigation is **difficult to understand for us, and the** interface design is all in a tumble."

Leading media archeologists of the world have met in Texas-City to discuss the loss of our digital heritage. After the discovery of nearly 300 CD-ROMs, PhotoCDs, DVDs and CD-is in a hidden chamber in the BGM, the Museum of Microsoft-founder Bill Gates last summer, the UN DAMN (United Nations Data Archive Media Network) had hoped to get more informations about the initial years of multimedia. Now there is a considerable disappointment among the attendees who are eager for information.

And Diderot suggested: „What we would need today is a work catalog of multimedia applications and a method how to analyze its complexity. Something like a critical canon with case studies. Today everything in hypermedia is regulated but at the begin of this era in the late 20th century, the design of these marvellous interactive works of art has been eternally creative. What a chance this would have been for our e-designers, researchers and educators today? Because of the data loss of silver discs a book, a critical canon would be helpful. It's really a pity that the scientists of the early 21st century had so less responsibility by archiving and analyzing these masterworks of the Neolithic Age of Multimedia."

Media archeologist D. W. Diderot with the last CD-ROM

Why we need a canon for Multimedia?

The »big idea« of Harald Kraemer

1. Information about multimedia in museums – **online and offline** – is mostly published in the form of project-oriented articles in conference proceedings like MW (Museums and the Web).
> To this day, we lack stringent analyses of multimedia applications in/for museums, that is, methodologically grounded studies and oeuvre catalogs providing exemplary case studies.

2. Multimedia „silver discs" tend to get lost.
> The following generations of students, designers and researchers will have no access on the digital data and on the design content of the masterworks of early multimedia design and unfortunately on our thoughts.

3. What are the multimedia applications one has to study in order to count as a professional media dramaturg, e-educator and designer in hypermedia for cultural contents?
> We need a critical canon (book) and a work catalog (dbms) to coach our young talents.

For these reasons I need support to continue and extend my recent research project **„Multimedia Classics – Hypermedia Hermeneutics"** concerning the analyzing work of meanwhile 700 multimedia applications.

» to be continued in Austin TX

ABOUT THE AUTHOR: HARALD KRAEMER Klybeckstrasse 115 CH-4057 Basel Switzerland Tel. +41.76.3360335 kraemer@transfusionen.de

His interest in analyzing, planning, designing, documenting, and archiving of digital cultures of knowledge is central for him and has influenced and enriched his life in many ways. As an art historian and media scientist he is familiar with the traditional methods of the Humanities as well as Media Art and Art Theory. As a systems analyst in Museum Informatics he knows the methods of analyzing and planning complex processes, and through his education as curator and in museology he has been trained in perception, communication, and exhibition-making. In 1998 he started to design and produce multimedia applications for museums – both offline and online – to learn how interactive technology can create pathways to knowledge. Some of his projects: Vienna Walk Demo (prototype of an interactive online film in 1998) / Virtual Transfer Musée Suisse (www.virtualtransfer.com), e-learning courses like Artcampus (Institute of Art History University of Bern, www.artcampus.ch) / Introduction into Pinyin (www.eastasianarthistory.com). Kraemer is a passionate teacher too. He trains his students in how to create interactive applications that are fascinating, stimulating and rich in content by analyzing multimedia masterworks online and offline. On the other hand he leads them into a critical viewing and perception by studying the writings of Paul Virilio, Robert Bresson, Otl Aicher, but also Cicero and Sunzi. After teaching Art & Media History, Design in theory and practise at the universities in Bern, Cologne, Constance, Luneburg, he is recently Docent at the Design Dept. at Zurich University of the Arts and at the Dept. for Image Sciences at Danube University Krems. He has a PhD in History of Art from University Trier and a MA in conceptual design for museums of the Viennese Institute for Cultural Studies. He has published widely on the subject of hypermedia, museum informatics, and digital collections, as well as contemporary art and knowledge transfer in/for museums. Currently he is working on „Multimedia Classics – Hypermedia Hermeneutics", a critical oeuvre catalog and a methodology of hypermedia. More: www.zhdk.ch/?person/detail&id=31762

Figure 32.6 Hyperherald – a fictive journal of the future (2013). © Harald Kraemer, Hong Kong.

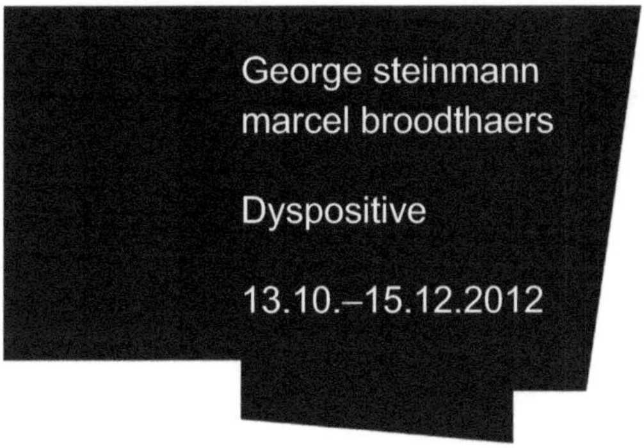

Figure 32.7 Exhibition poster, George Steinmann, Marcel Broodthaers –Dyspositive (2012) at Lotsremark Projekte, Basel.

In addition to classroom sessions, I offered parallel weekly museum visits and exhibition tours so that the students get in touch with the locations of the museums and art galleries in Hong Kong and the people who work there.

By comparing and discussing in front of 'real' works of art installed in 'real' exhibition spaces, my students get a critical view. They learn how a curator can create a flow through the exhibition, how to use an exhibition as a narrative and how visitors get manipulated by the exhibition design. That is why it is important for me to curate my own exhibition shows by select the artists and arranging their works of art in a stimulating way. I understand an exhibition as a whole and therefore, I am responsible for every single detail. That is the reason why I design not only the flow but also the appearances such as invitation cards and posters (see Figs 32.7 and 32.8). As a teacher, I have to teach my students a lesson, and if they see that I can create and design successful exhibition shows like 'The Age of Experience' (see Fig. 32.9), then they are following my example.

In a way, you are saying that you want people to see the museum from a different perspective. You go out to your audience instead of asking your audience to bring themselves closer to your work or to the museum. Is that correct?

It is more that I bring them out of balance and I bring them back into balance. I think if you confront the visitors with a situation or a question which is related to their own life in an unusual way, it will be more uncomfortable for them. So they are starting to think about it. Then, they want to find an answer; they want to know more. This is sustainable and they will come back. If you only give them information and facts they will be unsatisfied, because they can get these facts at any time and in all places.

If we want to change the relationship between museums and visitors, we have to educate the incoming curators in a good way. Since the beginning of my engagement at CityU, I have visited over 120 exhibitions, art fairs and auctions shows with my students, (see Fig. 32.10). These visits are an essential part of my course. By learning how to analyse the different functions, roles and designs of exhibitions my students learn to understand the complex interplay of the different factors in the system of art, museum and galleries as well as education and communication. They learn why exhibitions

Figure 32.8 Exhibition poster, Pendants Parlants (2012) at Kunsthaus Interlaken, Switzerland. © Harald Kraemer, Hong Kong.

Figure 32.9 Exhibition poster, age of experience (2015) at City University of Hong Kong.

Figure 32.10 Harald Kraemer at Art Basel Hong Kong 2016.

are fascinating, stimulating and rich in content. By planning and producing their own exhibitions, the students have to show how to transform the theory into practice. As a result of my newly-created course 'curatorial project', the students curated, planned, designed and produced four major art events to explore various elements about street art, all under the title STREET ART RELOADING, May 2016. So, they generated practical knowledge and got a real feedback from the visitors about their work. With these experiences, the students learn to understand where their own skills and abilities are and how to use them.

What is your teaching philosophy?

My partner Janine Stoll—a teacher and an art historian—said once that I am following the guidelines of Johann Heinrich Pestalozzi, a Swiss pedagogue and educational reformer. Pestalozzi's motto was 'Learning by head, hand and heart'. In a sense, I am really following these good old virtues. But on the other hand, I feel like a 'Gestalter' of knowledge. I am someone who is giving an idea a form or a shape, and this can be a book, an exhibition, a multimedia application or a course. I am teaching my students that systems and their properties should be viewed as wholes, not as collections of parts, and to demonstrate this I unbalance them first and then rebalance them. 'Unbalance so as to Rebalance'. This proverb of the French cinematographer Robert Bresson has changed my way of teaching.

Figure 32.11 Harald Kraemer at Christies Hong Kong 2015.

My friend, the Austrian artist Herbert Starek, made a portrait of me a few years ago and he gave this portrait the title 'Der kühne Interpret' which can be translated as 'The Bold Interpreter' (see Fig. 32.11). At first, I was astonished because I have never seen myself as a juggler, however I am really impressed at how closely this portrait fits me. Furthermore, I am leading my students into critical viewing and perception by studying the writings of Paul Virilio, Rudolf Arnheim, Robert Bresson, Otl Aicher, Guy Bonsiepe, Cicero, Zhuangzi (莊周) and Sun Tzu (孫子) (Fig. 32.12).

What are the other major projects you are currently working on?

In January 2017 my fund project 'Archiving ephemeral knowledge–Hong Kong martial arts as a documentation strategy for intangible cultural heritage' will start. I will invite specialists in the archiving of performing and performance arts to CityU to discuss, together with our specialists in motion capture of hakka kung fu, new strategies for the archiving and documentation of intangible cultural heritage. The results of the symposium will be evaluated by the International Council of Museums/International Committee for Documentation[7] and get published.

Recently, I have collected data about multimedia in museums from institutions and exhibitions in Hong Kong, Mainland China (Beijing, Hangzhou, Nanjing, Shanghai) and Taiwan. This will be the base for my next GRF application 'multimedia classics–hypermedia hermeneutics–transmedia narratives'. I am planning to combine the data material I have collected in museums in the US, Europe, Hong Kong, Mainland China

[7] ICOM/CIDOC (International Council of Museums/International Committee for Documentation) – Homepage. Available at: http://icom.museum/the-committees/international-committees/international-committee/international-committee-for-documentation/.

Figure 32.12 Herbert Starek, The Bold Interpreter (2011), Pigmentprint, 116×88cm. © Herbert Starek, Vienna.

and Taiwan to create an online archive for media in museums, as well as another handbook with excellent case studies for students and further generations of researchers.

As part of my MA Programme *curating art and media*, I will maintain the cooperation with museums in Hong Kong, Mainland China and Taiwan. Also, I have discovered that there is no useful handbook for my students which combines curatorship, arts management and exhibition management with case scenarios related to Mainland China and Hong Kong. So, I have started to create a practical handbook together with my students. The material they have prepared will be proofread and complemented by different curators and experts and published in 2017.

At the moment, I am planning several exhibition shows like 'The Age of Experience' in Vienna, and together with my partner, the exhibitions 'Interval in Space' in Hong Kong and Nairs in Switzerland.

In cooperation with Dr Florian Knothe, I am preparing the show *A Philosophy of Landscape. Robert Lettner and the Mustard Seed Garden of Painting* for the Hong Kong University Museum and Art Gallery[8] and another one with the title *The ornamental Utopia of Robert Lettner* for City University of Hong Kong.

Furthermore, I have to finish my oeuvre catalogue about the Austrian artist Robert Lettner by summer 2017.

[8] University Museum & Art Gallery – University of Hong Kong – Homepage. Available at: http://www.umag.hku.hk/en/.

The Legend Continues: How Bruce Lee's Legacy Contributes to Our Shared Understanding of Libraries, Archives and Museums

33

Shannon Lee
Bruce Lee Foundation, Los Angeles, CA, United States

Introduction

The Bruce Lee Foundation was founded in 2002. This charity, dedicated to Bruce Lee, has a much broader and more far-reaching scope than just martial arts, as it really focuses on philosophy, the way that Lee lived his life and his many contributions to martial arts and culture. Although not housed in a traditional brick and mortar building, the Bruce Lee Foundation is very much an example of a memory institution (an organisation maintaining a repository of public knowledge). This generic term is often used to refer to institutions such as libraries, archives, museums, monuments and providers of digital libraries which serve as memories for our society. Even though the Foundation houses an extensive collection of Lee's items including photographs, his library of books, clothing and training equipment, without a large budget they rely on their connections for donations and loans in order to collaborate with museums for exhibitions. In essence, by not having a museum of its own, the Foundation's collaborative exhibits are extensions that endeavour to provide access to archival materials in a public forum. In the following interview, Shannon Lee (chairperson of the Bruce Lee Foundation, Fig. 33.1) discusses *Bruce Lee: kung fu–art–life*, a multifaceted exhibition that is uniquely segmented to examine the cultural journey of Bruce Lee, the man growing up in Hong Kong; Bruce Lee the actor and the filmmaker; Bruce Lee the martial artist; and finally Bruce Lee the icon. From the dynamically designed entryway – the mirrors and the water quote – the exhibit sets the tone for audiences to immerse themselves in the experience.

Could you begin this interview by first introducing yourself? Your training and background, and your current roles and duties at the Bruce Lee Foundation?

I am the chairperson at the Bruce Lee Foundation.[1] Bruce Lee is also my father. I also run the other side of the business i.e., licensing and entertainment, so I am immersed in all things Bruce Lee!

[1] Bruce Lee Foundation – Homepage. Available at: https://bruceleefoundation.org/.

Inside the World's Major East Asian Collections. http://dx.doi.org/10.1016/B978-0-08-102145-3.00033-9

Figure 33.1 Shannon Lee.

My training and background for all of this is really just life. I do not hold any kind of business degree, charitable organisations degree or training. My degree comes from trying to live life to the fullest and having Bruce Lee as a father and mentor throughout my life. I was also a student of Jeet Kune Do and other forms of martial arts for many years, so I do have that background as well. I also have a creative background. I acted for a number of years, I like to write and I have a degree in music: so I sing. That's basically my background.

Could you give us a brief introduction to the Bruce Lee Foundation? When was the Foundation established? Who were the founders, and what are its services and functions?

The Bruce Lee Foundation was founded in 2002. Prior to that, there was another organisation that existed for about 5 years called the Bruce Lee Educational Foundation. That was founded by a group of students of my father's: first and second generation students. I participated in that, but more so on the periphery. That organisation had been primarily focused on martial arts and the preservation of Jeet Kune Do, but it was disbanded in 2001. While I felt that was a very important concept, I really felt there could be a charity dedicated to Bruce Lee that would have a much broader and more far-reaching scope. The charity could include the martial arts aspect but also focus on the philosophical teachings, looking at the way my father lived his life and helping to inspire and emulate that in the world.

So, in 2002, we founded the Bruce Lee Foundation. It had a very small number of board members: Firstly there were a handful of my father's original students, Taky Kimura, Allen Joe and Ted Wong (Ted Wong was my *sifu* in Jeet Kune Do). Secondly, there were a handful of professionals and friends that we pulled together to get it started. It was very much a grassroots organisation. We started with pretty much nothing and we initially started doing activities with which we were already familiar, such as giving seminars and continuing to educate people about Jeet Kune Do. About once a year, we would have an event and we started a small scholarship fund. In 2003 we awarded our first scholarship, and now many, many years later, we have grown and evolved somewhat. In fact, last year, in 2015, we hired our first director, a man by the name of Richard Grewer. We've also grown our scholarship programme, I want to say that we handed out seven scholarships last year. We have started to change and morph the types of events and programmes we do as well. In 2015, I gave a TED Talk[2] and I have done a lot more speaking engagements, I have gone to elementary schools, high schools, universities as well as martial arts schools to give talks about my father and his philosophies. We launched an initiative to create our own museum project, which we have been calling the Bruce Lee Action Museum.[3] As a part of that, we have mounted three exhibits: one in Hong Kong, one in Seattle and one in Sacramento. We also began a rebranding initiative to expand our programme centre outreach, and started a fundraising campaign and, in conjunction with the 75th birthday anniversary of my father, we had an event in downtown Las Vegas that was different to any event that we'd ever done. We had a lot of activities that were free and open to the public from yoga sessions, dance sessions and martial arts training sessions to film screenings etc.

We want to try and provide the global community with more information about who Bruce Lee was, what his teachings were and how that can be really affecting for people's lives. We have been looking at how to put that forth, and what we've been saying is that the Bruce Lee Foundation is about motivating action and inspiring confidence. One of the events we are going to be initiating this year is called 'Bruce Lee's Little Dragons', and it's a programme which we are going to pilot in Los Angeles, to provide access to martial arts instruction for children who cannot afford it or do not have access to it.

Could you provide a very brief introduction to the Bruce Lee exhibit at the Hong Kong Heritage Museum? What are some of the highlights of the exhibit?

First of all, I think the exhibit is really beautiful. The museum, and everyone we worked with there, did a fabulous job at creating a very multifaceted exhibition that is very well-rounded but also very engaging. I love the way that they have segmented the exhibit to have a look at Bruce Lee, the man; Bruce Lee, the actor and filmmaker; Bruce Lee, the martial artist; and then Bruce Lee, the icon. I love the entryway – the mirrors and the water quote – it is really dynamic and really sets the tone for you to immerse yourself in the experience. I love the way that each section has its own look and feel to it. The beginning section, that talks about his childhood and growing up, has a very 1950s Hong Kong feel to it. The movie section, with each film having its own set, is really fun and engaging. They have done some really special stuff with the heavy bag that moves, animations they've created and the beautiful statue they created as well. There is a lot of artistry, and you really got the sense that Hong Kong came together as a community.

[2] TED Talks – Homepage. Available at: https://www.ted.com/talks.

[3] Bruce Lee Action Museum – Homepage. Available at: http://www.bruceleeactionmuseum.org/.

Are the materials and artefacts at the museum currently on permanent loan to the Hong Kong Heritage Museum?

It's not permanent. I think the time period is 5 years. Of course, I think it has a couple of years left to go. We are open to discussions with them about what they want to do, if anything, beyond that. But we have not reached that point in time. I know the exhibit has been really popular, but I do not know what their plans are beyond the five-year loan.

Your father passed away in 1973, but his legacy continues to inspire filmmakers and audiences around the world. Could you tell us why there was such a long wait – almost 40 years – for such an exhibit to finally be set up in Hong Kong?

I think, in part, there needed to be some time because when my father first passed away there was a big outcry. There was this big transmigration of his films all around the world, a lot of activity was happening and people were getting to see, love and appreciate his films and himself: 10 years after his passing.

It took some time for people to really understand the larger impact of Bruce Lee. When he first passed away, he was seen as a movie star and that guy who did awesome kung fu movies. But they did not really know the depth of his character: he was truly a martial artist. A lot of people debated for many years whether or not Bruce Lee was actually a martial artist or if he just did that for the movies. I think that over time, people have not only come to understand the depth of who he was as a martial artist but also as a creative, a thinker, a writer and a self-educated man who had a very devout dedication to the path of self-actualization and self-cultivation. It was a combination of all of these things that contributed to the awesomeness they were encountering on screen. However, it really took time to cement the breadth of his legacy into consciousness. He was so ahead of his time in so many ways. I think that as the landscape has changed – as our world has become smaller and smaller – through the birth of technology, more and more people around the world are discovering Bruce Lee.

There were some efforts to create a museum in our former family residence in Hong Kong. The Hong Kong Government were in deep discussions with the property owner for a number of years, but in the end they were unable to acquire the property. I think that when that fell through, the Hong Kong Government really wanted to figure out what they could do, so they decided to try and mount this exhibition at the Hong Kong Heritage Museum.[4] Of course, it took a couple of years to do that. I know that there's always outcry in Hong Kong amongst the population, they say 'Why did it take so long'? From my point of view, I think Bruce Lee is worthy of discussion, worthy of remembrance and worthy of celebration and has been for the last 40 years. However, I do want to give recognition to Hong Kong for, to date, having the largest and most thorough exhibition in the world, and paying tribute and recognising my father for the impact he has made globally.

[4] Hong Kong Heritage Museum – Homepage. Available at: http://hk.heritage.museum/en_US/web/hm/highlights.html.

Can you tell us how this collaboration occurred between the museum and your foundation?

For me, if I can provide access to my father's legacy at little to no cost, I think that is a beautiful thing. The Hong Kong Heritage Museum approached us. The government had been in contact with us in the years prior when they were trying to acquire the property, my family's former residence. So they had connections and access to us already, and I've been back and forth to Hong Kong on numerous occasions. My father had been awarded a couple of awards by the Hong Kong Film Association over the years, and I have travelled there to accept those on his behalf. There was already a relationship there. When they approached us to do this, I really did not hesitate. We have always wanted to do our own project, however when it comes to museum and nonprofit work it is quite an undertaking to garner the enthusiasm, the funding and the wherewithal of dedicated individuals to get a project like that off the ground. When they came to us and said that they would like to run an exhibit for 5 years, in my mind, it was a no-brainer. I just felt that I had all these memorabilia and artefacts in my care and no one was getting to enjoy them or experience them because there was nowhere for them to be other than in our archive. It is my mission to be able to provide opportunities to share, and it is something we are working on in the Foundation. It seemed like a wonderful opportunity to work hand in hand with a top-notch facility, one that was on the other side of the world and, of course, one that was very important to the legacy of Bruce Lee. They reached out to me, and I said, 'Great'!

Speaking of items, there are more than 600 items of Bruce Lee memorabilia at this exhibition from local and overseas collectors. How did you decide which of these materials would showcase his life as a film star and martial artist, but also as a cultural phenomenon?

It took them a couple of years to mount the exhibit, and the culture and tourism board government members came here to Los Angeles and went through the archives. We showed them the things that we had, and we talked extensively with them about the various ways we could go about doing it. In the end, because it is their facility and their organisation, and they were the ones who were going to do the heavy lifting in terms of creating the exhibit, we really wanted them to take the lead in terms of the format of the exhibit. I really just saw myself in the role of aiding them to bring their vision into reality. I just wanted to be as supportive as I could. They were top-notch and professional from the beginning, and I thought that everything that they came up with was great.

My father's story is a very East–West story. He was born in the United States but grew up for a number of years in Hong Kong. He then came back to the United States and spent many years back and forth, and you really have to tell that story because it is the truth of the situation.

As chairperson of the Bruce Lee Foundation, could you please describe what a typical day at work looks like?

I oversee the entertainment and licensing divisions as well, so my days are a constant flow from one thing to another. At the beginning of the week – every Monday morning – I meet with the director of the foundation and the other members of the executive committee. We go over all of the things we are working on and that we need input and feedback on. For instance, I have just received two speaking requests, so I am looking over these to try and assess if they would be good to do. We are rebranding our website, scheduling for 2016 and looking at all of the different events that we're going to be doing. We're launching our pilot programme, the Little Dragons, 2016, so we are just moving as quickly as we can to come up with the next step: taking our action steps if you will. I just want to say that I'm really fortunate and blessed to have people working with me, and for me, who are dedicated, passionate, who get it and are all about wanting to spread the message of Bruce Lee. They do an excellent job and it gives me peace of mind.

Does the foundation continue to actively collect materials that contribute to the Bruce Lee legacy?

We do, but we don't do it in a majorly aggressive way. For one, we do not have a huge budget for that. However, we have had people donate things to us, and we have had people loan things to us. We have very good relationships with a number of the larger collectors. We ourselves have an extensive collection of my father's items including original photographs, his library of books, clothing, training equipment etc. Every now and again, yes, we will acquire something, and every now and then, we will be donated an item. In the cases where we are looking for a particular item that we do not have, we have a network of people who we can reach out to and say 'Hey, the people at the museum want to put this item in their exhibit. Would you be willing to loan it to them'?

The Bruce Lee Exhibition in Hong Kong has such a strong focus on the local and the global cultures. What other kinds of projects do you have in the future which will expand on this particular exhibit?

As you know, we are still continuing to work on the Bruce Lee Action Museum, and the exhibits we have mounted are extensions of that, such that we are trying to provide access to these archival materials in a public forum. We are also working on a plan to create an interactive, online resource version of the Action Museum. We want to be able to provide access to the writings and the books in an online research library and provide access globally so that anyone who has a computer can interact with us as well as (at some point down the line when we have physical space for that). We want to put our resources into creating a virtual experience so that people all around the globe can experience it, and you do not have to necessarily travel to be able to do that. That is one big thing that we are working on this year.

What do you want the audience to take home after seeing the exhibit in Hong Kong?

I think that people are attracted to the name Bruce Lee for a whole host of reasons. However, what I would hope is that the knowledge that they have, their preconceived notions or their understanding – however large or small prior to stepping into the exhibit – would be completely blown out of the water, or greatly expanded, by really encountering the man, who he was and also his processes. He really considered himself an eternal student and was always trying to grow, expand and cultivate himself and his knowledge. It is really funny, when I have people come here to the office, I show them some of the materials in the archive and every single person says 'Wow, I just really feel like I am wasting my time'! In the sense that he was so enthusiastic and so driven and accomplished amazing things in such a short period of time: it's really phenomenal. I really hope that people encounter that and realise that Bruce Lee was much more than just 'that guy who made some kung fu movies'. It is so true, and that's why I do what I do.

During the set up of the exhibition, were there any memorable moments that you wish to share with our readers? Did you encounter any difficulties or challenges during the set up?

It was definitely a lot of work. From choosing the items to packing and transiting the items safely. There were a couple of things that were very challenging i.e., moving a big, heavy bag and a big, wooden dummy. There was actually one piece that we were not able to send. My father has a tiger skin which was used in the film *Game of Death*, and it has been in his possession since the early 1970s. It was also in our home. Because of the treaties on importing and exporting tiger skins and the like, we could not get that item over to Hong Kong for the display. But really, I have to give proper accolade to the Hong Kong Heritage Museum. They were extremely professional. It is always a little nerve-racking when you have these one of a kind possessions that you do not want anything to happen to. But they really put me at ease with their professionalism and understanding of the processes.

Which parts of your job at the Bruce Lee Foundation do you find most rewarding?

I think the most rewarding for me is the actual interaction with the public and getting to excite and impact people's lives. It is always really amazing. Last year, we got over 700 scholarship applications. Going through those, reading the stories of all of these different people (you want to give scholarships to all of them), reaching out to the winners to let them know they have won and having events and seeing joy and enthusiasm on people's faces is very rewarding. My father's energy is extremely dynamic and engaging, and his words and his messages are so thought-provoking and impactful. I just love getting to see the effect of that on the faces of the people that I encounter and work with when I do these events.

Has setting up this exhibit at the museum helped you reconnect with your father on an emotional level?

Yes. I lost my father when I was four, so I obviously did not have the interaction with him that most people get to have with their parents (Fig. 33.2). So I do not have those stories about 'that time when he walked into the house' etc. However, because he was so amazingly prolific in terms of documenting his process; because I have all of his thoughts, philosophy, writings, books, notes and day timers; and because he had such

Figure 33.2 Shannon Lee and her father, Bruce Lee.

a huge impact on so many people's lives, anytime I do anything like this, I feel like it is an opportunity to know him more. It is an opportunity to see him through another lens that I do not have, because he's not here. However, I guess in some ways (in an interesting way) if he was here, then I would not necessarily have this point of view. It is very impactful for me. I get to have a continually evolving relationship with him even though he's not here.

Is there anything you would like to add before we close this interview?

I just really feel that my father's message, the way he lived his life, the way he was such an innovator but also someone who was very much in harmony with the world at the same time – he was just doing 'him' and not what other people were doing, right or wrong. He was on a path of cultivating himself and I think that message, and that example, is so important that it makes me want to do what I do. I hope that people will apply those messages to themselves as well because my father's message was always about self-actualization. It is not about being Bruce Lee: it's about being yourself. But you can use Bruce Lee as an example of how to do that.

I think that people are still discovering the depth and impact of him. In some ways because he was this action star, there was an easy gateway into loving Bruce Lee. But then, at the same time, I think that gets in the way a little bit of the real gift of Bruce Lee, which I just hope more and more people are discovering.

Collecting Memories of Hong Kong in the Canadian Context

34

Jack Leong
University of Toronto Libraries, Toronto, ON, Canada

Introduction

Named in honour of Richard Charles Lee, one of the foremost Hong Kong businessmen and philanthropists of his day, the Richard Charles Lee Canada–Hong Kong Library is Canada's only library focused on Hong Kong studies. A facility with a unique research collection of over 50,000 volumes covering Hong Kong studies, Hong Kong statistics, government information and Chinese–Canadian studies, the library features quiet study spaces and seminar areas to provide resources and space to accommodate the continuous growth of research interest in Hong Kong and its relation to Canada and other regions in the world. As a leading scholar of Hong Kong–Canada relations, Jack Leong has overseen the library's growth and many initiatives, including the Hong Kong–Canada crosscurrents project (2014–19). This project aims to provide coordination and depository infrastructure for the research, collection development and public education of the effects of migrations and cultural connections between Hong Kong and Canada from the 1960s to the 2010s. He has also overseen the Hong Kong basic law portal, which is an online gateway to basic law research materials from major institutions around the world.

Can you begin this interview by first introducing yourself? Namely your training, roles and duties as the director of the Richard Charles Lee Canada–Hong Kong Library?

My name is Jack Leong and I am the current director of the Richard Charles Lee Canada–Hong Kong Library.[1] I am its first and founding director. I will begin by explaining my major roles and duties in setting up this library and running it for the last 7 years.

When the library was set up in 2007, we already had a good collection of materials on Canada–Hong Kong studies. My major task, therefore, was to organise and set up this existing collection based on the layout of the new facility and the needs of our users. I implemented the migration of the catalogue records from the local system

[1] Richard Charles Lee Canada-Hong Kong Library – Homepage. Available at: http://hongkong.library.utoronto.ca/.

Inside the World's Major East Asian Collections. http://dx.doi.org/10.1016/B978-0-08-102145-3.00034-0

to the University of Toronto Libraries'[2] **o**nline **p**ublic **a**ccess **c**atalogue, allowing the collection to become searchable online. I also developed a fully-fledged public service for the library over the years. So, in addition to reference, tours and research consultation, I organised and coordinated more than 50 conferences, seminars and exhibits. Such events are important for a new library as they provide us with opportunities to promote the library, the collection and the services to the academic community and the general public.

As an administrator, I supervised the operations of the library and was responsible for staff management and professional development. In addition to providing services to the University of Toronto,[3] I also conducted research and published in academic journals and books. I am interested in Chinese–Canadian studies, international outreach for libraries and Hong Kong studies, particularly literature and science fiction. My PhD research examined science fiction, focusing on the motifs of cyberspace, cyborg and space travel. In the 1990s those motifs were very innovative.

After my PhD studies, I worked for 2 years as a library assistant at the Cheng Yu Tung East Asian Library of the University of Toronto. During this time, I found that a career as a librarian could combine my interests in computer science and literary studies, so I enrolled on the master's degree in library science at the University of Toronto.[4] After graduation, I became the information services librarian in the East Asian Library. When the university established the Richard Charles Lee Canada–Hong Kong Library, I became the first director.

Could you provide an introduction to the collection at the Richard Charles Lee Canada–Hong Kong Library?

The collection was largely inherited from the Canada–Hong Kong Resources Centre, which started gathering materials on Hong Kong and Hong Kong immigrants to Canada during the early 1990s. There have been many significant donations from our community and institutional partners in Hong Kong. The earliest publications in the library are from the 1920s on the topics of Chinese in British Columbia and the memorial service for the death of Dr Sun Yat-Sen. The collection focuses primarily on Hong Kong, Canada–Hong Kong relations and Hong Kong–Canadians. Many Chinese who came to Canada before the 1990s were either originally from Hong Kong, or stayed in Hong Kong for a couple of years before embarking on their journey across the Pacific. That is why it is important to have a substantial collection on Chinese–Canadians in the Canada–Hong Kong Library.

How old is the library? Can you tell us about its background and how it all got started?

The former incarnation of the library—the Canada–Hong Kong Resources Centre—was set up in 1994. It operated under the Canada–Hong Kong research project and

[2] University of Toronto Libraries – Homepage. Available at: https://onesearch.library.utoronto.ca/.

[3] University of Toronto – Homepage. Available at: https://www.utoronto.ca/.

[4] Cheng Yu Tung East Asian Library, University of Toronto – Homepage. Available at: http://www.library.utoronto.ca/east/index.html.

was administered by the University of Toronto[4] and York University.[5] Although it was located at the University of Toronto, it was not part of the University of Toronto Libraries system until 2005. The centre had been active for about 10 years before the library was founded and the newspaper database was created at that time. For 1994–99 its operations were funded by the Hong Kong and Shanghai Banking Corporation.[6] There was also a 1 million dollar donation to the University of Toronto for the Canada–Hong Kong research project, which consisted of a publication series and the centre. Dr Vivienne Poy generously funded operations for 1999–2004.

In Toronto, there is keen interest in Hong Kong among the scholars and general public. Indeed, Toronto has a significant number of Hong Kong immigrants and many Canadians live in Hong Kong, creating numerous interactions between Canada and Hong Kong. An initiative to set up a permanent facility for the Resources Centre was on the agenda of the university council in 2004–05. At the time, Dr Vivienne Poy was the university chancellor and a strong supporter of the initiative (Fig. 34.1). Dr Poy, and many other prominent figures from Canada and Hong Kong, had visited and used the Resources Centre and found it to be a valuable facility. After the university council's approval and successfully raising 3 million Canadian dollars to endow the facility, the Resources Centre was transformed into the Richard Charles Lee Canada–Hong Kong Library and became part of the University of Toronto Libraries. The library was officially opened on 6 March 2008.

Figure 34.1 A library event attended by close to 100 people. The speaker in the photo is the Honourable Dr Vivienne Poy, the first Canadian senator of Asian descent. 2015.

[5] York University – Homepage. Available at: http://www.yorku.ca/index.html.

[6] Hong Kong and Shanghai Banking Corporation Limited – Homepage. Available at: https://www.hsbc.com.hk/.

What is the size of the collection and what are some of its highlights?

The library has approximately 50,000 volumes, which includes over 2000 periodical titles. We also have about 1000 reels of microfilm and 7000 newspaper clippings. This is the largest research collection on Hong Kong–Canadian studies in the world.

One of our most significant collections are the newspaper clippings from Hong Kong in the 1980s and 1990s, held in microfiche format. The library also processes more than 100 titles from the Chinese community periodicals published in Toronto, Ottawa, Vancouver, Edmonton, Calgary and Winnipeg. Another notable holding comes from Dr Vivienne Poy's papers (1998–2012). This collection consists of her research and correspondence during her time in the Canadian Senate. All these papers are maintained in a filing system and they provide important information on Asian Canadian studies and Canadian politics. Recently, the library acquired Professor David Lai's research archive. Professor Lai is a renowned scholar in Chinese–Canadian studies and his collection covers more than 30 years of his research on many topics including Chinatowns, railroad workers and Chinese community organisations.

What best prepared you for the position of director of the library?

Apart from my library science education and research experience, public speaking, management and event coordination are important skills for my role as the director (Figs 34.2 and 34.3). For example, the library has been active in hosting conferences and library events, which have greatly promoted the library and facilitated material donations. I have been developing my event coordination skills since my high school days when I was the chair of the student association that organised many large-scale activities, including the graduation camp for about 200 students. In university, I continued to be active in student groups, assuming leadership roles for chairing meetings and planning events. These roles provided me with opportunities to practice my leadership, public speaking and management skills. My computer skills are also important for my position. There have been many changes in the library related to digital

Figure 34.2 Happy spring festival photo exhibition. From left to right: PRC Consul General Xue Bing, Jack Leong, University of Toronto Chief Librarian Larry Alford. 2016.

Figure 34.3 Jack Leong in front of the library. 2016.

technology, which my undergraduate training in computer science has helped me to deal with. It gave me an excellent foundation and understanding of the principles of new technologies essential to the new information environment.

What scholarly and professional associations are you a part of, and how do they assist you in your work?

The association in which I participate most actively in is International Federation of Library Associations and Institutions.[7] I am the chair of the Standing Committee on Library Services to Multicultural Populations Section, where I have been active since 2008. There have been a lot of discussions on how to provide better library services for a population that is so diverse, multilingual and multicultural. In 2014, I hosted the mid-year meeting for this section to discuss issues and services for Indigenous Peoples and diverse users. From 2008 to 2013, I was a member of the Hong Kong Library Association[8] because I wanted to get to know more librarians in Hong Kong. From 2013, I gradually phased this out. Although I had met many interesting people, it was more appropriate to shift back to North America. I have also been a member of the Council of East Asian Libraries[9] and Association for Asian Studies since 2006. Locally, I am the secretary and director of the Canadian Foundation for Asian Culture that organises activities for Toronto's Asian heritage month.

Who are the majority of the library's users?

In terms of numbers, the majority of our users are undergraduate students with an Asian background. They are taking courses related to Hong Kong or Chinese–Canadian

[7] IFLA (International Federation of Library Associations) – Homepage. Available at: http://www.ifla.org/.
[8] Hong Kong Library Association (HKLA) – Homepage. Available at: http://www.hkla.org/.
[9] Council of East Asian Libraries (CEAL) – Homepage. Available at: http://www.eastasianlib.org/.

programmes. The University of Toronto offers a course on the history of Hong Kong and many courses in various disciplines discuss the education, politics and finances of Hong Kong. There are also students from Hong Kong, China and Taiwan who want to use the space for its artistic atmosphere; it reminds them of the modernity of the Hong Kong environment. The users in terms of our research services and materials are, of course, graduate students and professors working in this field of study. These scholars are mainly from the University of Toronto or other universities in southern Ontario. The library has a visiting scholar programme, and the quality of our collection has attracted scholars from the United States, Hong Kong and the West Coast of Canada. Recently, a New York history professor working on Hong Kong's housing policy in the 1970s spent 3 days conducting research in the library.

Can you give us typical reference enquiries from researchers and scholars?

The range of questions is really diverse. Questions can be about history, public administration, education, finance, basic law or political reform. Research questions often require a lot of investigation before we can provide the relevant materials and answers. Often, people have already gone into the main collection and some of the libraries in their own neighbourhoods. They usually come to us with unique research needs (Figs 34.4 and 34.5).

As the director, how do you acquire your collection? Do you actively collect or do you accept gifts?

In the 1990s, our materials were mainly acquired by donation from local community and institutional partners in Hong Kong such as the Hong Kong University (HKU) Libraries. The coordinator at the time, Peter Yeung, was well connected and resourceful so we had a great foundation when we built the new library in 2007. After 2007, when I became the

Figure 34.4 Inside the Richard Charles Lee Canada–Hong Kong Library. 2008

Figure 34.5 Jack Leong helping a patron at the service desk. 2008.

director, we continued the previous arrangement with the HKU Libraries[10] and the acquisition of materials held by Hong Kong immigrants in Toronto and elsewhere. At this point, the library also began to have an annual budget to acquire commercially published materials. I work with vendors from Hong Kong and read the publication lists in North America to acquire relevant materials. We have a collection development policy that specifies the subjects and geographic scope for our collection so we can focus our resources and avoid duplications with other libraries at University of Toronto Libraries, which has 44 libraries.

In the past few years, the library has been involved in the digitisation of some of its collections. What are some of the projects and what are the future plans for these digital collections?

With Canadian Heritage funding support, we have digitised materials related to the 1997 Handover in collaboration with the Simon Fraser University. We are currently in the process of digitising *Shing Wah Daily News* (醒華日報)[11] using the official archival copy originally held by the publisher. We continue to look for opportunities to digitise other materials, pending resources and copyright clearance. As part of the University of Toronto Libraries system, our plans for these digital collections align with the main library system. At the moment, University of Toronto Libraries is developing a central repository for digital materials called Collections UofT (http://collections.library.utoronto.ca). In partnership with humanities scholars, funders and other stakeholders, the library preserves and provides access to digital projects using the Islandora software to build this repository. Collections UofT has begun to take in a portion of the digital humanities collections that are part of University of Toronto's vast academic resources, digital projects and research output.

[10] University of Hong Kong Libraries – Homepage. Available at: http://lib.hku.hk/.

[11] *Shing Wah Daily News* (醒華日報) – Homepage. Available at: http://www.multiculturalcanada.ca/swdn2.

Large numbers of citizens who immigrated to Canada in the past 20 years have since returned to Hong Kong. How has this affected the Richard Charles Lee Canada–Hong Kong Library in terms of its outreach? Has the tide of reverse migration hindered or helped the library?

That is a very interesting question. The flow of migration has always been in two directions with people moving back and forth across the Pacific, probably relating to different stages of their lives and different pull and push factors in the two countries. Recently, I have been doing research on Chinese railway workers in the 1850s and 1860s. Even in the 19th century, people were going back and forth across the Pacific. I think we are seeing a continuation of that phenomenon.

Although the number of people returning to Hong Kong rose a bit in 1997 when they realised that there were few political changes, in the last few decades there has been more of a tendency to settle down in Toronto or Canada in general. I see this as a positive trend for the library as it strengthens the ties and networks between Canada and Hong Kong. For example, there are two professors from Toronto who recently moved back to Hong Kong to head up a department and school in the higher education sector of Hong Kong. They act as excellent ambassadors for the library outreach and international project. This phenomenon also creates a strong foundation for research and collection development projects such as the Hong Kong Canada crosscurrents projects (港加交匯研究計劃).[12]

Can you tell us a bit about the Hong Kong Canada crosscurrents project? How did it start and what are some of its plans?

This collaborative project has been in process since 2014 and will be concluded in 2019. It was first proposed by Professor Henry Yu in 2012, following a discussion with Dr Vivienne Poy and myself. When the Chinese–Canadian stories digital project[13] concluded in 2012, we agreed it was logical to shift the focus to a more contemporary immigration narrative around Hong Kong. It was officially launched in February 2014, and a project website was created in May 2014 to provide online access to the updates and databases created by the project. The intention is to provide coordination and a depository infrastructure for the research, collection development and public education of the effects of migrations and cultural connections between Hong Kong and Canada from the 1960s to the 2010s. The project will harness contributions from researchers, librarians and archivists to create powerful new research tools and collections in the online environment, with online and interactive learning resources for schoolteachers and students. This project also serves as a platform for the library's collection development, faculty liaison and community outreach and advancement. Project members included researchers,

[12] Hong Kong Canada Crosscurrents Projects (港加交匯研究計劃) – Homepage. Available at: https://hongkong.library.utoronto.ca/crosscurrents/welcome.

[13] Chinese Canadian Stories project – Homepage. Available at: http://ccs.library.ubc.ca/en/index.html.

librarians and community leaders. Besides the library, other institutional partners consist of St. John's College at the University of British Columbia,[14] Hong Kong Economic and Trade Office in Canada,[15] HKU Libraries, David Lam Centre at the Simon Fraser University,[16] York Centre for Asian Research[17] and Macau University Library.[18]

[14] St. John's College, University of British Columbia – Homepage. Available at: http://stjohns.ubc.ca/.
[15] Hong Kong Economic and Trade Office, Canada – Homepage. Available at: http://www.hketotoronto.gov.hk/contact-us/index.php.
[16] David Lam Centre, Simon Fraser University – Homepage. Available at: http://www.sfu.ca/davidlamcentre.html.
[17] York Centre for Asian Research – Homepage. Available at: http://ycar.apps01.yorku.ca/.
[18] Macau University Library – Homepage. Available at: http://library.umac.mo/.

The Rise of the C. V. Starr East Asian Library, University of California, Berkeley

35

Toshie Marra
University of California, Berkeley, CA, United States

Introduction

The East Asian collection at the University of California, Berkeley, was seeded by the deposit in 1896 of John Fryer's Chinese Library, which Fryer later bequeathed to the University. The East Asiatic Library (renamed 'East Asian' in 1991) was established in 1947 as a branch within the University Library system. The Center for Chinese Studies Library began as an off-campus reading room under the auspices of the Center for Chinese Studies in 1957. In 2008, the East Asian Library and Center for Chinese Studies Library merged and integrated their collections in the C. V. Starr East Asian Library. The merger consolidated Berkeley's Chinese language holdings; the move into new quarters improved accessibility to the entire collection and ensured that the Library would have room for growth in the coming decades. As the first freestanding library in the US constructed exclusively for an East Asian collection, the C. V. Starr East Asian Library is a facility that occupies a prominent central campus location next to Memorial Glade and Doe Library (Fig. 35.2), reflecting the university's role as a worldwide Pacific Rim hub for students and researchers of East Asian studies.

Could we begin this interview by first introducing yourself, for example, your training and background, and your major roles and duties at the Japanese Collection at C. V. Starr East Asian Library?

I was born and lived in Japan until I finished my BA degree. For my BA degree, I studied at the Osaka University for Foreign Studies (now a part of Osaka University[1]) with specialisation in Italian language and literature. Then, I came to live in the US, first in Princeton, New Jersey, and later in California. While I was working as a library assistant for Japanese collection at the Richard C. Rudolph East Asian Library, University of California, Los Angeles (UCLA),[2] I earned a master's degree in library

[1] Osaka University – Homepage. Available at: http://www.osaka-u.ac.jp/en.

[2] Richard C. Rudolph East Asian Library, University of California, Los Angeles (UCLA) – Homepage. Available at: http://www.library.ucla.edu/eastasian.

Inside the World's Major East Asian Collections. http://dx.doi.org/10.1016/B978-0-08-102145-3.00035-2

and information science from UCLA Graduate School of Education and Information Studies with a specialisation in cataloguing and preservation, and eventually I obtained the position of Japanese Studies Librarian at UCLA East Asian Library. After having worked at UCLA for 22 years, I took the current position of the Librarian for Japanese Collection at the C. V. Starr East Asian Library, University of California, Berkeley,[3] in 2012 (see Fig. 35.1 for a photo of Toshie Marra and her assistant).

Figure 35.1 Toshie Marra and Matthew Mewhinney, student assistant at her office in the C. V. Starr East Asian Library.

Figure 35.2 C. V. Starr East Asian Library, University of California, Berkeley.

[3] C. V. Starr East Asian Library, University of California – Homepage. Available at: http://www.lib.berkeley.edu/libraries/east-asian-library.

The following summarises my major areas of responsibilities at the C. V. Starr East Asian Library, UC Berkeley:

Collection development and management

The Librarian for Japanese Collection has primary responsibility for enhancing the collections and user-centred services in support of research, teaching and scholarship related to Japanese studies. Evaluates and selects Japanese language materials in all formats and media, including electronic, that are appropriate to the research and teaching needs of the UC Berkeley campus. Manages acquisitions funds, prepares requests for funds, and expends funds. Coordinates acquisitions with UC campuses and other libraries as appropriate, either through existing agreements or by exploring additional areas of cooperation. Selects materials for storage or withdrawal, preservation, microfilming or digitisation. Works with the Director to identify and initiate applications for grant funds to improve access to, or conservation of, the Japanese collection. Represents the Library in regional, national and international cooperative programs and special projects concerning Japanese collections and materials.

Instruction, training and outreach

Responsible for library and research instruction needs in Japanese studies. Provides library tours, drop-in or course-integrated lectures and standalone research instruction sessions as needed. Prepares teaching materials and guides to library resources and serves as liaison to faculty in Japanese studies.

Reference and research services

Cultivates and sustains strong connections with faculty and students associated with key academic departments and centres on campus. Provides reference and consultation services for faculty, graduate students and undergraduate students in Japanese studies.

Any reason you chose you come live in USA?

I came to live in the US because of my marriage. My late husband, Michael F. Marra, was a professor of Japanese literature at Department of Asian Languages & Cultures, UCLA.[4]

You mentioned that strong connections with faculty and students associated with key academic departments; could you tell me which are considered the key departments? What are the needs to set up strong connections with faculty and students? What kind of activities or programmes are involved for setting up this connection?

The key departments for me are those academic departments that hold faculty members with research focus on Japan. Most of such faculty members are listed at the Center for Japanese Studies' website.[5]

[4] Department of Asian Languages & Cultures, UCLA – Homepage. Available at: http://www.alc.ucla.edu/.
[5] Center for Japanese Studies, University of California, Berkeley – Homepage. Available at: http://ieas.berkeley.edu/cjs/.

I need to keep close work relationships with faculty members in order to make sure that my collection development efforts would go along with faculty's current research and instructional needs. When I began my work at UC Berkeley in 2012, I arranged individual interviews with most of the core faculty members in Japanese studies to learn their and their students' research interests. I also attend many lectures, symposiums and workshops organised by the Center for Japanese Studies, (University of California, Berkeley).

I should also provide any support to faculty and students for facilitating their research activities. For example, in May 2015, I organised a 3-day workshop for reading Kuzushiji texts at UC Berkeley campus with an instructor invited from the National Institute of Japanese Literature (NIJL),[6] in which some UC Berkeley faculty members and graduate students participated in addition to many Japanese studies librarians from North America [the workshop was a part of the 3-year Kuzushiji Workshop series organized in coordination between the NIJL and the AAS/CEAL Committee on Japanese Materials (CJM), Subcommittee on Japanese Rare Books and co-sponsored by the Center for Japanese Studies and the C. V. Starr East Asian Library].

Please provide a brief introduction to the Japanese and Asian Collection at C. V. Starr East Asian Library.

In the following, I summarize the Library's collections based on the information provided at the Library's website: UC Berkeley's C. V. Starr East Asian Library contains one of the most comprehensive collections of materials in East Asian languages in the US. Its combined holdings, totalling over 1 million volumes in Chinese, Japanese, Korean and other East Asian languages, make it one of the top two such collections in the US outside of the Library of Congress.[7]

The Library's collections concentrate on the humanities and social sciences. Materials range from full-text electronic databases, books, periodicals and newspapers to block-printed maps, manuscripts, rare Chinese, Japanese and Korean imprints and rubbings of some of the earliest inscriptions in the Chinese tradition.[8]

The Library traces its origins to the deposit in 1896 of the private library of John Fryer, the University's first holder of the Agassiz Chair of Oriental Languages and Literature. Other early gifts, such as the library of Kiang Kang-hu, the Horace G. Carpentier Endowment and the collection of E. T. Williams, expanded the size and scope of the core collection.

The C. V. Starr East Asian Library possesses some particularly noteworthy special collections. The 100,000-volume Mitsui acquisition brought to Berkeley a handful of smaller collections, including the Asami, Teihyōkaku, Gakken, Motoori and Sōshin collections. The Asami Library contains 4000 volumes of classical Korean imprints and Korean manuscripts, including a fine manuscript of

[6] National Institute of Japanese Literature (国文学研究資料館) – Homepage. Available at: https://www.nijl.ac.jp/index_e.html.

[7] Library of Congress – Homepage. Available at: http://www.loc.gov/.

[8] Chinese Stone Rubbings Collection at East Asian Library, University of California, Berkeley – Homepage. Available at: http://vm136.lib.berkeley.edu/EAL/stone/.

the 18th-century anthology of Korean poetry, Haedong kayo, compiled by Kim Su-jang. The Teihyōkaku collection of Chinese rubbings, which has been augmented by the East Asian Library over the years, is one of the largest and richest collections of its kind outside East Asia. The Gakken collection is noted for its *kanshibun* (Chinese verse and prose written by Japanese literati). The Motoori and Sōshin collections are rich in woodblock editions of the Tokugawa and early Meiji periods. The Mitsui acquisition also included approximately 7000 volumes of manuscripts and some 2300 early Japanese maps.

The Ho-Chiang collection of Buddhist sutras in manuscript and print documents the development of Buddhism in China, Japan and Korea. The Mongolian and Manchu collections include an exceedingly rare 17th-century work, *Tai sang-ni acabume karulara bithe*. Among the pre-1949 xylographs of the Tibetan collection is a body of Tantric texts of the Nyingmapa sect and an 18th-century Narthang edition of the Kanjur section of the Buddhist canon.

The 8850-volume Murakami Library dedicated to belletristic writing of the Meiji through early Shōwa periods includes a large number of first editions, of particular interest not only for the illustrations and bindings, but also for the prefaces not reprinted in later editions. This and the collections above are housed in the Starr Library's Fong Yun Wah Rare Book Room.[9] The Library's rare holdings range in subject matter and date from oracle bones of the Shang dynasty (17th–11th century BCE) to political posters of the Cultural Revolution.

Materials formerly in Berkeley's Center for Chinese Studies Library and now in the Starr's general collection provide a rich resource for the study of contemporary China: over 1800 contemporary films on 4000 discs, 6000 volumes of provincial and local gazetteers and, in the series *Wen shi zi liao* (文史资料), over 11,000 volumes of first-person accounts of political movements, military actions and economic conditions that China witnessed between the last years of the Qing dynasty and the early decades of the People's Republic.

The Library also has extensive holdings in various nonprint media – audio and videocassettes, microform and CD-ROMs – and a growing offering of electronic resources.

What is the size of the collections? Could you describe the highlights of the collection?

Based on the latest statistics published by the Council on East Asian Libraries (CEAL),[10] the total holdings of UC Berkeley's East Asian Library number 1,121,717 volumes as of 30 June 2015, consisting of 579,920 for Chinese, 412,604 for Japanese, 108,754 for Korean, and 20,439 for non-Chinese, Japanese and Korean (CJK)–language materials. For highlights of the collection, please see the above.

[9] Fong Yun Wah Rare Book Room – Homepage. Available at: http://guides.lib.berkeley.edu/c.php?g=351532&p=2385251.

[10] Council on East Asian Libraries (CEAL) – Homepage. Available at: http://www.eastasianlib.org/.

What best prepared you for the position of Japanese Studies Librarian at C. V. Starr East Asian Library?

I have spent the past over 25 years working with Japanese collections at UCLA and UC Berkeley, both part of the University of California system. This extended experience has provided me with a substantial knowledge of research materials and collections for Japanese studies in various formats, including print and electronic. I have been also actively involved in professional activities at the regional and national level, including with CEAL (I served on the Executive Board as Treasurer from 2006 to 2009 and as a Member-At-Large from 2012 to 2015, and as Chair of the Subcommittee on Japanese Rare Books under the Committee on Japanese Materials[11] from 2000 to 2014 and as Co-chair since 2014) and the North American Coordinating Council on Japanese Library Resources[12] (I served as Chair-Elect in 2003 and as Chair from 2004 to 2006).

In addition, my interest and experience working with Japanese old and rare books helps me perform the current position at the C. V. Starr East Asian Library. Prior to serving on the Subcommittee on Japanese Rare Books, from 1994 to 1996, I catalogued over 500 titles of rare Japanese materials produced before 1868 at UCLA, and from 1996 to 1997, I did an internship at the Otani University Library[13] in Kyoto for a year-long period, during which I catalogued rare Japanese Buddhist materials held by the Library.

What scholarly and professional associations are you a part of, and how do they assist you in your work?

I am a member of the Association for Asian Studies (AAS),[14] CEAL and the American Library Association.[15] I regularly attend annual meetings of AAS and CEAL, including preconferences and workshops, which I find very useful to keep abreast of current trends and practices in East Asian studies librarianship.

Who are the majority of C. V. Starr East Asian Library's users? That is, who comes to see you about your collections? Are they mostly professors or students from higher education institutions, or are they people from outside the postsecondary sector, that is, the general public?

The majority of our library users are faculty and graduate students at UC Berkeley, including many visiting scholars, as well as local residents from California. We also have many visitors, mostly professors and students from higher education institutions, not only from the US, but also from other countries, especially from East Asia.

[11] Subcommittee on Japanese Rare Books, Committee on Japanese Materials, CEAL – Homepage. Available at: http://www.eastasianlib.org/cjm/jrb.html.

[12] North American Coordinating Council on Japanese Library Resources – Homepage. Available at: http://guides.nccjapan.org/homepage.

[13] Otani University – Homepage. Available at: http://www.otani.ac.jp/english/.

[14] Association for Asian Studies (AAS) – Homepage. Available at: https://www.asian-studies.org/.

[15] American Library Association (ALA) – Homepage. Available at: http://www.ala.org/.

Could you give examples of typical reference/research inquiries issued by the researchers or scholars at the C. V. Starr East Asian Library?

A typical reference inquiry is like: Could you give any guidance to find appropriate resources to conduct a research on …?

As Japanese Studies Librarian, how do you acquire and evaluate your collection?

We acquire library materials through purchase as well as gifts. I have not yet had a chance to evaluate any particular sections from our Library's Japanese collection systematically. However, I regularly use WorldCat[16] database to check holdings of other North American libraries before I decide to acquire any materials for our Library, which has given me some idea about our Library's strengths and weaknesses.

In the past few years, the C. V. Starr East Asian Library has been engaged in the digitisation of some of its collections. What are some of the projects and what future plans are there for the digital collections?

For digitised collections that are publicly available, please see the Library's webpage at http://www.lib.berkeley.edu/libraries/east-asian-library/digitized-collections to access the following collections:

- Ann Tompkins (Tang Fandi) and Lincoln Cushing Chinese Poster Collection[17]
- Chinese Stone Rubbings
- Japanese Historical Maps[18]

In addition, the following collections have been digitised:

- Asami collection of Korean rare books[19] (over 800 titles and 3800 volumes available by Internet Archive)
- Chinese rare books (375 titles available both on the library's online catalog OskiCat and in the National Central Library of Taiwan's repository)
- Japanese Sugoroku collection[20] (ca. 150 sheets digitised by the Art Research Center, Ritsumeikan University)
- A large number of modern, nonrare books have been contributed to Google Books Project and HathiTrust from the University of California, including UC Berkeley (as of January 8, 2017, over 8100 Chinese and 12,000 Japanese items are available in HathiTrust)

[16] WorldCat – Homepage. Available at: https://www.worldcat.org/.

[17] Ann Tompkins (Tang Fandi) and Lincoln Cushing Chinese Poster Collection at East Asian Library, University of California, Berkeley – Homepage. Available at: http://www.docspopuli.org/ChinaPosters.html.

[18] Japanese Historical Maps – East Asian Library, University of California, Berkeley – Homepage. Available at: http://www.davidrumsey.com/japan/.

[19] Asami Collection and Korean Rare Books – C. V. Starr East Asian Library, University of California, Berkeley. Available at: https://archive.org/details/starr.

[20] Sugoroku from the Collection of University of California, Berkeley. Available at: http://www.dh-jac.net/db7/sugoroku/FMPro?-db=sugoroku.fmj&-lay=Layout2&-format=search.htm&-view.

As for future, we are planning to digitise:

- Japanese Copperplate Print Collection, 1855–1920 (475 items with over 2400 images) with support from the Art Research Center, Ritsumeikan University[21,22]
- Yuen Ren Chao Collection (over 230,000 items of personal papers, letters, diary, etc.)

How does the collection catalogue and provide access for users? With a non-Roman script, what challenges does this present to cataloguing? Is there any?

The materials acquired by the East Asian Library are catalogued with OCLC Connexion[23] by the Library's technical service staff members who are native speakers of Chinese, Japanese or Korean languages. Catalogued materials are searchable in the UC Berkeley Library's online catalog OskiCat, UC System's union catalogue Melvyl[24] and in WorldCat. As OCLC has been supporting CJK cataloguing for several decades already, I am not aware of any major challenges with cataloguing with CJK script for modern publications. However, when we catalogue old books, we occasionally encounter the Chinese characters that are impossible to be reproduced in OCLC Connexion, which would cause searching problems.

The themes and information needs of libraries, archives and museums (LAMs, as some have referred to them) have increasingly converged. What are your experiences and thoughts about these cultural institutions whose work and best practices now often overlap?

LAMs often hold same kinds of materials, but they handle their materials differently. For example, many libraries in North America use OCLC Connexion for cataloguing their holdings, but archives and museums may use different systems, often their own original systems, for processing their collections. This situation might cause some challenges for our users to locate certain materials, especially those held by archives and museums. I think it is important for us working at these institutions to communicate, share information and work together, whenever possible, to better serve our users.

As an example of such experiences, the Subcommittee on Japanese Rare Books attempted to bring these institutions together to provide information about their Japanese old and rare books collections by compiling the Directory of North American Collections of Old and Rare Japanese Books, Other Print Materials, and Manuscripts (the directory was first published in October 2003 in the *Journal of East*

[21] Art Research Center, Ritsumeikan University – Homepage. Available at: http: //www.arc.ritsumei.ac.jp/en/index.html.

[22] A part of the digital images from the Japanese Copperplate Print Collection is available at: http://www.dh-jac.net/db/nishikie-e/search_ucb.php?enter=ucb.

[23] OCLC Connexion – Homepage. Available at: http://www.oclc.org/en-US/connexion.html.

[24] Melvyl – Homepage. Available at: http://melvyl.worldcat.org/.

Asian Libraries[25] and has evolved into the Directory of Overseas Collections of Old and Rare Japanese Books, Other Print Materials, and Manuscripts, now available at the National Institute of Japanese Literature website[26]).

Which part(s) of your job as librarian do you find most rewarding?

I find my job most rewarding when I could help my library users to find information or resources that they wanted to find. I also find my job rewarding when I feel I am making contributions in improving access for researchers to reach research materials.

Could you give an example of a librarian–user experience that you find most rewarding?

For example, I felt satisfied when I could help one of my faculty members to receive a donation of books that originally belonged to his teacher in Japan who had passed away. Because of the distance, it required good coordination and planning for the transfer of this private collection to our library, but the collection certainly has a special meaning for this faculty and I am glad that I could take a part in this acquisition.

Do you have any questions for me? Is there anything you would like to share with the readers before we conclude this interview?

Nothing particularly.

[25] Toshie Marra, Hideyuki Morimoto, and Reiko Yoshimura, "Directory of North American Collections of Old and Rare Japanese Books, Other Print Materials, and Manuscripts," Journal of East Asian Libraries, 131 (October 2003): 68–109. Available at: http://scholarsarchive.byu.edu/jeal/vol2003/iss131/8/.
[26] Directory of Overseas Collections of Old and Rare Japanese Books, Other Print Materials, and Manuscripts – Homepage. Available at: http://base1.nijl.ac.jp/~overseas/.

The Birth and Creation of a Leading Collection of Asian Materials at Princeton University

36

Martin Heijdra
Princeton University, Princeton, NJ, United States

Introduction

As one of the eminent institutions in North America, Princeton University's East Asian Library (EAL; Fig. 36.2) collects materials in practically all subjects in Chinese, Japanese and Korean, as well as works on Chinese, Japanese and Korean linguistics and literature in Western languages. Although the Gest Library originally began only with the acquisition of many rare books, it has become a growing collection that supports all kinds of research done in the Department and Programme of East Asian Studies. As a librarian whose tenure at Princeton University has been long and fortuitous, Dr. Martin Heijdra (Fig. 36.1) explains the makeup of the East Asian collection, which reflects the strengths of the academic department. Thus, the Library's East Asian collection is comprehensive in works particularly on literature and history.

Can we begin this interview by first introducing yourself, that is, your training, your background and your major roles and duties now that you are the head of the EAL? But you can also speak to your previous role as a librarian at the Princeton University Library.

My name is Martin Heijdra, and as for my background, I am not American; I am originally from Holland. I earned a master's degree in Chinese and Japanese studies at Princeton University.[1] I studied in China in 1977 and 2 years in Japan from 1979 to 1981. I came to Princeton University in 1983 as a graduate student, and I have stayed in Princeton ever since. During the later years of my studies at Princeton, I also worked at the Library. As they were in need of some help, I started as a graduate student, and eventually I was appointed as a Chinese Studies Librarian, or the Chinese Bibliographer, as it was called then.

Probably until a year ago, my main task was as a Chinese Bibliographer, which means I was responsible for collection development and offered research assistance to students,

[1] Princeton University – Homepage. Available at: https://www.princeton.edu/main/.

Inside the World's Major East Asian Collections. http://dx.doi.org/10.1016/B978-0-08-102145-3.00036-4

Figure 36.1 Dr Martin Heijdra.

Figure 36.2 East Asian Library – Princeton University Library.

graduate students and faculty. I was also the Head of Public Services, which meant I took care of the general aspects of the Library. When the previous head of the EAL retired last November, I was appointed Acting Head Librarian, and now I have officially become the Director. Since we are still looking for a replacement Chinese Bibliographer or, rather, Chinese Studies Librarian, I am also still concurrently performing the duties of the Chinese Bibliographer. My role as Director is really more generalized outreach: more contacts with colleagues elsewhere and getting local projects going.

How many different languages have you mastered? How much of that do you use those different languages in your day-to-day work?

As I am from Holland, I know Dutch, English, German and French; I use these daily, since in my work, I am responsible for Western-language collections development in East Asian Studies. Since many universities in the US do not prioritise East Asian studies in Western languages outside English, I think it is important that some universities keep cognisance of non-English Western languages. It is not quite coincidental that the one place that also still does much collection development for East Asian Studies in European languages is Columbia University,[2] where they also have a Dutch person for that. I also know Chinese, Japanese, some Russian, Italian, some Swedish, languages like that, which I very occasionally use. In my daily work, I use both Japanese and Chinese, but Chinese is, of course, my most frequently used language.

Do you see yourself as a scholar librarian? Given your strong research capability and your extensive research output and reputation in the field of Chinese studies, were there any reasons why you chose a career in librarianship instead of as a full-time academic in which you could have devoted more time and energy into research and teaching?

I see myself as a facilitator between scholars and librarians. I became a librarian really by happenstance: I remained in the US after not having finished my thesis yet and needed to work on campus at Princeton as an international student in order to continue with my student visa. So in a way, I happened to fall accidentally into my work for the Library. I eventually received a green card and 'continuing appointment', which is basically the equivalent of tenure, so that is how I finally decided to stay here.

As a librarian, I have been able to indulge myself in a lot of different fields because to be a good librarian, you have to have a very broad point of view, and I feel that it seems that at every moment, I have to jump into a new field. Having a scholarly background is very important. Even though we might not need to be a particular specialist, you need to have some experience in different fields, and most of all, one has to know what doing research is all about. I am by training a historian, and somehow I have come to think that historians are the broadest of all specialists; they are the most interdisciplinary. But even so, helping students with data and economics is something different than helping them with written sources, and here at Princeton, graduates and undergraduates do not do the same kinds of studies. Because of one's scholarly

[2] Columbia University – Homepage. Available at: http://www.columbia.edu/.

background, you can also be an intermediary person between vendors and scholars. Often with databases, I tell database vendors what we are looking for: what is lacking in the field, what I think scholars are looking for and what does not exist yet.

On the other hand, I get frequent telephone calls from scholars who tell me they just got this amount from their department or from their university in order to buy some database, but it is limited. Thus, they ask me what they should get and what they are able to afford, and I can help them. With that said, I am also still a historian, and I am currently the treasurer for the Society of Ming Studies.[3] I also work on the history of the book in China and Japan, and I am the book review editor for the journal *East Asian Publishing and Society*.[4]

You mentioned your background as a Ming Dynasty specialist and also the history of the book in China. How does your research interests inform your work as a librarian and now particularly as the head of an EAL?

Princeton is known for rare books, and I happened to learn a little bit on the job about Ming Dynasty era books. I have had a constant interaction with those books. Thus, I do tend to get some questions from Ming historians who want to know about particular Ming studies resources. For book history, I have specialised in the history of East Asian typography, both in the modern period and in the Ming period. I try to study both Chinese and Japanese typography; it's the one subject in which I really try to go beyond Chinese studies, so that has very much influenced my work as a Chinese studies librarian. My understanding both Japanese and Chinese languages helps me with rare book projects. It is important to remember that dealing with rare books is not the only thing that the East Asian librarian should do, but having that background will help with general reference work. I have already been asked to be an advisor for a particular Ming studies biographical database. I do not know whether I will do much for it, but of course, one often gets that kind of request, and it keeps informing my work as a librarian.

Could you provide a brief introduction to the collections of the EAL at Princeton, and could you also give us the collection highlights?

We are one of the major collections in North America. At the moment, the Chinese collection is ranked fourth according to the Library of Congress and is tied with Berkeley in size. Our Japanese collection is relatively smaller. When people generally think of Princeton University Chinese, they think of two things: rare books and electronic databases. We have around 5000 titles of pre-1911 books, with some 100,000 volumes. We also really invest in e-resources that advance the research of our students and faculty. But it is not electronic books we concentrate on, but databases, which really change the way scholars can do their work. For example, we now can search the full text of old gazetteers, which really has completely changed how you search that

[3] Society of Ming Studies – Homepage. Available at: http://mingstudies.arts.ubc.ca/.

[4] *East Asian Publishing and Society* – Homepage. Available at: http://www.brill.com/publications/journals/east-asian-publishing-and-society.

type of materials. That is why having access to such types of databases is much more important than whether or not you have an electronic copy of a book.

What are some of these databases that are more often used by scholars?

We have a whole range of databases. We have hundreds of Chinese studies databases alone, but we are working to expand our current Japanese ones as well. People sometimes ask for materials from the Qing archives, the Academia Sinica (AS)[5] or the National Library of China.[6] Of course, then there are also requests for statistical databases, used by completely different kinds of users. One recent database we just got is an image database because there are so many requests for visual material as an object of study. Such a database was really lacking until recently, but even the new one is actually unsatisfactory; it's not on the level of US databases for art at all, so we still have to wait for better ones.

Who are the majority of the Asian collection users? Are they mostly professors or students from higher education, or are they people who are outside the secondary centre?

Princeton, in general, is a very undergraduate research–oriented library. East Asian studies, however, are an exception, partly because of language. Thus, I can say that for me, we built our collection for graduate students. Professors actually already have a specialised field and some of them use the Library frequently too, but they normally get some of the things they need themselves, unlike graduate students. We also have outside users, people from other institutions in the neighbourhood. When I get requests from others, I try to help them if I have time. People in Ming history will come to me, of course. But I would say that my priorities in the selection process are the needs of graduate students.

Could you give examples of typical reference inquiries issued by the researchers or scholars at the EAL during your time there?

In Princeton, undergraduates need to write junior and senior theses, and the questions of these undergraduates are very different from those of graduate students. In the last few weeks, I had received questions about Ai Weiwei's attitudes towards the earthquake, leftover women in China's rural areas, the history of the Akutagawa Prize, Yu Mi Ri, who is a Korean author in Japan, a question about a policy shift in meritocratic membership appointments post-1989 in the Chinese Communist Party, as well as the reception of K-pop in English. For graduate students, I have answered questions on the history of city maps in China, where to find legal case studies for the Ming Dynasty and questions about dictionaries and textbooks for Manchu learning. Those are the kinds of questions that I get. So as you see, the questions are diverse. What happens here is that the professors want the students to come to me to talk about their proposed thesis topics to see whether it's a doable question; even

[5] Academia Sinica – Homepage. Available at: https://www.sinica.edu.tw/main_e.shtml.

[6] National Library of China – Homepage. Available at: http://www.nlc.cn/newen/.

when it's doable, it may not be doable for undergraduates, and then sometimes it's not doable at all. At other times, the research question needs just some tweaking to make it into a researchable question.

What are the major advantages or practical operational reasons for Ivy League institutional libraries in the US to hire scholars with PhDs majoring in sinology and Japanology to manage the EAL collections?

At Princeton, with my duties as a liaison librarian, I will occasionally teach a part of a class session. However, I do not teach a whole course. That is the responsibility of the professors. Librarians at Princeton rarely teach courses for credit. As for bibliographic instruction, I have been doing that more in some years than others. When professors prefer to teach bibliographic instruction themselves, I will defer to them; at other times, I will do more. But most students have their very own research interests, so those I deal with one-to-one. However, as an academic librarian, I do think that you need to know what scholarship is about, and you need to know that there exist different kinds of scholarship within your own subject area. Thus, having a PhD is good. On the other hand, I do not really think that having a PhD while never having any experience in librarianship is what an academic librarian is all about either; you need both.

That said, I think it is very important for academic liaison librarians to have subject expertise. For such positions, we normally at Princeton tend to look at people who have the subject background. Still, I do think that I was very lucky into being hired without a master's of library science (MLS) degree and having no library background at all. But they had been looking for a subject librarian for 2 years before they took me on as a graduate student, and they could take their time in evaluating me. But I do occasionally get graduate students or professors who send their students up to me and say, 'We think this student might be happy as a librarian'. Then I tell them it's better to get an MLS degree. If you have the right attitude, you will learn a lot; if you do not have the right attitude or background, it really does not matter whether you have the degree or not. An MLS degree is used at a lot of places as a kind of entry barrier. Only the very highest Ivy League library might take a chance with somebody with a PhD rather than an MLS degree. In most cases, the MLS is required, but it's not that difficult to get one. Or so I hear…

It sounds like you had a lot of experience doing research in academic libraries, but did you also work in one?

No. When I was hired, I had to be trained from the beginning; I had no other library experience than as a user, so I was lucky to be in a situation where they took a chance on me. In the beginning, I did not plan to become a librarian at all. It was only in order to being able to stay at Princeton and finish my PhD. That being said, looking back way before I was a graduate student, I remember having been in Hong Kong in 1978, where I collected catalogues from bookstores and I was going through them, and I still remember when I was looking through them I thought, 'Of course I cannot buy this book, but somebody should buy it because of its historical importance, someone will need this for their study'. And from the very beginning, I always read bibliographies. It is one of the first things I read in a book. So somehow I always had had a librarian's attitude already.

Do you feel that in some situations, librarians with PhD degrees usually receive more respect from their academic counterparts? Are they more open to suggestions from librarians with PhDs as well as more likely to involve them as research and teaching partners?

The sad thing is, yes. I cannot tell you the number of times I have been introduced as 'He's somebody from the library, but he's not just a librarian'. There has been a bit of change in recent times because there are professors who realise that they need help with databases, on how to use them. They also need help with how to manipulate big data. So there is now a kind of realisation that there are people with specialisations that the professors themselves do not possess. I do think that having gone through the same process of doing research for a PhD, knowing what scholarship is about and having a PhD does qualify you as being kind of an equal for some of the professors. What I sometimes notice is that people from other institutions, when they come to Princeton, might have different or lower expectations of librarians. It takes some time for them to realise that at Princeton, there are subject librarians who can be seen as their intellectual peers or have something of their own to teach them, and they might come from a background where that was not the case, where the librarian was the person whom the professor told to buy a book and where they were basically book buyers reacting to the recommendation of the professors. It takes time for them to relearn that type of expectation.

Are librarians considered faculty at Princeton, and what is the probation period for librarians to be tenured?

Although we do not really have tenure, we have something similar to it. There is a kind of a 3-year or 5-year process. After that, you come up for continuing appointment, to be decided on by your peers in a committee comprised of librarians. Librarian appointments are screened heavily at the beginning of hiring; some positions take a long time to fill. If you are considered to be right person, especially as a subject librarian, it might actually not be as difficult to get continuing appointment as it is to get tenure. But then again, there are those who do not get continuing appointment and who then have to leave.

As the Chinese Librarian, how do you acquire and evaluate your collection?

Basically, Chinese books are selected individually, one by one. Princeton is one of the very last holdouts in the library world where it is still considered that it is the subject librarian's personal responsibility to build your collection; it cannot be completely automated. That is what you will be judged on; you are selecting with your own mind and what you think is valuable to the research collection. Therefore, it's not just what people need right now; it's not just patron-driven acquisitions, it is what you think the current and future library needs 20 or 30 years from now. We start feeling that we are one of the few libraries in which librarians are evaluated that way. If a professor comes to me and says, 'Can you buy this book?', I sometimes think I did not do my job well; I should have bought that book before she or he even knew about that title.

How do we evaluate our collection? I would say that would probably be currently one of my weakest aspects in my position. I do not really have the time to evaluate backwards how we are doing. Of course, I react to the requests from users, fill what we do not have, and I try immediately to adjust myself to a need to expand into a new direction. It is our job as subject librarians to be proactive.

You talked a bit earlier about databases. In the past few years, the EAL has been engaged in the digitisation of some of its rare books, most recently as a part of the Chiang Ching Kuo Foundation Funds. Could you tell us more about it?

The Chiang Ching Kuo Foundation Funds project was in collaboration with the AS. The thing is, we digitised 200 rare book titles selected by us and them; the previous director of the Library made a lot of specialised, informed selections for that project. The AS was supposed to make this available in some way or enough for a combined database, but that actually never materialised. Thus, now we decided to make this available ourselves, in some cases having to redo some work within our own systems. That work now has been done, and we are close to finishing it and releasing the digitised works from within our own Princeton University Digital Library (PUDL) framework (see http://pudl.princeton.edu/). Thus, what we digitised is much more than what you can see currently. At the EAL, we always had a page where we made available a few specially requested items in an easy format which were not available yet on the main PUDL site in order to give already electronic access to a subset of our material, those which had been asked by individual users (see https://library.princeton.edu/eastasian/diglib/).

So the EAL electronic text site is not the main site where the whole collection will be released; the main site is the PUDL, where all Chinese digitised titles will be made available soon. What we have on our own EAL site are a few medical texts and some other books we digitised upon demand. We said, 'Hey, people need this. Let's make a scaled-down pdf with watermarks so that users can use it immediately'. These works on our site don't have what I think in many libraries is called 'structural maps', which allow people to jump easily from Chapter 1 to Chapter 2 or Chapter 3, or to Illustration A, B and C. Making those 'strucmaps' takes a lot of time, and even though that work was done for the AS site originally, it wasn't released to the public, and we now have to do it again ourselves on our own platform.

In addition to that, unfortunately Princeton is not really set up to digitise works for people, even when they have grants. If I get a request for something and I decide it is not yet available elsewhere, but worth digitising, I can often get it into the general digitisation workflow at Princeton. I can perhaps have 10 or 20 titles digitised a year.

The unfortunate fact is, people can't immediately get it because it takes time to get it through the pipeline. The good thing is: it will be free. That is how things are done here. So the digitisation of East Asian books is continuing on a small scale; every year, we can digitise about 20 texts or so.

In East Asian libraries, it is a balancing act in terms of priorities between the various areas of languages, expertise and collections. What are your experiences as a librarian, both as a Chinese-language librarian and now as head of the EAL in terms of balancing and prioritising those tensions that may exist?

You talk about tensions, and you are totally right; in a lot of libraries, I hear there are those tensions. Thankfully, we traditionally have not had those tensions that much here. Even as a Chinese Studies librarian, I was already responsible for electronic databases in both Japanese and Chinese because of my technological experience and because I have both a Japanese and Chinese background. Also, my research in typography goes really across both languages. I have a Dutch MA in Japanology, and although I am a sinologist, most of my dissertation was based upon the work of Japanese sinologists. Some tensions may always be there, but as Director of the EAL, I already have been trying to develop our Japanese rare books holdings, together with our Japanese librarian, and with our Korean librarian, I also maintain an interest in Korean rare books. Thus, I very much wish we can continue not to have those tensions in the future. The same is true of our professors: the professors in Chinese and Japanese studies work very well together, and I think I work well with all of them too.

How does the collection catalogue provide access to users? With the non-Roman script, what challenges does this present to cataloguing?

The cataloguers do not report to me, but we have a very close relationship. The main question is: how do you provide access, especially to books in storage? Almost every set of records needs a talk between the Chinese Studies librarian and the cataloguer. While they do not report to me, they are on site, so we have constant interaction, and that is very important.

For non-Roman scripts, in cataloguing, here that is not very much a library issue (even if occasionally a technical one). There was a time when I was the primary non-Roman script specialist on campus, and that included helping Arabic, Hebrew, Syriac users, anything you could think of. That has become a little less necessary as operating systems have become much more capable, and so has the new generation of system specialists, so I do not necessarily have to do much of that anymore. At the Library, for a long time, I have been basically on every committee that involves a part of the library systems that uses non-Roman scripts. Princeton has always been trying to pay attention to non-Roman scripts. Our Head of Cataloguing is an Arabic specialist, and our Head of Collection Development has a South Asian background, so we never have to defend the position that non-Roman scripts are important.

Which part of your job at the EAL do you find most rewarding?

It's difficult to say because I clearly like all aspects of my job. One of the difficulties of becoming the Director is having to get rid of some parts that I very much like doing. Perhaps the most rewarding part is being able to translate between the technology, the people, and the scholars; the scholars and the databases and between the vendors and the students in order to make sure that all things work between these parties, and being able to relay the requirements for our field of study, which are not necessarily the same requirements as, say, my subject librarian colleagues in economics or so, to vendors and system specialists. I do think that even if I am not primarily defining myself as a scholar anymore, but as a librarian, I like to make contributions to the field by bringing people together or like being the person who brings into contact people who should be talking to each other.

I understand that there are librarians from many countries who are managing significant Chinese collections in their libraries, yet they are without your qualification, namely, the PhD degree, knowledge, research capabilities and output. In your opinion, for a person who happens to be a good administrator, but without your level of scholarly knowledge or interest in Chinese history, to work at the EAL or at other Ivy League institutions, would this work at all?

Nobody can know everything, and having some knowledge and some background and not using it also does not work, but I do think you need to know what scholarship is and you need to know what people are doing in your field: what questions do they ask, what sources do they use and what needs do they have? Otherwise, just being a good manager is not enough; you need to have those other skills. Thus, I think a background in scholarship is necessary. If you are just a manager or do everything with approval plans, or just use a PDA, it might be okay for certain types of libraries, but it would not be OK for a place like Harvard, Princeton or another great research library. I think at those institutions, people will be expected to have more knowledge (which is not to say that people at other places do not have that too). At this moment, you also need to have a technological background; you have to know how databases work or should work. Just being a scholar is also not sufficient.

How does your work as a librarian and your work as a researcher in Chinese studies differ from those that are carried out by librarians and researchers in the same field in Taiwan and mainland China?

I must admit I do not know too much about this area, as I do not have as much interaction as I should with librarians in those areas. I think the main difference is we do Chinese studies, East Asian studies and Japanese studies; East Asia is our subject, and yet, for our colleagues in Asia, they use their languages for everything, not just East Asian Studies. It's different for them; they are also studying us!

Thus, I start feeling that what we need from them is not the same thing as what they need from us, and we have to realise that fact. Another difference is that when we give presentations and we introduce, for instance, our database development or digitisation projects, they are surprised at our level of interaction with scholarship and scholars.

The librarians there do not have as much direct relation or contact with the students or professors. A librarian there is a much less integrated in liaison work, and they do not have constant interaction. Of course, I also think sometimes that's true in the US as well; I know that sometimes Acquisitions does not have as close a relationship with subject librarians or with Public Services as we have here in Princeton. Yet, I think that if you lack one of these three parts, a librarian can't do his or her job really well.

I think that – I know much less of Taiwan – it's not that in China there are not a lot of people with great subject expertise, but they do not have that constant interaction with the user. Therefore, they also do not see their results. Their goal is that they want to incorporate that. But it takes time for a library culture to change. But of course, their experience with Chinese vendors, publishers, etc., is superior to our own, and one always learns a lot when talking to Chinese colleagues, so we all learn from each other.

Speaking of librarians from different areas in the world, East Asian librarians in Europe versus East Asian librarians in North America, in terms of their professional status, all in all, how are they different from each other?

Although European, I've never worked in Europe, but what I do know from some of my good friends from over there is that they are often more of a one- or two-person organisation. East Asian librarians tend to do everything themselves there. While I do a lot of different tasks here, I do not do everything. I have never catalogued nor know how in detail cataloguing works because I have never done that.

What I see as a major difference is the size of the collections. We in North America have so much more money to spend. I think that is really the big difference. I'm glad to be at an institution where I do not have to fight with my colleagues about money. I have to write reports if I want to buy special things, but it is not a fight for the last dollar.

Bringing It All Together

In an op-ed piece in the New York Times, 'The Chinese Want Their Art Back', Chinese art has become a prized liquid asset for superrich collectors, who, instead of putting their treasures on display, often deposit them in carefully guarded, climate-controlled warehouses. The irony is that the Chinese government, led by President Xi Jinping, is doing the same with its new policy to build a 'foundation for China to compete in the world' has motivated the government and loyal antique collectors to salvage those lost treasurers across the world.

This is quite a shift from the Chinese Cultural Revolution (1966–76), when galleries, libraries and museums were ransacked and countless antiquities destroyed. UNESCO[1] has estimated that 1.67 million Chinese relics are held by 200-plus museums in 47 other countries. Many Chinese want many of them back. The party has taken its new stance on culture at a time of rising nationalism. China openly promotes efforts to repatriate works pillaged during its self-defined 'century of humiliation', from the Opium Wars of the 1840 and 1850s to the establishment of the People's Republic in 1949.

Of course, many artworks never come up for auction. In January 2013, some 25 Chinese artworks were stolen in a second theft from a museum in Norway. The museum closed its China collection to visitors and, under an arrangement brokered by a Chinese entrepreneur, 7 of 21 marble plinths taken from the Old Summer Palace were promised to Peking University. Of course, this is just merely a story that sets the tone for the conclusion of this book. Chinese collections are one matter, but what about the rest of East Asia? Through the interviews we have collected in this book, we see a wide array of challenges and opportunities for the world of librarians, archivists and curators.

This book does not intend to be comprehensive in breadth. Owing to limitations caused by language barriers, as well as the authors' backgrounds, the contents of this book inevitably draw on the experience of the authors and therefore suggest a more 'Chinese-oriented theme'. Furthermore, owing to various political reasons, we have unfortunately not been able to interview any library, archive and museum (LAM) professionals practicing in the People's Republic of China.

Nevertheless, this book has covered a number of world-leading LAMs in many cities and cultural capitals throughout the world. The series of interviews featured in this book have provided a unique, yet insightful perspective on the professional lives and practices amongst a wide array of librarians, archivists and curators practicing in diversely different cultural and social, as well as institutional settings. By advocating a better understanding, we hope this book could help raise the overall status and

[1] United Nations Educational, Scientific and Cultural Organization (UNESCO) – Homepage. Available at: http://en.unesco.org/.

recognition of the LAM profession, thereby contributing to a more long-lasting effect on the artistic quality, as well as the future survival of various art forms.

In the following concluding section, the authors would like to summarise some of the key themes and issues arising across the interviews, and they are as follows:

Digital repositories and impacts on the evolution of scholarly activities worldwide

LAM resources form versatile and powerful repository archives that play an increasingly important role in the texts we access, use and create. In turn, it shapes how scholars, researchers, students and LAM professionals practice in different parts of the world. Such virtual repositories also vastly facilitated: integration, customisation and accessibility.

Digital repositories continue to create endless and boundless possibilities. Not only do they allow researchers to more readily access collections of artefacts that represent 'other' voices, digital repositories also allow for people representing those other voices to contribute to such LAM resources. In digital spaces, people can become both users and producers of LAM resources. Digital repositories have undoubtedly lessened the time and manual labour required for retrieving sought materials (regardless of whether they are textual, audio or visual images, or images of 3-D objects). From an end user's viewpoint, engagement with digital archives is usually not as time-consuming as work in the predigital era.

During the predigital era, finding which search terms to use to yield sought texts required much time. We needed to reply mostly on printed catalogues to look for the sought information. Even before the online repositories were made available, standalone OPAC (**O**nline **P**ublic **A**ccess **C**atalogue) served slightly better than an online inventory list, but did not allow instant access to the images of the original materials that were sought. Before digital repositories were made available, users also needed to go through basic training in order to familiarise themselves with the classification system, OPAC interface or setup of inventory lists, which could be drastically different from one intuition to another, let alone the different languages that one has to master when using the OPAC or card catalogue in a foreign country. Digital repositories are borne less of time-intensive engagement and more of fast access; they are also accessible and images are downloaded via mobile devices, thereby fulfilling instant gratification.

Digital archives, through their classification systems and searching and retrieval functions, enable information in multimodal format. With few exceptions (e.g., Google Search by Image), words remain the requisite search criteria, and texts require linguistic metadata to maximise search and retrieval possibilities. For instance, Google Images has a rather robust image search, but it relies solely on linguistic tags. Researchers need to rely on words for figure types, characters, postures and attributes rather than sketches or drawings of image elements ('Search Images'). Researchers, in other words, can search for images, but not by using images. Such functionality subtly reinforces a hierarchy between these modes, placing words above images.

From the viewpoint of LAM professionals, digital repositories also allow image, video and text to be consolidated and served on a single platform, offering new opportunities for creating scholarly and learning activities while transforming from textual materiality to multimodality. It forces us to reconsider what kinds of new scholarship and scholarly activities were previously not possible during the existing textual storage and card catalogue retrieval systems era.

New digital technologies, such as virtual and gaming worlds where video and audio dominate, might allow for models that accommodate other kinds of scholarly texts and activities, particularly if we can move sentiment away from associating these technologies primarily with play. With the possibilities of such digital technologies, definitions and boundaries between scholarly and nonscholarly endeavours and entertainment versus academic activities are increasingly becoming blurred or overlapping.

Not surprisingly, the structure of much of our research instructions and methodology has also undertaken drastic changes because of this digital paradigm. LAMs need to resist our assumptions not only about what LAM resources might prove, but also about what these resources themselves might be. Digital repositories have certainly facilitated the creation of LAM resources for rhetoric and composition, allowing for larger, more visible and more comprehensive collections of texts that can legitimise and extend the work of the field. Scholars' individual websites and blogs that provide records of scholarly activity and ongoing conversations surrounding their teaching and study of writing (e.g., Culture Cat, Digital Digs and Virtual Politics) also constitute important digital objects, which digital repositories ask us to rethink what constitutes scholarly productions as they blur the lines between academic and nonacademic texts.

In digital spaces, the boundaries around these categories become fluid, and texts move more freely between them. Certain digital repositories even have the potential to promote tourism, and resources in digital format are increasingly being used for gaming design and commercials.

Historical myths versus historical facts: digital archives for historic research and international understanding

Since World War II, many countries have faced a challenge of bridging different historical understanding and interpretations, or the so-called question of different historical recognitions. Generally speaking, it is difficult for historians, who have been in the past constrained to writing national histories, to write an internationally common history. However, historians who have taken on the challenge contributed much for sharing historical records and opening up the records of different countries. A very rapid increase of accessibility to historical data through digital archives, needless to say, greatly eases historical research. Historians who favoured original documents had concealed their use of digital archives until recently. Now, historians do not hesitate to make public citations and references to JACAR (Japan Center for Asian Historical Records)[2] data. JACAR is now even regarded by many historians as a kind of 'international common good'.

[2] JACAR (Japan Center for Asian Historical Records) – Homepage. Available at: http://www.jacar.go.jp/english/index.html.

With the technology afforded by digital archives, one can have instant access to historical records of different historical facts that leads to a fuller historical understanding. The nature of current communication among peers of scholarly institutions can encounter barriers, such as differing politics between China and other nations that raise censorship questions, or politics surrounding JACAR, and how its materials are identified for inclusion and exclusion, and the importance of these materials to other Asian countries. In addition to democratising history, digital archives will also make historical studies more scientific. Historians used to be aristocratic, monopolising historical documents and thus the power of historical interpretation. Digital archives now prevent historians from holding such privileges. Thus broadened use by the public of digital archives and open reviewing by peer historians will make historical research not only more democratised, but also more scientific and one of the greatest contributions to social science research today.

Technical challenges faced by library, archive and museum professionals

The series of interviews appearing in this book suggest that librarians, archivists and curators are coping with their own limitations in current and archaic language, scripts and cultural knowledge when overseeing these collections and providing access. We see LAMs compensate by employing a number of techniques. Some libraries hire subject experts with an MA or PhD in Chinese historiography or in Chinese language and literature instead of professionals with only the MLIS degree. In the case of the International Dunhuang Project,[3] where international collaborative projects come to play, it brings in experts and scholars from all over the world with different skills, knowledge and expertise to examine and to understand a collection or even single work that is of immeasurable cultural or historical value.

At the Oriental Institute of the Czech Academy of Sciences, it deals with its non-Latin script by hiring external workers with the proper knowledge background for specific projects that need translation.

At the Peter the Great Museum of Ethnology and Anthropology (Kunstkamera), Dr. Vladimir Davydov, Head of the Siberian Ethnography Department, explains that there are some linguists and Eastern studies specialists at their Museum who provide research consultation and help deal with the problems caused by old languages and scripts, or, in other words, to collaborate with other neighbouring departments within the Museum. In cases where they are unable to find the appropriate experts within to decode scripts, they would then consult with specialists from other organisations, such as the Institute of Linguistics or Institute of Eastern manuscripts of the Russian Academy of Sciences. They would usually ask for assistance in advance when they are planning to publish archival documents containing scripts in foreign languages or languages of indigenous peoples of Siberia.

[3] International Dunhuang Project (IDP) – Homepage. Available at: http://idp.bl.uk/.

At the British Library, it has successfully completed cataloguing projects with a cycle of paid interns with strong language skills in languages, such as Mongolian, in which the permanent team struggles to catalogue because of the different range of languages and scripts involved. Even without cataloguing experience, the interns complete the information required simply by typing them in a spreadsheet, which was eventually converted into a machine-readable cataloguing (MARC) record. In the UK, depending on their services or collections, the British Library would have curators working for them, and the British museums would employ librarians.

At the Vatican, staff includes librarians and curators coming from all corners of the world, bringing in different knowledge and language skills. In Taiwan, Dr. Leo Lin points out that at his Department of International Cooperation at the National Central Library, national libraries are increasingly investing their manpower and resources in conducting exchanges and cooperation on an international level with the aim of improving our services and professional knowledge.

As you can see, collaborations on a cross-cultural and cross-national level have become increasingly necessary due to the reason that the implementation of such large cultural projects (either digital or nondigital) simply requires integrated scholarship and technological knowledge, as well as interprofessional skills. For the reason that such complicated knowledge and skillsets are often held by different professionals coming from different fields of training, librarians and archivists have the requisite training and expertise in creating, maintaining and preserving the contents of the documents, as well as ensuring the contents meet the needs of their end users. On the other hand, curators are expected to serve as scholars in their respective fields, providing primary research and initiatives in understanding, interpreting and analysing the contents of the materials they hold, thereby allowing the largest user groups to manipulate the contents for scholarly discovery and research on a global scale.

Indeed, collections can even wax and wane in support with different eras and political contexts. In the case of the National Palace Museum in Taiwan, it has been able to work collaboratively with its counterparts across the straights with mainland China. Both the Forbidden City Museum and Palace Museum in Taiwan jointly organise an international symposium each year, while the staff and researchers frequently share work experiences and research findings. As political and economic systems shift, new opportunities will continue to open up for LAMs in the way they operate.

Concluding remarks

Prof. Ji Xianlin (季羡林), a famous formally recognised 'Master of Chinese Traditional Culture (國學大師 gouxuedashi)', said it well in 1988 during a Duhuang seminar in Beijing: 'The site of Duhuang is located in China, and the research of Duhuang belongs to the world' (Sha, 2009, p. 102).[4] He also maintained that 'cultural exchange

[4] Sha, W. T. (沙武田). (2009). 敦煌学的故事 (Stories about Dunhuang studies). In Dunhuang Institution. yo (Ed.), 敦煌壁画故事与历史传说 (Stories and historical legends about the Dunhuang murals) (pp. 101–102). Lanzhou: Gansu People's Press.

is the main drive for humankind's progress. Only by learning from each other's strong points to make up for shortcomings can people constantly progress, the ultimate target of which is to achieve a kind of Great Harmony'.[5] These statements made by Prof. Ji are simple and yet profound; they are also the core essence and message of this interview book.

Our virtual journey traveling from country to country now comes to an end. We have explored history and culture from a multidimensional perspective through meaningful dialogues with a variety of seasoned LAM experts. The experiences and feedback shared by them have also enabled us to re-examine the viewpoints of other cultures in the modern globalised context. We sincerely hope that you have enjoyed these stories. But it does not mean our journey to the East is over. There is still a vast number of leading East Asian LAM professionals practising in different parts of the world, waiting for us, to be interviewed, with still many successful stories all around the globe to be spread.

[5] "Ji Xianlin: A Gentle Academic Giant." China.org, 19 August 2005. Available at: http://www.china.org.cn/english/NM-e/139052.htm.

Bibliography

Askin, N. (2015). Collaboration and crowdsourcing: The future of LAM convergence. *See Also, 1*(1).

Barsky, E., & Cho, A. (2007). Introducing Web 2.0: Social search for health librarians. *Journal of the Canadian Health Libraries Association, 28*(2), 59–61.

Blogposts written by Sara Chiesura on for the Asia, Pacific and Africa Collections, the British Library. Available at: https://bl.academia.edu/SaraChiesura.

Cho, A. (2007). An introduction to mashups for health librarians. *Journal of the Canadian Health Libraries Association, 28*(1), 19–22.

Cho, A. (2011). Bringing history to the library: University-community engagement in the academic library. *Computers in Libraries, 31*(4), 15.

Cho, A. (2013). YouTube and academic libraries: Building a digital collection. *Journal of Electronic Resources Librarianship, 25*(1), 39–50.

Cho, A. (2014a). Collaboration as outreach in the 21st Century academic library. In C. Smallwood (Ed.), *Bringing the arts into the library*. Chicago: American Library Association.

Cho, A. (2014b). Diversity pathways in librarianship: Some of the challenges faced and lessons learned as a Canadian-born Chinese male librarian. In D. Lee, & M. Kumaran (Eds.), *Aboriginal and visible minority librarians: Oral histories from Canada*. Lanham: Rowman & Littlefield.

Cho, A. (2015). Chinese character metadata: The key to ensure consistency for cataloging and discoverability of Chinese-language materials. *International Journal of Metadata, Semantics and Ontologies, 10*(1), 28–36.

Cho, A., & Con, A. (2013). Partnerships linking cultures: Multicultural librarianship in British Columbia's public libraries. In C. Smallwood, & K. Becnel (Eds.), *Library services for multicultural patrons to encourage library use*. New York: Scarecrow Press.

Cho, A., & Giustini, D. (2008). Web 3.0 and health librarians: An introduction. *Journal of the Canadian Health Libraries Association, 29*(1), 13–18.

Cho, A., & Giustini, D. (2011). Web 3.0 and health librarians: What does the future hold? In P. Younger, & P. Morgan (Eds.), *Using Web 2.0 for Health Information*. London: Facet.

Cho, A., & Li, Y. (2011). Libraries in a digital frontier: Preserving Chinese Canadian cultural heritage. In *Digital libraries: For cultural heritage, knowledge dissemination, and future creation* (pp. 35–38). Berlin Heidelberg: Springer.

Cho, A., Lin, J., & Wong-Chu, J. (2015). *AlliterAsian: Twenty years of ricepaper magazine*. Arsenal Press.

Giustini, D., Hooker, D., & Cho, A. (2009). Social cataloguing: An overview for health librarians. *Journal of the Canadian Health Libraries Association, 30*(4), 133–138.

Lo, P. (2015a). Comparative study on M-learning usage among LIS students from Hong Kong, Japan and Taiwan. *The Journal of Academic Librarianship*. http://dx.doi.org/10.1016/j.acalib.2015.07.005.

Lo, P. (2015b). Enhanced and changing roles of school librarians under the digital age. *New Library World*. http://dx.doi.org/10.1108/NLW-05-2015-0037.

Lo, P. (2015c). Information for inspiration: Understanding information-seeking behaviour and library usage of students at the Hong Kong Design Institute. *Australian Academic & Research Libraries*. http://dx.doi.org/10.1080/00048623.2015.1019604.

Lo, P. (2015d). *Preserving local documentary heritage: Conversations with special library managers and archivists in Hong Kong*. Hong Kong: City University of HK Press.

Lo, P. (2015e). Why librarianship? A comparative study between University of Tsukuba, University of Hong Kong, University of British Columbia and Shanghai University. *Australian Academic & Research Libraries*. http://dx.doi.org/10.1080/00048623.2015.1059993.

Lo, P. (2016). *Conversations with the World's leading Orchestra and Opera librarians*. Lanham, MD: Rowman & Littlefield.

Marcum, D. (2014). Archives, libraries, museums: Coming back together? *Information and Culture*, *49*(1), 74–89.

Marty, P. F. (2009). An introduction to digital convergence: Libraries, archives, and museums in the information age. *Museum Management and Curatorship*, *24*(4), 295–298.

Marty, P. F. (2010). An introduction to digital convergence: Libraries, archives, and museums in the information age. *The Library*, *80*(1). Available at: http://www.jstor.org/stable/10.1086/648549.

RLG's conference "Libraries, archives and museums – Three-ring circus, one big show?" and rare books and manuscripts section in 2006: "Libraries, archives and museums in the twenty-first century: Intersecting missions, converging futures?".

VanderBerg, R. (2012). Converging libraries, archives and museums: Overcoming distinctions, but for what gain? *Archives and Manuscripts*, *40*(3), 136–146.

Waibel, G., & Erway, R. (2009). Think globally, act locally: Library, archive, and museum collaboration. *Museum Management and Curatorship*, *24*(4), 323–335.

Yu, H. (2007). Towards a Pacific History of the Americas. *Amerasia Journal*, *33*(2), xiviii–xix.

Index

'*Note*: Page numbers followed by "f" indicate figures, "t" indicate tables and "b" indicate boxes.'

M

N

O

MIX
Papier | Fördert
gute Waldnutzung
FSC® C083411

Kolibri 360 GmbH
Ferdinand-Jühlke-Straße 7
99095 Erfurt, Deutschland
produktsicherheit@kolibri360.de